Pro iOS Persistence

Using Core Data

Michael Privat
Robert Warner

Apress®

Pro iOS Persistence

ISBN-13 (pbk): 978-1-4302-6028-8

ISBN-13 (electronic): 978-1-4302-6029-5

Managing Director: Welmoed Spahr
Lead Editor: Steve Anglin
Development Editor: Matthew Moodie
Technical Reviewers: Ethan Mateja and Ron Natalie
Editorial Board: Steve Anglin, Gary Cornell, Louise Corrigan, Jim DeWolf, Jonathan Gennick, Robert Hutchinson, Michelle Lowman, James Markham, Matthew Moodie, Jeff Olson, Jeffrey Pepper, Douglas Pundick, Ben Renow-Clarke, Gwenan Spearing, Matt Wade, Steve Weiss
Coordinating Editor: Jill Balzano
Copy Editor: Lori Jacobs
Compositor: SPi Global
Indexer: SPi Global
Artist: SPi Global
Cover Designer: Anna Ishchenko

Distributed to the book trade worldwide by Springer Science+Business Media New York, 233 Spring Street, 6th Floor, New York, NY 10013. Phone 1-800-SPRINGER, fax (201) 348-4505, e-mail orders-ny@springer-sbm.com, or visit www.springeronline.com. Apress Media, LLC is a California LLC and the sole member (owner) is Springer Science + Business Media Finance Inc (SSBM Finance Inc). SSBM Finance Inc is a Delaware corporation.

For information on translations, please e-mail rights@apress.com, or visit www.apress.com.

Apress and friends of ED books may be purchased in bulk for academic, corporate, or promotional use. eBook versions and licenses are also available for most titles. For more information, reference our Special Bulk Sales–eBook Licensing web page at www.apress.com/bulk-sales.

Any source code or other supplementary material referenced by the author in this text is available to readers at www.apress.com/9781430260288. For detailed information about how to locate your book's source code, go to www.apress.com/source-code/.

I dedicate this book to my loving wife, Kelly, and my children, Matthieu and Chloé.

—Michael Privat

I dedicate this book to my beautiful wife, Sherry, and our wonderful children: Tyson, Jacob, Mallory, Camie, and Leila.

—Rob Warner

Contents at a Glance

Contents

About the Authors

Michael Privat is a senior developer at Availity, LLC, located in Jacksonville, Florida. He oversees the design and implementation of the various components that make up the transaction processing platform. He coauthored *Pro Core Data for iOS* (Apress, 2011) and *Beginning OS X Lion Apps Development* (Apress, 2011). He has published several iOS apps, including Ghostwriter Notes, Budget Tracker, and Fluid Notes. He earned an engineering degree in computer science from the University of Nice, France before joining MIT to do research on applied artificial intelligence. He currently lives in France with his wife, Kelly, and their children: Matthieu and Chloé.

Rob Warner is a senior technical staff member for Availity, LLC, based in Jacksonville, Florida, where he works with various technologies to deliver solutions in the health care sector. He coauthored *Pro Core Data for iOS* (Apress, 2011), *Beginning OS X Lion Apps Development* (Apress, 2011), and *The Definitive Guide to SWT and JFace* (Apress, 2004); he blogs at www.grailbox.com. He earned his bachelor's degree in English from Brigham Young University and is working on his master's degree in computer science at Georgia Tech. He lives in Jacksonville, Florida, with his wife, Sherry, and their five children: Tyson, Jacob, Mallory, Camie, and Leila.

About the Technical Reviewers

Ron Natalie has 35 years of experience developing large-scale applications in C, Objective-C, and C++ on Unix, OS X, and Windows. He has a degree in electrical engineering from the Johns Hopkins University and has taught professional courses in programming, network design, and computer security.

He splits his time between Virginia and North Carolina with his wife, Margy.

Ethan Mateja is a software engineer currently working as an iOS mobile architect for Ubiquiti Networks and providing private consulting support to a wide variety of clients. With 12 years of experience as a full stack engineer, Ethan's experience spans writing server-side software for the U.S. Department of Defense to significant mobile projects with Actian Inc, Paypal, Salesforce, and other Bay Area startups.

As a husband and father of two, Ethan enjoys living in the heart of the San Mateo County redwoods where his passion for discovery and wonder of nature are a part of daily life. Citing his natural surroundings as an inspiration for his love of problem solving, Ethan regularly embraces long hikes in the woods to ponder the most impenetrable engineering challenges.

Acknowledgments

Writing a book is a time-consuming effort that takes a lot of time away from the family. It's a sacrifice that my wife, Kelly, and my two children, Matthieu and Chloé, allowed me to make with the promise to catch up once the project is complete. I am very grateful for their patience and for allowing me to finish this project. I am now realizing that the catching up time has come and I am very excited about that.

With every edition we get new readers who don't hesitate to let us know what they liked or disliked, and what they would like to see in the next edition. I am grateful for all the passion some exhibit when talking about this book, and I am also grateful for all those who bring their ideas to help us improve with each edition.

A project like this often seems overwhelming at first. The more we think through the chapters, decide how to organize them, and conjecture about everything that needs to be said, the more we get the feeling we've stretched ourselves very thin. But the amazing Apress team has been there for us the whole way. They really took a lot of the weight off our shoulders by providing guidance, by helping organize our work, and by providing the collaborative tools we needed. They are truly a next-generation publishing company.

This book would not exist without the support of Availity, the company I work for. Everyone from leadership, including Trent Gavazzi, Mary Anne Orenchuk, Jack Hunt, and Steve Vaughn, often came to check on how the book was going. Some of our engineers also liked offering suggestions and voicing their support: Rob McGuinness, Ed McNeil, Herve Devos, Kelly Burton. They are all great to work with and I thank them all for their support.

Finally, I would like to dedicate a paragraph to the coauthor of this book, who refuses to admit, publicly at least, that he's awesome. Rob Warner loves producing quality work. He is infatuated with the beauty of software designs and languages and can even turn code into prose. I thank him for the opportunity to work with him once again.

—Michael Priva

My daughter Leila has reminded me several times that she merits more of a starring role in this book than I've given her in past books, so this is my opportunity to show her and the rest of my family what stars they are in my life. I love my beautiful wife, Sherry, and my wonderful children, Tyson, Jacob, Mallory, Camie, and Leila. I'm grateful for their encouragement and support—even when said encouragement takes the form of calling me a nerd. I'm so blessed y'all are in my life.

I'm also thankful to my parents, who bought us our first computer (an Atari 400), encouraged our learning, and buy copies of every book I write even though they never read them. My siblings and in-laws always do a great job of asking how the book is coming and politely feigning interest in the subject matter. I have a great family.

This has been another great writing experience with the incredible folks at Apress, and I thank them for their patience and insight. The army of folks required to bring a book to fruition has never been more apparent, so I'm clearer now than I've ever been that many people have invested thankless time and effort into this book's publication. Special thanks to Steve Anglin, Jill Balzano, Anamika Panchoo, Matthew Moodie, Douglas Pundick, Ron Natalie, and anyone else who had a hand in publishing this book.

Thanks as well to all our readers for their questions, feedback, praise, and criticism. We pour our minds and hearts into making this the best information we can, and we are always seeking for ways to improve the material or make it more accessible.

Working with Michael on yet another project is an amazing privilege. I continue to hope he doesn't tire of me, as I learn so much every time I work with him. I thank him for his patience, dedication, persistence, and expertise.

I work for an amazing company. Availity gives me the opportunity to produce and make a difference every day. Working with an array of such bright people keeps me on my toes! I don't have space to name them all, of course, but I'll add a particular thanks to the folks in leadership (Trent Gavazzi, Jack Hunt, Mary Anne Orenchuk, Taryn Tresca, and Steve Vaughn) for their support. Thanks as well to Geoff Packwood for periodically checking in to make sure we're moving the pile forward. I also get to work every day with an awesome team—Lori Creel, Mary Horn, Robert McGuinness, Robert Ventrone, and Ambur Wilson—as we try to build greatness.

—Rob Warner

Introduction

The world has gone mobile, and it seems that iOS apps lead the charge. People use their iPhone, iPads, and soon their Apple Watches to consume, produce, and store a diversity of information. As you develop applications to run on these Apple devices, you'll appreciate the polish that Apple has spread on its persistence framework: Core Data. No other mobile platform offers a persistence layer that approaches Core Data's power, ease of use, or flexibility. With each release of the iOS Software Development Kit (SDK), Apple grows and improves the Core Data framework.

We've written and rewritten this book several times as Core Data has continued to grow. Last summer, as we neared completion of this book, Apple surprised us all with the announcement of its new Swift programming language. After discussion between ourselves and with the folks at Apress, we concluded that the proper response to Swift's advent was to rewrite anew and incorporate every example in this book in both Objective-C and Swift. We have some bruises and scars from that experience, of course, as all the Swift early adopters can attest. With each new release of Xcode, we had to revisit chapters we thought done because some bits of code no longer compiled under the new Xcode. We believe we've caught all the errant ?s and !s, but apologize in advance if any slipped through.

What You'll Need

To follow along with this book, you'll need a Mac running OS X Mavericks or OS X Yosemite, and you'll need Xcode 6. You'll be happiest if you're running the latest point version of Xcode 6, particularly if you use the Swift code samples. Language support for Swift continues to improve with each release of Xcode. You can download the latest version of Xcode 6 from the Mac App Store.

This text doesn't cover beginning iOS development, whether in Objective-C or Swift, so you should have at least a basic understanding of either Objective-C or Swift, and also of Cocoa Touch and iOS development.

What You'll Find

This book approaches iOS persistence and Core Data from both theoretical and practical perspectives, so you'll learn generally how Core Data works and how its pieces fit together, and also you'll be guided step-by-step how to incorporate this powerful persistence framework into your applications. You'll see how to implement every topic we treat both in Objective-C and in Swift. We cover a range of topics, including how to build your Core Data data models, how to query your data, how to migrate data across model versions, how to encrypt data, how to use Core Data on different threads, how to store data in the cloud, and how to tune performance.

You can read the book cover to cover, but for the best results we recommend you read it in front of your computer, typing in the code samples to understand how they work and what they do. We also recommend that you keep this book as a reference for your ongoing Core Data needs and challenges.

How This Book Is Organized

We've organized this book to build from basic principles to advanced topics, so you'll probably gain the most if you work through the book from front to back. Chapter titles clearly mark the subject matter they contain, however, so if you're looking for information on a specific topic, feel free to jump directly to that chapter.

Source Code and Errata

You can download the source code for this book from the Apress web site at `www.apress.com`. We've released all the code under the MIT license (`http://opensource.org/licenses/MIT`), so feel free to use it in your own projects, whether personal or commercial. Check the errata section of the Apress web site for any corrections to code or text.

How to Contact Us

We'd love to hear from you! You can find us here:

> Michael Privat
>
> Email: `mprivat@mac.com`
>
> Twitter: `@michaelprivat`
>
> Blog: `http://michaelprivat.com`

> Rob Warner
>
> Email: `rwarner@grailbox.com`
>
> Twitter: `@hoop33`
>
> App.net: `@hoop33`
>
> Blog: `http://grailbox.com`

Touring Core Data

That computer in your purse or pocket—the one that purportedly places phone calls—stores gigabytes' worth of data: pictures, e-mails, texts, tweets, restaurant reviews, high scores, books, what your friends ate for breakfast, and countless other combinations of zeros and ones that inform and entertain you every day. As Apple's offering to manage data, Core Data manages much of that information, and the percentage of Core Data–managed information on iOS devices continues to grow. In this chapter, we'll discover why.

This chapter explains what Core Data is and what components Core Data comprises. It outlines and explains the basic classes that Core Data uses and how they work together. It shows how to set up Core Data in your applications, whether you take advantage of Xcode's Core Data code generation or add Core Data functionality by hand. It also shows the basics of creating an object model for your objects, storing objects, and retrieving them.

In this chapter, you build two applications: one that tells Xcode to set up Core Data for you and one to which you add Core Data by hand. Neither application has an interface beyond a blank screen, but, rather, they both focus on Core Data interaction. Applications in later chapters will have actual user interfaces, but be patient and focus on learning the basics of Core Data. The information you learn in this chapter will provide a solid foundation for you throughout the rest of this book and with your own Core Data projects.

What Is Core Data?

Imagine computers couldn't store data. Imagine each time you powered on your iPhone or iPad, you started fresh with each application you worked with. All your documents were gone: your school papers, your budget projection spreadsheets, your crafted pitch presentations for another round of venture capitalist funding, all vanished. You're back to Level 1 on Angry Birds. You have no more grumpy cat pictures. Your texts from last night have disappeared (which, for some of you, might be a good thing). In short, your device is the classic tabula rasa, day after day, blank and empty of any data, and not very useful.

What those imaginary computers lack is persistence: the ability to store and retrieve data over time. We want to persist information, like our pictures and our high scores and our documents. Core Data, Apple's solution for persistence, allows applications to persist data of any form and retrieve it.

Core Data isn't technically a database, although it usually stores its data in one (an SQLite database, to be precise). It's not an object-relational mapper (ORM), though it can feel like one. It's truly an object graph, allowing you to create, store, and retrieve objects that have attributes and relationships to other objects. Its simplicity and power allow you to persist data of any form, from basic data models to complex.

Core Data Components

Newcomers to Core Data often express dismay at the complexity of the framework, but as we'll see, that initial response is unfounded. Cocoa's predilection for long names probably contributes to the mistaken sense of the complexity; after all, NSPersistentStoreCoordinator is a mouthful. Once you get past the long names, however, and understand the purpose of each of the classes, you'll recognize both the elegance and the simplicity of the Core Data framework.

We can divide the Core Data classes into two groups: the ones we generally set up once, when our programs launch, and the ones we work with throughout the running time of our programs. In addition, Cocoa provides a set of classes that Core Data uses that aren't limited in scope to Core Data. Core Data leverages classes like NSPredicate and NSSortDescriptor, which are also used in other contexts in Cocoa applications, to augment its capabilities. We'll touch on those other classes throughout this book.

Let's first discuss the classes we set up once, when our programs launch. These classes are

- NSPersistentStore
- NSPersistentStoreCoordinator
- NSManagedObjectModel

The NSPersistentStore class represents a persistent store: a place on your device's file system that actually stores data. This is usually an SQLite database, though Core Data also offers other types of persistent stores:

- XML (OS X only)
- Atomic
- In-memory

XML stores, which are available only on OS X, store data (as you'd guess) in XML files. Atomic stores, so named because they read and write the entire data store when accessed, can be useful if you want to create your own file format for storing files. Core Data provides one atomic store implementation called the binary store type, and you can create custom stores based on atomic stores. Understand, though, that atomic stores tend to be slower, especially as your data set grows large, because they write and read the data files atomically. In-memory stores are useful if you don't require your data to persist beyond the current launch of the application but still want to use the power of Core Data to interact with the data. Most, if not all, of your persistent stores will be SQLite stores, though. They're fast, since they can read and write partial data, and they persist data beyond just the current launch of your applications. Each of your applications will often have one persistent store, though they can have more than one.

The NSPersistentStoreCoordinator class represents a persistent store coordinator, which coordinates among persistent stores, object models, and object contexts. The persistent store coordinator uses an object model, which we'll see next, and ties it to one or more persistent stores. It also coordinates the storage and retrieval of objects between one or more managed object contexts and one or more persistent stores. It's in a sense the hub of Core Data, tying together all the Core Data classes. Luckily for you, though, it's easy to create and configure, and then it performs all its complicated magic for you while your application runs.

The NSManagedObjectModel class represents a managed object model or, more simply, an object model, which looks so much like a data model that you're forgiven for thinking of it in that way. Just as an entity-relationship (ER) diagram defines tables, columns, and relationships, an object model defines entities, attributes, and relationships. You can create an object model in code, but Xcode provides an object model editor that lets you visually create object models that your application loads and uses.

You use the next two classes throughout the runtime of your applications. They are

- NSManagedObjectContext
- NSManagedObject

The NSManagedObjectContext class represents a managed object context, or just an object context. Your applications can use one or more of these, though often they'll use only one. Object contexts provide places for objects to live, and the Apple documentation calls it a "scratch pad." You create objects in the object context, retrieve objects from the object context, and tell the object context to save itself. The object context takes care of talking to the persistent store coordinator to actually store and retrieve objects. You'll talk to the object contexts a lot in your Core Data applications.

The NSManagedObject class represents a managed object, or an object that Core Data manages. You can think of these as rows in a database. Managed objects have attributes and relationships, as defined by an object model, and use key-value coding (KVC) so you can easily set and get their data. You can also create a subclass of NSManagedObject to create properties that match your object model and convenience methods to work with your managed objects.

Figure 1-1 shows the Core Data classes and how they work together.

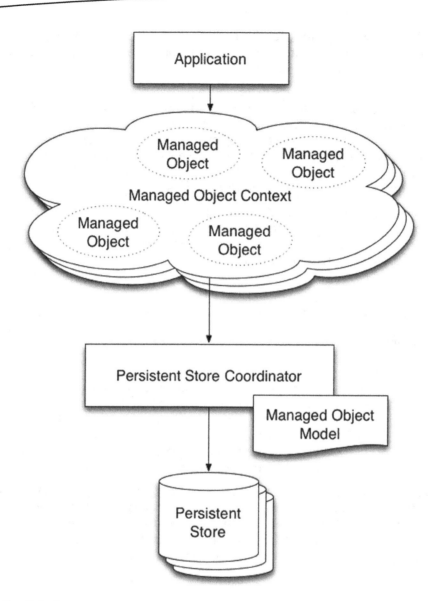

Figure 1-1. *The Core Data classes*

Creating a New Core Data Project

Theory and diagrams work well for gaining an understanding of how something works, but actual working code cements the concepts into true comprehension. We've talked about theory and seen a diagram; now, let's see Core Data in practice. In this section, we create an Xcode project that uses Core Data from its outset. Later in this chapter, we show how to add Core Data to an existing project.

This first application, not so imaginatively named CoreDataApp, stores Person objects with a single attribute, name. It has a blank screen for an interface, so you can't interact with it. You run it, it creates data in an SQLite database, and then we use the sqlite3 command-line application to browse the database.

Creating the Project

Launch Xcode and create a new single view application project. Call it CoreDataApp and set the organization identifier to book.persistence. Make sure the Use Core Data check box is checked, as shown in Figure 1-2, and create and save the project. Throughout this book, we use Objective-C as the primary language, but we include Swift versions of the listings as well.

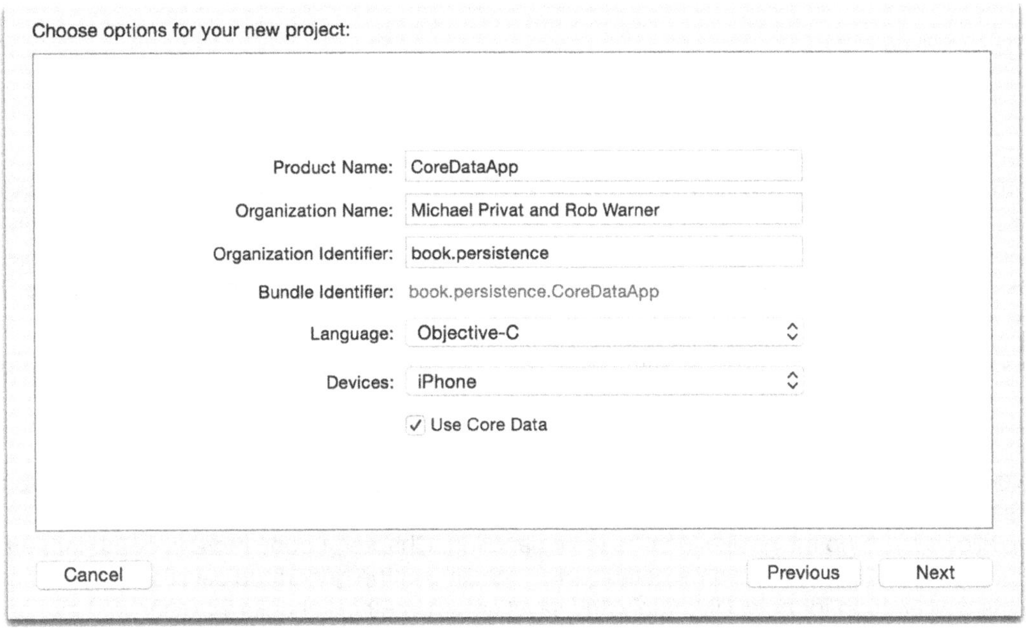

Figure 1-2. Creating the CoreDataApp project

Touring the Core Data Components

By checking the Use Core Data check box, you've instructed Xcode to add the Core Data framework to your project. If you selected Objective-C as the project language, Xcode has added the Core Data header file, CoreData/CoreData.h, to the project's AppDelegate.h file. If you selected Swift as the language, you'll find the line import CoreData in the project's AppDelegate.swift file.

You've also told Xcode to create a model that will be loaded into an NSManagedObjectModel instance in your application. To see this, expand the CoreDataApp folder in Xcode's Project Navigator. You should see an entry called CoreDataApp.xcdatamodeld, which is a directory that contains the various artifacts that make up the project's data model. When we build the application, Xcode will compile this to a directory called CoreDataApp.momd inside the application bundle. This directory will contain the artifacts that CoreDataApp loads to create the NSManagedObjectModel instance.

Finally, you've told Xcode to create properties in your application delegate class, AppDelegate, to materialize the Core Data stack. Open the header file, AppDelegate.h, which should match Listing 1-1.

Listing 1-1. AppDelegate.h

```
#import <UIKit/UIKit.h>
#import <CoreData/CoreData.h>

@interface AppDelegate : UIResponder <UIApplicationDelegate>

@property (strong, nonatomic) UIWindow *window;

@property (readonly, strong, nonatomic) NSManagedObjectContext *managedObjectContext;
@property (readonly, strong, nonatomic) NSManagedObjectModel *managedObjectModel;
@property (readonly, strong, nonatomic) NSPersistentStoreCoordinator *persistentStoreCoordinator;

- (void)saveContext;
- (NSURL *)applicationDocumentsDirectory;

@end
```

You should recognize the three Core Data properties: managedObjectContext, managedObjectModel, and persistentStoreCoordinator. Xcode puts them all in the application delegate class, which works fine, but application delegate classes tend to grow to unwieldy sizes. When we add Core Data to an existing project later in this chapter, we use a different approach that partitions the Core Data stack to a different class.

You should also notice two methods that Xcode has created to help us with Core Data interaction.

```
- (void)saveContext;- (NSURL *)applicationDocumentsDirectory;
```

The saveContext method gives us a central location for saving the managed object context. We can save the managed object context from anywhere in the code, of course, but having one place to do the save allows us to do things like localize error handling. Chapter 4 goes more in depth into error handling. Xcode has generated some default error handling in the generated saveContext method that works well enough for now. Ultimately, the saveContext method checks whether we have any changes floating in the managed object context by calling its hasChanges method, and then calls save.

The applicationDocumentsDirectory method returns, as you would imagine, this application's documents directory. The persistent store coordinator calls this method to determine where on the file system to create the persistent store.

The Swift version of the generated project doesn't have a header file, of course, but it has the same properties, as well as corresponding calls for the method declarations we just examined (saveContext and applicationDocumentsDirectory:). The source doesn't group the properties for the Core Data stack together, but if you read through AppDelegate.swift, you'll find them, initialized using closures (not shown here), as Listing 1-2 shows.

Listing 1-2. Core Data properties in AppDelegate.swift

```
lazy var managedObjectModel: NSManagedObjectModel
lazy var persistentStoreCoordinator: NSPersistentStoreCoordinator?
lazy var managedObjectContext: NSManagedObjectContext?
```

Initializing the Core Data Components

Xcode's generated code for Core Data initializes the Core Data stack lazily, when its components are first accessed. You can certainly use this approach for all your Core Data applications, and for CoreDataApp we'll leave the default Xcode implementation. You also, however, can set up your Core Data stack when your application launches. We also use that approach in this book.

The Core Data stack for CoreDataApp initializes when you first access the managed object context, materialized by the managedObjectContext property. Listing 1-3 contains the code for managedObjectContext's Objective-C accessor, and Listing 1-4 shows the same accessor in Swift.

Listing 1-3. The Accessor for `managedObjectContext` in Objective-C

```objc
// Returns the managed object context for the application.
// If the context doesn't already exist, it is created and bound to the persistent store coordinator
for the application.
- (NSManagedObjectContext *)managedObjectContext
{
  if (_managedObjectContext != nil) {
    return _managedObjectContext;
  }

  NSPersistentStoreCoordinator *coordinator = [self persistentStoreCoordinator];
  if (coordinator != nil) {
    _managedObjectContext = [[NSManagedObjectContext alloc] init];
    [_managedObjectContext setPersistentStoreCoordinator:coordinator];
  }
  return _managedObjectContext;
}
```

Listing 1-4. The Accessor for `managedObjectContext` in Swift

```swift
lazy var managedObjectContext: NSManagedObjectContext? = {
  // Returns the managed object context for the application (which is already bound to the
  persistent store coordinator for the application.) This property is optional since there are
  legitimate error conditions that could cause the creation of the context to fail.
  let coordinator = self.persistentStoreCoordinator
  if coordinator == nil {
    return nil
  }
  var managedObjectContext = NSManagedObjectContext()
  managedObjectContext.persistentStoreCoordinator = coordinator
  return managedObjectContext
}()
```

As the comment generated by Xcode attests, the accessor checks to see whether the managedObjectContext property (synthesized as _managedObjectContext) has been created. If so, the accessor returns it. If not, it retrieves the persistentStoreCoordinator property, allocates and initializes the managed object context, and sets its persistent store coordinator to the retrieved persistentStoreCoordinator.

The accessor for persistentStoreCoordinator, shown in Listing 1-5 (Objective-C) and Listing 1-6 (Swift), does its own lazy initialization. Note that we've removed the long comment about error handling, which Chapter 4 covers. As you can see, this code checks whether the persistentStoreCoordinator property (synthesized as _persistentStoreCoordinator) has been created. If not, it determines the URL (uniform resource locator) for the persistent store by tacking the file name, CoreDataApp.sqlite (or CoreDataAppSwift.sqlite), onto the directory returned by the applicationDocumentsDirectory helper discussed earlier in this chapter, and stores it in storeURL. It then allocates the persistentStoreCoordinator property, initializes it with the managed object model returned by the managedObjectModel accessor, and adds a persistent store that points to the URL created in storeURL.

Listing 1-5. The Objective-C Accessor for persistentStoreCoordinator

```objc
// Returns the persistent store coordinator for the application.
// If the coordinator doesn't already exist, it is created and the application's store added to it.
- (NSPersistentStoreCoordinator *)persistentStoreCoordinator
{
  if (_persistentStoreCoordinator != nil) {
    return _persistentStoreCoordinator;
  }
    NSURL *storeURL = [[self applicationDocumentsDirectory] URLByAppendingPathComponent:
    @"CoreDataApp.sqlite"];

  NSError *error = nil;
  _persistentStoreCoordinator = [[NSPersistentStoreCoordinator alloc] initWithManagedObjectModel:
  [self managedObjectModel]];
  if (![_persistentStoreCoordinator addPersistentStoreWithType:NSSQLiteStoreType configuration:
  nil URL:storeURL options:nil error:&error]) {
    /* Comment deleted */
    NSLog(@"Unresolved error %@, %@", error, [error userInfo]);
    abort();
  }

  return _persistentStoreCoordinator;
}
```

Listing 1-6. The Swift Accessor for persistentStoreCoordinator

```swift
lazy var persistentStoreCoordinator: NSPersistentStoreCoordinator? = {
    // The persistent store coordinator for the application. This implementation creates and return
    a coordinator, having added the store for the application to it. This property is optional since
    there are legitimate error conditions that could cause the creation of the store to fail.
    // Create the coordinator and store
    var coordinator: NSPersistentStoreCoordinator? = NSPersistentStoreCoordinator(managedObjectMode
    l: self.managedObjectModel)
    let url = self.applicationDocumentsDirectory.URLByAppendingPathComponent("CoreDataAppSwift.
    sqlite")
    var error: NSError? = nil
    var failureReason = "There was an error creating or loading the application's saved data."
```

```
if coordinator!.addPersistentStoreWithType(NSSQLiteStoreType, configuration: nil, URL: url,
options: nil, error: &error) == nil {
    coordinator = nil
    // Report any error we got.
    let dict = NSMutableDictionary()
    dict[NSLocalizedDescriptionKey] = "Failed to initialize the application's saved data"
    dict[NSLocalizedFailureReasonErrorKey] = failureReason
    dict[NSUnderlyingErrorKey] = error
    error = NSError(domain: "YOUR_ERROR_DOMAIN", code: 9999, userInfo: dict)
    // Replace this with code to handle the error appropriately.
    // abort() causes the application to generate a crash log and terminate. You should not use
    this function in a shipping application, although it may be useful during development.
    NSLog("Unresolved error \(error), \(error!.userInfo)")
    abort()
}

    return coordinator
}()
```

We have one more piece of lazy initialization to review, found in the accessor for managedObjectModel and shown in Listing 1-7 (Objective-C) and Listing 1-8 (Swift). This code, like the other accessors, returns the managedObjectModel property (synthesized as _managedObjectModel) if it has been initialized. Otherwise, the code initializes it by storing the URL for the compiled managed object model, CoreDataApp.momd (CoreDataAppSwift.momd), in the modelURL variable, allocating the managedObjectModel property, and initializing it with the URL to the managed object model.

Listing 1-7. The Objective-C Accessor for managedObjectModel

```
// Returns the managed object model for the application.
// If the model doesn't already exist, it is created from the application's model.
- (NSManagedObjectModel *)managedObjectModel
{
  if (_managedObjectModel != nil) {
    return _managedObjectModel;
  }
  NSURL *modelURL = [[NSBundle mainBundle] URLForResource:@"CoreDataApp" withExtension:@"momd"];
  _managedObjectModel = [[NSManagedObjectModel alloc] initWithContentsOfURL:modelURL];
  return _managedObjectModel;
}
```

Listing 1-8. The Swift Accessor for managedObjectModel

```
lazy var managedObjectModel: NSManagedObjectModel = {
    // The managed object model for the application. This property is not optional. It is a fatal
error for the application not to be able to find and load its model.
    let modelURL = NSBundle.mainBundle().URLForResource("CoreDataAppSwift", withExtension: "momd")!
    return NSManagedObjectModel(contentsOfURL: modelURL)!
}()
```

The lazy-initialization approach works just fine and ensures that all pieces of the Core Data stack get initialized when they're needed. Feel free to continue to use this approach in your Core Data–based applications. The second application we build in this chapter, PersistenceApp, takes a different approach: it contains all the Core Data interactions in a single class, `Persistence`, that directly initializes the Core Data stack. Feel free to use either approach in your Core Data applications.

Creating a Managed Object Model

Xcode has created an empty object model for us, `CoreDataApp.xcdatamodeld` (or `CoreDataAppSwift.xcdatamodeld`), which you can see by selecting it in the Xcode Project Navigator (see Figure 1-3).

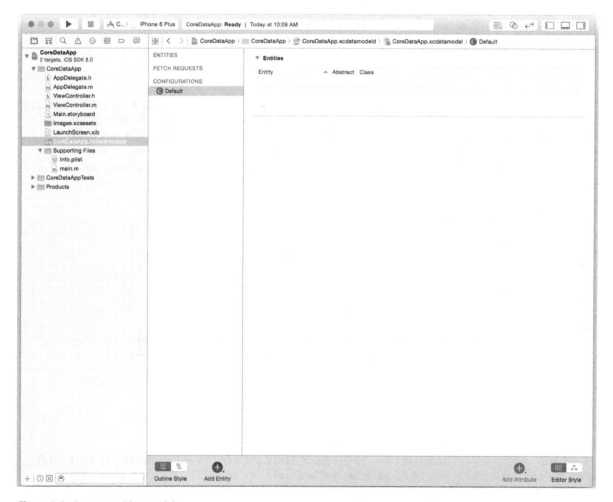

Figure 1-3. An empty object model

For the CoreDataApp application, we want to create a single entity called Person that has a single attribute called name. Note the convention of capitalizing the entity name and lowercasing the attribute name; this naming approach is optional but conforms well to standard coding practices. We use it throughout the book.

To create this entity, click the Add Entity button at the bottom of the Xcode window. This will create an entity called Entity. Rename it Person. Then, click the + button under Attributes and create an attribute called name and change its type from Undefined to String. Your object model should now match Figure 1-4.

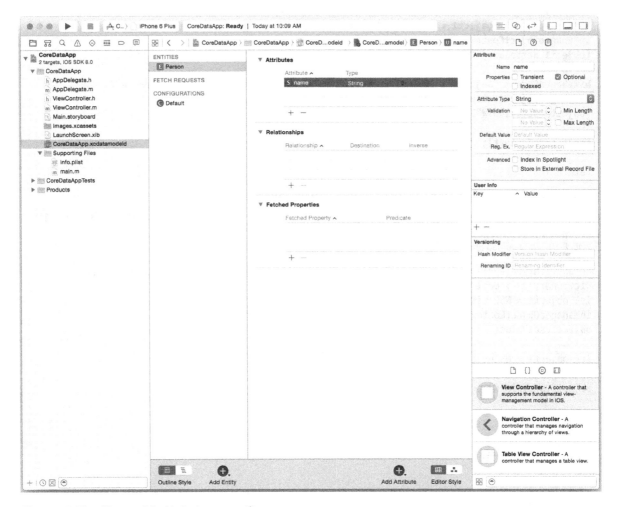

Figure 1-4. *The object model with the* Person *entity*

Xcode will compile and load this object model into the managedObjectModel property.

Adding Some Objects

Before running the CoreDataApp application, open AppDelegate.m, add code to the applicati on:didFinishLaunchingWithOptions: method to initialize the Core Data stack by accessing the managedObjectContext property, create some managed objects, and save the managed object context. Listing 1-9 shows the updated method.

Listing 1-9. The Updated application:didFinishLaunchingWithOptions: Method

```
- (BOOL)application:(UIApplication *)application didFinishLaunchingWithOptions:(NSDictionary *)
launchOptions {
  NSManagedObject *object1 = [NSEntityDescription insertNewObjectForEntityForName:@"Person"
  inManagedObjectContext:self.managedObjectContext];
  [object1 setValue:@"Tarzan" forKey:@"name"];

  NSManagedObject *object2 = [NSEntityDescription insertNewObjectForEntityForName:@"Person"
  inManagedObjectContext:self.managedObjectContext];
  [object2 setValue:@"Jane" forKey:@"name"];

  [self saveContext];

  return YES;
}
```

If you're working with Swift, open AppDelegate.swift instead, and update as shown in Listing 1-10.

Listing 1-10. The updated application:didFinishLaunchingWithOptions: function

```
func application(application: UIApplication!, didFinishLaunchingWithOptions launchOptions:
NSDictionary!) -> Bool {
  let object1 = NSEntityDescription.insertNewObjectForEntityForName("Person",
  inManagedObjectContext: self.managedObjectContext!) as NSManagedObject
  object1.setValue("Tarzan", forKey: "name")

  let object2 = NSEntityDescription.insertNewObjectForEntityForName("Person",
  inManagedObjectContext: self.managedObjectContext!) as NSManagedObject
  object2.setValue("Jane", forKey: "name")

  saveContext()

  return true
}
```

This code creates two new Person managed objects, object1 and object2, and sets their name attributes to "Tarzan" and "Jane," respectively. Note that managed objects use Cocoa's standard KVC to set values for attributes. You can also create custom classes for your entities with direct accessors for attributes, so that you can write code as follows:

```
object1.name = @"Tarzan";
```

Chapter 2 discusses custom classes.

We create the managed objects by inserting them into a managed object context: our managedObjectContext property. By accessing that property, we start the chain that initializes our entire Core Data stack.

After creating the two managed objects, this code saves the managed object context using the saveContext helper, before throwing a blank window onto the screen. Build and run the application to create the managed objects in the persistent store and see the blank window. Then stop the application.

Viewing the Data

The CoreDataApp application doesn't have any code to display the contents of its persistent store. How, then, can we verify that the application actually created and stored data? For that, we examine the SQLite database file, CoreDataApp.sqlite or CoreDataAppSwift.sqlite, directly. When you run the application in the iOS Simulator, the application writes this file to a directory below your home directory. The easiest way to find this file is to open a terminal and type

```
find ~ -name 'CoreDataApp.sqlite'
```

Once you locate the file, change to that directory and open the file using the sqlite3 application.

```
sqlite3 CoreDataApp.sqlite
```

Alternatively, you can open the file directly using the find command:

```
find ~ -name 'CoreDataApp.sqlite' -exec sqlite3 {} \;
```

Let's first examine the database schema by typing the .schema command at the sqlite> prompt.

```
sqlite> .schema
CREATE TABLE ZPERSON ( Z_PK INTEGER PRIMARY KEY, Z_ENT INTEGER, Z_OPT INTEGER, ZNAME VARCHAR );
CREATE TABLE Z_METADATA (Z_VERSION INTEGER PRIMARY KEY, Z_UUID VARCHAR(255), Z_PLIST BLOB);
CREATE TABLE Z_PRIMARYKEY (Z_ENT INTEGER PRIMARY KEY, Z_NAME VARCHAR, Z_SUPER INTEGER, Z_MAX INTEGER);
```

You see three tables, two of which (Z_METADATA and Z_PRIMARYKEY) Core Data uses for database management tasks. The third, ZPERSON, stores Person entities. You can see it has a column called ZNAME, of type VARCHAR, for storing the name attribute. Note that this schema, including tables, table names, and column names, among others, are undocumented implementation details subject to change. You can't rely on these patterns and should never access SQLite databases directly in any of your Core Data–based applications. For testing purposes, however, like what we're doing here, you're safe to mess around.

Let's verify that the CoreDataApp application created and stored the two Person managed objects:

```
sqlite> select * from zperson;
1|1|1|Tarzan
2|1|1|Jane
sqlite> .quit
```

You can confirm that, indeed, the CoreDataApp application has successfully used the Core Data framework to create and store data.

Adding Core Data to an Existing Project

Now that you understand how Core Data works, you can see how easy it is to add to an existing project. Just follow the same steps that Xcode does when you check the Use Core Data check box.

- Import the Core Data header file (CoreData/CoreData.h) or add @import CoreData for Objective-C, or add import CoreData for Swift.

- Add a managed object model to your application.

- Add code to your application to initialize the Core Data stack and grant access to the managed object context.

You can mimic Xcode's generated code for initializing the Core Data stack or follow a different pattern. We use both approaches throughout this book. However you approach the problem, the basic steps are the same.

Creating a Core Data-less Application

To add Core Data to an existing application, we must first have a Core Data-less application to add to. Create a new Xcode project using the single view application template and call it PersistenceApp. Be sure to uncheck the Use Core Data check box (see Figure 1-5).

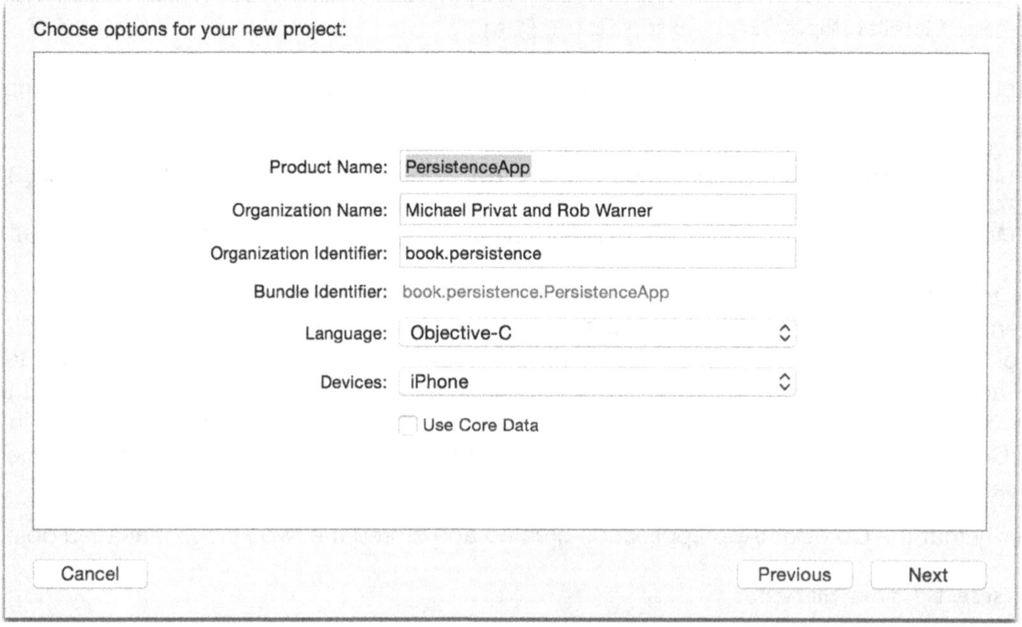

Choose options for your new project:

Product Name:	PersistenceApp
Organization Name:	Michael Privat and Rob Warner
Organization Identifier:	book.persistence
Bundle Identifier:	book.persistence.PersistenceApp
Language:	Objective-C
Devices:	iPhone
	☐ Use Core Data

Cancel   Previous   Next

Figure 1-5. Creating the PersistenceApp project

Adding the Core Data Framework

Your application must link against the Core Data framework, aptly named `CoreData.framework`, in order to use Core Data classes. While adding the Core Data framework to your project used to require a dozen mouse clicks, Xcode's recent updates have introduced the notion of module imports. To link the Core Data framework to your project, simply add an `@import CoreData;` directive when you need access to Core Data classes in your Objective-C project, or `import CoreData` in your Swift project. Xcode will do the rest of the linking work.

Adding a Managed Object Model

A Core Data–based application requires a managed object model, so add a new file to the PersistenceApp group using the Core Data ⊙ Data Model template. Yes, even Xcode calls it a data model, not a managed object model. You can call the model whatever you'd like; you just have to match the name when creating your persistence store. For the sake of convention, though, call it `PersistenceApp.xcdatamodeld`. When you're done, you should have an empty Core Data model called `PersistenceApp.xcdatamodeld`, as shown in Figure 1-6.

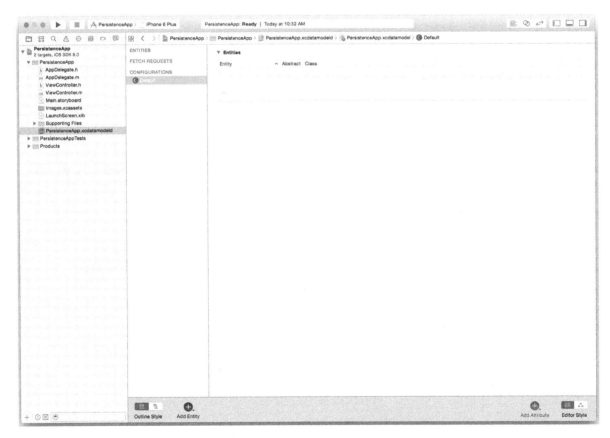

Figure 1-6. The empty `PersistenceApp.xcdatamodeld` managed object model

We'll add entities and attributes to the model later. For now, we'll continue to focus on adding everything necessary for Core Data to the application.

Adding and Initializing the Core Data Stack

For the PersistenceApp application, we're going to put all the Core Data stuff into a separate class called Persistence, and add an instance of that class as a property in our AppDelegate class. This will allow us to keep our AppDelegate class's code cleaner and provide a clean interface for Core Data access.

Create a new file in the PersistenceApp group using the Source ⊙ Cocoa Touch Class template, call it Persistence, and make it a subclass of NSObject. Now, if you're doing this in Objective-C, add the Core Data properties and helper method declarations to Persistence.h, as shown in Listing 1-11.

Listing 1-11. Persistence.h

```
#import <Foundation/Foundation.h>
@import CoreData;

@interface Persistence : NSObject

@property (readonly, strong, nonatomic) NSManagedObjectContext *managedObjectContext;
@property (readonly, strong, nonatomic) NSManagedObjectModel *managedObjectModel;
@property (readonly, strong, nonatomic) NSPersistentStoreCoordinator *persistentStoreCoordinator;

- (void)saveContext;
- (NSURL *)applicationDocumentsDirectory;

@end
```

In the implementation file, Persistence.m, add implementations for the two helper methods, which don't deviate much from the Xcode-generated versions, as shown in Listing 1-12.

Listing 1-12. Helper Method Implementations in Persistence.m

```
- (void)saveContext {
  NSError *error;
  if ([self.managedObjectContext hasChanges] && ![self.managedObjectContext save:&error]) {
    NSLog(@"Unresolved error %@, %@", error, [error userInfo]);
    abort();
  }
}

- (NSURL *)applicationDocumentsDirectory {
  return [[[NSFileManager defaultManager] URLsForDirectory:NSDocumentDirectory
  inDomains:NSUserDomainMask] lastObject];
}
```

Notice that we don't check whether the managedObjectContext property is nil before saving, because we're going to create it when the Persistence instance is initialized so we know it won't be nil. We retain the naive error handling, though, for now.

To initialize the Core Data stack, add an implementation for init that creates the managed object model, the persistent store coordinator, and the managed object context, as shown in Listing 1-13.

Listing 1-13. Initializing the Core Data Stack in Persistence.m

```objc
- (id)init {
  self = [super init];
  if (self != nil) {
    // Initialize the managed object model
    NSURL *modelURL = [[NSBundle mainBundle] URLForResource:@"PersistenceApp"
    withExtension:@"momd"];
    _managedObjectModel = [[NSManagedObjectModel alloc] initWithContentsOfURL:modelURL];

    // Initialize the persistent store coordinator
    NSURL *storeURL = [[self applicationDocumentsDirectory] URLByAppendingPathComponent:
    @"PersistenceApp.sqlite"];

    NSError *error = nil;
    _persistentStoreCoordinator = [[NSPersistentStoreCoordinator alloc]
    initWithManagedObjectModel:self.managedObjectModel];
    if (![_persistentStoreCoordinator addPersistentStoreWithType:NSSQLiteStoreType
                                      configuration:nil
                                                URL:storeURL
                                            options:nil
                                              error:&error]) {
      NSLog(@"Unresolved error %@, %@", error, [error userInfo]);
      abort();
    }

    // Initialize the managed object context
    _managedObjectContext = [[NSManagedObjectContext alloc] init];
    [_managedObjectContext setPersistentStoreCoordinator:self.persistentStoreCoordinator];
    }
  return self;
}
```

In Chapter 9, we modify this approach to use threads for better performance, but for now we perform all the initialization on the main thread.

To finish initializing the Core Data stack, we add a Persistence property to the application delegate and create it when the application loads. Open AppDelegate.h, add a forward declaration for Persistence, and add the property, so that the file matches Listing 1-14.

Listing 1-14. `AppDelegate.h`

```
#import <UIKit/UIKit.h>

@class Persistence;

@interface AppDelegate : UIResponder <UIApplicationDelegate>

@property (strong, nonatomic) UIWindow *window;
@property (strong, nonatomic) Persistence *persistence;

@end
```

Next, open `AppDelegate.m` and add an import for `Persistence.h`:

```
#import "Persistence.h"
```

As the last step of initializing the Core Data stack, allocate and initialize the `persistence` property in the `application:didFinishLaunchingWithOptions` method. This method should now match Listing 1-15.

Listing 1-15. Allocating and Initializing the persistence Property

```
- (BOOL)application:(UIApplication *)application didFinishLaunchingWithOptions:(NSDictionary *)
launchOptions {
  self.persistence = [[Persistence alloc] init];
  return YES;
}
```

If you're building this project in Swift, your work follows the same sort of pattern, albeit without the header files. In your `Persistence` class, add a variable for your managed object context. We'll do all the initialization in the closure for this managed object context variable. You also add helpers for saving the context and getting the application document directory. Listing 1-16 shows the updated `Persistence.swift` file, and Listing 1-17 shows the additions to `AppDelegate.swift` to create a Persistence instance. Note that the Core Data stack will initialize when we create the Persistence instance; if we wanted, instead, to initialize Core Data when the managed object context is first accessed, we'd simply add the `@lazy` annotation to the managed object context variable.

Listing 1-16. `Persistence.swift` Updated for Core Data

```
import Foundation
import CoreData

class Persistence: NSObject {

  var managedObjectContext: NSManagedObjectContext? = {
    // Initialize the managed object model
    let modelURL = NSBundle.mainBundle().URLForResource("PersistenceAppSwift", withExtension:
    "momd")!
    let managedObjectModel = NSManagedObjectModel(contentsOfURL: modelURL)
```

```
  // Initialize the persistent store coordinator
  let storeURL = Persistence.applicationDocumentsDirectory.URLByAppendingPathComponent("Persisten
  ceAppSwift.sqlite")
  var error: NSError? = nil
  let persistentStoreCoordinator = NSPersistentStoreCoordinator(managedObjectModel:
  managedObjectModel!)
  if persistentStoreCoordinator.addPersistentStoreWithType(NSSQLiteStoreType, configuration: nil,
  URL: storeURL, options: nil, error: &error) == nil {
    abort()
  }

  // Initialize the managed object context
  var managedObjectContext = NSManagedObjectContext()
  managedObjectContext.persistentStoreCoordinator = persistentStoreCoordinator

  return managedObjectContext
}()

func saveContext() {
  var error: NSError? = nil

  if {
    if managedObjectContext.hasChanges && !managedObjectContext.save(&error) {
      abort()
    }
  }
}

class var applicationDocumentsDirectory: NSURL {
  let urls = NSFileManager.defaultManager().URLsForDirectory(.DocumentDirectory, inDomains:
  .UserDomainMask)
  return urls[urls.endIndex-1] as NSURL
}
}
```

Listing 1-17. The Updated AppDelegate.swift

```
import UIKit
import CoreData

@UIApplicationMain
class AppDelegate: UIResponder, UIApplicationDelegate {

  var window: UIWindow?
  var persistence: Persistence?

  func application(application: UIApplication!, didFinishLaunchingWithOptions launchOptions:
  NSDictionary!) -> Bool {
    persistence = Persistence()
    return true
  }
  /* Code snipped */
}
```

The Core Data stack now properly initializes when the application runs, but without an object model or any objects in it, we can't really see evidence of that. The next step is to create an object model.

Creating the Object Model

At this point, we've added all the Core Data pieces to the application that Xcode would have done for us had we checked the Use Core Data check box. For an application that you manually add Core Data to, you create the object model in the same way that you did for an application for which you checked Xcode's Use Core Data check box.

For PersistenceApp, we store gadgets that have a name and a price. Open the object model, PersistenceApp.xcdatamodeld, in Xcode's Project Navigator, and add a Gadget entity with a String attribute called name and a Float attribute called price. Your data model should match Figure 1-7.

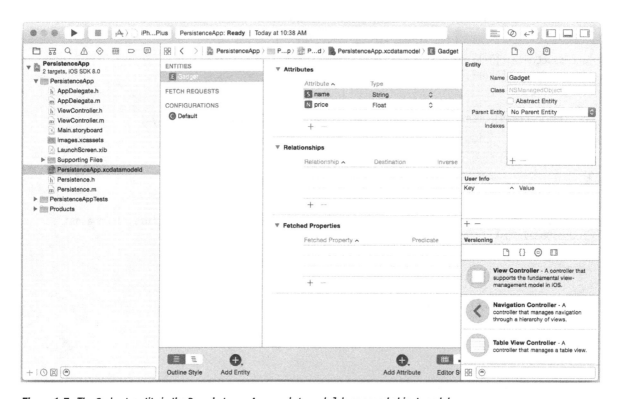

Figure 1-7. The Gadget entity in the PersistenceApp.xcdatamodeld managed object model

Now that we have an object model, we can create some objects in it.

Adding Objects to PersistenceApp

Once again, we use the application:didFinishLaunchingWithOptions method to add objects to the object model. This time, however, we'll do that work in another method that we call from application: didFinishLaunchingWithOptions. Also, instead of relying on the sqlite3 command-line tool to view the stored data, we fetch the objects from the persistent store and log them to the console—again, from a separate method. To begin, add calls to the two methods that we will create in application:didFinishLaunchingWithOptions, so that the code matches Listing 1-18 (Objective-C) or Listing 1-19 (Swift).

Listing 1-18. Adding Calls to Create and Fetch Objects (Objective-C)

```objectivec
- (BOOL)application:(UIApplication *)application didFinishLaunchingWithOptions:(NSDictionary *)
launchOptions {
  self.persistence = [[PAPersistence alloc] init];
  [self createObjects];
  [self fetchObjects];

  return YES;
}
```

Listing 1-19. Adding Calls to Create and Fetch Objects (Swift)

```swift
func application(application: UIApplication!, didFinishLaunchingWithOptions launchOptions:
NSDictionary!) -> Bool {
  persistence = Persistence()

  createObjects()
  fetchObjects()

  return true
}
```

Then, create implementations for the new methods. The createObjects method should look familiar; as before, you create the objects in the managed object context, then save the context. This code creates four Gadget instances: an iPad, an iPad Mini, an iPhone, and an iPod touch. The prices for them are in US dollars, and may or may not be accurate! Listing 1-20 shows the Objective-C code, and Listing 1-21 shows the Swift code. One thing to notice: since KVC requires object values, not primitives, the prices we set on the objects are NSNumber instances, not primitive floats.

Listing 1-20. The Objective-C createObjects Method

```objectivec
- (void)createObjects {
  NSManagedObject *iPad = [NSEntityDescription insertNewObjectForEntityForName:@"Gadget"
  inManagedObjectContext:self.persistence.managedObjectContext];
  [iPad setValue:@"iPad" forKey:@"name"];
  [iPad setValue:@499.0f forKey:@"price"];

  NSManagedObject *iPadMini = [NSEntityDescription insertNewObjectForEntityForName:@"Gadget"
  inManagedObjectContext:self.persistence.managedObjectContext];
  [iPadMini setValue:@"iPad Mini" forKey:@"name"];
  [iPadMini setValue:@329.0f forKey:@"price"];

  NSManagedObject *iPhone = [NSEntityDescription insertNewObjectForEntityForName:@"Gadget"
  inManagedObjectContext:self.persistence.managedObjectContext];
  [iPhone setValue:@"iPhone" forKey:@"name"];
  [iPhone setValue:@199.0f forKey:@"price"];
```

```
  NSManagedObject *iPodTouch = [NSEntityDescription insertNewObjectForEntityForName:@"Gadget"
inManagedObjectContext:self.persistence.managedObjectContext];
  [iPodTouch setValue:@"iPod touch" forKey:@"name"];
  [iPodTouch setValue:@299.0f forKey:@"price"];

  [self.persistence saveContext];
}
```

Listing 1-21. The Swift createObjects function

```
func createObjects() {
  if let persistence = persistence {
    let iPad = NSEntityDescription.insertNewObjectForEntityForName("Gadget",
    inManagedObjectContext: persistence.managedObjectContext!) as NSManagedObject
    iPad.setValue("iPad", forKey: "name")
    iPad.setValue(499, forKey: "price")

    let iPadMini = NSEntityDescription.insertNewObjectForEntityForName("Gadget",
    inManagedObjectContext: persistence.managedObjectContext!) as NSManagedObject
    iPadMini.setValue("iPad Mini", forKey: "name")
    iPadMini.setValue(329, forKey: "price")

    let iPhone = NSEntityDescription.insertNewObjectForEntityForName("Gadget",
    inManagedObjectContext: persistence.managedObjectContext!) as NSManagedObject
    iPhone.setValue("iPhone", forKey: "name")
    iPhone.setValue(199, forKey: "price")

    let iPodTouch = NSEntityDescription.insertNewObjectForEntityForName("Gadget",
    inManagedObjectContext: persistence.managedObjectContext!) as NSManagedObject
    iPodTouch.setValue("iPod Touch", forKey: "name")
    iPodTouch.setValue(299, forKey: "price")

    persistence.saveContext()
  }
  else {
    println("Error, persistence layer not initialized")
  }
}
```

The fetchObjects method fetches the objects from the persistent store and uses NSLog (or println)
to log them to the console. To fetch objects, we use the NSFetchRequest class, which represents
a fetch request. A fetch request is tied to a particular entity and contains all the criteria describing
what you want to fetch from that entity. With a fetch request, you can do things like set limits, specify
criteria that objects must match, sort the results, and use advanced aggregators to massage the
results the fetch request returns. Chapter 2 explains more about how to use NSFetchRequest, and
then Chapter 3 goes deeper into the powers of fetching data. At this point, however, we stay simple
in our usage of NSFetchRequest and just fetch all of the objects from our Gadget entity.

Before iOS 5.0, you typically created and used an NSFetchRequest instance by allocating
and initializing one, creating an NSEntityDescription instance, and setting the entity for the
NSFetchRequest instance to the NSEntityDescription instance, as shown in Listing 1-22.

Listing 1-22. Pre-iOS 5.0 NSFetchRequest Creation

```
NSFetchRequest *fetchRequest = [[NSFetchRequest alloc] init];
[fetchRequest setEntity:[NSEntityDescription entityForName:@"Gadget"
                              inManagedObjectContext:self.persistence.managedObjectContext]];
```

In iOS 5.0, Apple added a couple of convenience methods for NSFetchRequest so you don't have to create an NSEntityDescription instance or take two lines of code to tie your NSFetchRequest instance to an entity. One is an initializer that takes an entity name, and the other is a class method that takes an entity name. Listing 1-23 shows two ways to create an NSFetchRequest instance in iOS 5.0 or later.

Listing 1-23. Creating NSFetchRequest Instances in iOS 5.0 and Later

```
NSFetchRequest *fetchRequest1 = [[NSFetchRequest alloc] initWithEntityName:@"Gadget"];
NSFetchRequest *fetchRequest2 = [NSFetchRequest fetchRequestWithEntityName:@"Gadget"];
```

You can use any of the approaches. You might notice, however, that the pre-iOS 5.0 approach specified the managed object context for the entity, while the iOS 5.0-and-later approach does not. How, then, does the NSFetchRequest instance know which managed object context to use to find the entity?

The answer to that is that actually executing a fetch request is a method on the managed object context. For the later approaches, the managed object context uses the fetch request's entity name to look up the actual NSEntityDescription when it executes the fetch request. Listing 1-24 shows how to execute a fetch request.

Listing 1-24. Executing a Fetch Request

```
NSError *error;
NSManagedObjectContext *managedObjectContext = ...; // Get from somewhere
NSArray *objects = [managedObjectContext executeFetchRequest:fetchRequest error:&error];
```

You can pass nil for error if you don't care about any error results, but you'll usually want error information so you can handle the errors. Again, Chapter 4 covers error handling.

With this nascent knowledge of fetch requests, we can implement the fetchObjects method, as shown in Listing 1-25 (Objective-C) or Listing 1-26 (Swift). This method creates a fetch request, executes it against the managed object context, and displays the results in the console.

Listing 1-25. The Objective-C fetchObjects Method

```
- (void)fetchObjects {
  // Fetch the objects
  NSFetchRequest *fetchRequest = [NSFetchRequest fetchRequestWithEntityName:@"Gadget"];
  NSArray *objects = [self.persistence.managedObjectContext executeFetchRequest:fetchRequest
  error:nil];

  // Log the objects
  for (NSManagedObject *object in objects) {
    NSLog(@"%@", object);
  }
}
```

Listing 1-26. The Swift fetchObjects function

```swift
func fetchObjects() {
  if let persistence = persistence {
    let fetchRequest = NSFetchRequest(entityName: "Gadget")
    var error : NSError?
    let objects = persistence.managedObjectContext!.executeFetchRequest(fetchRequest, error: &error)
as [NSManagedObject]
    if let error = error {
      println("Something went wrong: \(error.localizedDescription)")
    }

    for object in objects {
      println(object)
    }
  }
  else {
    println("Error, persistence layer not initialized")
  }
}
```

Build and run the application. You should see a blank screen in the iOS Simulator, and in the Xcode Console you should see output that looks something like the following:

```
2014-07-07 21:49:40.537 PersistenceApp[8878:83583] <NSManagedObject: 0x7faa21e380b0> (entity:
Gadget; id: 0xd000000000040000 <x-coredata://D2570307-5795-4E9A-96C9-7B477D27AB5D/Gadget/p1> ;
data: {
    name = "iPad Mini";
    price = 329;
})
2014-07-07 21:49:40.538 PersistenceApp[8878:83583] <NSManagedObject: 0x7faa21e386a0> (entity:
Gadget; id: 0xd000000000080000 <x-coredata://D2570307-5795-4E9A-96C9-7B477D27AB5D/Gadget/p2> ;
data: {
    name = "iPod touch";
    price = 299;
})
2014-07-07 21:49:40.538 PersistenceApp[8878:83583] <NSManagedObject: 0x7faa21e38580> (entity:
Gadget; id: 0xd0000000000c0000 <x-coredata://D2570307-5795-4E9A-96C9-7B477D27AB5D/Gadget/p3> ;
data: {
    name = iPhone;
    price = 199;
})
2014-07-07 21:49:40.538 PersistenceApp[8878:83583] <NSManagedObject: 0x7faa21e37340> (entity:
Gadget; id: 0xd000000000100000 <x-coredata://D2570307-5795-4E9A-96C9-7B477D27AB5D/Gadget/p4> ;
data: {
    name = iPad;
    price = 499;
})
```

If you're running the Swift version of the app, the output is a little more compact, as the following shows:

```
<NSManagedObject: 0x7be633a0> (entity: Gadget; id: 0x7be68180 <x-coredata://9796AAF7-58AA-4B3A-86B8-
A1897330E17F/Gadget/p1> ; data: {
    name = iPad;
    price = 499;
})
<NSManagedObject: 0x7be66d60> (entity: Gadget; id: 0x7be681e0 <x-coredata://9796AAF7-58AA-4B3A-86B8-
A1897330E17F/Gadget/p2> ; data: {
    name = iPhone;
    price = 199;
})
<NSManagedObject: 0x7be666b0> (entity: Gadget; id: 0x7be681d0 <x-coredata://9796AAF7-58AA-4B3A-86B8-
A1897330E17F/Gadget/p3> ; data: {
    name = "iPad Mini";
    price = 329;
})
<NSManagedObject: 0x7be66e20> (entity: Gadget; id: 0x7be68250 <x-coredata://9796AAF7-58AA-4B3A-86B8-
A1897330E17F/Gadget/p4> ; data: {
    name = "iPod Touch";
    price = 299;
})
```

As before, you can also explore the SQLite database using `sqlite3`, but the log messages evidence that the objects were stored and retrieved.

Wrapping Up

In this chapter, you learned what Core Data is and what it's used for. You learned about the importance of persistence for data. You learned about the components of Core Data and how they work together. You built two Core Data–based applications: one that makes Xcode set up for you, and one in which you set up Core Data for yourself. You stored data in your Core Data persistent stores and retrieved them.

The applications you built in this chapter used anemic object models. In the next chapter, we build on the knowledge from this chapter to create more complex object models. You'll also learn about concepts like sorting and using predicates, and you'll understand the power of the Core Data object model.

Building Data Models

You can create applications with the most intuitive user interfaces that perform tasks users can't live without, but if you don't model your data correctly, your applications will become difficult to maintain, will underperform, and might even become unusable. This chapter explains how to model your data to support, not undermine, your applications.

In the previous chapter, you've built a simple iOS application using Xcode's Empty Application template. In this chapter, we model a bookstore and build an application to store information about the books we have. As in the previous chapter, we don't build any user interface code yet, maintaining the focus on Core Data.

Designing Your Database

The American philosopher Ralph Waldo Emerson once said, "A foolish consistency is the hobgoblin of little minds." People often wield that quote to defend carelessness or inattention to detail. We hope we're not falling into that trap as we flip-flop inconsistently between claiming Core Data is not a database and treating it as if it were. This section discusses how to design your data structures, and likening this process to modeling a relational database greatly helps not only the discussion but also the resulting design. The analogy breaks down in spots, however, as all analogies do, and we point out those spots throughout this discussion.

Core Data entity descriptions look, act, smell, and taste an awful lot like tables in a relational database. Attributes seem like columns in the tables, relationships feel like joins on primary and foreign keys, and entities appear like rows. If your model sits on a SQLite persistent store, Core Data actually realizes the entity descriptions, attributes, relationships, and entities as the database structures you'd expect. Remember, though, that your data can live in memory only or in some flat-file atomic store that has no tables or rows or columns or primary and foreign keys. Core Data abstracts the data structure from a relational database structure, simplifying both how you model and how you interact with your data. Allow for that abstraction in your mental model of how Core Data modeling works or you will fill your Core Data model with cruft, work against Core Data, and produce suboptimal data structures.

Newcomers to Core Data who have data modeling experience decry the lack of an autoincrement field type, believing that they have the responsibility, as they do in traditional data modeling, to define a primary key for each table. Core Data has no autoincrement type because you don't define any primary keys. Core Data assumes the responsibility to establish and maintain the uniqueness of each managed object, whether it's a row in a table or not.

Having no primary keys means having no foreign keys either; Core Data manages the relationships between entities, or tables, and performs any necessary joins for you. Get over the discomfort of not defining primary and foreign keys quickly, because agonizing over this implementation detail isn't worth your effort or angst.

> **Tip**   Here's a rule of thumb to remember as you create your Core Data models: worry about data, not data storage mechanisms.

Relational Database Normalization

Relational database theory espouses a process called normalization that's used for designing a data model. Normalization aims to reduce or eliminate redundancy and provide efficient access to the data inside the database. The normalization process divides into five levels, or forms, and work continues on a sixth form. The five normal forms carry definitions only a logician can love, or perhaps even understand; they read something like the following:

A relation R is in fourth normal form (4NF) if and only if, wherever there exists an MVD in R, say A -> -> B, then all attributes of R are also functionally dependent on A. In other words, the only dependencies (FDs or MVDs) in R are of the form K -> X (i.e. a functional dependency from a candidate key K to some other attribute X). Equivalently: R is in 4NF if it is in BCNF and all MVD's in R are in fact FDs.

(www.databasedesign-resource.com/normal-forms.html)

We have neither sufficient pages in this book nor the inclination to walk through formal definitions for each of the normal forms and then explain what they mean. Instead, this section describes each of the normal forms in relation to Core Data and provides data modeling advice. Note that adherence to a given normal form requires adherence to all the normal forms that precede it.

A database that conforms to first normal form (1NF) is considered normalized. To conform to this level of normalization, each row in the database must have the same number of fields. For a Core Data model, this means that each managed object should have the same number of attributes. Since Core Data doesn't allow you to create variable numbers of attributes in your entities, your Core Data models are automatically normalized.

Second normal form (2NF) and third normal form (3NF) deal with the relationships between non-key fields and key fields, dictating that non-key fields should be facts about the entire key field to which they belong. Since your Core Data model has no key fields, you shouldn't run afoul of these concerns.

You should, however, make sure that all the attributes for a given entity describe that entity, and not something else. For example, a Category entity that describes a category for books shouldn't have an author field since the author describes a book, not the category the book belongs to.

The next two normal forms, fourth normal form (4NF) and fifth normal form (5NF), can be considered the same form in the Core Data world. They deal with reducing or eliminating data redundancy, pushing you to move multiple-value attributes into separate entities and create to-many relationships between the entities. In Core Data terms, 4NF says that entity attributes shouldn't be used to store multiple values. Instead, you should move these attributes to a separate entity and create a to-many relationship between the entities. Consider, for example, the categories and books in the model in the bookstore application we build in this chapter. A model that would violate 4NF and 5NF would have a single entity, Category, with an additional attribute, book. We would then create a new category managed object for each book, so that we'd have several redundant Category objects. Instead, the bookstore data model will include a Category entity and separate Book entities.

Building a Simple Model

Create a new single view application project in Xcode so we can start building a simple model. Pursuing our imaginative app naming series, name this new application BookStore and set the language to your choice as shown in Figure 2-1.

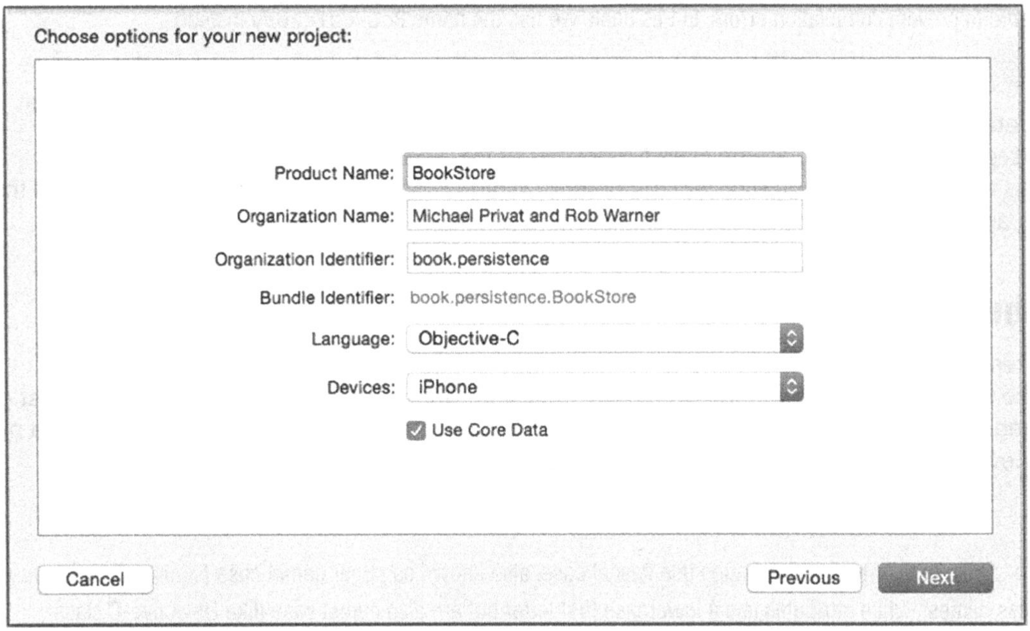

Figure 2-1. Creating the BookStore project

At this time, you should already be familiar with all the Core Data components described in Chapter 1. Find the object model (named BookStore.xcdatamodeld) Xcode has created and open it. As expected, it is empty.

> **Tip**   In Chapter 1, we showed you how to keep your application delegate clean of Core Data initialization and move this over to a class like Persistence. It is your choice to replicate this pattern in this chapter or keep the Xcode template as is and continue.

Entities

Just as you would when designing an object-oriented application, you should take a moment to think about the level of details your Core Data model requires in order to design the right set of model objects. In the case of modeling a book library, we want to quickly be able to locate books within the library by category. So, we start our model with a BookCategory entity. Click the Add Entity button at the bottom of the Xcode window and rename the newly created entity to BookCategory.

> **Tip**   There is already a class called Category in the Objective-C runtime, so it is best to avoid using this name to prevent compilation errors. In this book, we use the name BookCategory instead.

Core Data represents objects in the runtime as instances of NSManagedObject. Select the BookCategory entity and open the Data Model inspector. Note how the BookCategory entity is mapped to the class NSManagedObject by default. While designing your models, keep in mind that entities are akin to classes (hence the similar naming convention).

Attribues

Attributes are the properties used to describe an entity. Imagine what would be necessary to describe the category for the purpose of the BookStore application. We would want to at least give the category a name so that librarians can quickly know what the category refers to. To add a name, add a new attribute called name to the BookCategory entity and change its type to String.

> **Tip**   Take note of how entity names use Pascal case, also known as upper camel case (similar to Objective-C class names), while attributes use a lowercase first letter but are also camel case (like Objective-C class properties).

At this point, your model should look like Figure 2-2.

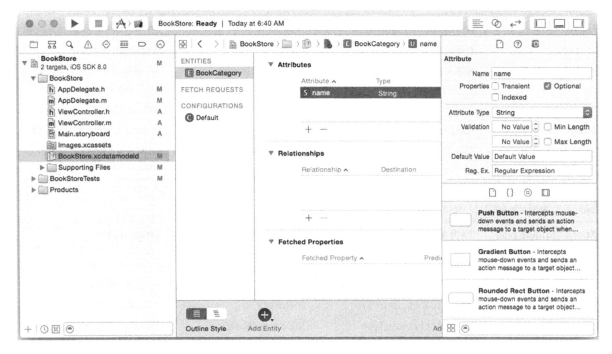

Figure 2-2. The BookCategory *entity with a* name *attribute*

Core Data supports a limited set of attributes types as described in Table 2-1 (for Objective-C code) and Table 2-2 (for Swift code).

Table 2-1. Available Attribute Types in Objective-C

Xcode attribute type	Objective-C attribute type	Objective-C data type	Description
Int16	NSInteger16AttributeType	NSNumber	A 16-bit integer
Int32	NSInteger32AttributeType	NSNumber	A 32-bit integer
Int64	NSInteger64AttributeType	NSNumber	A 64-bit integer
Decimal	NSDecimalAttributeType	NSDecimalNumber	A base-10 subclass of NSNumber
Double	NSDoubleAttributeType	NSNumber	An object wrapper for double

(continued)

Table 2-1. (continued)

Xcode attribute type	Objective-C attribute type	Objective-C data type	Description
Float	NSFloatAttributeType	NSNumber	An object wrapper for float
String	NSStringAttributeType	NSString	A character string
Boolean	NSBooleanAttributeType	NSNumber	An object wrapper for a Boolean value
Date	NSDateAttributeType	NSDate	A date object
Binary Data	NSBinaryDataAttributeType	NSData	Unstructured binary data
Transformable	NSTransformableAttributeType	Any non-standard type	Any type transformed into a supported type

Table 2-2. Available Attribute Types in Swift

Xcode attribute type	Swift attribute type	Swift data type	Description
Int16	Integer16AttributeType	NSNumber	A 16-bit integer
Int32	Integer32AttributeType	NSNumber	A 32-bit integer
Int64	Integer64AttributeType	NSNumber	A 64-bit integer
Decimal	DecimalAttributeType	NSDecimalNumber	A base-10 subclass of NSNumber
Double	DoubleAttributeType	NSNumber	An object wrapper for double
Float	FloatAttributeType	NSNumber	An object wrapper for float
String	StringAttributeType	String	A character string
Boolean	BooleanAttributeType	NSNumber	An object wrapper for a Boolean value
Date	DateAttributeType	NSDate	A date object
Binary Data	BinaryDataAttributeType	NSData	Unstructured binary data
Transformable	TransformableAttributeType	Any non-standard type	Any type transformed into a supported type

Most of these types are straightforward because they map directly to Objective-C data types. Using them is just a matter of leveraging the key/value accessors of the NSManagedObject instances. The Transformable type is the only type that doesn't have an Objective-C counterpart. It is used for custom types, which you use for any type not already supported by Core Data. Use Transformable as the type when the attribute you're trying to persist doesn't fit neatly into one of the supported data types. For example, if your managed object needs to represent a color and needs to persist it, it would make sense to use the CGColorRef type. In this case you need to set the Core Data type to transient and `Transformable` and provide Core Data with the mechanism for transforming the attribute into supported data types. Custom attributes make sense to use when you create your own managed objects that extend from `NSManagedObject`, and we talk about them in more detail in Chapter 7.

Key-Value Coding

`NSManagedObject` instances are key-value coding (KVC) compliant. KVC is a mechanism for accessing the properties of an object using a predefined naming convention. `NSManagedObject` provides implementations for KVC methods, both for Objective-C and for Swift. Here are the method declarations in Objective-C:

```
- (void)setValue:(id)value forKey:(NSString *)key
```

and

```
- (id)valueForKey:(NSString *)key
```

Here are their Swift counterparts:

```
func setValue(_ value: AnyObject!, forKey key: String!)
```

and

```
func valueForKey(_ key: String!) -> AnyObject!
```

Accessing an attribute in your code becomes a trivial matter, as this Objective-C snippet shows:

```
NSManagedObject *myCategory = ....
// Get the current value for the name attribute
NSString *name = [myCategory valueForKey:@"name"];
// Set the value for the name attribute to Magazines
[myCategory setValue:@"Magazines" forKey:@"name"];
```

Here is the Swift counterpart to that code:

```
var myCategory = ....
// Get the current value for the name attribute
var name: AnyObject! = myCategory.valueForKey("name")
// Set the value for the name attribute to Magazines
myCategory.setValue("Magazines", forKey: "name")
```

Generating Classes

Your code can always use `NSManagedObject` instances and KVC, but as your model grows and you have many different entities, it will inevitably become very confusing to call everything a managed object. For this reason, Core Data allows you to map entities directly to custom classes. All their attributes are mapped to Objective-C properties and everything becomes a lot simpler to manage.

In Xcode, select the `BookCategory` entity. In the menu, select Editor ➤ Create NSManagedObject Subclass… and follow the prompts until you click Create.

> **Tip**   If you check the Use scalar properties for primitive data types checkbox, the code generator will use
> primitive types instead of NSNumber to store numeric values. When deciding whether to use scalar values or
> not, consider how you are going to access the data. For example, scalar values are easier to access and use
> in arithmetic operations, but they cannot be added to a collection without being wrapped into an NSNumber.

A new class called BookCategory has been added to your Xcode project. As expected for the
Objective-C version, BookCategory.h looks like Listing 2-1.

Listing 2-1. BookCategory.h

```
#import <Foundation/Foundation.h>
#import <CoreData/CoreData.h>

@interface BookCategory : NSManagedObject

@property (nonatomic, retain) NSString * name;

@end
```

If you're creating this project in Swift, you'll instead have a file called BookCategory.swift, shown in
Listing 2-2.

Listing 2-2. BookCategory.swift

```
import Foundation
import CoreData

class BookCategory: NSManagedObject {

    @NSManaged var name: String

}
```

In either language, BookCategory is a subclass of NSManagedObject and has a simple property of
type NSString (Objective-C) or String (Swift) called name. This matches the model. The mapping
between this class and the entity is kept in the model itself. Go back to the model and select the
BookCategory entity. Open the Data Model inspector and see that its associated class is now
BookCategory (the newly created class).

If you're doing this project in Swift, you have a little more work to do, unless some future version
of Xcode corrects this issue. Unlike Objective-C, Swift has namespaces. When Swift compiles
your classes, it puts them into the namespace of their containing modules, which usually matches
the project's name. This means that your BookCategory class is really named BookStoreSwift.
BookCategory (if you named your project BookStoreSwift as we did). The Core Data model, however,
just shows BookCategory for the class. If you run the program now, you'll get an error message in the
console that looks something like:

```
CoreData: warning: Unable to load class named 'BookCategory' for entity 'BookCategory'.  Class not
found, using default NSManagedObject instead.
```

To correct this issue, you can either update the name of the class in the Core Data model to BookStoreSwift.BookCategory, or add an attribute to the BookCategory class to tell Core Data that the class really is named BookCategory after all, as Listing 2-3 shows.

Listing 2-3. Using the @objc attribute to Rename the Class for Objective-C

```
import Foundation
import CoreData

@objc(BookCategory)
class BookCategory: NSManagedObject {

    @NSManaged var name: String

}
```

The @objc(name) attribute changes the class's name, as far as any Objective-C classes are concerned, to name, so we can specify the un-namespaced version that our model specifies.

Accessing the name attributes is now even simpler and more familiar than before:

```
BookCategory *myCategory = ....
// Get the current value for the name attribute
NSString *name = myCategory.name;
// Set the value for the name attribute to Magazines
myCategory.name = @"Magazines";
```

In Swift, it looks like the following:

```
var myCategory = ....
// Get the current value for the name attribute
var name: AnyObject! = myCategory.name
// Set the value for the name attribute to Magazines
myCategory.name = "Magazines"
```

Relationships

As you normalize your data model, you'll likely create several entities, depending on the complexity of the data you're modeling. Relationships allow you to tie entities together. Core Data allows you to tune the relationships you create to accurately reflect how your data relate to each other. Start with adding a Book entity to your model. At this point, leave it with no attributes until we figure out what needs to go there.

In the BookStore application, you can see an obvious relationship between a category and the books it contains. For now, we will keep the problem reasonably simple by stating that a book can belong to only one category. Let's reflect this relationship in the model.

Select the BookCategory entity and in the Relationships section, click the + button. Xcode creates a new relationship for you to configure. Enter books for the name, and select Book as the destination, and leave the inverse blank for now. In the Data Model inspector tab in Xcode, change the type to To Many to indicate that this relationship will point to possibly multiple books. This is called a one-to-many relationship. Figure 2-3 shows what the model looks like so far.

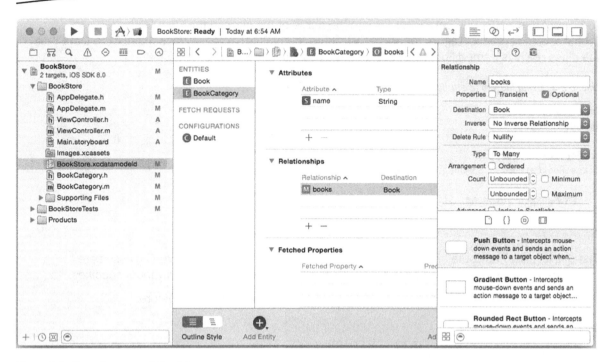

Figure 2-3. A one-to-many relationship

Leaving the Inverse field blank gives you compiler warnings. You can ignore these warnings and run your application without specifying an inverse relationship—after all, these are compiler warnings, not compiler errors—but you could face unexpected consequences. Core Data uses bidirectional relationship information to maintain the consistency of the object graph (hence the Consistency Error) and to manage undo and redo information. If you leave a relationship without an inverse, you imply that you will take care of the object graph consistency and undo/redo management. The Apple documentation strongly discourages this, however, especially in the case of a To-Many relationship. When you don't specify an inverse relationship, the managed object at the other end of the relationship isn't marked as changed when the managed object at this end of the relationship changes. Consider, for example, if a player object is deleted and it has no inverse relationship back to its team. Any optionality rules or delete rules aren't enforced when the object graph is saved.

In order to comply and help Core Data, add the inverse relationship—that is, for a given book, the category that it belongs to. Select the Book entity and add a new relationship. Set the name to category, the destination to BookCategory, and the inverse to books. If you go back to the BookCategory entity and select the books relationship, you will see that its inverse is now automatically set as well.

Relationship Properties

Let's take a look at the options available for configuring relationships. Select the books relationship and open the Data Model inspector as shown in Figure 2-3.

The first field, Name, becomes the name of the key NSManagedObject uses to reference the relationship. By convention, it's the name of the referenced entity in lower case. In the case of a To Many relationship, the name field conventionally is pluralized. Note that these guidelines are conventions only, but you will make your data models more understandable, maintainable, and easier to work with if you follow them. You can see that the BookStore data model follows these conventions—in the Book entity, the relationship to the BookCategory entity is called category. In the BookCategory entity, the relationship to the Book entity, a To Many relationship, is called books.

The Properties field has two options, both checkboxes, which you can set independently of each other. The first, Transient, allows you to specify that a relationship should not be saved to the persistent store. A transient relationship still has support for undo and redo operations, but it disappears when the application exits, giving the relationship the lifespan of a Hollywood marriage. Some possible uses for transient relationships include the following:

> Relationships between entities are temporal and shouldn't survive beyond the current run of the application.

> Relationship information can be derived from some external source of data, whether another Core Data persistent store or some other source of information.

In most cases, you'll want your relationships to be persistent and you'll leave the Transient checkbox unchecked.

The second property checkbox, Optional, specifies whether this relationship requires a non-nil value. Think of this like a nullable vs. non-nullable column in a database. If you check the Optional checkbox, a managed object of this entity type can be saved to the persistent store without having anything specified for this relationship. If unchecked, however, saving the context will fail. If the Book entity in the data model for the BookStore application, for example, left this checkbox unchecked, every book entity would have to belong to a category. Setting the "category" value for a book to nil (or never setting it at all) would cause all calls to save: to fail with the following error description, "category is a required value."

We cover the next field, Delete Rule, in the section "Delete Rule."

The Type field has two options: To Many and To One. To One means that this relationship has exactly one managed object (or zero, depending on optionality settings) on each end of the relationship. For the BookStore application, making the books relationship on the Category entity a To One type would mean that only one book could exist in a given category, which would obviously be counterintuitive for a book category. If the entities were Frame and Picture, however, a To One type would make sense, as a frame typically has only one picture in it. Setting this field to To Many means the destination entity can have many managed objects that relate to each managed object instance of this entity type.

The next field, Count, sets limits on the number of managed objects of the destination entity type that can relate to each managed object of this entity type, and has effect only if the type is set to To Many. You can specify values for Minimum and/or Maximum, and Core Data will enforce the rules you set. Note that you can set one without setting the other—you don't have to set both. Exceeding the limits you set causes the save: operation to fail with a "Too many items" or a "Too few items" error message. Note that the Optional setting overrides the Minimum Count setting: if Optional is checked and Minimum Count is 1, saving the context when the relationship count is zero succeeds.

Delete Rule

The Delete Rule setting allows you to specify what happens if you try to delete a managed object of this entity type. Table 2-3 lists the four possibilities and what they mean.

Table 2-3. *Delete Rule Options*

Rule name	Description
Cascade	The source object is deleted and any related destination objects are also deleted.
Deny	If the source object is related to any destination objects, the deletion request fails and nothing is deleted.
Nullify	The source object is deleted and any related destination objects have their inverse relationships set to nil.
No Action	The source object is deleted and nothing changes in any related destination objects.

Be careful how you set the Delete Rule for your relationships. In the BookStore application, for example, if you set the Delete Rule for the books relationship in the BookCategory entity to "Cascade," deleting a category would delete all the books related to it. This is probably not what you want. If you set that rule to "Deny" and a category had any books in it, trying to delete the category would result in an error on any attempts to save the context with the message "category is not valid." Setting the Delete Rule to "Nullify" would preserve the books in the persistent store, though they would no longer belong to any category.

The "No Action" option represents another way, like not specifying an inverse relationship, that Core Data allows you to accept responsibility for managing object graph consistency. If you specify this value for the Delete Rule, Core Data allows you to delete the source object but pretends to the destination objects that the source object still exists. For the BookStore application, this would mean removing a category but still telling customers that the books they are looking for are available, but they are not in any category for the customers to browse. You won't find many compelling reasons to use the "No Action" setting, except perhaps for performance reasons when you have many destination objects. Chapter 9 discusses performance tuning with Core Data.

Ordered Properties

The Arrangement field specifies whether Core Data should maintain the order in which entities are added to the relationship, and applies only to a To Many relationship. To maintain the order, you check the Ordered checkbox. In the case of the BookStore application, we don't care about the order in which books are added to a category, so to see an example of an ordered relationship, create a Page entity and create a To Many relationship called pages from Book to Page. Obviously in the case of pages, we want to maintain the order, so set the Arrangement field of the pages relationship to Ordered by checking the checkbox in the relationship properties. Don't forget to set the inverse relationship.

The model should look as shown in Figure 2-4.

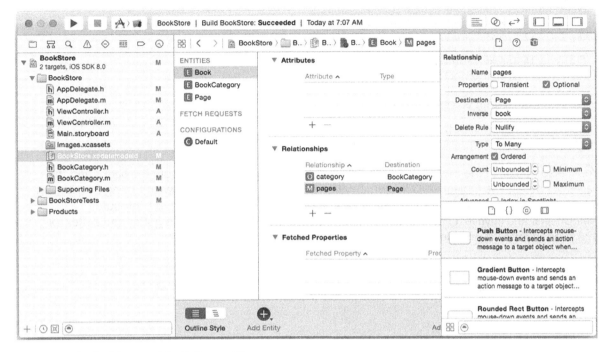

Figure 2-4. *The BookStore model with three entities*

Refresh the custom objects by selecting all three entities in the model (click the first one and shift+click on the last one) and, in the Xcode menu, select Editor ➤ Create NSManagedObject Subclass... then follow the prompts until you can click Create. Xcode will ask you for permission to replace the existing BookCategory class. Click Replace and you should have three custom Core Data managed objects: BookCategory, Book, and Page. If you have chosen to generate these classes in Swift, don't forget to either update the class names in the Core Data model to include the namespace (e.g., BookStoreSwift.Book), or to add the @objc() attribute to the class (e.g., @objc(Book)).

Open BookCategory.h and note how the unordered relationship to books is represented as an NSSet.

```
@property (nonatomic, retain) NSSet *books;
```

Now open Book.h and see how the ordered relationship is represented with an NSOrderedSet.

```
@property (nonatomic, retain) NSOrderedSet *pages;
```

You can see this in Swift by first looking in BookCategory.swift to see the NSSet:

```
@NSManaged var books: NSSet
```

And then looking at the NSOrderedSet in Book.swift:

```
@NSManaged var pages: NSOrderedSet
```

The `NSOrderedSet` class provides accessors that work with indices, allowing you to specify a strict order. Listing 2-4 shows the Objective-C method declarations, and Listing 2-5 shows the Swift declarations.

Listing 2-4. NSOrderedSet accessors in Objective-C

```
- (id)objectAtIndex:(NSUInteger)idx;
- (NSUInteger)indexOfObject:(id)object;
```

Listing 2-5. NSOrderedSet accessors in Swift

```
func objectAtIndex(_ index: Int) -> AnyObject!
func indexOfObject(_ object: AnyObject!) -> Int
```

You'll also notice, in the Swift version, the `@NSManaged` attribute in front of both the `books` and the `pages` variables. The Objective-C implementation file `BookCategory.m`, shown in Listing 2-6, has an attribute called `@dynamic` in front of the name and books properties. Both these attributes (`@NSManaged` and `@dynamic`) do the same thing: they tell the compiler that the getter and setter for that property will be provided at runtime, not compile time.

Listing 2-6. BookCategory.m

```
#import "BookCategory.h"
#import "Book.h"

@implementation BookCategory

@dynamic name;
@dynamic books;

@end
```

Storing and Retrieving Data

Now that we've created a basic data model, let's add some attributes to the entities we've created so that we can experiment with storing and retrieving data.

Select the `Page` entity and add a new `text` attribute of type `String`. We will use this to store the text on a given page. Select the `Book` entity and add a `title` attribute of type `String` and a `price` of type `Float`. Once done, regenerate all the custom Core Data objects for all three entities. Since we have numeric types and we prefer to access them through primitive types, be sure to check the Use scalar properties for primitive data types checkbox.

At this point, your project and model should look as illustrated in Figure 2-5.

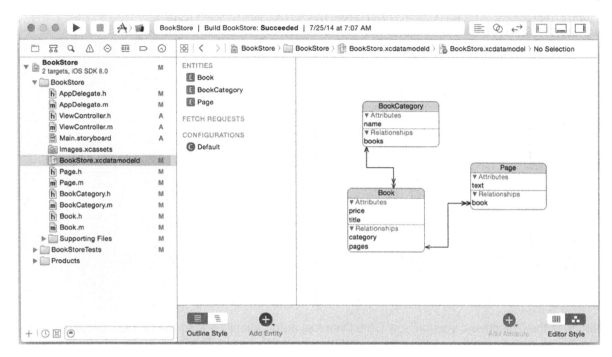

Figure 2-5. The BookStore model and generated custom classes

Listing 2-7 shows the Book.h header file, and Listing 2-8 shows the Book.swift file.

Listing 2-7. Book.h

```objc
#import <Foundation/Foundation.h>
#import <CoreData/CoreData.h>

@class BookCategory, Page;

@interface Book : NSManagedObject

@property (nonatomic, retain) NSString * title;
@property (nonatomic) float price;
@property (nonatomic, retain) BookCategory *category;
@property (nonatomic, retain) NSOrderedSet *pages;
@end

@interface Book (CoreDataGeneratedAccessors)

- (void)insertObject:(Page *)value inPagesAtIndex:(NSUInteger)idx;
- (void)removeObjectFromPagesAtIndex:(NSUInteger)idx;
- (void)insertPages:(NSArray *)value atIndexes:(NSIndexSet *)indexes;
- (void)removePagesAtIndexes:(NSIndexSet *)indexes;
```

```
- (void)replaceObjectInPagesAtIndex:(NSUInteger)idx withObject:(Page *)value;
- (void)replacePagesAtIndexes:(NSIndexSet *)indexes withPages:(NSArray *)values;
- (void)addPagesObject:(Page *)value;
- (void)removePagesObject:(Page *)value;
- (void)addPages:(NSOrderedSet *)values;
- (void)removePages:(NSOrderedSet *)values;
@end
```

Listing 2-8. Book.swift

```swift
import Foundation
import CoreData

class Book: NSManagedObject {

    @NSManaged var title: String
    @NSManaged var price: Float
    @NSManaged var category: BookCategory
    @NSManaged var pages: NSOrderedSet

}
```

Notice in the Objective-c version how Core Data has automatically added the proper collection accessors, making the use of our objects and their properties easy. The Swift version, however, can't generate corresponding runtime accessors, so they're not present.

Inserting New Managed Objects

With our Core Data model fleshed out, we're ready to put objects into it. Upon startup, we want to populate our Core Data store with some categories and books. For now, we will use hard-coded data. Open AppDelegate.m (Objective-C) or AppDelegate.swift (Swift) and edit the application:didFinishLaunchingWithOptions: method to invoke an initStore method, as shown in Listing 2-9 (Objective-C) or Listing 2-10 (Swift).

Listing 2-9. Creating a Hook to Preload Data (Objective-C)

```objc
- (void)initStore {
  // Load data here
}

- (BOOL)application:(UIApplication *)application didFinishLaunchingWithOptions:(NSDictionary *)
  launchOptions {
  [self initStore];
  return YES;
}
```

Listing 2-10. Creating a Hook to Preload Data (Swift)

```swift
func initStore() {
  // Load data here
}

func application(application: UIApplication!, didFinishLaunchingWithOptions launchOptions:
NSDictionary!) -> Bool {
  initStore()
  return true
}
```

Now all we have to do is create our objects and push them into the persistent store. Edit the AppDelegate.m or AppDelegate.swift file so that the initStore method looks like Listing 2-11 (Objective-C) or Listing 2-12 (Swift). For the Objective-C version, you also must add the following import statements:

```objc
#import "BookCategory.h"
#import "Book.h"
#import "Page.h"
```

Also worth noting is that the Objective-C version takes advantage of the dynamically-generated addBooks: method for adding books. Since Swift doesn't have that support, we instead must retrieve the mutable set of books using NSManagedObject's mutableSetValueForKeyPath function, and then add the books to the NSManagedSet object that it returns.

Listing 2-11. The Objective-C initStore Method for Adding New Objects

```objc
- (void)initStore {
  BookCategory *fiction = [NSEntityDescription insertNewObjectForEntityForName:@"BookCategory"
  inManagedObjectContext:self.managedObjectContext];
  fiction.name = @"Fiction";

  BookCategory *biography = [NSEntityDescription insertNewObjectForEntityForName:@"BookCategory"
  inManagedObjectContext:self.managedObjectContext];
  biography.name = @"Biography";

  Book *book1 = [NSEntityDescription insertNewObjectForEntityForName:@"Book"
  inManagedObjectContext:self.managedObjectContext];
  book1.title = @"The first book";
  book1.price = 10;

  Book *book2 = [NSEntityDescription insertNewObjectForEntityForName:@"Book"
  inManagedObjectContext:self.managedObjectContext];
  book2.title = @"The second book";
  book2.price = 15;

  Book *book3 = [NSEntityDescription insertNewObjectForEntityForName:@"Book"
  inManagedObjectContext:self.managedObjectContext];
  book3.title = @"The third book";
  book3.price = 10;
```

```
[fiction addBooks:[NSSet setWithArray:@[book1, book2]]];
[biography addBooks:[NSSet setWithArray:@[book3]]];

[self.managedObjectContext save:nil];
}
```

Listing 2-12. The Swift initStore function;. for Adding New Objects

```swift
func initStore() {
    var fiction = NSEntityDescription.insertNewObjectForEntityForName("BookCategory",
    inManagedObjectContext: self.managedObjectContext) as BookCategory
    fiction.name = "Fiction"

    var biography = NSEntityDescription.insertNewObjectForEntityForName("BookCategory",
    inManagedObjectContext: self.managedObjectContext) as BookCategory
    biography.name = "Biography"

    var book1 = NSEntityDescription.insertNewObjectForEntityForName("Book", inManagedObjectContext:
    self.managedObjectContext) as Book
    book1.title = "The first book"
    book1.price = 10

    var book2 = NSEntityDescription.insertNewObjectForEntityForName("Book", inManagedObjectContext:
    self.managedObjectContext) as Book
    book2.title = "The second book"
    book2.price = 15

    var book3 = NSEntityDescription.insertNewObjectForEntityForName("Book", inManagedObjectContext:
    self.managedObjectContext) as Book
    book3.title = "The third book"
    book3.price = 10

    var fictionRelation = fiction.mutableSetValueForKeyPath("books")
    fictionRelation.addObject(book1)
    fictionRelation.addObject(book2)

    var biographyRelation = biography.mutableSetValueForKeyPath("books")
    biographyRelation.addObject(book3)

    self.saveContext()
}
```

The code is easy to read. Note, however, that you can't allocate a managed object directly. Instead, you must obtain it from the managed object context. That is, of course, so the context can manage it.

The initStore method creates two categories and three books. It adds the two first books to the "fiction" category and the third book to the "biography" category. We purposely overlooked the Page entity here to not overcrowd the example.

Launch the app to execute this code. Once you get the white screen on the simulator, you can quit. In Chapter 1 we showed you how to find and view the SQLite store that backs your data store. Open the database file, BookStore.sqlite, with sqlite3 in a Terminal window.

The .schema command confirms that our data model is correctly created.

```
sqlite> .schema
CREATE TABLE ZBOOK ( Z_PK INTEGER PRIMARY KEY, Z_ENT INTEGER, Z_OPT INTEGER, ZCATEGORY INTEGER,
ZPRICE FLOAT, ZTITLE VARCHAR );
CREATE TABLE ZBOOKCATEGORY ( Z_PK INTEGER PRIMARY KEY, Z_ENT INTEGER, Z_OPT INTEGER, ZNAME VARCHAR );
CREATE TABLE ZPAGE ( Z_PK INTEGER PRIMARY KEY, Z_ENT INTEGER, Z_OPT INTEGER, ZBOOK INTEGER,
Z_FOK_BOOK INTEGER, ZTEXT VARCHAR );
CREATE TABLE Z_METADATA (Z_VERSION INTEGER PRIMARY KEY, Z_UUID VARCHAR(255), Z_PLIST BLOB);
CREATE TABLE Z_PRIMARYKEY (Z_ENT INTEGER PRIMARY KEY, Z_NAME VARCHAR, Z_SUPER INTEGER, Z_MAX
INTEGER);
CREATE INDEX ZBOOK_ZCATEGORY_INDEX ON ZBOOK (ZCATEGORY);
CREATE INDEX ZPAGE_ZBOOK_INDEX ON ZPAGE (ZBOOK);
```

And a couple of queries show that our data have been loaded:

```
sqlite> .header on
sqlite> .mode column
sqlite> select * from ZBOOKCATEGORY;
Z_PK        Z_ENT       Z_OPT       ZNAME
----------  ----------  ----------  ----------
1           2           1           Biography
2           2           1           Fiction
sqlite> select * from ZBOOK;
Z_PK        Z_ENT       Z_OPT       ZCATEGORY   ZPRICE      ZTITLE
----------  ----------  ----------  ----------  ----------  --------------
1           1           1           1           10.0        The third book
2           1           1           2           10.0        The first book
3           1           1           2           15.0        The second boo
```

Of course, we if run the application once again, new entities will be loaded and we will have
duplicates.

```
sqlite> select * from ZBOOKCATEGORY;
Z_PK        Z_ENT       Z_OPT       ZNAME
----------  ----------  ----------  ----------
1           2           1           Fiction
2           2           1           Biography
3           2           1           Biography
4           2           1           Fiction
```

This is because the initStore method assumes (wrongfully) that the store is empty when it runs.
We could, of course, create a new persistent store upon startup by deleting the BookStore.sqlite
file, but this might be a little overdone. There may be information from previous sessions we might
want to use in the future. For safety, we will simply clear the entities we care about.

First let's create a utility method, called deleteAllObjects, for clearing entities by entity name. You
can find the Objective-C code for this method in Listing 2-13 and the Swift code in Listing 2-14.
You pass this method the name of the entity for which you wish to delete all objects. This method
fetches all objects for that entity and then deletes them.

Listing 2-13. The Objective-C deleteAllObjects Method

```objc
- (void)deleteAllObjects:(NSString *)entityName {
  NSFetchRequest *fetchRequest = [NSFetchRequest fetchRequestWithEntityName:entityName];

  NSError *error;
  NSArray *items = [self.managedObjectContext executeFetchRequest:fetchRequest error:&error];

  for (NSManagedObject *managedObject in items) {
    [self.managedObjectContext deleteObject:managedObject];
  }

  if (![self.managedObjectContext save:&error]) {
    NSLog(@"Error deleting %@ - error:%@", entityName, error);
  }
}
```

Listing 2-14. The Swift deleteAllObjects Function

```swift
func deleteAllObjects(entityName: String) {
  let fetchRequest = NSFetchRequest(entityName: entityName)

  let objects = self.managedObjectContext?.executeFetchRequest(fetchRequest, error: nil)
  for object in objects as [NSManagedObject] {
    self.managedObjectContext?.deleteObject(object)
  }

  var error: NSError? = nil
  if !self.managedObjectContext!.save(&error) {
    println("Error deleting \(entityName) - error:\(error)")
  }
}
```

Edit the initStore method to clear all books and categories before running by adding the following two lines at the beginning of the Objective-C method:

```objc
- (void)initStore {
  [self deleteAllObjects:@"Book"];
  [self deleteAllObjects:@"BookCategory"];
  ...
}
```

Your Swift function should look like this:

```swift
func initStore() {
  deleteAllObjects("Book")
  deleteAllObjects("BookCategory")
  ...
}
```

Now run the application once again and see how the store is clean no matter how many times we run it.

```
sqlite> select * from ZBOOKCATEGORY;
Z_PK        Z_ENT       Z_OPT       ZNAME
----------  ----------  ----------  ----------
3           2           1           Fiction
4           2           1           Biography
sqlite> select * from ZBOOK;
Z_PK        Z_ENT       Z_OPT       ZCATEGORY   ZPRICE      ZTITLE
----------  ----------  ----------  ----------  ----------  ---------------
4           1           1           3           10.0        The first book
5           1           1           3           15.0        The second boo
6           1           1           4           10.0        The third book
```

You might notice that the primary key counter doesn't reset (the Z_PK column in the tables)—it continues to increment as you add and delete objects. Remember that this is an implementation detail, so you can ignore it. Let Core Data handle it.

Retrieving Managed Objects

We've briefly touched, through code samples, on how to retrieve objects from the persistent store. Let's take a closer look at how to pull information. For this, create a new method called showExampleData. Edit application:didFinishLaunchingWithOptions: to add a call to this new method right after calling initStore, as Listing 2-15 (Objective-C) and Listing 2-16 (Swift) show.

Listing 2-15. Calling showExampleData (Objective-C)

```
- (BOOL)application:(UIApplication *)application didFinishLaunchingWithOptions:(NSDictionary *)
  launchOptions {
  [self initStore];
  [self showExampleData];
  return YES;
}
```

Listing 2-16. Calling showExampleData (Swift)

```
func application(application: UIApplication!, didFinishLaunchingWithOptions launchOptions:
NSDictionary!) -> Bool {
  initStore()
  showExampleData()
  return true
}
```

Now add the showExampleData method shown in Listing 2-17 (Objective-C) and Listing 2-18 (Swift). This method uses NSLog or println to log all the books in the persistent store to the Xcode console.

Listing 2-17. The showExampleData Method in Objective-C

```
- (void)showExampleData {
  NSFetchRequest *fetchRequest = [NSFetchRequest fetchRequestWithEntityName:@"Book"];

  NSArray *books = [self.managedObjectContext executeFetchRequest:fetchRequest error:nil];
  for (Book *book in books) {
    NSLog(@"Title: %@, price: %.2f", book.title, book.price);
  }
}
```

Listing 2-18. The showExampleData Function in Swift

```
func showExampleData() {
  let fetchRequest = NSFetchRequest(entityName: "Book")

  let books = self.managedObjectContext?.executeFetchRequest(fetchRequest, error: nil)
  for book in books as [Book] {
    println(String(format: "Title: \(book.title), price: %.2f", book.price))
  }
}
```

The method creates a new fetch request for the Book entity and executes it. Because the fetch request has no selection criteria, it simply returns all objects it finds in the persistent store that match the given entity (i.e., Book). If you run the application, you get the following output in the console:

```
BookStore[84975:c07] Title: The first book, price: 10.00
BookStore[84975:c07] Title: The third book, price: 10.00
BookStore[84975:c07] Title: The second book, price: 15.00
```

You may notice that the books may or may not be in order; in the preceding log, for example, the book with the title "The third book" comes before the book with the title "The second book." Remember that the books relationship is not ordered, so the order isn't deterministic.

Predicates

In the preceding fetch, we fetched all books from the Book entity, without any way to narrow the scope of what Core Data returned. Core Data does have mechanisms, however, to return only subsets of data. Core Data uses the NSPredicate class from the Foundation framework to specify how to select the objects that should be part of the result set when executing a fetch request. Predicates can be built in two ways: you can either build the object and its graph manually or you can use the query language NSPredicate implements. You will find that most of the time you will prefer the convenience and readability of the latter method.

In this section we look at both ways of building predicates for each example in order to help draw a parallel between the query language and the NSPredicate object graph. Understanding both ways will help you determine your preferred approach. You can also mix and match the approaches depending on your applications and data scenarios.

The predicate query language builds an NSPredicate object graph from a string representation that has similarities to an SQL 'WHERE' clause. The method that builds a predicate from the language is the class method predicateWithFormat:(NSString *). For instance, if you want to get the managed object that represents the book "The first book," you build the predicate by calling [NSPredicate predicateWithFormat:@"title = 'The first book'"].

To test this, modify the showExampleData method as shown in Listing 2-19 (Objective-C) and Listing 2-20 (Swift).

Listing 2-19. The Objective-C showExampleData Method with a Predicate

```
- (void)showExampleData {
  NSFetchRequest *fetchRequest = [NSFetchRequest fetchRequestWithEntityName:@"Book"];
  fetchRequest.predicate = [NSPredicate predicateWithFormat:@"title = 'The first book'"];

  NSArray *books = [self.managedObjectContext executeFetchRequest:fetchRequest error:nil];
  for (Book *book in books) {
    NSLog(@"Title: %@, price: %.2f", book.title, book.price);
  }
}
```

Listing 2-20. The Swift showExampleData Function with a Predicate

```
func showExampleData() {
  let fetchRequest = NSFetchRequest(entityName: "Book")
  fetchRequest.predicate = NSPredicate(format: "title='The first book'")

  let books = self.managedObjectContext?.executeFetchRequest(fetchRequest, error: nil)
  for book in books as [Book] {
    println(String(format: "Title: \(book.title), price: %.2f",  book.price))
  }
}
```

Run this and this time, the output finds only one book as expected.

```
BookStore[85253:c07] Title: The first book, price: 10.00
```

In its simplest form, a predicate executes a test on an object. If the test succeeds, then the object is part of the result set. If the test is negative, then the object isn't included in the result set. The preceding example, title = 'The first book' is an example of a simple predicate. The key path title and the constant string value 'The first book' are called expressions. The operator '=' is called a comparator.

NSPredicate objects are made by compositing NSExpression instances. The example could have been written as shown in Listing 2-21 (Objective-C) and Listing 2-22 (Swift).

Listing 2-21. An Objective-C Predicate Using the NSPredicate Object Graph

```objc
- (void)showExampleData {
  NSFetchRequest *fetchRequest = [NSFetchRequest fetchRequestWithEntityName:@"Book"];

  NSExpression *exprTitle = [NSExpression expressionForKeyPath:@"title"];
  NSExpression *exprValue = [NSExpression expressionForConstantValue:@"The first book"];
  NSPredicate *predicate = [NSComparisonPredicate predicateWithLeftExpression:exprTitle
  rightExpression:exprValue modifier:NSDirectPredicateModifier type:NSEqualToPredicateOperatorType
  options:0];
  fetchRequest.predicate = predicate;

  NSArray *books = [self.managedObjectContext executeFetchRequest:fetchRequest error:nil];
  for (Book *book in books) {
    NSLog(@"Title: %@, price: %.2f", book.title, book.price);
  }
}
```

Listing 2-22. A Swift Predicate Using the NSPredicate Object Graph

```swift
func showExampleData() {
  let fetchRequest = NSFetchRequest(entityName: "Book")

  let exprTitle = NSExpression(forKeyPath: "title")
  let exprValue = NSExpression(forConstantValue: "The first book")
  let predicate = NSComparisonPredicate(leftExpression: exprTitle, rightExpression: exprValue,
  modifier: .DirectPredicateModifier, type: .EqualToPredicateOperatorType, options: nil)
  fetchRequest.predicate = predicate

  let books = self.managedObjectContext?.executeFetchRequest(fetchRequest, error: nil)
  for book in books as [Book] {
    println(String(format: "Title: \(book.title), price: %.2f",  book.price))
  }
}
```

Running the application again will reveal the same result as before, as expected.

You've seen that predicates can be written in two ways. Obviously, the first one was simpler and more readable. In some advanced cases, however, the only option is the second. This could be the case, for example, in an application that lets users build queries and then composes the user's selections and filters into predicates.

In Chapter 3 we study predicates more closely and explain the ins and outs of predicate building.

Fetched Properties

Fetched properties are a convenient way to retrieve subsets of data based on a predefined predicate. Imagine, for example, that we want to add a property to BookCategory to get the "bargain books" (i.e., all the books cheaper than $12). We can define what a bargain book is directly in the model. Open `BookStore.xcdatamodeld` and select the `BookCategory` entity. Click the + sign below the Fetched Properties section to create a new fetched property and name it `bargainBooks`. Open the Data Model inspector, and in the Destination drop-down, pick Book. For the predicate, enter

```
SELF.price < 12 AND (SELF.category=$FETCH_SOURCE)
```

Figure 2-6 shows the `bargainBooks` fetched property.

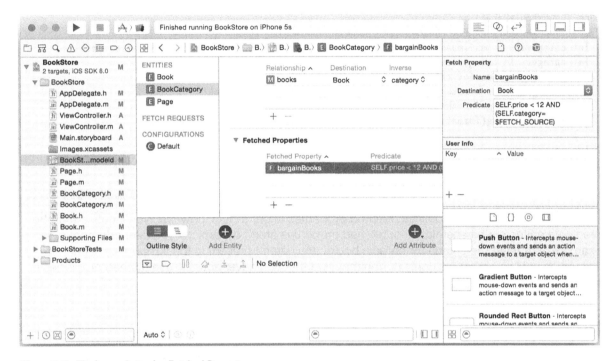

Figure 2-6. *The* `bargainBooks` *Fetched Property*

The `SELF` keyword relates to the destination (i.e., Book). The `$FETCHED_SOURCE` keyword refers to the `BookCategory` object. So the preceding code reads something like "this book belongs to the list if its price is less than $12 and its category is the calling category."

Then in the code, rewrite the `showExampleData` method as shown in Listing 2-23 (Objective-C) or Listing 2-24 (Swift) to illustrate how to use the fetched property.

Listing 2-23. Using a Fetched Property in Objective-C

```
- (void)showExampleData {
  NSFetchRequest *fetchRequest = [NSFetchRequest fetchRequestWithEntityName:@"BookCategory"];
  NSArray *categories = [self.managedObjectContext executeFetchRequest:fetchRequest error:nil];
  for (BookCategory *category in categories) {
    // Retrieve the bargain books for the current category
    NSArray *bargainBooks = [category valueForKey:@"bargainBooks"];
```

```
    // Now simply display them
    NSLog(@"Bargains for category: %@", category.name);
    for (Book *book in bargainBooks) {
      NSLog(@"Title: %@, price: %.2f", book.title, book.price);
    }
  }
}
```

Listing 2-24. Using a Fetched Property in Swift

```
func showExampleData() {
  let fetchRequest = NSFetchRequest(entityName: "BookCategory")
  let categories = self.managedObjectContext?.executeFetchRequest(fetchRequest, error: nil)
  for category in categories as [BookCategory] {
    println("Bargains for category: \(category.name)")
    let bargainBooks = category.valueForKey("bargainBooks") as [Book!]
    for book in bargainBooks {
      println(String(format: "Title: \(book.title), price: %.2f",  book.price))
    }
  }
}
```

We first fetch the categories. Then, for each category, we get the bargain books and display their titles.

Despite the convenience of defining fetched properties in our model, however, you'll notice that the predicate editor is a bit anemic. Also, fetched properties aren't dynamic; if you later add books, for example, that meet the criteria for bargain books, they aren't present in the bargainBooks fetched properties until you reset the context. You may find that you never actually use fetched properties in your applications.

Notifications

When trying to keep a user interface synchronized with the data it represents, you will often find it useful to be notified when data change. Core Data comes with mechanisms for handling notifications on data changes.

Notification upon Creation

Sometimes you need to be notified each time an instance of a specific type of managed object is created. You may have requirements, for example, to create derived data that aren't present in the store (cache files, perhaps, or simply for auditing reasons). Pretend we want to get a log entry every time a new book is created. We can use Core Data's notifications, which call our custom Core Data class's awakeFromInsert method each time a new object is created. In your implementation, you should call super's implementation, and then perform your work. Open Book.m or Book.swift and override the awakeFromInsert method as shown in Listing 2-25 (Objective-C) and Listing 2-26 (Swift).

Listing 2-25. Core Data Notifications Through the awakeFromInsert *Method (Objective-C)*

```objc
- (void)awakeFromInsert {
  [super awakeFromInsert];
  NSLog(@"New book created");
}
```

Listing 2-26. Core Data Notifications Through the awakeFromInsert *Function (Swift)*

```swift
override func awakeFromInsert() {
  super.awakeFromInsert()
  println("New book created")
}
```

Since our application reloads the persistent store every time it launches, you will get three new book creation notifications each time you run it.

```
BookStore[85678:c07] New book created
BookStore[85678:c07] New book created
BookStore[85678:c07] New book created
```

Notification upon Fetch

Similarly, in some cases you want to be notified when an object is retrieved from the persistent store. For example, if your objects contain vectors to draw an image, upon fetching the object, you may want to render a thumbnail image. For storage reasons, you might decide that it's redundant to persist the actual thumbnail and therefore you have to compute it when the object is fetched. To receive this notification, you override the awakeFromFetch method. As with awakeFromInsert, you should call the super implementation first. Still in Book.m or Book.swift, override the awakeFromFetch method as shown in Listing 2-27 (Objective-C) and Listing 2-28 (Swift).

Listing 2-27. Core Data Notifications Through the awakeFromFetch *Method (Objective-C)*

```objc
- (void)awakeFromFetch {
  [super awakeFromFetch];
  NSLog(@"Book fetched: %@", self.title);
}
```

Listing 2-28. Core Data Notifications Through the awakeFromFetch *Method (Swift)*

```swift
override func awakeFromFetch() {
  super.awakeFromFetch()
  println("Book fetched: \(self.title)")
}
```

When you run this, you get the following output:

```
BookStore[85678:c07] Book fetched: The first book
BookStore[85678:c07] Book fetched: The second book
BookStore[85678:c07] Book fetched: The third book
BookStore[85678:c07] New book created
BookStore[85678:c07] New book created
BookStore[85678:c07] New book created
```

You get the fetches first because of the cleanup in the deleteAllObjects method. First the books are read and deleted, then the three new books are added.

You might notice something a little strange, however, in the application's output. Even though you fetch the book with the title "The first book" in the showExampleData method, as evidenced in the log

```
BookStore[85678:c07] Title: The first book, price: 10.00
```

You don't see another log message saying "Book fetched," even though showExampleData clearly executes a fetch request. This means that your awakeFromFetch isn't necessarily called every time you execute a fetch request that returns it—it's called only when it's re-initialized from the persistent store during a fetch. If the object has already been initialized from the persistent store, and is sitting in your managed object context, executing a fetch request won't call awakeFromFetch.

Though that may sound confusing, you can remember this behavior by focusing more on the "awake" part of the method name, rather than the "fetch" part. The object "awakes" when it is loaded into memory, so this method is called when a managed object is loaded into memory and that happened because of a fetch.

In Chapter 9, we talk about a concept called "faulting." Faulting comes into play when the awakeFromFetch method is called, so be sure to read that chapter for more information.

Notification upon Change

By far the most useful notification is on data change. If you are displaying a book in your user interface and its title changes, you may want to the user interface to reflect this change. Since NSManagedObject is KVC compliant, all the usual principles of key-value observing (KVO) can be applied and notifications can be fired on data modifications. The KVO model is very simple and decentralized, with only two objects at play: the observer and the observed. The observer must be registered with the observed object and the observed object is responsible for firing notifications when its data change. The default implementation of NSManagedObject automatically handles the firing of notifications.

Registering an Observer

In order to receive change notifications, you must register the observer with the observed object using the addObserver:forKeyPath:options:context: method. The registration is valid for a given key path only, which means that it is valid only for the named attribute or relationship. The advantage is that it gives you a very fine level of control over which notifications fire.

The options give you an even finer level of granularity by specifying what information you want to receive in your notifications. Table 2-4 below shows the Objective-C options, which can be combined with a bitwise OR (for example, NSKeyValueObservingOptionOld | NSKeyValueObservingOptionNew to specify both old and new).

Table 2-4. *The Objective-C Notification Options*

Option	Description
NSKeyValueObservingOptionOld	The change dictionary will contain the old value under the lookup key NSKeyValueChangeOldKey
NSKeyValueObservingOptionNew	The change dictionary will contain the new value under the lookup key NSKeyValueChangeNewKey

The Swift versions of these options have briefer names, as Table 2-5 shows. The keys in the change directory, however, remain the same.

Table 2-5. *The Swift Notification Options*

Option	Description
Old	The change dictionary will contain the old value under the lookup key NSKeyValueChangeOldKey
New	The change dictionary will contain the new value under the lookup key NSKeyValueChangeNewKey

Let's register the app delegate to be an observer to title changes for the book named "The first book." Open AppDelegate.m or AppDelegate.swift and edit showExampleData, returning to the simpler version that fetches the first book, as shown in Listing 2-29 (Objective-C) and Listing 2-30 (Swift). While we're in the method, after registering for event notification, we also change the book title to "The new title."

Listing 2-29. *Registering for KVO in Objective-C*

```
- (void)showExampleData {
  NSFetchRequest *fetchRequest = [NSFetchRequest fetchRequestWithEntityName:@"Book"];
  fetchRequest.predicate = [NSPredicate predicateWithFormat:@"title = 'The first book'"];

  NSArray *books = [self.managedObjectContext executeFetchRequest:fetchRequest error:nil];
  for (Book *book in books) {
    NSLog(@"Title: %@, price: %.2f", book.title, book.price);

    // Register this object for KVO
    [book addObserver:self
          forKeyPath:@"title"
            options:NSKeyValueObservingOptionOld | NSKeyValueObservingOptionNew
            context:nil];
    book.title = @"The new title";
  }
}
```

Listing 2-30. Registering for KVO in Swift

```
func showExampleData() {
  let fetchRequest = NSFetchRequest(entityName: "Book")
  fetchRequest.predicate = NSPredicate(format: "title='The first book'")

  let books = self.managedObjectContext?.executeFetchRequest(fetchRequest, error: nil)
  for book in books as [Book] {
    println(String(format: "Title: \(book.title), price: %.2f",  book.price))

    // Register this object for KVO
    book.addObserver(self, forKeyPath: "title", options: .Old | .New, context: nil)
    book.title = "The new title"
  }
}
```

Don't build and run the application yet, however, as it will crash because you've registered to receive a notification, but you haven't yet written code to handle the notification once you've received it. Read on to the next section to understand how to receive notifications you've registered for.

Receiving the Notifications

Registering to receive the change notifications is one thing. Actually receiving the notifications is another. To receive change notifications, you override the observeValueForKeyPath:ofObject: change:context: method in the observer class. Still in AppDelegate.m or AppDelegate.swift, add the method shown in Listing 2-31 (Objective-C) and Listing 2-32 (Swift).

Listing 2-31. Receiving the Change Notification (Objective-C)

```
- (void)observeValueForKeyPath:(NSString *)keyPath
                      ofObject:(id)object
                        change:(NSDictionary *)change
                       context:(void *)context {
  NSLog(@"Changed value for %@: %@ -> %@", keyPath,
        [change objectForKey:NSKeyValueChangeOldKey],
        [change objectForKey:NSKeyValueChangeNewKey]);
}
```

Listing 2-32. Receiving the Change Notification (Swift)

```
override func observeValueForKeyPath(keyPath: String,
  ofObject object: AnyObject,
  change: [NSObject : AnyObject],
  context: UnsafeMutablePointer<()>) {
  println("Changed value for \(keyPath): \(change[NSKeyValueChangeOldKey]!) -> \(change[NSKeyValue
ChangeNewKey]!)")
}
```

Run the application once again and you will get the following output, indicating that the title change notification has been received:

```
Changed value for title: The first book -> The new title
```

Conclusion

For applications that depend on data, which means most applications, the importance of designing your data model correctly cannot be overstated. The Xcode data modeling tool provides a solid interface for designing and defining your data models, and throughout this chapter you have learned to navigate the many options available as you create entities, attributes, and relationships. Make sure to understand the implications of how you've configured your data model, so that your applications can run efficiently and correctly.

In most cases, you should avoid options in your model that wrest control from Core Data and make you manage the consistency of the object graph yourself. Core Data will almost always do a better job of managing object graph consistency than you will. When you must take control, make sure to debug your solutions well to prevent application crashes or data corruption.

While you can work with NSManagedObject directly, you will find that as you build larger applications, you will inevitably feel the need to use subclasses, as we discussed in this chapter, in order to keep your objects and their properties clearly delineated in code.

In the next chapter, we take an in-depth look at building predicates for advanced queries.

Chapter 3

Advanced Querying

Simple applications and simple data models can usually skate on simple queries to serve up the data specific to the applications' requirements. Nontrivial applications, however, usually have more complex data models and more intricate requirements surrounding that data. To meet those application requirements and interact with the more complex data, you need more advanced approaches to querying your data. This chapter discusses advanced querying techniques for Core Data and will equip you with the requisite tools for extracting the data combinations you need for your data-rich applications.

Most of the classes we discuss in this chapter aren't tied to Core Data but, rather, apply to any of the collection classes. You use NSPredicate, NSExpression, NSSortDescriptor, aggregation operators, functions, and the lot to filter any type of collection, not just Core Data result sets. Some classes, and some methods of these classes, in fact, apply only to general collections and don't work with Core Data. Keep in mind, however, that once you have fetched a result set from Core Data, you have a standard NSArray collection that you can manipulate outside Core Data's confines as you wish.

Building WordList

Whether you're playing Words with Friends, Scrabble, or some other word game, you'll find more success if you know the words that the game you're playing allows. In this chapter, we build an application called WordList that downloads a popular word list from the Internet and runs various queries against it to demonstrate advanced queries. The application isn't fancy—you can see the user interface (UI) in Figure 3-1—and it won't guarantee victory or even improved scores. You may, however, learn a new word or two that you can play in your favorite word game and impress your friends.

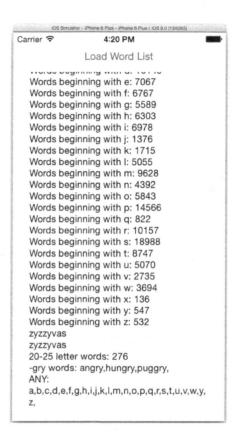

Figure 3-1. The WordList application

Creating the Application

In Xcode, create a new project using the Single View Application template. Set the Product Name to WordList, select the language you'd like to use, uncheck Use Core Data (we'll be adding it ourselves), and click Next to let Xcode go to work to create your project.

Next, add Core Data to the WordList application by following the steps outlined previously.

- Add an @import CoreData (Objective-C) or import CoreData (Swift) directive wherever you need access to the Core Data classes.

- Add the WordList data model, WordList.xcdatamodeld.

- Add the Persistence class, which encapsulates WordList's Core Data interaction.

The header file for the Objective-C Persistence class, shown in Listing 3-1, declares the properties and methods for realizing the Core Data stack. It should look familiar—you saw it first in Chapter 1's Persistence class.

Listing 3-1. Persistence.h

```objectivec
@import CoreData;

@interface Persistence : NSObject

@property (readonly, strong, nonatomic) NSManagedObjectContext *managedObjectContext;
@property (readonly, strong, nonatomic) NSManagedObjectModel *managedObjectModel;
@property (readonly, strong, nonatomic) NSPersistentStoreCoordinator *persistentStoreCoordinator;

- (void)saveContext;
- (NSURL *)applicationDocumentsDirectory;

@end
```

Listing 3-2 shows the Objective-C implementation file, `Persistence.m`.

Listing 3-2. Persistence.m

```objectivec
#import "Persistence.h"

@implementation Persistence

- (id)init
{
  self = [super init];
  if (self != nil) {
    // Initialize the managed object model
    NSURL *modelURL = [[NSBundle mainBundle] URLForResource:@"WordList" withExtension:@"momd"];
    _managedObjectModel = [[NSManagedObjectModel alloc] initWithContentsOfURL:modelURL];

    // Initialize the persistent store coordinator
    NSURL *storeURL = [[self applicationDocumentsDirectory] URLByAppendingPathComponent:@"WordList.
    sqlite"];

    NSError *error = nil;
    _persistentStoreCoordinator = [[NSPersistentStoreCoordinator alloc]
    initWithManagedObjectModel:self.managedObjectModel];
    if (![_persistentStoreCoordinator addPersistentStoreWithType:NSSQLiteStoreType
                                      configuration:nil
                                               URL:storeURL
                                           options:nil
                                             error:&error]) {
      NSLog(@"Unresolved error %@, %@", error, [error userInfo]);
      abort();
    }

    // Initialize the managed object context
    _managedObjectContext = [[NSManagedObjectContext alloc] init];
    [_managedObjectContext setPersistentStoreCoordinator:self.persistentStoreCoordinator];
  }
  return self;
}
```

```objc
#pragma mark - Helper Methods

- (void)saveContext
{
  NSError *error = nil;
  if ([self.managedObjectContext hasChanges] && ![self.managedObjectContext save:&error]) {
    NSLog(@"Unresolved error %@, %@", error, [error userInfo]);
    abort();
  }
}

- (NSURL *)applicationDocumentsDirectory
{
  return [[[NSFileManager defaultManager] URLsForDirectory:NSDocumentDirectory
inDomains:NSUserDomainMask] lastObject];
}

@end
```

Finally, Listing 3-3 shows the Swift implementation, `Persistence.swift`. Notice that we sneak in an extension at the bottom of the file that we'll later use to make formatting output simpler.

Listing 3-3. Persistence.swift

```swift
import Foundation
import CoreData

class Persistence: NSObject {

  var managedObjectContext: NSManagedObjectContext = {
    // Initialize the managed object model
    let modelURL = NSBundle.mainBundle().URLForResource("WordListSwift", withExtension: "momd")
    let managedObjectModel = NSManagedObjectModel(contentsOfURL: modelURL!)

    // Initialize the persistent store coordinator
    let storeURL = Persistence.applicationDocumentsDirectory.URLByAppendingPathComponent("WordListS
    wift.sqlite")
    var error: NSError? = nil
    let persistentStoreCoordinator = NSPersistentStoreCoordinator(managedObjectModel:
    managedObjectModel!)
    if persistentStoreCoordinator.addPersistentStoreWithType(NSSQLiteStoreType, configuration: nil,
    URL: storeURL, options: nil, error: &error) == nil {
      abort()
    }

    // Initialize the managed object context
    var managedObjectContext = NSManagedObjectContext()
    managedObjectContext.persistentStoreCoordinator = persistentStoreCoordinator

    return managedObjectContext
  }()
```

```
func saveContext() {
  var error: NSError? = nil
  let managedObjectContext = self.managedObjectContext
  if managedObjectContext != nil {
    if managedObjectContext.hasChanges && !managedObjectContext.save(&error) {
      abort()
    }
  }
}

class var applicationDocumentsDirectory: NSURL {
  let urls = NSFileManager.defaultManager().URLsForDirectory(.DocumentDirectory, inDomains:
  .UserDomainMask)
  return urls[urls.endIndex-1] as NSURL
}
}

extension Float {
    func format(f: String) -> String {
        return NSString(format: "%\(f)f", self)
    }
}
```

In your application delegate, AppDelegate, add a Persistence property and initialize the Core
Data stack when WordList launches. For the Objective-C version, Listing 3-4 shows the updated
AppDelegate.h file, and Listing 3-5 shows the updated application:didFinishLaunchingWithOptions:
method in AppDelegate.m. Be sure to import Persistence.h at the top of AppDelegate.m. For the
Swift version, see Listing 3-6.

Listing 3-4. AppDelegate.h

```
#import <UIKit/UIKit.h>

@class Persistence;

@interface AppDelegate : UIResponder <UIApplicationDelegate>

@property (strong, nonatomic) UIWindow *window;
@property (strong, nonatomic) Persistence *persistence;

@end
```

Listing 3-5. The Updated application:didFinishLaunchingWithOptions: Method

```
- (BOOL)application:(UIApplication *)application didFinishLaunchingWithOptions:(NSDictionary *)
launchOptions {
  self.persistence = [[Persistence alloc] init];
  return YES;
}
```

Listing 3-6. The Updated AppDelegate. `swift`

```
import UIKit
import CoreData

@UIApplicationMain
class AppDelegate: UIResponder, UIApplicationDelegate {

  var window: UIWindow?
  var persistence: Persistence?

  func application(application: UIApplication!, didFinishLaunchingWithOptions launchOptions:
NSDictionary!) -> Bool {
    persistence = Persistence()
    return true
  }
  /* Code snipped */
}
```

WordList now initializes the Core Data stack, but it has an empty data model. In the next section, we build the data model so that WordList can store and manage the word list.

Building the Data Model

You should have already created the data model, `WordList.xcdatamodeld`, in the previous section. In this section, you add the entities, attributes, and relationships that the WordList application requires.

The source data for the WordList application is a list of words, so we could model the data as a single entity with a single attribute to store the text of a word. The other pieces of data that WordList requires—the length of the word and the category it belongs to, as determined by its first letter—can be calculated from the word itself. We're not going to model the data that way, however, for two reasons. First, that would thwart the purpose of the chapter; we want some attributes and relationships so we can use Core Data's advanced querying capabilities. The second reason isn't so artificial, however: performance. As you use Core Data in your applications, remember that your database server isn't some high-powered server that crunches numbers and data at lightning speeds. It's an iOS device, crowded with applications and running processes and a CPU (central processing unit) that balances size, weight, performance, and battery life. Just because you can calculate something at runtime doesn't mean you should. Precalculating and storing metadata can be a way to improve the performance and efficiency of your Core Data applications. We discuss performance at greater depth in Chapter 9.

For the WordList data model, create two entities: `WordCategory` and `Word`. In the `WordCategory` entity, add an attribute of type `String` named `firstLetter`. In the `Word` entity, add two attributes: `text`, of type `String`, and `length`, of type `Integer 16`. Then, create a to-many relationship from `WordCategory` to `Word`, with a Nullify delete rule, and call it `words`. Don't forget to create the inverse relationship from `Word` back to `WordCategory` called `wordCategory`. When you're finished, the data model should match Figure 3-2.

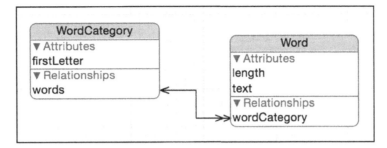

Figure 3-2. The WordList data model

Creating the User Interface

The WordList UI provides a button to reload the source data (the list of words) from the Internet and a text area to display statistics about the data. To accomplish this sparse interface, open Main.storyboard and drag a button to the top center of the view and a text view filling the rest of the view below that. Set up the constraints to maintain the controls like this; the easiest way to accomplish this is to select them, click the Resolve Auto Layout issues icon in the bottom right of Xcode (it looks like a triangle between two vertical lines), and select Add Missing Constraints.

In ViewController.h, declare a method to handle button presses—the touch-up inside event—and a property to point to the text area. Your code should match Listing 3-7. For Swift, open ViewController.swift and add analogs for the same things: a function to handle button presses and a variable to point to the text area, as Listing 3-8 shows.

Listing 3-7. ViewController.h

```
#import <UIKit/UIKit.h>

@interface ViewController : UIViewController

@property (nonatomic, strong) IBOutlet UITextView *textView;

- (IBAction)loadWordList:(id)sender;

@end
```

Listing 3-8. ViewController.swift

```
import UIKit

class ViewController: UIViewController {

    @IBOutlet weak var textView: UITextView!

    @IBAction func loadWordList(sender: AnyObject) {
    }
}
```

The view you've created should look like Figure 3-3.

Figure 3-3. The WordList UI

For Objective-C, add an empty method implementation in ViewController.m for loadWordList:. For both Objective-C and Swift, wire the touch-up inside event for the button to the loadWordList: selector. Also, wire the text view in the interface to the textView property.

We'll come back to the UI code in a moment, to respond to button presses and update the statistics. First, however, we're going to add code to the persistence layer, Persistence, to load the word list and provide statistics.

Loading and Analyzing the Word List

We delegate responsibility for loading the data model and providing statistics about that data to the Persistence class. We declare two methods in that class: one for taking an NSString containing all the words, parsing it, and loading it and one for returning an NSString containing statistics about the word list. Declare these methods for the Objective-C version in Persistence.h, as Listing 3-9 shows.

Listing 3-9. Two Method Declarations in `Persistence.h`

```
- (void)loadWordList:(NSString *)wordList;
- (NSString *)statistics;
```

The `loadWordList:` method does three things.

- Deletes all existing data, in case the user has already loaded the word list;

- Creates the word categories; and

- Loads the words.

Start by creating a helper method, `deleteAllObjectsForEntityWithName:`, which deletes all data in a given entity. Listing 3-10 shows the Objective-C implementation of this method, and Listing 3-11 shows the Swift implementation.

Listing 3-10. `deleteAllObjectsForEntityWithName:` *in* `Persistence.m`

```
- (void)deleteAllObjectsForEntityWithName:(NSString *)name {
  NSLog(@"Deleting all objects in entity %@", name);

  NSFetchRequest *fetchRequest = [NSFetchRequest fetchRequestWithEntityName:name];
  fetchRequest.resultType = NSManagedObjectIDResultType;

  NSArray *objectIDs = [self.managedObjectContext executeFetchRequest:fetchRequest error:nil];
  for (NSManagedObjectID *objectID in objectIDs) {
    [self.managedObjectContext deleteObject:[self.managedObjectContext objectWithID:objectID]];
  }

  [self saveContext];

  NSLog(@"All objects in entity %@ deleted", name);
}
```

Listing 3-11. `deleteAllObjectsForEntityWithName` *in* `Persistence.swift`

```
func deleteAllObjectsForEntityWithName(name: String) {
    println("Deleting all objects in entity \(name)")
    var fetchRequest = NSFetchRequest(entityName: name)
    fetchRequest.resultType = .ManagedObjectIDResultType

    if let managedObjectContext = managedObjectContext {
        var error: NSError? = nil
        let objectIDs = managedObjectContext.executeFetchRequest(fetchRequest, error: &error)
        for objectID in objectIDs! {
            managedObjectContext.deleteObject(managedObjectContext.objectWithID(objectID as
            NSManagedObjectID))
        }

        saveContext()

        println("All objects in entity \(name) deleted")
    }
}
```

This method introduces a performance optimization—rather than fetching all the objects for an entity, we fetch only the object identifiers for the matching objects. We do this by setting the resultType property of the fetch request to NSManagedObjectIDResultType. After fetching all the object identifiers into an array, we iterate through them and tell the managed object context to delete the object for the identifier. When we're done, we save the context.

The loadWordList: method uses the method you just created to delete all WordCategory and Word instances. It then creates 26 WordCategory instances —one each for letters "a" through "z." It then parses the word list and adds the words to our Core Data object graph, setting the text, length, and category for each and logging a message after every 100 words it adds so we can track the progress in Xcode's console. Finally, it saves the managed object context. Listing 3-12 shows the Objective-C loadWordList: method, and Listing 3-13 shows the Swift loadWordList function.

Listing 3-12. loadWordList: in Persistence.m

```
- (void)loadWordList:(NSString *)wordList {
  // Delete all the existing words and categories
  [self deleteAllObjectsForEntityWithName:@"Word"];
  [self deleteAllObjectsForEntityWithName:@"WordCategory"];

  // Create the categories
  NSMutableDictionary *wordCategories = [NSMutableDictionary dictionaryWithCapacity:26];
  for (char c = 'a'; c <= 'z'; c++) {
    NSString *firstLetter = [NSString stringWithFormat:@"%c", c];
    NSManagedObject *wordCategory = [NSEntityDescription insertNewObjectForEntityForName:
    @"WordCategory" inManagedObjectContext:self.managedObjectContext];
    [wordCategory setValue:firstLetter forKey:@"firstLetter"];
    [wordCategories setValue:wordCategory forKey:firstLetter];
    NSLog(@"Added category '%@'", firstLetter);
  }

  // Add the words from the list
  NSUInteger wordsAdded = 0;
  NSArray *newWords = [wordList componentsSeparatedByCharactersInSet:[NSCharacterSet
  whitespaceAndNewlineCharacterSet]];
  for (NSString *word in newWords) {
    if (word.length > 0) {
      NSManagedObject *object = [NSEntityDescription insertNewObjectForEntityForName:@"Word"
      inManagedObjectContext:self.managedObjectContext];
      [object setValue:word forKey:@"text"];
      [object setValue:[NSNumber numberWithInteger:word.length] forKey:@"length"];
      [object setValue:[wordCategories valueForKey:[word substringToIndex:1]]
      forKey:@"wordCategory"];
      ++wordsAdded;
      if (wordsAdded % 100 == 0)
        NSLog(@"Added %lu words", wordsAdded);
    }
  }
  NSLog(@"Added %lu words", wordsAdded);
  [self saveContext];
  NSLog(@"Context saved");
}
```

Listing 3-13. loadWordList in Persistence.swift

```
func loadWordList(wordList: String) {
    // Delete all the existing words and categories
    deleteAllObjectsForEntityWithName("Word")
    deleteAllObjectsForEntityWithName("WordCategory")

    // Create the categories
    var wordCategories = NSMutableDictionary(capacity: 26)
    for c in "abcdefghijklmnopqrstuvwxyz" {
        let firstLetter = "\(c)"
        var wordCategory: AnyObject! = NSEntityDescription.insertNewObjectForEntityForName
        ("WordCategory", inManagedObjectContext: self.managedObjectContext!)
        wordCategory.setValue(firstLetter, forKey: "firstLetter")
        wordCategories.setValue(wordCategory, forKey: firstLetter)
        println("Added category '\(firstLetter)'")
    }

    // Add the words from the list
    var wordsAdded = 0
    let newWords = wordList.componentsSeparatedByCharactersInSet(NSCharacterSet.
    whitespaceAndNewlineCharacterSet())
    for word in newWords {
        if countElements(word) > 0 {
            var object: AnyObject! = NSEntityDescription.insertNewObjectForEntityForName
            ("Word", inManagedObjectContext: self.managedObjectContext!)
            object.setValue(word, forKey: "text")
            object.setValue(countElements(word), forKey: "length")
            object.setValue(wordCategories.valueForKey((word as NSString).substringToIndex(1)),
            forKey: "wordCategory")
            wordsAdded++
            if wordsAdded % 100 == 0 {
                println("Added \(wordsAdded) words")
                saveContext()
                println("Context saved")
            }
        }
    }
    saveContext()
    println("Context saved")
}
```

You might notice something curious about the way this code handles the word categories it creates. Instead of just storing the word categories in Core Data and fetching the correct word category to set in a word's wordCategory relationship, this code puts the word categories in an NSMutableDictionary instance. This is a performance optimization; it's much faster to look up the appropriate category for a word in a dictionary than to have Core Data explore its object graph for the same category. As you use Core Data in your applications, don't be afraid to go outside Core Data where appropriate to improve performance.

Getting a Count

The method to provide statistics about our word list, statistics, returns an NSString that we can plop into the text view in WordList's UI. We'll start simply, displaying the number of words in the word list. We'll continue to add to this method throughout this chapter as we learn more about querying Core Data. Add the code shown in Listing 3-14 to Persistence.m or the code shown in Listing 3-15 to Persistence.swift to return the number of words in the word list.

Listing 3-14. statistics in Persistence.m

```
- (NSString *)statistics {
  NSMutableString *string = [[NSMutableString alloc] init];
  [string appendString:[self wordCount]];
  return string;
}
```

Listing 3-15. statistics in Persistence.swift

```
func statistics() -> String {
    var string = NSMutableString()

    string.appendString(wordCount())
    return string
}
```

Now implement the wordCount method shown in Listing 3-16 (Objective-C) and Listing 3-17 (Swift).

Listing 3-16. wordCount in Persistence.m

```
- (NSString *)wordCount {
  NSFetchRequest *fetchRequest = [NSFetchRequest fetchRequestWithEntityName:@"Word"];
  NSUInteger count = [self.managedObjectContext countForFetchRequest:fetchRequest error:nil];
  return [NSString stringWithFormat:@"Word Count: %lu\n", count];
}
```

Listing 3-17. wordCount in Persistence.swift

```
func wordCount() -> String {
    let fetchRequest = NSFetchRequest(entityName: "Word")
    var error: NSError? = nil
    let count = self.managedObjectContext!.countForFetchRequest(fetchRequest, error: &error)
    return "Word Count: \(count)\n"
}
```

This method creates a fetch request, but instead of calling executeFetchRequest:error:, it calls a different method on our managed object context: countForFetchRequest:error:. This method, instead of returning the results from the fetch request, returns the count of items that the fetch request would return. In this case, it returns the number of objects in the Word entity, which gives us the number of words.

Displaying the Statistics

Finally, we add code to the interface to handle presses on the Load Word List button and display statistics about the word list. Listing 3-18 (Objective-C) and Listing 3-19 (Swift) shows the updated ViewController.m or ViewController.swift file, respectively. This code adds an updateStatistics method that calls Persistence's statistics method that we just implemented and sets the text of the text view to the returned value. It calls the updateStatistics method both when the view is about to appear and after the word list loads.

The loadWordList: implementation asynchronously loads the list of words from the appropriate URL (uniform resource locator) and hands over that list of words to the application's persistence layer for storage. On completion, it updates the statistics in the text view.

Listing 3-18. ViewController.m

```objc
#import "ViewController.h"
#import "AppDelegate.h"
#import "Persistence.h"

@implementation ViewController

- (void)viewWillAppear:(BOOL)animated {
  [super viewWillAppear:animated];
  [self updateStatistics];
}

- (void)updateStatistics {
  AppDelegate *appDelegate = (AppDelegate *)[[UIApplication sharedApplication] delegate];
  self.textView.text = [appDelegate.persistence statistics];
}

- (IBAction)loadWordList:(id)sender {
  // Hide the button while we're loading
  [(UIButton *)sender setHidden:YES];

  // Load the words
  NSURL *url = [NSURL URLWithString:@"https://dotnetperls-controls.googlecode.com/files/enable1.
  txt"];
  NSURLRequest *request = [NSURLRequest requestWithURL:url];
  NSLog(@"Loading words");
  [NSURLConnection sendAsynchronousRequest:request
                                     queue:[NSOperationQueue mainQueue]
                         completionHandler:^(NSURLResponse *response, NSData *data, NSError *error)
{
                           NSString *words = [[NSString alloc] initWithData:data
encoding:NSUTF8StringEncoding];
                           NSInteger statusCode = [(NSHTTPURLResponse *)response statusCode];
                           // Check for successful load
                           if (words != nil && statusCode == 200) {
                             // Give the word list to the persistence layer
                             AppDelegate *appDelegate = (AppDelegate *)[[UIApplication
                             sharedApplication] delegate];
```

```objc
                              [appDelegate.persistence loadWordList:words];
                            }
                            else {
                              // Load failed; show any errors
                              NSLog(@"Error: %lu", statusCode);
                              if (error != NULL)
                                NSLog(@"Error: %@", [error localizedDescription]);
                            }

                            // Show the button
                            [(UIButton *)sender setHidden:NO];

                            // Update the text view with statistics
                            [self updateStatistics];
                          }];
}

@end
```

Listing 3-19. ViewController.swift

```swift
import UIKit

class ViewController: UIViewController {
    @IBOutlet weak var textView: UITextView!

    override func viewWillAppear(animated: Bool) {
        super.viewWillAppear(animated)
        updateStatistics()
    }

    func updateStatistics() {
        let appDelegate = UIApplication.sharedApplication().delegate as AppDelegate
        textView.text = appDelegate.persistence?.statistics()
    }

    @IBAction func loadWordList(sender: AnyObject) {
        // Hide the button while we're loading
        (sender as UIButton).hidden = true

        // Load the words
        let url = NSURL(string: "https://dotnetperls-controls.googlecode.com/files/enable1.txt")
        let request = NSURLRequest(URL: url!)
        println("Loading words")

        NSURLConnection.sendAsynchronousRequest(request, queue: NSOperationQueue.mainQueue()) {
        (response: NSURLResponse!, data: NSData!, error: NSError!) -> Void in
            let words = NSString(data: data, encoding: NSUTF8StringEncoding)
```

```
        // Check for successful load
        if error == nil && response != nil && (response as NSHTTPURLResponse).statusCode == 200
{
            // Give the word list to the persistence layer
            let appDelegate = UIApplication.sharedApplication().delegate as AppDelegate
            appDelegate.persistence?.loadWordList(words!)
        }
        else {
            // Load failed; show any errors
            if response != nil { println("Error: \((response as NSHTTPURLResponse).statusCode)")
}
            println("Error: \(error.localizedDescription)")
        }

        // Show the button
        (sender as UIButton).hidden = false

        // Update the text view with statistics
        self.updateStatistics()
    }
  }
}
```

Build and run the application, and then tap the Load Word List button. After a few seconds, depending on the speed of your Internet connection and the speed of your computer, you should see the Load Word List button reappear and the word count display in the text area of the application, as shown in Figure 3-4.

Figure 3-4. The WordList application with the word count

Throughout the rest of this chapter, we update the `statistics` method in `Persistence` to perform more queries on the word list data and return more information to display in the UI.

Querying Relationships

The next output we add to the displayed statistics about our word list is the number of words that start with each letter. The query language used in predicates for fetch requests supports traversing the relationships defined in your data model. You do this by referencing the relationship by name in your predicate, and by using dot notation to access the properties of the entity referred to by the relationship. For example, for the `Word` entity, `wordCategory.firstLetter` refers to the `wordCategory` relationship in `Word`, which refers to the `WordCategory` entity, and to the `firstLetter` attribute in the `WordCategory` entity.

We can use the `wordCategory` relationship defined in the `Word` entity to fetch words by the category they belong to. To do this, we iterate through the alphabet and fetch the count of the words whose `wordCategory` has the `firstLetter` set to the current letter. We create a method, `wordCountForCategory:`, that takes a letter and fetches the count for that letter. That code looks like Listing 3-20 (Objective-C) or Listing 3-21 (Swift).

Listing 3-20. wordCountForCategory: in Persistence.m

```
- (NSString *)wordCountForCategory:(NSString *)firstLetter {
  NSFetchRequest *fetchRequest = [NSFetchRequest fetchRequestWithEntityName:@"Word"];
  fetchRequest.predicate = [NSPredicate predicateWithFormat:@"wordCategory.firstLetter = %@",
  firstLetter];
  NSUInteger count = [self.managedObjectContext countForFetchRequest:fetchRequest error:nil];
  return [NSString stringWithFormat:@"Words beginning with %@: %lu\n", firstLetter, count];
}
```

Listing 3-21. wordCountForCategory in Persistence.swift

```
func wordCountForCategory(firstLetter: String) -> String {
    var fetchRequest = NSFetchRequest(entityName: "Word")
    fetchRequest.predicate = NSPredicate(format: "wordCategory.firstLetter = %@", argumentArray:
    [firstLetter])

    var error: NSError? = nil
    let count = self.managedObjectContext!.countForFetchRequest(fetchRequest, error: &error)

    return "Words beginning with \(firstLetter): \(count)\n"
}
```

Then, we update the statistics method to iterate through the alphabet, calling
wordCountForCategory: for each letter and appending the results to the statistics. Listing 3-22
(Objective-C) or Listing 3-23 (Swift) shows that code.

Listing 3-22. The Updated statistics Method in Persistence.m

```
- (NSString *)statistics {
  NSMutableString *string = [[NSMutableString alloc] init];
  [string appendString:[self wordCount]];
  for (char c = 'a'; c <= 'z'; c++) {
    [string appendString:[self wordCountForCategory:[NSString stringWithFormat:@"%c", c]]];
  }
  return string;
}
```

Listing 3-23. The Updated statistics Function in Persistence.swift

```
func statistics() -> String {
    var string = NSMutableString()
    string.appendString(wordCount())

    for c in "abcdefghijklmnopqrstuvwxyz" {
        string.appendString(wordCountForCategory("\(c)"))
    }

    return string
}
```

Now when you build and run the application, you should see the word count by letter, as shown in Figure 3-5. Note that you don't need to reload the word list each time you run the application; the words are already stored in Core Data, and our queries run against the existing data.

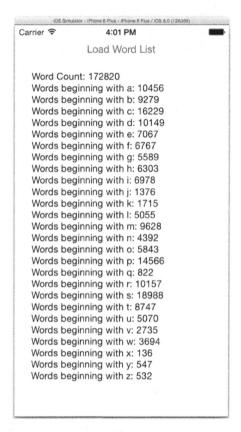

Figure 3-5. The WordList application with the word count by letter

Understanding Predicates and Expressions

Chapter 2 discusses predicates and the two ways to build them.

- Using the query language; and
- Using the NSExpression class to manually build predicates.

In the wordCountForCategory: method we just implemented, we use the predicate query language to filter the fetch results. The predicate query language has similarities to a structured query language (SQL) WHERE clause: you state the attributes and relationships you want to filter on (the columns), the values these properties should be compared to, and how they should be compared. For example, we can retrieve the word "zyzzyvas" from our word list with the predicate "text = 'zyzzyvas'." The predicate query language is usually simpler to write and easier to use than the NSExpression class to build predicates. The query language doesn't cover all the cases that NSExpression does, however, and you also might find scenarios in which you prefer using NSExpression, so understanding both approaches is essential for fetching the data you target.

Put simply, a predicate executes a test on an object. If the test passes, the object is fetched, and if it fails, the object is not fetched. A predicate contains two or more expressions and one or more comparators. In the predicate in the preceding paragraph, the attribute text and the constant string 'zyzzyvas' are expressions, and the operator = is the comparator, which compares the text value of a Word to 'zyzzyvas' and returns the Word object if they match.

To build an equivalent predicate using NSExpression, you would create two expressions: one for text and one for "zyzzyvas", and then create an NSComparisonPredicate instance to compare the two expressions to see whether they're equal. That code looks like Listing 3-24 (Objective-C) or Listing 3-25 (Swift).

Listing 3-24. Building a Predicate with NSExpression (Objective-C)

```
NSExpression *expressionText = [NSExpression expressionForKeyPath:@"text"];
NSExpression *expressionZyzzyvas = [NSExpression expressionForConstantValue:@"zyzzyvas"];
NSPredicate *predicate = [NSComparisonPredicate predicateWithLeftExpression:expressionText
                                                rightExpression:expressionZyzzyvas
                                                modifier:NSDirectPredicateModifier
                                                    type:NSEqualToPredicateOperatorType
                                                options:0];
```

Listing 3-25. Building a Predicate with NSExpression (Swift)

```
let expressionText = NSExpression(forKeyPath: "text")
let expressionZyzzyvas = NSExpression(forConstantValue: "zyzzyvas")
let predicate = NSComparisonPredicate(leftExpression: expressionText, rightExpression:
expressionZyzzyvas, modifier: .DirectPredicateModifier, type: .EqualToPredicateOperatorType,
options: NSComparisonPredicateOptions.convertFromNilLiteral())
```

This code is clearly more complex, but it accomplishes the same thing as the query language predicate. Over the next few sections, we dig deeper into how to create predicates this way. Before going further, however, prove that both approaches work by adding methods to retrieve the word "zyzzyvas" both ways in the WordList application and display the results in the text view. Also, log the predicate created using NSExpression by calling NSPredicate's predicateFormat method. Listing 3-26 shows the Objective-C code, and Listing 3-27 shows the Swift code.

Listing 3-26. Using Both the Query Language and NSExpression (Objective-C)

```
- (NSString *)statistics {
  NSMutableString *string = [[NSMutableString alloc] init];
  [string appendString:[self wordCount]];
  for (char c = 'a'; c <= 'z'; c++) {
    [string appendString:[self wordCountForCategory:[NSString stringWithFormat:@"%c", c]]];
  }
  [string appendString:[self zyzzyvasUsingQueryLanguage]];
  [string appendString:[self zyzzyvasUsingNSExpression]];
  return string;
}

- (NSString *)zyzzyvasUsingQueryLanguage {
  NSFetchRequest *fetchRequest = [NSFetchRequest fetchRequestWithEntityName:@"Word"];
```

```objc
    fetchRequest.predicate = [NSPredicate predicateWithFormat:@"text = 'zyzzyvas'"];
    NSArray *words = [self.managedObjectContext executeFetchRequest:fetchRequest error:nil];
    return words.count == 0 ? @"" : [NSString stringWithFormat:@"%@\n", [words[0]
    valueForKey:@"text"]];
}
- (NSString *)zyzzyvasUsingNSExpression {
    NSExpression *expressionText = [NSExpression expressionForKeyPath:@"text"];
    NSExpression *expressionZyzzyvas = [NSExpression expressionForConstantValue:@"zyzzyvas"];
    NSPredicate *predicate = [NSComparisonPredicate predicateWithLeftExpression:expressionText
                                                    rightExpression:expressionZyzzyvas
                                                modifier:NSDirectPredicateModifier
                                                    type:NSEqualToPredicateOperatorType
                                                options:0];
    NSLog(@"Predicate: %@", [predicate predicateFormat]);
    NSFetchRequest *fetchRequest = [NSFetchRequest fetchRequestWithEntityName:@"Word"];
    fetchRequest.predicate = predicate;
    NSArray *words = [self.managedObjectContext executeFetchRequest:fetchRequest error:nil];
    return words.count == 0 ? @"" : [NSString stringWithFormat:@"%@\n", [words[0]
    valueForKey:@"text"]];
}
```

Listing 3-27. Using Both the Query Language and NSExpression (Swift)

```swift
func statistics() -> String {
    var string = NSMutableString()

    string.appendString(wordCount())

    for c in "abcdefghijklmnopqrstuvwxyz" {
        string.appendString(wordCountForCategory("\(c)"))
    }

    string.appendString(zyzzyvasUsingQueryLanguage())
    string.appendString(zyzzyvasUsingNSExpression())

    return string
}

func zyzzyvasUsingQueryLanguage() -> String {
    var fetchRequest = NSFetchRequest(entityName: "Word")
    fetchRequest.predicate = NSPredicate(format: "text = 'zyzzyvas'", argumentArray: [])

    var error: NSError? = nil
    if let words = self.managedObjectContext!.executeFetchRequest(fetchRequest, error: &error) {
        if words.isEmpty { return "" }
        else {
            let word: AnyObject! = words[0].valueForKey("text")
            return "\(word)\n"
        }
```

```
        else { return "" }
    }
}

func zyzzyvasUsingNSExpression() -> String {
    let expressionText = NSExpression(forKeyPath: "text")
    let expressionZyzzyvas = NSExpression(forConstantValue: "zyzzyvas")
    let predicate = NSComparisonPredicate(leftExpression: expressionText, rightExpression:
expressionZyzzyvas, modifier: .DirectPredicateModifier, type: .EqualToPredicateOperatorType,
options: nil)

    println("Predicate: \(predicate.predicateFormat)")

    var fetchRequest = NSFetchRequest(entityName: "Word")
    fetchRequest.predicate = predicate

    var error: NSError? = nil
    if let words = self.managedObjectContext!.executeFetchRequest(fetchRequest, error: &error) {
        if words.isEmpty { return "" }
        else {
            let word: AnyObject! = words[0].valueForKey("text")
            return "\(word)\n"
        }
    }
    else { return "" }
}
```

If you run the WordList application, you should see the word "zyzzyvas" appear twice in the text view. You should also see the text version of the predicate in the logs.

```
Predicate: text == "zyzzyvas"
```

Viewing Your SQL Queries

For developers more familiar with SQL statements than with NSPredicates and NSExpressions, you can instruct your application to log the SQL statements it uses when performing fetch requests. This can help you understand how Core Data interprets your predicates and expressions, making debugging your fetch requests simpler.

To turn on SQL debugging for your application, edit the Run scheme in Xcode to add these arguments in the Arguments Passed on Launch section.

```
-com.apple.CoreData.SQLDebug 1
```

Note the dash in front. Your Xcode scheme setup should match Figure 3-6.

Figure 3-6. Adding -com.apple.CoreData.SQLDebug 1 to the arguments passed on launch

Add these arguments to the WordList Run schema, then launch the application. You should now see the SQL statements WordList uses to fetch its data, along with other information, like query duration, in the Xcode console. The output should look something like the following:

```
2014-07-30 11:45:15.647 WordList[65858:2586192] CoreData: sql: SELECT COUNT( DISTINCT t0.Z_PK) FROM
ZWORD t0 JOIN ZWORDCATEGORY t1 ON t0.ZWORDCATEGORY = t1.Z_PK WHERE  t1.ZFIRSTLETTER = ?
2014-07-30 11:45:15.699 WordList[65858:2586192] CoreData: annotation: total count request execution
time: 0.0528s for count of 10456.
```

You can actually coax Core Data into giving you even more SQL information in the console by specifying 2 or 3 instead of 1—the higher the number, the more information Core Data will log. Try, for example, changing the launch arguments to the following:

```
-com.apple.CoreData.SQLDebug 3
```

Run the WordList application again and look in the console for even richer information, such as the following:

```
2014-07-31 15:29:04.797 WordList[73416:2971038] CoreData: sql: SELECT COUNT( DISTINCT t0.Z_PK) FROM
ZWORD t0 JOIN ZWORDCATEGORY t1 ON t0.ZWORDCATEGORY = t1.Z_PK WHERE  t1.ZFIRSTLETTER = ?
2014-07-31 15:29:04.797 WordList[73416:2971038] CoreData: details: SQLite bind[0] = "s"
2014-07-31 15:29:04.822 WordList[73416:2971038] CoreData: annotation: count request <NSFetchRequest:
0x7fc6a292d850> (entity: Word; predicate: (wordCategory.firstLetter == "s"); sortDescriptors:
((null)); type: NSCountResultType; ) returned 18988
2014-07-31 15:29:04.822 WordList[73416:2971038] CoreData: annotation: total count request execution
time: 0.0254s for count of 18988.
```

Seeing the actual SQL statements that Core Data derives from your predicates and expressions can help you troubleshoot and verify how you're retrieving data.

Creating Single-Value Expressions

Expressions can represent either single values or collections of values. NSPredicate supports four types of single-value expressions, as shown in Table 3-1.

Table 3-1. The Four Types of Single-Value Expressions

Type	Static Initializer Method (Objective-C)	Initializer (Swift)	Description
Constant value	+expressionForConstantValue:	init(forConstantValue obj: AnyObject!)	Represents a constant value
Evaluated object	+expressionForEvaluatedObject	expressionForEvaluatedObject()	Represents the object being evaluated for inclusion in the result set
Key path	+expressionForKeyPath:	init(forKeyPath keyPath: String!)	The value represented by the specified key path
Variable	+expressionForVariable:	init(forVariable string: String!)	A value from the variable bindings dictionary associated with the evaluated object

The zyzzyvasUsingNSExpression method in the WordList application creates two single-value expressions: one using a key path and one using a constant expression. The expressionText expression resolves to the value stored in the key path "text" of a Word entity.

```
NSExpression *expressionText = [NSExpression expressionForKeyPath:@"text"]; // Objective-C
let expressionText = NSExpression(forKeyPath: "text") // Swift
```

The constant value expression, expressionZyzzyvas, represents the constant value "zyzzyvas".

```
NSExpression *expressionZyzzyvas = [NSExpression expressionForConstantValue:@"zyzzyvas"];
// Objective-C
let expressionZyzzyvas = NSExpression(forConstantValue: "zyzzyvas") // Swift
```

You might not use the evaluated object type often, if at all, when using Core Data. The evaluated object type refers to the NSManagedObject instance itself, and usually you'll want to query the attributes and relationships of the objects, not the objects themselves. We can do something like query for certain object IDs, which might meet some esoteric need of your application. We leave other ideas for use up to the reader.

Creating Collection Expressions

The single-value expressions allow predicates to compare objects against single values to determine inclusion in the result set. Sometimes you want to compare objects against multiple values, however, to determine whether to include them. A collection expression contains the multiple NSExpression instances that predicates use for evaluation. In this section, we examine the Aggregate expression type, which you create using NSExpression's +expressionForAggregate: static initializer in Objective-C, or init(forAggregate collection: [AnyObject]!) initializer in Swift.

Although Apple's documentation for NSExpression says, "Aggregate expressions are not supported by Core Data," in practice this isn't always true. Let's suppose, for example, that we wanted to retrieve words that have between 20 and 25 letters, inclusively. We would create two NSExpression instances, one for the constant value 20 and one for the constant value 25, and then create an aggregate expression that contains them both. We would then use that aggregate expression in our predicate. Listing 3-28 shows how to create that aggregate expression in Objective-C, and Listing 3-29 shows how to create it in Swift.

Listing 3-28. Creating an Aggregate Expression in Objective-C

```
NSExpression *lower = [NSExpression expressionForConstantValue:@20];
NSExpression *upper = [NSExpression expressionForConstantValue:@25];
NSExpression *expr  = [NSExpression expressionForAggregate:@[lower, upper]];
```

Listing 3-29. Creating an Aggregate Expression in Swift

```
let lower = NSExpression(forConstantValue: 20)
let upper = NSExpression(forConstantValue: 25)
let expr  = NSExpression(forAggregate: [lower, upper])
```

To incorporate this into the WordList application, add the Objective-C method shown in Listing 3-30 or the Swift function shown in Listing 3-31, which takes a range (an NSRange instance) and finds the count of words whose length lies in that range. Then, add a call to it in the statistics method.

```
[string appendString:[self wordCountForRange:NSMakeRange(20, 25)]]; // Objective-C
string.appendString(wordCountForRange(NSMakeRange(20, 25))) // Swift
```

Listing 3-30. Using an Aggregate Expression to Find Words with a Length in Range (Objective-C)

```
- (NSString *)wordCountForRange:(NSRange)range {
  NSExpression *length = [NSExpression expressionForKeyPath:@"length"];
  NSExpression *lower = [NSExpression expressionForConstantValue:@(range.location)];
  NSExpression *upper = [NSExpression expressionForConstantValue:@(range.length)];
  NSExpression *expr = [NSExpression expressionForAggregate:@[lower, upper]];
  NSPredicate *predicate = [NSComparisonPredicate predicateWithLeftExpression:length
                                                  rightExpression:expr
                                                modifier:NSDirectPredicateModifier
                                                  type:NSBetweenPredicateOperatorType
                                                options:0];
  NSLog(@"Aggregate Predicate: %@", [predicate predicateFormat]);
  NSFetchRequest *fetchRequest = [NSFetchRequest fetchRequestWithEntityName:@"Word"];
```

```
  fetchRequest.predicate = predicate;
  NSUInteger count = [self.managedObjectContext countForFetchRequest:fetchRequest error:nil];
  return [NSString stringWithFormat:@"%lu-%lu letter words: %lu\n", range.location, range.length,
  count];
}
```

Listing 3-31. Using an Aggregate Expression to Find Words with a Length in Range (Swift)

```swift
func wordCountForRange(range: NSRange) -> String {
    let length = NSExpression(forKeyPath: "length")
    let lower = NSExpression(forConstantValue: range.location)
    let upper = NSExpression(forConstantValue: range.length)
    let expr = NSExpression(forAggregate: [lower, upper])
    let predicate = NSComparisonPredicate(leftExpression: length, rightExpression: expr, modifier:
    .DirectPredicateModifier, type: .BetweenPredicateOperatorType, options: nil)

    println("Aggregate predicate: \(predicate.predicateFormat)")

    var fetchRequest = NSFetchRequest(entityName: "Word")
    fetchRequest.predicate = predicate

    var error: NSError? = nil
    let count = self.managedObjectContext!.countForFetchRequest(fetchRequest, error: &error)

    return "\(range.location)-\(range.length) letter words: \(count)\n"
}
```

The next section, "Comparing Expressions Using Different Predicate Types," covers the different predicate types, including NSBetweenPredicateOperatorType.

Run the WordList application, and you should see a line in the output like the following:

```
20-25 letter words: 276
```

You can also see, in the Xcode console, that the predicate's query language incorporates the two constant values in a BETWEEN clause, as we'd expect.

```
length BETWEEN {20, 25}
```

Comparing Expressions Using Different Predicate Types

In addition to expressions, predicates require comparators to evaluate whether to include objects in their result sets. The NSComparisonPredicate class, a subclass of NSPredicate, compares two expressions with each other using the type of comparator you specify when you create it. You can, for example, require that the expressions are equal for the evaluated object to be included in the result set. We saw this when comparing Word objects with the constant expression "zyzzyvas": only words with that exact text were returned.

We also saw a "between" type comparator with the wordCountForRange: method, which required that a word have a length between two integers for inclusion in the result set. NSComparisonPredicate offers a slew of other comparison types to fit other comparison needs. See Table 3-2 for a list of the comparison types. The Query Language and Logical Description columns use L and R to represent the left expression and right expression being compared, respectively. The Swift types are the same as the Objective-C types, except that the Objective-C types begin with NS and the Swift types do not.

Table 3-2. The Comparison Types

Objective-C or Swift Type	Query Language	Logical Description
(NS)LessThanPredicateOperatorType	L < R	L less than R
(NS)LessThanOrEqualToPredicateOperatorType	L <= R	L less than or equal to R
(NS)GreaterThanPredicateOperatorType	L > R	L greater than R
(NS)GreaterThanOrEqualToPredicateOperatorType	L >= R	L greater than or equal to R
(NS)EqualToPredicateOperatorType	L = R	L equal to R
(NS)NotEqualToPredicateOperatorType	L != R	L not equal to R
(NS)MatchesPredicateOperatorType	L MATCHES R	L matches the R regular expression
(NS)LikePredicateOperatorType	L LIKE R	L = R where R can contain * wildcards
(NS)BeginsWithPredicateOperatorType	L BEGINSWITH R	L begins with R
(NS)EndsWithPredicateOperatorType	L ENDSWITH R	L ends with R
(NS)InPredicateOperatorType	L IN R	L is in the collection R
(NS)ContainsPredicateOperatorType	L CONTAINS R	L is a collection that contains R
(NS)BetweenPredicateOperatorType	L BETWEEN R	L is a value between the two values of the array R

Note   NSLikePredicateOperatorType is a simplified version of NSMatchesPredicateOperatorType. While NSMatchesPredicateOperatorType can use complex regular expressions, NSLikePredicateOperatorType uses simple wildcard replacement (*) characters, so that the expression text LIKE 'b*ball' would match baseball and basketball but not football.

We can use NSEndsWithPredicateOperatorType, for example, to find all the words that end with the letters "gry." Listing 3-32 shows the endsWithGryWords method in Objective-C, and Listing 3-33 shows it in Swift, to do just that. Don't forget to add a call to it in your statistics method, and then build and run the application to see "puggry, hungry, angry" (in no particular order) added to the output.

Listing 3-32. The endsWithGryWords Method in Objective-C

```objc
- (NSString *)endsWithGryWords {
  NSExpression *text = [NSExpression expressionForKeyPath:@"text"];
  NSExpression *gry = [NSExpression expressionForConstantValue:@"gry"];
  NSPredicate *predicate = [NSComparisonPredicate predicateWithLeftExpression:text
                                                 rightExpression:gry
                                        modifier:NSDirectPredicateModifier
                                            type:NSEndsWithPredicateOperatorType
                                         options:0];
  NSLog(@"Predicate: %@", [predicate predicateFormat]);
  NSFetchRequest *fetchRequest = [NSFetchRequest fetchRequestWithEntityName:@"Word"];
  fetchRequest.predicate = predicate;
  NSArray *gryWords = [self.managedObjectContext executeFetchRequest:fetchRequest error:nil];
  return [NSString stringWithFormat:@"-gry words: %@\n",
          [[gryWords valueForKey:@"text"] componentsJoinedByString:@","]];
}
```

Listing 3-33. The endsWithGryWords Method in Swift

```swift
func endsWithGryWords() -> String {
    let text = NSExpression(forKeyPath: "text")
    let gry = NSExpression(forConstantValue: "gry")
    let predicate = NSComparisonPredicate(leftExpression: text, rightExpression: gry, modifier:
    .DirectPredicateModifier, type: .EndsWithPredicateOperatorType, options: nil)

    println("Predicate: \(predicate.predicateFormat)")

    var fetchRequest = NSFetchRequest(entityName: "Word")
    fetchRequest.predicate = predicate

        let list = NSMutableString()
var error: NSError? = nil
    if let gryWords = self.managedObjectContext!.executeFetchRequest(fetchRequest, error: &error) {
        for word in gryWords {
            list.appendString(((word as NSManagedObject).valueForKey("text") as String)+",")
        }
    }
    return "-gry words: \(list)\n"
}
```

You can look in the Xcode console to see that the query language equivalent of this predicate is

```
text ENDSWITH "gry"
```

Using Different Comparison Modifiers

The third parameter to the NSComparisonPredicate static initializer method we've been using is modifier, and we've been passing NSDirectPredicateModifier exclusively for this parameter. If the left expression is a collection rather than a single object, however, you have a few more modifiers to choose from, as shown in Table 3-3. As with the predicate type constants, the Objective-C constants begin with NS and the Swift ones do not.

Table 3-3. The Comparison Predicate Modifiers

Modifier	Query Language Example	Description
(NS)DirectPredicateModifier	X	Compares the left expression directly to the right expression
(NS)AllPredicateModifier	ALL X	Compares the left expression (a collection) to the right expression, returning YES only if all the values match
(NS)AnyPredicateModifier	ANY X	Compares the left expression (a collection) to the right expression, returning YES if any of the values match

The NSAllPredicateModifier constant, as the table shows, evaluates to the query language expression ALL X, and returns YES only if all the values in the collection match the predicate. Otherwise, it returns NO. The NSAnyPredicateModifier constant, on the other hand, which evaluates to ANY X, returns YES if at least one of the values in the collection matches the predicate. Otherwise, it returns NO.

Remember earlier in this chapter when we mentioned that Apple's documentation claims that Core Data doesn't support aggregate expressions? In the case of NSAllPredicateModifier, this is true. If you try to run an ALL X query, your application will crash. You can use the NSAnyPredicateModifier, however, as the anyWordContainsZ method shown in Listing 3-34 (Objective-C) and Listing 3-35 (Swift) illustrate. This method lists all the categories for which any word contains the letter "z." Add the method and a call to it in statistics, build and run the application, and you'll see that all categories except "x" have at least one word that contains the letter "z."

Listing 3-34. The anyWordContainsZ Method (Objective-C)

```
- (NSString *)anyWordContainsZ {  NSExpression *text = [NSExpression
expressionForKeyPath:@"words.text"];
  NSExpression *z = [NSExpression expressionForConstantValue:@"z"];
  NSPredicate *predicate = [NSComparisonPredicate predicateWithLeftExpression:text
                                                  rightExpression:z
                                           modifier:NSAnyPredicateModifier
                                               type:NSContainsPredicateOperatorType
                                            options:0];
  NSLog(@"Predicate: %@", [predicate predicateFormat]);
  NSFetchRequest *fetchRequest = [NSFetchRequest fetchRequestWithEntityName:@"WordCategory"];
  fetchRequest.predicate = predicate;
  NSArray *categories = [self.managedObjectContext executeFetchRequest:fetchRequest error:nil];
  return [NSString stringWithFormat:@"ANY: %@\n",
        [[categories valueForKey:@"firstLetter"] componentsJoinedByString:@","]];
}
```

Listing 3-35. The anyWordContainsZ Method (Swift)

```
func anyWordContainsZ() -> String {
    let text = NSExpression(forKeyPath: "words.text")
    let z = NSExpression(forConstantValue: "z")
    let predicate = NSComparisonPredicate(leftExpression: text, rightExpression: z,
    modifier:.AnyPredicateModifier, type: .ContainsPredicateOperatorType, options: nil)
```

```
    println("Predicate: \(predicate.predicateFormat)")

    var fetchRequest = NSFetchRequest(entityName: "WordCategory")
    fetchRequest.predicate = predicate

    let list = NSMutableString()
    var error: NSError? = nil
    if let categories = self.managedObjectContext!.executeFetchRequest(fetchRequest, error: &error)
{

        for word in categories {
            list.appendString(((word as NSManagedObject).valueForKey("firstLetter") as String)+",")
        }
    }

    return "ANY: \(list)\n"
}
```

Using Different Options

The final parameter to the NSComparisonPredicate static initializer is options, for which we've been blithely passing 0 (or NSComparisonPredicatOptions.convertFromNilLiteral() for Swift). You actually have four other values to choose from for this parameter for string comparison comparators only. Each option has an equivalent code you can use in the query language by appending the code between square brackets right after the operator. Table 3-4 lists the available options, codes, and how to use them in the query language. Again, the Objective-C options begin with NS, and the Swift ones do not.

Table 3-4. The String Comparison Options

Option	Code	Description	Query Language Example
(NS)CaseInsensitivePredicateOption	c	The comparison is case-insensitive	"X" =[c] "x"
(NS)DiacriticInsensitivePredicateOption	d	The comparison overlooks accents	"è" =[d] "e"
(NS)NormalizedPredicateOption	n	Indicates that the operands have been preprocessed (made all the same case, accents removed, etc.), so NSCaseInsensitivePredicateOption and NSDiacriticInsensitivePredicateOption options can be ignored	"abc" =[n] "abc"
(NS)LocaleSensitivePredicateOption	l	The comparison takes the current locale into consideration	"straße =[l] "strasse"`

You can specify multiple options using bitwise OR flags, or put multiple codes together if using the query language. To compare both case insensitively and diacritic insensitively, for example, you would pass for the options parameter.

NSCaseInsensitivePredicateOption | NSDiacriticInsensitivePredicateOption

Using the query language, you'd do something like the following:

"È" =[cd] "e"

Although our list of words doesn't contain any accented or non-English characters, we can verify that the case-insensitive option works. Create a new method called caseInsensitiveFetch: that takes an NSString parameter. In that method, convert the string to upper case, then fetch the word using the NSCaseInsensitivePredicateOption option. Listing 3-36 (Objective-C) and Listing 3-37 (Swift) show what your method or function should look like.

Listing 3-36. The caseInsensitiveFetch: Method (Objective-C)

```
- (NSString *)caseInsensitiveFetch:(NSString *)word {
  NSExpression *text = [NSExpression expressionForKeyPath:@"text"];
  NSExpression *allCapsWord = [NSExpression expressionForConstantValue:[word uppercaseString]];
  NSPredicate *predicate = [NSComparisonPredicate predicateWithLeftExpression:text
                                              rightExpression:allCapsWord
                                         modifier:NSDirectPredicateModifier
                                             type:NSEqualToPredicateOperatorType
                                          options:NSCaseInsensitivePredicateOption];
  NSLog(@"Predicate: %@", [predicate predicateFormat]);
  NSFetchRequest *fetchRequest = [NSFetchRequest fetchRequestWithEntityName:@"Word"];
  fetchRequest.predicate = predicate;
  NSArray *words = [self.managedObjectContext executeFetchRequest:fetchRequest error:nil];
  return [NSString stringWithFormat:@"%@\n", words.count == 0 ? @"" : [words[0]
valueForKey:@"text"]];
}
```

Listing 3-37. The caseInsensitiveFetch: Function (Swift)

```
func caseInsensitiveFetch(word: String) -> String {
    let text = NSExpression(forKeyPath: "text")
    let allCapsWord = NSExpression(forConstantValue: word.uppercaseString)
    let predicate = NSComparisonPredicate(leftExpression: text, rightExpression: allCapsWord,
modifier: .DirectPredicateModifier, type: .EqualToPredicateOperatorType, options:
.CaseInsensitivePredicateOption)

    println("Predicate: \(predicate.predicateFormat)")

    var fetchRequest = NSFetchRequest(entityName: "Word")
    fetchRequest.predicate = predicate

    var error: NSError? = nil
    if let words = self.managedObjectContext!.executeFetchRequest(fetchRequest, error: &error) {
        if words.isEmpty { return "" }
```

```
        else {
            let word: AnyObject! = words[0].valueForKey("text")
            return "\(word)\n"
        }
    }
    else { return "" }
}
```

Then, add a call to that method in your `statistics` method, passing the word of your choice, as follows:

```
[string appendString:[self caseInsensitiveFetch:@"qiviut"]]; // Objective-C
string.appendString(caseInsensitiveFetch("qiviut")) // Swift
```

You should see the query-language equivalent in your Xcode console, and your word in the WordList display area. The query-language equivalent looks as follows:

```
text ==[c] "QIVIUT"
```

Adding It Up: Using Compound Predicates

We've been using predicates with one criterion, whether it has been words that belong to a certain category or words that match a specific text. You often must combine criteria, however, to extract the data you're really after. You can form predicates by combining multiple subpredicates using the logical operators OR, AND, and NOT. You might, for example, want to find all the 20-letter words that end in "-ing," or words that have a "q" but not a "u." For these types of predicates, you need multiple criteria.

Core Data allows you to build compound predicates using the `NSCompoundPredicate` class. You build them using one of the three static initializers (or the same-named functions in Swift) shown in Table 3-5.

Table 3-5. Static Initializers for Creating Compound Predicates

Initializer Name	Query Language Example	Description
+andPredicateWithSubpredicates:	P1 AND P2 AND P3	Returns YES only if all subpredicates return YES
+orPredicateWithSubpredicates:	P1 OR P2 OR P3	Returns YES if at least one of the subpredicates returns YES
+notPredicateWithSubpredicate:	NOT P	Returns YES if its only subpredicate returns NO

To get a list of the 20-letter words that end in "-ing," create a method called `twentyLetterWordsEndingInIng`, as shown in Listing 3-38 (Objective-C) and Listing 3-39 (Swift), and add a call to it in the `statistics` method. This code creates a predicate that compares the length of each word to 20. It creates another predicate that compares the ending of each word to "-ing." It then creates a compound predicate that combines the two predicates using the logical operator AND.

Listing 3-38. Using Compound Predicates in Objective-C

```objc
- (NSString *)twentyLetterWordsEndingInIng {
  // Create a predicate that compares length to 20
  NSExpression *length = [NSExpression expressionForKeyPath:@"length"];
  NSExpression *twenty = [NSExpression expressionForConstantValue:@20];
  NSPredicate *predicateLength = [NSComparisonPredicate predicateWithLeftExpression:length
                                                     rightExpression:twenty
                                                     modifier:NSDirectPredicateModifier
                                                     type:NSEqualToPredicateOperatorType
                                                     options:0];

  // Create a predicate that compares text to "ends with -ing"
  NSExpression *text = [NSExpression expressionForKeyPath:@"text"];
  NSExpression *ing = [NSExpression expressionForConstantValue:@"ing"];
  NSPredicate *predicateIng = [NSComparisonPredicate predicateWithLeftExpression:text
                                                  rightExpression:ing
                                                  modifier:NSDirectPredicateModifier
                                                  type:NSEndsWithPredicateOperatorType
                                                  options:0];

  // Combine the predicates
  NSPredicate *predicate = [NSCompoundPredicate andPredicateWithSubpredicates:@[predicateLength,
  predicateIng]];
  NSLog(@"Compound predicate: %@", [predicate predicateFormat]);

  NSFetchRequest *fetchRequest = [NSFetchRequest fetchRequestWithEntityName:@"Word"];
  fetchRequest.predicate = predicate;
  NSArray *words = [self.managedObjectContext executeFetchRequest:fetchRequest error:nil];
  return [NSString stringWithFormat:@"%@\n", [[words valueForKey:@"text"]
  componentsJoinedByString:@","]];
}
```

Listing 3-39. Using Compound Predicates in Swift

```swift
func twentyLetterWordsEndingInIng() -> String {
    // Create a predicate that compares length to 20
    let length = NSExpression(forKeyPath: "length")
    let twenty = NSExpression(forConstantValue: 20)
    let predicateLength = NSComparisonPredicate(leftExpression: length, rightExpression: twenty,
    modifier: .DirectPredicateModifier, type: .EqualToPredicateOperatorType, options: nil)

    // Create a predicate that compares text to "ends with -ing"
    let text = NSExpression(forKeyPath: "text")
    let ing = NSExpression(forConstantValue: "ing")
    let predicateIng = NSComparisonPredicate(leftExpression: text, rightExpression: ing, modifier:
    .DirectPredicateModifier, type: .EndsWithPredicateOperatorType, options: nil)

    // Combine the predicates
    let predicate = NSCompoundPredicate.andPredicateWithSubpredicates([predicateLength,
    predicateIng])
```

```
println("Compound predicate: \(predicate.predicateFormat)")

var fetchRequest = NSFetchRequest(entityName: "Word")
fetchRequest.predicate = predicate

let list = NSMutableString()
var error: NSError? = nil
if let words = self.managedObjectContext!.executeFetchRequest(fetchRequest, error: &error) {
    for word in words {
        list.appendString(((word as NSManagedObject).valueForKey("text") as String)+",")
    }
}

return "\(list)\n"
}
```

When you build and run WordList, you'll see the four 20-letter words that end in "-ing" in the WordList UI. You'll also see the query language equivalent in the Xcode console, which looks like the following:

```
length == 20 AND text ENDSWITH "ing"
```

When you have to filter your data against multiple criteria to fetch what you want, remember to combine predicates into a compound predicate and let Core Data do the work of applying all the criteria for you. Oh, and if you build the compound predicate referred to previously, to find words that contain a "q" but not a "u," you'll see the 21 words that match.

Aggregating

Aggregating data refers to gathering global statistics on a collection using a collection operator. Collection operators are part of the Key-Value Coding paradigm and can be added to a key path to indicate that an aggregation operation should be executed. The syntax for using these aggregation operators is

```
(key path to collection).@(operator).(key path to argument property)
```

For example, to refer to the average length of the words in the word list, you'd use

```
words.@avg.length
```

The Apple documentation refers to these operators as Set and Array Operators, as you can use them on any collection, not just Core Data result sets. You can also use them as part of a predicate; for example, to get all the categories that have more than 10,000 words, you'd use a predicate with the query language.

```
words.@count > 10000
```

Table 3-6 lists the operators, which are the same in Objective-C or Swift.

Table 3-6. The Aggregation Operators

Operator	Constant	Description
avg	NSAverageKeyValueOperator	Computes the average of the argument property in the collection
count	NSCountKeyValueOperator	Computes the number of items in the collection (does not use an argument property)
min	NSMinimumKeyValueOperator	Computes the minimum value of the argument property in the collection
max	NSMaximumKeyValueOperator	Computes the maximum value of the argument property in the collection
sum	NSSumKeyValueOperator	Computes the sum value of the argument property in the collection

Using @count to Retrieve Counts

The @count function returns a count of the number of objects that match the predicate. We can use this to return a list of letters that have a high number of words, which we arbitrarily set at more than 10,000, as described previously. The fetch request we set up to retrieve these data target the Category entity and fetch the category objects whose count of word relationships exceeds 10,000. This gives us the letters that begin more than 10,000 words.

We use the query language to set up this predicate, as seen in the highCountCategories method shown in Listing 3-40 (Objective-C) and Listing 3-41 (Swift).

Listing 3-40. Using the @count Function in Objective-C

```
- (NSString *)highCountCategories {
  NSPredicate *predicate = [NSPredicate predicateWithFormat:@"words.@count > %d", 10000];
  NSLog(@"Predicate: %@", [predicate predicateFormat]);

  NSFetchRequest *fetchRequest = [NSFetchRequest fetchRequestWithEntityName:@"WordCategory"];
  fetchRequest.predicate = predicate;
  NSArray *categories = [self.managedObjectContext executeFetchRequest:fetchRequest error:nil];
  return [NSString stringWithFormat:@"High count categories: %@\n",
        [[categories valueForKey:@"firstLetter"] componentsJoinedByString:@","]];
}
```

Listing 3-41. Using the @count Function in Swift

```
func highCountCategories() -> String {
    let predicate = NSPredicate(format: "words.@count > %d", argumentArray: [10000])
    println("Predicate: \(predicate.predicateFormat)")

    var fetchRequest = NSFetchRequest(entityName: "WordCategory")
    fetchRequest.predicate = predicate
```

```
    let list = NSMutableString()
    var error: NSError? = nil
    if let categories = self.managedObjectContext!.executeFetchRequest(fetchRequest, error: &error)
{

        for word in categories {
            list.appendString(((word as NSManagedObject).valueForKey("firstLetter") as String)+",")
        }
    }

    return "High count categories: \(list)\n"
}
```

This code creates a predicate that checks the count of the words relationship, verifying that it's greater than 10,000, and then creates a fetch request for the WordCategory entity that uses that predicate. It returns the qualifying letters in a comma-separated list.

Add a call to this method in the statistics method. Then, build and run the application to see the letters that have more than 10,000 words: a, c, d, p, r, and s.

Getting the Average Length of All Words—Two Ways

Using the aggregation operators directly on collections is straightforward: fetch the data using a Core Data fetch request, then apply the operator. Listing 3-42 (Objective-C) and Listing 3-43 (Swift), for example, show how to retrieve the average word length directly.

Listing 3-42. Getting the Average Word Length from the Collection in Objective-C

```
- (NSString *)averageWordLengthFromCollection {
  NSFetchRequest *fetchRequest = [NSFetchRequest fetchRequestWithEntityName:@"Word"];
  NSArray *words = [self.managedObjectContext executeFetchRequest:fetchRequest error:nil];
  return [NSString stringWithFormat:@"Average from collection: %.2f\n",
          [[words valueForKeyPath:@"@avg.length"] floatValue]];
}
```

Listing 3-43. Getting the Average Word Length from the Collection in Swift

```
func averageWordLengthFromCollection() -> String {
    var fetchRequest = NSFetchRequest(entityName: "Word")

    var error: NSError? = nil
    let words = self.managedObjectContext!.executeFetchRequest(fetchRequest, error: &error)

    var formattedAverage = "0"
    if let words = words {
        if let avg = (words as NSArray).valueForKeyPath("@avg.length") as? Float {
            let format = ".2"
            formattedAverage = avg.format(format)
        }
    }
    return "Average from collection: \(formattedAverage)\n"
}
```

This code fetches all the words, then applies the @avg operator using the following code:

```
[words valueForKeyPath:@"avg.length"] // Objective-C
(words as NSArray).valueForKeyPath("@avg.length") as Float // Swift
```

Add a call to it in the `statistics` method, then run it to see that the average length is 9.09 characters.

You can see, however, that you're trading simplicity for efficiency. This code reads in all the words, then calculates the average of the lengths. We can instead use `NSExpression` and another class, `NSExpressionDescription`, to fetch only the average using Core Data. To begin, we use another Objective-C static initializer that `NSExpression` offers: `+expressionForFunction:arguments:`, which takes a predefined function name and an array of `NSExpression` objects. The Swift counterpart is similar: a function in the format `init(forFunction name: String!, arguments parameters: [AnyObject]!)` that also takes a predefined function name and an array of `NSExpression` objects.

The predefined function names are similar to, but don't quite match, the aggregator function names. The Apple-provided documentation lists them all, but we highlight only the few shown in Table 3-7.

Table 3-7. Some of the Predefined Functions for +expressionForFunction:arguments:

Function Name	Description
average:	Returns an average of the values in the array
sum:	Returns the sum of the values in the array
count:	Returns the count of the values in the array
min:	Returns the minimum value in the array
max:	Returns the maximum value in the array

Since we want the average word length, we use the `average:` predefined function and we pass an `NSExpression` that represents the length property of the words. Listing 3-44 shows the Objective-C code and Listing 3-45 shows the Swift code to create this expression.

Listing 3-44. Create an NSExpression using +expressionForFunction:arguments:

```
NSExpression *length = [NSExpression expressionForKeyPath:@"length"];
NSExpression *average = [NSExpression expressionForFunction:@"average:" arguments:@[length]];
```

Listing 3-45. Create an NSExpression using init(forFunction name: String!, arguments parameters: [AnyObject]!)

```
let length = NSExpression(forKeyPath: "length")
let average = NSExpression(forFunction: "average:", arguments: [length])
```

Next, we set up an `NSExpressionDescription` instance to describe what we want to fetch from our Core Data store. An `NSExpressionDescription` represents a property on a Core Data entity that doesn't actually appear in the Core Data model, which is perfect for an expression that fetches the average (since it doesn't actually exist in our model). As a property, an `NSExpressionDescription` has a name and a type, as well as an expression. Listing 3-46 (Objective-C) and Listing 3-47 (Swift) show how to create the `NSExpressionDescription` for fetching the word length average.

Listing 3-46. Creating an NSExpressionDescription for the Word Length Average (Objective-C)

```
NSExpressionDescription *averageDescription = [[NSExpressionDescription alloc] init];
averageDescription.name = @"average";
averageDescription.expression = average;
averageDescription.expressionResultType = NSFloatAttributeType;
```

Listing 3-47. Creating an NSExpressionDescription for the Word Length Average (Swift)

```
var averageDescription = NSExpressionDescription()
averageDescription.name = "average"
averageDescription.expression = average
averageDescription.expressionResultType = .FloatAttributeType
```

To finish, we create a fetch request, and then set its propertiesToFetch property to an array
containing the NSExpressionDescription we just created. We also set the fetch request's
resultType property to a dictionary, so we can reference the NSExpressionDescription we created
by the name we set: "average". We execute the fetch request and extract the average value
from the result dictionary. Listing 3-48 (Objective-C) and Listing 3-49 (Swift) show the complete
averageWordLengthFromExpressionDescription method. Call it from your statistics method and run
to see that, however you get the average, you get 9.09 characters.

Listing 3-48. Getting the Average Word Length Using an Expression Description (Objective-C)

```
- (NSString *)averageWordLengthFromExpressionDescription {
  NSExpression *length = [NSExpression expressionForKeyPath:@"length"];
  NSExpression *average = [NSExpression expressionForFunction:@"average:" arguments:@[length]];

  NSExpressionDescription *averageDescription = [[NSExpressionDescription alloc] init];
  averageDescription.name = @"average";
  averageDescription.expression = average;
  averageDescription.expressionResultType = NSFloatAttributeType;

  NSFetchRequest *fetchRequest = [NSFetchRequest fetchRequestWithEntityName:@"Word"];
  fetchRequest.propertiesToFetch = @[averageDescription];
  fetchRequest.resultType = NSDictionaryResultType;
  NSArray *results = [self.managedObjectContext executeFetchRequest:fetchRequest error:nil];
  return [NSString stringWithFormat:@"Average from expression description: %.2f\n",
        [[results[0] valueForKey:@"average"] floatValue]];
}
```

Listing 3-49. Getting the Average Word Length Using an Expression Description (Swift)

```
func averageWordLengthFromExpressionDescription() -> String {
    let length = NSExpression(forKeyPath: "length")
    let average = NSExpression(forFunction: "average:", arguments: [length])

    var averageDescription = NSExpressionDescription()
    averageDescription.name = "average"
    averageDescription.expression = average
    averageDescription.expressionResultType = .FloatAttributeType
```

```
var fetchRequest = NSFetchRequest(entityName: "Word")
fetchRequest.propertiesToFetch = [averageDescription]
fetchRequest.resultType = .DictionaryResultType

var error: NSError? = nil
let results = self.managedObjectContext!.executeFetchRequest(fetchRequest, error: &error)

var formattedAverage = "0"
if let results = results {
    if let avg = (words as NSArray).valueForKeyPath("@avg.length") as? Float {
        let format = ".2"
        formattedAverage = avg.format(format)
    }
}
return "Average from collection: \(formattedAverage)\n"
}
```

Using a Function as an Rvalue

You can also use a function in the right side of your predicate. Suppose, for example, we wanted to get the text of the longest word from the word list. We can't simply use the @max(length) aggregator, because that returns the length of the longest word, not the longest word itself. Instead, we want to return the word object whose length equals the maximum length value, so the predicate tests the length against the max: function as follows:

length = max:(length)

Listing 3-50 (Objective-C) and Listing 3-51 (Swift) show the longestWords method (after all, you could have more than one word with the same length) that uses this predicate. Using SQL Logging, you can see that the SQL that Core Data uses has an inner SELECT statement, as you'd expect. The inner SELECT statement gets the maximum length of a word, and the outer SELECT statement gets all the words with that length.

```
SELECT 0, t0.Z_PK, t0.Z_OPT, t0.ZLENGTH, t0.ZTEXT, t0.ZWORDCATEGORY FROM ZWORD t0 WHERE  t0.ZLENGTH
= (SELECT max(t1.ZLENGTH) FROM ZWORD t1)
```

Listing 3-50. The longestWords: Method (Objective-C)

```
- (NSString *)longestWords {
  NSFetchRequest *fetchRequest = [NSFetchRequest fetchRequestWithEntityName:@"Word"];
  NSPredicate *predicate = [NSPredicate predicateWithFormat:@"length = max:(length)"];
  NSLog(@"Predicate: %@", [predicate predicateFormat]);
  fetchRequest.predicate = predicate;
  NSArray *words = [self.managedObjectContext executeFetchRequest:fetchRequest error:nil];
  return [NSString stringWithFormat:@"Longest words: %@\n",
          [[words valueForKey:@"text"] componentsJoinedByString:@","]];
}
```

Listing 3-51. The `longestWords:` Function (Swift)

```swift
func longestWords() -> String {
    var fetchRequest = NSFetchRequest(entityName: "Word")
    let predicate = NSPredicate(format: "length = max:(length)", argumentArray: [])

    println("Predicate: \(predicate.predicateFormat)")

    fetchRequest.predicate = predicate

    let list = NSMutableString()
    var error: NSError? = nil
    if let words = self.managedObjectContext!.executeFetchRequest(fetchRequest, error: &error) {
        for word in words {
            list.appendString(((word as NSManagedObject).valueForKey("text") as String)+",")
        }
    }
    return "Longest words: \(list)\n"
}
```

After adding a call to this method in `statistics` and running WordList, you can see that the longest word is the 28-letter gem "ethylenediaminetetraacetates."

Using Subqueries

In some cases, you want to fetch objects based on criteria that pertain to other related objects. Suppose, for example, you want to fetch all the word categories that have at least one 25-letter word. Without subqueries, you'd normally have to fetch these data in two steps.

1. Fetch all the word categories.

2. For each word category, fetch the count of words with 25 letters.

Subquery expressions allow you to combine those steps into a single query. Your entire predicate and logic can be expressed as

```
SUBQUERY(words, $x, $x.length == 25).@count > 0
```

The general format for subqueries is

```
SUBQUERY(collection_expression, variable_expression, predicate)
```

The `collection_expression` parameter refers to the collection property in the entity you're fetching, so we use `words` to reference the `words` collection. The `variable_expression` can be called anything you'd like; it's the variable that will temporarily hold each item in the collection as the subquery iterates through the collection. The `predicate` is, of course, the test for inclusion in the result set.

As with other expression types, you can create subqueries using the query language, as shown previously, or you can build them manually with `NSExpression`. The `NSExpression` class has a static initializer called `+expressionForSubQuery:usingIteratorVariable:predicate:` (or the Swift counterpart init(forSubquery expression: NSExpression!, usingIteratorVariable variable: String!, predicate predicate: AnyObject!)) for creating subquery expressions. The parameters to that method line up with the query language format: the first parameter is the collection expression to evaluate. The second is the name of the temporary variable to use during iteration. Finally, the last is the predicate to use for evaluation.

The wordCategoriesWith25LetterWords method shown in Listing 3-52 (Objective-C) and Listing 3-53 (Swift) uses the subquery described earlier to get all the categories that have at least one 25-letter word. Add a call to it in your statistics method to see that two categories, "i" and "p," have at least one 25-letter word.

Listing 3-52. Using a Subquery in Objective-C

```
- (NSString *)wordCategoriesWith25LetterWords {
  NSFetchRequest *fetchRequest = [NSFetchRequest fetchRequestWithEntityName:@"WordCategory"];
  NSPredicate *predicate = [NSPredicate predicateWithFormat:@"SUBQUERY(words, $x, $x.length = 25)
  .@count > 0"];
  fetchRequest.predicate = predicate;
  NSLog(@"Subquery Predicate: %@", [predicate predicateFormat]);
  NSArray *categories = [self.managedObjectContext executeFetchRequest:fetchRequest error:nil];
  return [NSString stringWithFormat:@"Categories with 25-letter words: %@\n",
          [[categories valueForKey:@"firstLetter"] componentsJoinedByString:@","]];
}
```

Listing 3-53. Using a Subquery in Swift

```
func wordCategoriesWith25LetterWords() -> String {
    var fetchRequest = NSFetchRequest(entityName: "WordCategory")
    let predicate = NSPredicate(format: "SUBQUERY(words, $x, $x.length = 25).@count > 0",
    argumentArray: [])

    println("Subcategoy predicate: \(predicate.predicateFormat)")

    fetchRequest.predicate = predicate

    let list = NSMutableString()
    var error: NSError? = nil
    if let categories = self.managedObjectContext!.executeFetchRequest(fetchRequest, error: &error)
{
        for word in categories {
            list.appendString((((word as NSManagedObject).valueForKey("firstLetter") as String)+",")
        }
    }

    return "Categories with 25-letter words: \(list)\n"
}
```

Sorting

Until now, we've accepted the output order of any fetch request as Core Data chose to return it, but Core Data allows you to set a sort order for any fetch request. You can select multiple columns for the sort, as well as the sort direction for each column. To sort a fetch request, you set the fetch request's sortDescriptors property to an array of NSSortDescriptor instances. Each NSSortDescriptor stores the column (or property) it sorts on, as well as the order to sort.

To sort all the words that start with "z" in ascending length order, for example, you'd create an NSSortDescriptor as follows:

```
[NSSortDescriptor sortDescriptorWithKey:@"length" ascending:YES] // Objective-C
NSSortDescriptor(key: "length", ascending: true) // Swift
```

That would sort the words in ascending length order but arbitrarily sort the words that have the same length. We can add another sort descriptor that sorts the words in descending alphabetical order, as follows:

```
[NSSortDescriptor sortDescriptorWithKey:@"text" ascending:NO] // Objective-C
NSSortDescriptor(key: "text", ascending: false) // Swift
```

The order in which you put your sort descriptors in the array that you use to set your fetch request's sortDescriptors is significant. The results will be sorted according to the order of the sort descriptors. In our example, that means that words of the same length will be grouped together, sorted in descending alphabetical order.

Listing 3-54 (Objective-C) and Listing 3-55 (Swift) show the zWords method that sorts the words starting with "z" using those two sort descriptors.

Listing 3-54. Sorting the Results in Objective-C

```objc
- (NSString *)zWords {
  NSFetchRequest *fetchRequest = [NSFetchRequest fetchRequestWithEntityName:@"Word"];
  NSPredicate *predicate = [NSPredicate predicateWithFormat:@"text BEGINSWITH 'z'"];
  NSSortDescriptor *lengthSort = [NSSortDescriptor sortDescriptorWithKey:@"length" ascending:YES];
  NSSortDescriptor *alphaSort = [NSSortDescriptor sortDescriptorWithKey:@"text" ascending:NO];

  fetchRequest.predicate = predicate;
  fetchRequest.sortDescriptors = @[lengthSort, alphaSort];

  NSLog(@"Predicate: %@", predicate);
  NSArray *words = [self.managedObjectContext executeFetchRequest:fetchRequest error:nil];
  return [NSString stringWithFormat:@"Z words:\n%@\n",
          [[words valueForKey:@"text"] componentsJoinedByString:@"\n"]];
}
```

Listing 3-55. Sorting the Results in Swift

```swift
func zWords() -> String {
    var fetchRequest = NSFetchRequest(entityName: "Word")
    let predicate = NSPredicate(format: "text BEGINSWITH 'z'", argumentArray: [])
```

```
println("Predicate: \(predicate.predicateFormat)")

let lengthSort = NSSortDescriptor(key: "length", ascending: true)
let alphaSort = NSSortDescriptor(key: "text", ascending: false)

fetchRequest.predicate = predicate
fetchRequest.sortDescriptors = [lengthSort, alphaSort]

let list = NSMutableString()
var error: NSError? = nil
if let words = self.managedObjectContext!.executeFetchRequest(fetchRequest, error: &error) {
    for word in words {
        list.appendString(((word as NSManagedObject).valueForKey("text") as String)+",")
    }
}

return "Z words: \(list)\n"
}
```

Remember to add a call to the zWords method in `statistics` to see the execution of the sort.

Summary

This chapter might or might not have helped you become a better Words with Friends player, but it should certainly have improved your skills at querying your Core Data stores. Whether using the query language syntax or building your predicates using NSExpression, you should be able to formulate the queries to extract your data to meet your applications' requirements. Don't forget to use tools like SQL Logging and logging the predicate format to tweak your queries and understand exactly what your application is doing when it fetches data.

Chapter 4

Attending to Data Quality

If you have been diligently following the previous chapters, you should already be reasonably well versed in using the basics of Core Data. Dealing with errors, whether system errors or user errors, and seeding data are issues you must deal with when writing high-quality apps. This chapter is designed to help you fend off the real-world problems that arise when you apply all the theory to the real world of app development. We continue on with the BookStore application from Chapter 2.

Seeding Data

A question we hear often concerns how to distribute a persistent store that already contains some data. Many applications, for example, include a list of values for users to pick from to categorize the data they enter, and developers need to populate the data store with those values. You can approach this problem in several ways, including creating a SQLite database yourself and distributing that with your application instead of allowing Core Data to create the database itself, but this approach has its drawbacks, especially if a future version of your application augments this list of values. You really shouldn't overwrite the user's database file with a new, otherwise blank one that has more values in its list.

Another popular option is to use multiple persistent stores. One is used to contain the user's data while the other is a static data store containing the seed values only. This solution works, but only if your app does not allow the user to augment the seeded lists. For example, if we seeded the BookStore app with a static list of categories in a separate store, we could never allow users to add their own, which would be very limiting.

If you've been following along with the examples in this book, you've already preloaded data into your data stores many times. Think about the applications in this book that don't have edit user interfaces and how you got data into those. That's right: you created managed objects in code and then saved the managed object context. Unfortunately, this solution also has problems of its own. For instance, if the seed data set is enormous, it will take forever for the app to insert all the records one at a time, horribly degrading the user experience. If you've tried the WordList application from Chapter 3, you probably noticed that inserting the nearly 170k words in the list took a few seconds from the time the list was downloaded to the time it was fully inserted into the store.

From experience, we find that the optimum option for seeding data lies somewhere between showing up with a fully loaded backing store and manually inserting rows. The remainder of this section expands on this idea by employing an initial seed that can be used if this is the first time ever that the user runs the app. When the app is updated, that list can be modified incrementally by hand because the bulk of the data will already be there.

In the BookStore application from Chapter 2, we seeded the data store by hard-coding a list of categories and books. We will use the seeded data store as our static seed. Go back to Chapter 2 (or download the source code—you can find the code samples for this chapter in the Source Code/Download area of the Apress web site [www.apress.com]) and run the app one last time, just to make sure we have created a seeded store.

Open the Terminal app on your Mac and find the BookStore.sqlite file (after you have run the app from Chapter 2 at least once). Once you find it, copy the file to your desktop and rename it seed.sqlite.

If you want to use the fast track, you can usually do it using this command from the Terminal prompt (all on one line):

```
find ~ -name BookStore.sqlite -exec cp {} ~/Desktop/seed.sqlite \;
```

Your desktop should now have a file called seed.sqlite, which contains all the seed data. One of the cardinal rules of software development is "Trust you did everything right, but verify anyway." From the terminal, run sqlite3 ~/Desktop/seed.sqlite.

From the SQLite prompt, run

```
sqlite> select * from ZBOOKCATEGORY;
```

and you should see the data

Z_PK	Z_ENT	Z_OPT	ZNAME
3	2	1	Fiction
4	2	1	Biography

Again, if you run

```
sqlite> select * from ZBOOK;
```

the book data should be present.

Z_PK	Z_ENT	Z_OPT	ZCATEGORY	ZPRICE	ZTITLE
4	1	1	4	10.0	The third book
5	1	1	3	15.0	The second boo
6	1	1	3	10.0	The first book

Use the .quit command to exit the SQLite prompt.

At this point, we have our original seed data. Make a copy of the BookStore Xcode project from Chapter 2. From this point on, we will work on that copy.

> **Note** It is important to make a copy so that when we launch the app, it is launched for the first time and therefore gets seeded. To be sure, go to the iOS simulator and remove the BookStore app from the simulated device (press and hold on the icon as on the real device).

Open the new BookStore project in Xcode.

> **Important** Do not run the new app until we're ready, or else it'll create a data store before we've implemented the seeding procedure.

Let's start with unhooking the manual seeding we created as part of Chapter 2. Open `AppDelegate.m` or `AppDelegate.swift` and go to the `persistentStoreCoordinator` method. For Objective-C, change the following line:

```
NSURL *storeURL = [[self applicationDocumentsDirectory]
URLByAppendingPathComponent:@"BookStore.sqlite"];
```

to

```
NSURL *storeURL = [[self applicationDocumentsDirectory]
URLByAppendingPathComponent:@"BookStoreEnhanced.sqlite"];
```

For Swift, change this line:

```
let storeURL = AppDelegate.applicationDocumentsDirectory.URLByAppendingPathComponent
("BookStoreSwift.sqlite")
```

to

```
let storeURL = AppDelegate.applicationDocumentsDirectory.URLByAppendingPathComponent
("BookStoreEnhancedSwift.sqlite")
```

This will change the name of the SQLite file used to back Core Data and make it easier for us to identify later in this chapter.

The next step, still in `AppDelegate.m` or `AppDelegate.swift`, is to blank out the `initStore` method, but keep the method around. We'll put our new code in there later.

While you're there, delete the `deleteAllObjects` method.

Finally, update the showExampleData method to simply list all the books in the store, as shown in Listing 4-1 (Objective-C) and Listing 4-2 (Swift).

Listing 4-1. Showing the Books in the Store (Objective-C)

```
- (void)showExampleData {
  NSFetchRequest *fetchRequest = [NSFetchRequest fetchRequestWithEntityName:@"Book"];
  NSArray *books = [self.managedObjectContext executeFetchRequest:fetchRequest error:nil];
  for (Book *book in books) {
    NSLog(@"Title: %@, price: %.2f", book.title, book.price);
  }
}
```

Listing 4-2. Showing the Books in the Store (Swift)

```
func showExampleData() {
  let fetchRequest = NSFetchRequest(entityName: "Book")
  let books = self.managedObjectContext?.executeFetchRequest(fetchRequest, error: nil)
  for book in books as [Book] {
    println(String(format: "Title: \(book.title), price: %.2f", book.price))
  }
}
```

Using the Seed Store

The first thing the app does when it starts, before executing any Core Data operations, is call the initStore method. This is exactly what we want because it'll allow us to place our seed before Core Data initializes.

Let's add the seed.sqlite file to the project. From your Desktop folder drag the seed.sqlite file onto the Xcode project navigator. Typically, you want to add the file to the Supporting Files group to keep your project organized.

When you drop the file into the Supporting Files group, Xcode gives you some options. Make sure you check Copy items into destination group's folder. In the Add to targets section, make sure BookStore is checked as well.

Your folder should look something like Figure 4-1 (Objective-C) or Figure 4-2 (Swift).

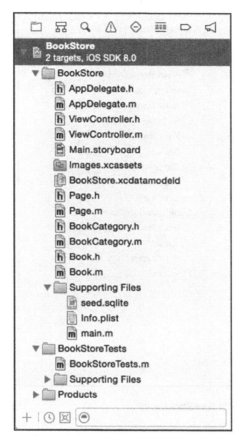

Figure 4-1. Adding the `seed.sqlite` *file to BookStore (Objective-C)*

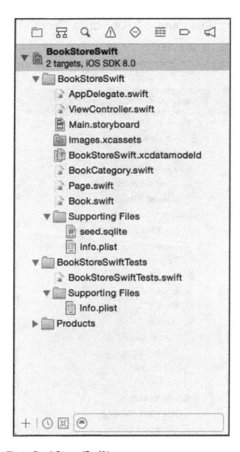

Figure 4-2. Adding the seed.sqlite file to BookStore (Swift)

Now we're ready to create the initial seed. Change the implementation of the initStore method as shown in Listing 4-3 (Objective-C) or Listing 4-4 (Swift).

Listing 4-3. Initial Seeding in Objective-C

```
- (void)initStore {
  NSFileManager *fm = [NSFileManager defaultManager];

  NSString *seed = [[NSBundle mainBundle] pathForResource: @"seed" ofType: @"sqlite"];
  NSURL *storeURL = [[self applicationDocumentsDirectory] URLByAppendingPathComponent:
  @"BookStoreEnhanced.sqlite"];
  if (![fm fileExistsAtPath:[storeURL path]]) {
    NSLog(@"Using the original seed");
    NSError *error = nil;
    if (![fm copyItemAtPath:seed toPath:[storeURL path] error:&error]) {
      NSLog(@"Error seeding: %@", error);
      return;
    }

    NSLog(@"Store successfully initialized using the original seed");
}
```

```
  else {
    NSLog(@"The original seed isn't needed. There is already a backing store.");
  }
}
```

Listing 4-4. Initial Seeding in Swift

```
func initStore() {
  let fm = NSFileManager.defaultManager()

  let seed = NSBundle.mainBundle().pathForResource("seed", ofType: "sqlite")
  if let seed = seed {
      let storeURL = AppDelegate.applicationDocumentsDirectory.URLByAppendingPathComponent
      ("BookStoreEnhancedSwift.sqlite")

      if !fm.fileExistsAtPath(storeURL.path!) {
          println("Using the original seed")
          var error: NSError? = nil
          if !fm.copyItemAtPath(seed, toPath: storeURL.path!, error: &error) {
              println("Seeding error: \(error?.localizedDescription)")
              return
          }
          println("Store successfully initialized using the original seed.")
      }
      else {
          println("The seed isn't needed. There is already a backing store.")
      }
  }
  else {
      println("Could not find the seed.")
  }
}
```

Now you can launch the app. You'll notice that even though we've removed all the hard-coded initialization code, your app will have data from the seed.

The output should look something like the following:

```
Using the original seed
Store successfully initialized using the original seed
Book fetched: The second book
Title: The second book, price: 15.00
Book fetched: The third book
Title: The third book, price: 10.00
Book fetched: The first book
Title: The first book, price: 10.00
```

If you quit and launch it again, you should get the following:

```
The original seed isn't needed. There is already a backing store.
Book fetched: The second book
Title: The second book, price: 15.00
Book fetched: The third book
Title: The third book, price: 10.00
Book fetched: The first book
Title: The first book, price: 10.00
```

We are now at the point were we can create an original seed for your app and it populates the seed in a flash, even if you have hundreds of thousands of rows, because it does it by copying the whole file at once instead of manually inserting each row individually.

If your seed data never change, you're done! If on the other hand you want to update the seed in the future, keep on reading.

Updating Seeded Data in Subsequent Releases

Let's assume we want to update our seed data with a fourth book. Whether users have been using your app for a while or they are getting introduced to the app directly from the latest version, they all need to be able to get that fourth book.

There are two parts to keeping everything in working order. First, you need to update your seed.sqlite so that it contains all the seed data. Second, you need to make sure existing users get the additional data.

Updating the Seed Data Store

Let's start with updating the seed. This is the easy part. In order to achieve this, all we have to do is add the new book, with code, into the current data store, and then use that as the new seed.

Open AppDelegate.m or AppDelegate.swift and at the end of the initStore method, after all the seeding work, add the code in Listing 4-5 (Objective-C) or Listing 4-6 (Swift) to add the fourth book to one of the categories.

Listing 4-5. Adding a Fourth Book to the Seed (Objective-C)

```
- (void)initStore {
  ...

  NSFetchRequest *fetchRequest = [NSFetchRequest fetchRequestWithEntityName:@"BookCategory"];
  NSArray *categories = [self.managedObjectContext executeFetchRequest:fetchRequest error:nil];
  Category *category = [categories lastObject];
  Book *book4 = [NSEntityDescription insertNewObjectForEntityForName:@"Book"
  inManagedObjectContext:self.managedObjectContext];
  book4.title = @"The fourth book";
  book4.price = 12;

  [category addBooks:[NSSet setWithObjects:book4, nil]];

  [self saveContext];
}
```

Listing 4-6. Adding a Fourth Book to the Seed (Swift)

```swift
func initStore() {
  ...

  let fetchRequest = NSFetchRequest(entityName: "BookCategory")
  let categories = self.managedObjectContext?.executeFetchRequest(fetchRequest, error: nil)

  let category = categories?.last as BookCategory
  var book4 = NSEntityDescription.insertNewObjectForEntityForName("Book",
  inManagedObjectContext: self.managedObjectContext!) as Book
  book4.title = "The fourth book"
  book4.price = 12

  var booksRelation = category.valueForKeyPath("books") as NSMutableSet
  booksRelation.addObject(book4)
  saveContext()
}
```

Launch the app (only once or else it'll keep adding) and the output should show that the fourth book has been added.

```
The original seed isn't needed. There is already a backing store.
New book created
Book fetched: The second book
Title: The second book, price: 15.00
Book fetched: The third book
Title: The third book, price: 10.00
Book fetched: The first book
Title: The first book, price: 10.00
Title: The fourth book, price: 12.00
```

At this point, we need to collect the data store and make that the seed. Let's start with putting it on the Desktop by running the following at the Terminal prompt:

```
find ~ -name BookStoreEnhanced.sqlite -exec cp {} ~/Desktop/seed.sqlite \;
```

Check that the seed looks right by running the following command from the Terminal prompt:

```
sqlite3 ~/Desktop/seed.sqlite "select ZTITLE from ZBOOK";
```

You should see the new book in there.

```
ZTITLE
--------------
The second book
The third book
The first book
The fourth book
```

Okay, now that we've made a new seed, let's go back to clean up our BookStore app. First remove the code you just added to initStore so that the fourth book no longer gets added. The initStore method should revert to the way it was shown in Listing 4-3 or Listing 4-4.

Since we don't want to cheat, we need to reset the app so it forgets all about the fourth book and gets re-seeded from the old seed. In the iOS simulator, press and hold the BookStore icon and delete the app. Then launch it again. It should re-seed with our old seed and show only three books.

```
Using the original seed
Store successfully initialized using the original seed
Book fetched: The second book
Title: The second book, price: 15.00
Book fetched: The third book
Title: The third book, price: 10.00
Book fetched: The first book
Title: The first book, price: 10.00
```

Now let's put the new seed in place. In Xcode, right-click on the seed.sqlite file and select "Show in Finder." Using Finder, simply drag and drop the new seed we just made in the Desktop folder onto the old seed. Finder will ask you how you want to manage the file conflict. Just pick "Replace." That's it: the new seed is in place.

At this point, people who download your app for the first time will get the fourth book. Those who would get it as an update would not see the new book since the seed would not be used. We have to take care of these users.

Updating Existing Users

There are several options for updating data from the seed. The one you should choose depends largely on the requirements of your app. For example, sometimes it is possible to just dump the data store and replace it with the seed. This is the case if the user does not store anything in that store.

If you must update the store while preserving the users' data, you should consider manually updating it so that updates are incremental.

Let's edit the initStore method once again to support incremental updates. We want to pick up the new records we want to add (in this case, there's only one—the fourth book) and if they're not already there, then apply all the updates that were released at the same time. Then repeat that block for each new version of the app that you create. Listing 4-7 (Objective-C) and Listing 4-8 (Swift) shows the initStore method that manages incremental updates.

Listing 4-7. Initial Seeding and Incremental Updates (Objective-C)

```
- (void)initStore {
  NSFileManager *fm = [NSFileManager defaultManager];

  NSString *seed = [[NSBundle mainBundle] pathForResource: @"seed" ofType: @"sqlite"];
  NSURL *storeURL = [[self applicationDocumentsDirectory]
  URLByAppendingPathComponent:@"BookStoreEnhanced.sqlite"];
  if(![fm fileExistsAtPath:[storeURL path]]) {
    NSLog(@"Using the original seed");
    NSError * error = nil;
```

```objc
  if (![fm copyItemAtPath:seed toPath:[storeURL path] error:&error]) {
    NSLog(@"Error seeding: %@",error);
    return;
  }

  NSLog(@"Store successfully initialized using the original seed");
}
else {
  NSLog(@"The original seed isn't needed. There is already a backing store.");

  // Update 1
  {
    NSFetchRequest *request = [NSFetchRequest fetchRequestWithEntityName:@"Book"];
    request.predicate = [NSPredicate predicateWithFormat:@"title=%@", @"The fourth book"];
    NSUInteger count = [self.managedObjectContext countForFetchRequest:request error:nil];
    if(count == 0) {
      NSLog(@"Applying batch update 1");

      NSFetchRequest *fetchRequest = [NSFetchRequest fetchRequestWithEntityName:@"BookCategory"];
      NSArray *categories = [self.managedObjectContext executeFetchRequest:fetchRequest error:nil];

      BookCategory *category = [categories lastObject];
      Book *book4 = [NSEntityDescription insertNewObjectForEntityForName:@"Book"
      inManagedObjectContext:self.managedObjectContext];
      book4.title = @"The fourth book";
      book4.price = 12;

      [category addBooks:[NSSet setWithObjects:book4, nil]];

      [self.managedObjectContext save:nil];

      NSLog(@"Update 1 successfully applied");
    }
  } }
}
```

Listing 4-8. Initial Seeding and Incremental Updates (Swift)

```swift
func initStore() {
    let fm = NSFileManager.defaultManager()

    let seed = NSBundle.mainBundle().pathForResource("seed", ofType: "sqlite")
    if let seed = seed {
        let storeURL = AppDelegate.applicationDocumentsDirectory.URLByAppendingPathComponent
        ("BookStoreEnhancedSwift.sqlite")

        if !fm.fileExistsAtPath(storeURL.path!) {
            println("Using the original seed")
            var error: NSError? = nil
```

```
              if !fm.copyItemAtPath(seed, toPath: storeURL.path!, error: &error) {
                  println("Seeding error: \(error?.localizedDescription)")
                  return
              }
              println("Store successfully initialized using the original seed.")
          }
          else {
              println("The seed isn't needed. There is already a backing store.")

            // Update 1
            if let managedObjectContext = self.managedObjectContext {
                let fetchRequest1 = NSFetchRequest(entityName: "Book")
                fetchRequest1.predicate = NSPredicate(format: "title=%@",
                argumentArray: ["The fourth book"])
                if managedObjectContext.countForFetchRequest(fetchRequest1, error: nil) == 0 {
                    println("Applying batch update 1")
                    let fetchRequest = NSFetchRequest(entityName: "BookCategory")
                    let categories = managedObjectContext.executeFetchRequest(fetchRequest, error: nil)

                    let category = categories?.last as BookCategory
                    var book4 = NSEntityDescription.insertNewObjectForEntityForName("Book",
                    inManagedObjectContext: managedObjectContext) as Book
                    book4.title = "The fourth book"
                    book4.price = 12

                    var booksRelation = category.valueForKeyPath("books") as NSMutableSet
                    booksRelation.addObject(book4)

                    saveContext()
                    println("Update 1 successfully applied")
                }
            }
          }
      }
  }
  else {
      println("Could not find the seed.")
  }
}
```

You can finally run the app and since you had launched the first version already, it will not re-seed but instead will update the app incrementally.

```
The original seed isn't needed. There is already a backing store.
Applying batch update 1
New book created
Update 1 successfully applied
Book fetched: The second book
Title: The second book, price: 15.00
Book fetched: The third book
Title: The third book, price: 10.00
Book fetched: The first book
Title: The first book, price: 10.00
Title: The fourth book, price: 12.00
```

And if you run it again, it doesn't apply any new seed or update.

```
The original seed isn't needed. There is already a backing store.
Book fetched: The second book
Title: The second book, price: 15.00
Book fetched: The third book
Title: The third book, price: 10.00
Book fetched: The first book
Title: The first book, price: 10.00
Title: The fourth book, price: 12.00
```

The last test scenario is to delete your app from the simulator once again and launch it to simulate what a new user will get.

```
Using the original seed
Store successfully initialized using the original seed
Book fetched: The second book
Title: The second book, price: 15.00
Book fetched: The third book
Title: The third book, price: 10.00
Book fetched: The first book
Title: The first book, price: 10.00
Title: The fourth book, price: 12.00
```

It simply uses the seed and does not try to apply any updates. In all cases, the complete set of seed data is available.

Undoing and Redoing

Golfers call it a mulligan. Schoolyard children call it a do-over. Computer users call it Edit and Undo. Whatever you call it, you've realized that you've blundered and want to take back your last action. Not all scenarios afford you that opportunity, to which many broken-hearted lovers will attest, but Core Data forgives and allows you to undo what you've done using the standard Cocoa NSUndoManager mechanism. This section instructs you how to use it to allow your users to undo their Core Data changes.

The Core Data undo manager, an object of type NSUndoManager, lives in your managed object context, and NSManagedObjectContext provides a getter and a setter for the undo manager. Unlike Core Data on Mac OS X, however, the managed object context in iOS's Core Data doesn't provide an undo manager by default for performance reasons. If you want to undo capabilities for your Core Data objects, you must set the undo manager in your managed object context yourself.

If you want to support undoing actions in your iOS application, you typically create the undo manager when you set up your managed object context, which usually happens in the getter for the managed object context. The BookStore application, for example, sets up the managed object context in the application delegate, as shown in Listing 4-9 (Objective-C) or Listing 4-10 (Swift). Simply set the undo manager there and you are all set.

Listing 4-9. Setting up the Undo Manager (Objective-C)

```objc
- (NSManagedObjectContext *)managedObjectContext {
  if (_managedObjectContext != nil) {
    return _managedObjectContext;
  }

  NSPersistentStoreCoordinator *coordinator = [self persistentStoreCoordinator];
  if (!coordinator) {
    return nil;
  }
  _managedObjectContext = [[NSManagedObjectContext alloc] init];
  [_managedObjectContext setPersistentStoreCoordinator:coordinator];

  // Add the undo manager
  [_managedObjectContext setUndoManager:[[NSUndoManager alloc] init]];

  return _managedObjectContext;
}
```

Listing 4-10. Setting up the Undo Manager (Swift)

```swift
lazy var managedObjectContext: NSManagedObjectContext? = {
    // Initialize the managed object model
    let modelURL = NSBundle.mainBundle().URLForResource("BookStoreSwift", withExtension: "momd")
    let managedObjectModel = NSManagedObjectModel(contentsOfURL: modelURL!)

    // Initialize the persistent store coordinator
    let storeURL = AppDelegate.applicationDocumentsDirectory.URLByAppendingPathComponent
    ("BookStoreEnhancedSwift.sqlite")
    var error: NSError? = nil
    let persistentStoreCoordinator = NSPersistentStoreCoordinator(managedObjectModel:
    managedObjectModel!)

    if(persistentStoreCoordinator.addPersistentStoreWithType(NSSQLiteStoreType, configuration: nil,
    URL: storeURL, options: nil, error: &error) == nil) {
        self.showCoreDataError()
        return nil
    }

    var managedObjectContext = NSManagedObjectContext()
    managedObjectContext.persistentStoreCoordinator = persistentStoreCoordinator

    // Add the undo manager
    managedObjectContext.undoManager = NSUndoManager()

    return managedObjectContext
}()
```

Once the undo manager is set into the managed object context, it tracks any changes in the managed object context and adds them to the undo stack. You can undo those changes by calling the undo method of NSUndoManager, and each change (actually, each undo group, as explained in the section "Undo Groups") is rolled back from the managed object context. You can also replay changes that have been undone by calling NSUndoManager's redo method.

The undo and redo methods perform their magic only if the managed object context has any change to undo or redo, so calling them when no changes can be undone or redone does nothing. You can check, however, if the undo manager can undo or redo any changes by calling the canUndo and canRedo methods, respectively.

Undo Groups

By default, the undo manager groups all changes that happen during a single pass through the application's run loop into a single change that can be undone or redone as a unit. This means, for example, that in the WordList application of Chapter 3, all word creations belong to the same group because they are all created during a for-loop without releasing control of the thread until done.

You can alter this behavior by turning off automatic grouping completely and managing the undo groups yourself. To accomplish this, pass NO to setGroupsByEvent. You become responsible, then, for creating all undo groups, because the undo manager will no longer create them for you. You create the undo group by calling beginUndoGrouping to start creating the group and endUndoGrouping to complete the undo group. These calls must be matched, or an exception of type NSInternalInconsistencyException is raised. You could, for example, create an undo group for each word creation in WordList so that you can undo the creation one word at a time. The grouping strategy depends largely on the specific requirements of your application.

Limiting the Undo Stack

By default, the undo manager tracks an unlimited number of changes for you to undo and redo. This can cause memory issues, especially on iOS devices. You can limit the size of the undo stack by calling NSUndoManager's setLevelsOfUndo: method, passing an unsigned integer that represents the number of undo groups to retain on the undo stack. You can inspect the current undo stack size, measured in the number of undo groups, by calling levelsOfUndo, which returns an unsigned integer. A value of 0 represents no limit. If you've imposed a limit on the size of the undo stack, the oldest undo groups roll off the stack to accommodate the newer groups.

Disabling Undo Tracking

Once you create an undo manager and set it into the managed object context, any changes you make to the managed object context are tracked and can be undone. You can disable undo tracking, however, by calling NSUndoManager's disableUndoRegistration method. To re-enable undo tracking, call NSUndoManager's enableUndoRegistration method. Disabling and enabling undo tracking use a reference counting mechanism, so multiple calls to disableUndoRegistration require an equal number of calls to enableUndoRegistration before undo tracking becomes enabled again.

Calling enableUndoRegistration when undo tracking is already enabled raises an exception of type NSInternalInconsistencyException, which will likely crash your application. To avoid this embarrassment, you can call NSUndoManager's isUndoRegistrationEnabled, which returns a BOOL, before calling enableUndoRegistration. For example, the following code checks whether undo tracking is enabled before enabling it:

```
if (![undoManager isUndoRegistrationEnabled]) {
    [undoManager enableUndoRegistration];
}
```

The isUndoRegistrationEnabled method disappeared in iOS 8, however, and doesn't exist in Swift, so you're responsible for keeping track of your diable/enable calls. You can clear the undo stack entirely by calling the removeAllActions method. This method has the side effect of re-enabling undo tracking.

Adding Undo to BookStore

Let's put all this into practice with the BookStore app. We've already added the undo manager at the beginning of this section. Let's create some code that'll add a few books and we'll undo the change at the end to show how it works.

Before we do anything else, since we'll be playing around with inserting data, let's force the app to use the original seed every time it launches. This will, of course, reset the app at every launch, so it would not be suitable for most production applications. In the context of our experiments, however, this is perfect because we will always start the app with a known data set, no matter how many changes we experiment with.

Update the initStore method to force it to use the seed, as shown in Listing 4-11 (Objective-C) or Listing 4-12 (Swift).

Listing 4-11. Forcing BookStore to Always Use the Seed (Objective-C)

```
- (void)initStore {
  NSFileManager *fm = [NSFileManager defaultManager];

  NSString *seed = [[NSBundle mainBundle] pathForResource: @"seed" ofType: @"sqlite"];
  NSURL *storeURL = [[self applicationDocumentsDirectory] URLByAppendingPathComponent:
  @"BookStoreEnhanced.sqlite"];

  if([fm fileExistsAtPath:[storeURL path]]) {
    [fm removeItemAtPath:[storeURL path] error:nil];
  }

  if(![fm fileExistsAtPath:[storeURL path]]) {
    NSLog(@"Using the original seed");
    ...
```

Listing 4-12. Forcing BookStore to Always Use the Seed (Swift)

```swift
func initStore() {
  let fm = NSFileManager.defaultManager()

  let seed = NSBundle.mainBundle().pathForResource("seed", ofType: "sqlite")
  if let seed = seed {
      let storeURL = AppDelegate.applicationDocumentsDirectory.URLByAppendingPathComponent
      ("BookStoreEnhancedSwift.sqlite")

      if fm.fileExistsAtPath(storeURL.path!) {
          fm.removeItemAtPath(storeURL.path!, error: nil)
      }

      if !fm.fileExistsAtPath(storeURL.path!) {
          println("Using the original seed")
          ...
```

This will do it—it will always delete the existing data store if it exists.

In AppDelegate.m or AppDelegate.swift, create a new method called insertSomeData and add the code shown in Listing 4-13 (Objective-C) or Listing 4-14 (Swift).

Listing 4-13. Setting up Data to Undo (Objective-C)

```objc
- (void)insertSomeData {
  NSFetchRequest *fetchRequest = [NSFetchRequest fetchRequestWithEntityName:@"BookCategory"];
  NSArray *categories = [self.managedObjectContext executeFetchRequest:fetchRequest error:nil];

  BookCategory *category = [categories lastObject];

  for(int i=5; i<10; i++) {
    Book *book = [NSEntityDescription insertNewObjectForEntityForName:@"Book"
    inManagedObjectContext:self.managedObjectContext];
    book.title = [NSString stringWithFormat:@"The %dth book", i];
    book.price = i;
    [category addBooksObject:book];
  }

  [self saveContext];
}
```

Listing 4-14. Setting up Data to Undo (Objective-C)

```swift
func insertSomeData() {
    let category = self.managedObjectContext?.executeFetchRequest(NSFetchRequest(entityName:
    "BookCategory"), error: nil)?.last as BookCategory?

    if let managedObjectContext = self.managedObjectContext {
        managedObjectContext.undoManager?.groupsByEvent = false
```

```
        if let category = category {
            for i in 5..<10 {
                var book = NSEntityDescription.insertNewObjectForEntityForName("Book",
                inManagedObjectContext: managedObjectContext) as Book
                book.title = "The \(i)th book"
                book.price = Float(i)

                var booksRelation = category.valueForKeyPath("books") as NSMutableSet
                booksRelation.addObject(book)
            }
            saveContext()
        }
    }
}
```

Use the new method by going to the `application:didFinishLaunchingWithOptions:` method and calling it right after `initStore` and right before `showExampleData`, as shown in Listing 4-15 (Objective-C) or Listing 4-16 (Swift).

Listing 4-15. Calling `insertSomeData` in Objective-C

```
- (BOOL)application:(UIApplication *)application didFinishLaunchingWithOptions:(NSDictionary *)
launchOptions {
  [self initStore];
  [self insertSomeData];
  [self showExampleData];
  return YES;
}
```

Listing 4-16. Calling `insertSomeData` in Swift

```
func application(application: UIApplication!, didFinishLaunchingWithOptions launchOptions:
NSDictionary!) -> Bool {
    initStore()
    insertSomeData()
    showExampleData()
    return true
}
```

If you launch the app, you will see the five new books created (in addition to those from the seed).

```
Using the original seed
Store successfully initialized using the original seed
New book created
New book created
New book created
New book created
New book created
Book fetched: The second book
Title: The second book, price: 15.00
Book fetched: The third book
```

```
Title: The third book, price: 10.00
Book fetched: The first book
Title: The first book, price: 10.00
Book fetched: The fourth book
Title: The fourth book, price: 12.00
Title: The 9th book, price: 9.00
Title: The 5th book, price: 5.00
Title: The 6th book, price: 6.00
Title: The 8th book, price: 8.00
Title: The 7th book, price: 7.00
```

Now let's utilize the undo manager by calling undo at the end of the insertSomeData method, as shown in Listing 4-17 (Objective-C) or Listing 4-18 (Swift). Since all of the inserts were made during the same iteration of the run loop, one call to undo should undo all five books.

Listing 4-17. Testing the Undo Manager (Objective-C)

```
- (void)insertSomeData {
  NSFetchRequest *fetchRequest = [NSFetchRequest fetchRequestWithEntityName:@"BookCategory"];
  NSArray *categories = [self.managedObjectContext executeFetchRequest:fetchRequest error:nil];

  BookCategory *category = [categories lastObject];

  for(int i=5; i<10; i++) {
    Book *book = [NSEntityDescription insertNewObjectForEntityForName:@"Book"
    inManagedObjectContext:self.managedObjectContext];
    book.title = [NSString stringWithFormat:@"The %dth book", i];
    book.price = i;
    [category addBooksObject:book];
  }

  [self.managedObjectContext.undoManager undo];
  [self saveContext];
}
```

Listing 4-18. Testing the Undo Manager (Swift)

```
func insertSomeData() {
    let category = self.managedObjectContext?.executeFetchRequest(NSFetchRequest(entityName:
"BookCategory"), error: nil)?.last as BookCategory?

    if let managedObjectContext = self.managedObjectContext {
        if let category = category {
            for i in 5..<10 {
                var book = NSEntityDescription.insertNewObjectForEntityForName("Book",
                inManagedObjectContext: managedObjectContext) as Book
                book.title = "The \(i)th book"
                book.price = Float(i)

                var booksRelation = category.valueForKeyPath("books") as NSMutableSet
                booksRelation.addObject(book)
            }
```

```
            managedObjectContext.undoManager?.undo()
            saveContext()
        }
    }
}
```

Run the method once again and notice that even though all the books were created, they are not in the store when we display the data since the change has been undone.

```
Using the original seed
Store successfully initialized using the original seed
New book created
New book created
New book created
New book created
New book created
Book fetched: The second book
Title: The second book, price: 15.00
Book fetched: The third book
Title: The third book, price: 10.00
Book fetched: The first book
Title: The first book, price: 10.00
Book fetched: The fourth book
Title: The fourth book, price: 12.00
```

If you add a call to redo right after the call to undo, as shown next, what was undone will be redone and the new books will be in the store when you display the data.

```
[self.managedObjectContext.undoManager redo]; // Objective-C
managedObjectContext.undoManager?.redo()      // Swift
```

Experimenting with the Undo Groups

In this section, we modify the data insert method to put each new book in its own undo group. The effect of that, of course, is that when the undo method is called, only one insert will be undone per call. Listing 4-19 (Objective-C) and Listing 4-20 (Swift) shows the updated code.

Listing 4-19. Managing Our Own Undo Groups (Objective-C)

```
- (void)insertSomeData {
  NSFetchRequest *fetchRequest = [NSFetchRequest fetchRequestWithEntityName:@"BookCategory"];
  NSArray *categories = [self.managedObjectContext executeFetchRequest:fetchRequest error:nil];

  BookCategory *category = [categories lastObject];

  // Tell the undo manager that from now on, we manage grouping
  [self.managedObjectContext.undoManager setGroupsByEvent:NO];
```

```
  for(int i=5; i<10; i++) {
    // Start a new group
    [self.managedObjectContext.undoManager beginUndoGrouping];

    Book *book = [NSEntityDescription insertNewObjectForEntityForName:@"Book"
    inManagedObjectContext:self.managedObjectContext];
    book.title = [NSString stringWithFormat:@"The %dth book", i];
    book.price = i;
    [category addBooksObject:book];

    // End the current group
    [self.managedObjectContext.undoManager endUndoGrouping];
  }

  [self.managedObjectContext.undoManager undo];
  [self saveContext];
}
```

Listing 4-20. Managing Our Own Undo Groups (Swift)

```
func insertSomeData() {
    let category = self.managedObjectContext?.executeFetchRequest(NSFetchRequest(entityName:
    "BookCategory"), error: nil)?.last as BookCategory?

    if let managedObjectContext = self.managedObjectContext {
        // Tell the undo manager that from now on, we manage grouping
        managedObjectContext.undoManager?.groupsByEvent = false

        if let category = category {
            for i in 5..<10 {
                // Start a new group
                managedObjectContext.undoManager?.beginUndoGrouping()

                var book = NSEntityDescription.insertNewObjectForEntityForName("Book",
                inManagedObjectContext: managedObjectContext) as Book
                book.title = "The \(i)th book"
                book.price = Float(i)

                var booksRelation = category.valueForKeyPath("books") as NSMutableSet
                booksRelation.addObject(book)

                // End the current group
                managedObjectContext.undoManager?.endUndoGrouping()
            }

            managedObjectContext.undoManager?.undo()
            saveContext()
        }
    }
}
```

Launch the app and since there is a call to undo, the ninth book is missing. Add a second call to undo in that method and notice how both the eighth and ninth books are missing.

Dealing with Errors

When you ask Xcode to generate a Core Data application for you, it creates boilerplate code for every vital aspect of talking to your Core Data persistent store. This code is more than adequate for setting up your persistent store coordinator, your managed object context, and your managed object model. In fact, if you go back to a non–Core Data project and add Core Data support, you'll do well to drop in the same code, just as Xcode generates it, to manage Core Data interaction. The code is production-ready.

That is, it is production-ready except in one aspect: error handling.

The Xcode-generated code alerts you to this shortcoming with a comment that says the following:

```
// Replace this implementation with code to handle the error appropriately.
// abort() causes the application to generate a crash log and terminate. You should not use this
function in a shipping application, although it may be useful during development.
```

The Xcode-generated implementation logs the error and aborts the application, which is a decidedly unfriendly approach. All users see when this happens is your application abruptly disappearing, without any clue as to why. If this happens in a live application, you'll get poor reviews and low sales.

Happily, however, you don't have to fall into this trap of logging and crashing. In this section, we explore strategies for handling errors in Core Data. No one strategy is the best, but this section should spark ideas for your specific applications and audiences and help you devise an error-handling strategy that makes sense.

Errors in Core Data can be divided into two major categories.

- Errors in normal Core Data operations
- Validation errors

The next sections discuss strategies for handling both types of errors.

Handling Core Data Operational Errors

All the examples in this book respond to any Core Data errors using the default, Xcode-generated error-handling code, dutifully outputting the error message to Xcode's console and aborting the application. This approach has two advantages.

- It helps diagnose issues during development and debugging.
- It's easy to implement.

These advantages help only you as developer, however, and do nothing good for the application's users. Before you publicly release an application that uses Core Data, you should design and implement a better strategy for responding to errors. The good news is that the strategy needn't be large or difficult to implement, because your options for how to respond are limited. Although applications are all different, in most cases you won't be able to recover from a Core Data error and should probably display an alert and instruct the user to close the application. Doing this explains to users what happened and gives them control over when to terminate the app. It's not much control, but hey—it's better than just having the app disappear.

Virtually all Core Data operational errors should be caught during development, so careful testing of your app should prevent these scenarios.

Currently, the BookStore app has user interface, albeit blank. We currently load the Core Data stack when the application launches, before the user interface displays. If we wait for the user interface to load before initializing Core Data, however, we'll have an easier time displaying an error message. Let's change the application to do that.

If you're working with Objective-C, open ViewController.m and add the imports and methods shown in Listing 4-21. If you're working with Swift, open ViewController.swift and add the functions that Listing 4-22 shows.

Listing 4-21. Updating ViewController.m

```
#import "AppDelegate.h"
#import "BookCategory.h"
#import "Book.h"
#import "Page.h"

- (NSURL *)applicationDocumentsDirectory {
  return [[[NSFileManager defaultManager] URLsForDirectory:NSDocumentDirectory
inDomains:NSUserDomainMask] lastObject];
}

- (NSManagedObjectContext*)managedObjectContext {
  AppDelegate *ad = [UIApplication sharedApplication].delegate;
  return ad.managedObjectContext;
}

- (void)saveContext {
  NSManagedObjectContext *managedObjectContext = self.managedObjectContext;
  if (managedObjectContext != nil) {
    NSError *error = nil;
    if ([managedObjectContext hasChanges] && ![managedObjectContext save:&error]) {
      // Replace this implementation with code to handle the error appropriately.
      // abort() causes the application to generate a crash log and terminate. You should not use
         this function in a shipping application, although it may be useful during development.
      NSLog(@"Unresolved error %@, %@", error, [error userInfo]);
      abort();
    }
  }
}
```

Listing 4-22. Updating ViewController.swift

```
lazy var managedObjectContext: NSManagedObjectContext? = {
    let appDelegate = UIApplication.sharedApplication().delegate as AppDelegate
    return appDelegate.managedObjectContext
}()
```

```
func saveContext() {
    var error: NSError? = nil
    if let managedObjectContext = self.managedObjectContext {
        if managedObjectContext.hasChanges && !managedObjectContext.save(&error) {
            let message = validationErrorText(error!)
            println("Error: \(message)")
        }
    }
}
```

Next, move the initStore, showExampleData, and insertSomeData methods from AppDelegate.m to ViewController.m, or from AppDelegate.swift to ViewController.swift.

We will have the controller call those methods once it has displayed its view. Add the method shown in Listing 4-23 to ViewController.m, or the function in Listing 4-24 to ViewController.swift.

Listing 4-23. Overriding the viewDidAppear: Method

```
-(void)viewDidAppear:(BOOL)animated {
  [super viewDidAppear:animated];
  [self initStore];
  [self showExampleData];
}
```

Listing 4-24. Overriding the viewDidAppear function

```
override func viewDidAppear(animated: Bool) {
    super.viewDidAppear(animated)
    if let managedObjectContext = self.managedObjectContext {
        self.initStore()
        self.showExampleData()
    }
}
```

Remove the calls to initStore, insertSomeData, and showExample data from application:didFinish LaunchingWithOptions: in AppDelegate.m or AppDelegate.swift.

Run the app and everything should work exactly the way it did before, except this time we're out of the startup sequence when we start interacting with Core Data.

To add error-handling code to the BookStore application, add a method to AppDelegate.m or AppDelegate.swift to dosplay the error. You can quibble with the wording, but remember that error messages aren't a paean to the muses, and the longer the message, the less likely it will be read. Listing 4-25 (Objective-C) and Listing 4-26 (Swift) contain implementations with short and simple messages—with only an extraneous exclamation mark to plead with the user to read it.

Listing 4-25. A Method to Show a Core Data Error (Objective-C)

```
- (void)showCoreDataError {
  UIAlertView *alert = [[UIAlertView alloc] initWithTitle:@"Error!" message:@"BookStore can't
  continue.\nPress the Home button to close the app." delegate:nil cancelButtonTitle:@"OK"
  otherButtonTitles: nil];
  [alert show];
}
```

Listing 4-26. A Method to Show a Core Data Error (Swift)

```
func showCoreDataError() {
    var alert = UIAlertController(title: "Error!", message: "BookStore can't continue.\nPress the
    Home button to close the app.", preferredStyle: UIAlertControllerStyle.Alert)
    alert.addAction(UIAlertAction(title: "OK", style: UIAlertActionStyle.Default, handler: nil))
    self.window?.rootViewController?.presentViewController(alert, animated: true, completion: nil)
}
```

Now, change the persistentStoreCoordinator accessor method to use this new method instead of logging and aborting. Listing 4-27 (Objective-C) and Listing 4-28 (Swift) show the updates to persistentStoreCoordinator.

Listing 4-27. The Updated persistentStoreCoordinator Method (Objective-C)

```
- (NSPersistentStoreCoordinator *)persistentStoreCoordinator {
    if (_persistentStoreCoordinator != nil) {
        return _persistentStoreCoordinator;
    }

    _persistentStoreCoordinator = [[NSPersistentStoreCoordinator alloc]
    initWithManagedObjectModel:[self managedObjectModel]];
    NSURL *storeURL = [[self applicationDocumentsDirectory]
    URLByAppendingPathComponent:@"BookStoreEnhanced.sqlite"];
    NSError *error = nil;
    if (![_persistentStoreCoordinator addPersistentStoreWithType:NSSQLiteStoreType
    configuration:nil URL:storeURL options:nil error:&error]) {
      [self showCoreDataError];
    }

    return _persistentStoreCoordinator;
}
```

Listing 4-28. The Updated persistentStoreCoordinator creation in the managedObjectContext Function (Swift)

```
if(persistentStoreCoordinator.addPersistentStoreWithType(NSSQLiteStoreType, configuration: nil,
URL: storeURL, options: nil, error: &error) == nil) {
    self.showCoreDataError()
    return nil
}
```

To force this error to display, run the BookStore application, and then close it. Go to the data model, add an attribute called foo of type String to the Book entity, and then run the application again. The persistent store coordinator will be unable to open the data store because the model no longer matches, and your new error message will display as Figure 4-3 shows.

Figure 4-3. Showing a Core Data Error condition

Of course, at this point your app should mark itself "unstable" so that it prevents further attempts to interact with Core Data, or else your users will find themselves dealing with a surge of alert boxes to dismiss. You may have noticed that the implementation of the viewDidAppear: method did not try to insert any new data. If it did, you would have to deal with catching more exceptions coming from the non-initialized persistent store. This is because we've never told the app that it was unstable so it keeps on trying to access the persistent store. Let's deal with it.

Add the following property in AppDelegate.h:

```
@property (nonatomic) BOOL unstable;
```

Or in AppDelegate.swift:

```
var unstable: Bool?
```

We will set this property as needed in showCoreDataError, as shown in Listing 4-29 (Objective-C) or Listing 4-30 (Swift).

Listing 4-29. Marking the App as Unstable (Objective-C)

```
- (void)showCoreDataError {
  self.unstable = YES;

  UIAlertView *alert = [[UIAlertView alloc] initWithTitle:@"Error!" message:@"BookStore can't
continue.\nPress the Home button to close the app." delegate:nil cancelButtonTitle:@"OK"
otherButtonTitles: nil];
  [alert show];
}
```

Listing 4-30. Marking the App as Unstable (Swift)

```
func showCoreDataError() {
    self.unstable = true

    var alert = UIAlertController(title: "Error!", message: "BookStore can't continue.\nPress the
    Home button to close the app.", preferredStyle: UIAlertControllerStyle.Alert)
    alert.addAction(UIAlertAction(title: "OK", style: UIAlertActionStyle.Default, handler: nil))
    self.window?.rootViewController?.presentViewController(alert, animated: true, completion: nil)
}
```

In ViewController.m or ViewController.swift, in viewDidAppear:, add the call to insertSomeData.

Finally, we make sure we don't cause extra damage by preventing inserts if the store isn't correctly initialized by editing the insertSomeData method, as shown in Listing 4-31 Objective-C) or Listing 4-32 (Swift).

Listing 4-31. Preventing Inserts If the App Is Unstable (Objective-C)

```
- (void)insertSomeData {
  NSFetchRequest *fetchRequest = [NSFetchRequest fetchRequestWithEntityName:@"BookCategory"];
  NSArray *categories = [self.managedObjectContext executeFetchRequest:fetchRequest error:nil];

  AppDelegate *ad = [UIApplication sharedApplication].delegate;
  if(ad.unstable) {
    NSLog(@"The app is unstable. Preventing updates.");
    return;
  }
...
```

Listing 4-32. Preventing Inserts If the App Is Unstable (Swift)

```
func insertSomeData() {
    let ad = UIApplication.sharedApplication().delegate as? AppDelegate

    if let unstable = ad?.unstable {
        if unstable {
            println("The app is unstable. Preventing updates.")
            return
        }
    }
...
```

Try launching the app. You should see the alert as well as the note in the log about preventing updates.

Don't forget to undo the change you made to the data model so that we can put the app back into working order. Simply delete the foo attribute, then launch to make sure the app runs fine.

Handling Validation Errors

If you've configured any properties in your Core Data model with any validation parameters and you allow users to input values that don't automatically meet those validation parameters, you can expect to have validation errors. Validations ensure the integrity of your data; Core Data won't store anything you've proclaimed invalid into the persistent store. Just because you've created the validation rules, however, doesn't mean that users are aware of them—or that they know that they can violate them. If you leave the Xcode-generated error handling in place, users won't know they've violated the validation rules even after they input invalid data. All that will happen is that your application will crash, logging a long stack trace that the users will never see. Bewildered users will be left with a crashing application, and they won't know why or how to prevent its occurrence. Instead of crashing when users enter invalid data, you should instead alert users and give them an opportunity to correct the data.

Validation on the database side can be a controversial topic, and for good reason. You can protect your data's integrity at its source by putting your validation rules in the data model, but you've probably made your coding tasks more difficult. Validation rules in your data model are one of those things that sound good in concept but prove less desirable in practice. Can you imagine, for example, using Oracle to do field validation on a web application? Yes, you can do it, but other approaches are probably simpler, more user-friendly, and architecturally superior. Validating user-entered values in code, or even designing user interfaces that prevent invalid entry altogether, makes your job easier and users' experiences better.

Having said that, however, we'll go ahead and outline a possible strategy for handling validation errors. Don't say we didn't warn you, though.

Detecting that users have entered invalid data is simple: just inspect the NSError object that you pass to the managed object context's save: method if an error occurs. The NSError object contains the error code that caused the save: method to fail, and if that code matches one of the Core Data validation error codes shown in Table 4-1, you know that some part of the data you attempted to save was invalid. You can use NSError's userInfo dictionary to look up more information about what caused the error. Note that if multiple errors occurred, the error code is 1560, NSValidationMultipleErrorsError, and the userInfo dictionary holds the rest of the error codes in the key called NSDetailedErrorsKey.

Table 4-1. Core Data Validation Errors

Constant	Code	Description
`NSManagedObjectValidationError`	1550	Generic validation error
`NSValidationMultipleErrorsError`	1560	Generic message for error containing multiple validation errors
`NSValidationMissingMandatoryPropertyError`	1570	Non-optional property with a `nil` value
`NSValidationRelationshipLacksMinimumCountError`	1580	To-many relationship with too few destination objects
`NSValidationRelationshipExceedsMaximumCountError`	1590	Bounded, to-many relationship with too many destination objects
`NSValidationRelationshipDeniedDeleteError`	1600	Some relationship with `NSDeleteRuleDeny` is nonempty
`NSValidationNumberTooLargeError`	1610	Some numerical value is too large
`NSValidationNumberTooSmallError`	1620	Some numerical value is too small
`NSValidationDateTooLateError`	1630	Some date value is too late
`NSValidationDateTooSoonError`	1640	Some date value is too soon
`NSValidationInvalidDateError`	1650	Some date value fails to match date pattern
`NSValidationStringTooLongError`	1660	Some string value is too long
`NSValidationStringTooShortError`	1670	Some string value is too short
`NSValidationStringPatternMatchingError`	1680	Some string value fails to match some pattern

You can choose to implement an error-handling routine that's familiar with your data model and thus checks only for certain errors, or you can write a generic error-handling routine that will handle any of the validation errors that occur. Though a generic routine scales better and should continue to work no matter the changes to your data model, a more specific error-handling routine may allow you to be more helpful to your users in your messaging and responses. Neither is the correct answer—the choice is yours for how you want to approach validation error handling.

To write a truly generic validation error-handling routine would be a lot of work. One thing to consider is that the NSError object contains a lot of information about the error that occurred, but not necessarily enough information to tell the user why the validation failed. Imagine, for example, that you have an entity Foo with an attribute bar that must be at least five characters long. If the user enters "abc" for bar, you'll get an NSError message that tells you the error code (1670), the entity (Foo), the attribute (bar), and the value (abc) that failed validation. The NSError object doesn't tell you why abc is too short—it contains no information that bar requires at least five characters. To arrive at that, you'd have to ask the Foo entity for the NSPropertyDescription for the bar attribute, get the validation predicates for that property description, and walk through the predicates to see what the minimum length is for bar. It's a noble goal but tedious and usually overkill. This is one place where violating "Don't Repeat Yourself" (DRY) and letting your code know something about the data model might be a better answer.

One other strange thing to consider when using validations in your data model is that they aren't enforced when you create a managed object; they're enforced only when you try to save the managed object context that the managed object lives in. This makes sense if you think it through, since creating a managed object and populating its properties happens in multiple steps. First, you create the object in the context, and then you set its attributes and relationships. So, for example, if you were creating the managed object for the Foo entity in the previous paragraph, you'd write code as follows:

```
NSManagedObject *foo = [NSEntityDescription insertNewObjectForEntityForName:@"Foo"
inManagedObjectContext:context]; // foo is invalid at this point; bar has fewer than five characters
[foo setValue:@"abcde" forKey:@"bar"];
```

The managed object foo is created and lives in the managed object context in an invalid state, but the managed object context ignores that. The next line of code makes the foo managed object valid, but it won't be validated until the managed object context is saved.

Handling Validation Errors in BookStore

In this section, you implement a validation error-handling routine for the BookStore application. It's generic in that it doesn't have any knowledge of which attributes have validation rules, but it is specific in that it doesn't handle all the validation errors—just the ones that you know you set on the model. Before doing that, however, you need to add some validation rules to BookStore's data model. Add a minimum value of 15 to the price attribute of the Book entity as shown in Figure 4-4.

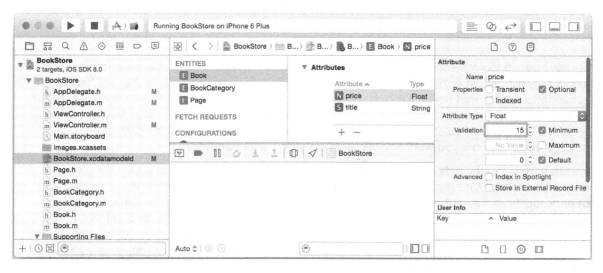

Figure 4-4. *Adding a validation rule*

Implementing the Validation Error-Handling Routine

The validation error-handling routine you write should accept a pointer to an NSError object and return an NSString that contains the error messages, separated by line feeds. Open ViewController.m or ViewController.swift, and add the method shown in Listing 4-33 (Objective-C) or Listing 4-34 (Swift).

Listing 4-33. Adding a Validation Error-Handling Routine (Objective-C)

```objc
- (NSString *)validationErrorText:(NSError *)error {
  // Create a string to hold all the error messages
  NSMutableString *errorText = [NSMutableString stringWithCapacity:100];
  // Determine whether we're dealing with a single error or multiples, and put them all
  // in an array
  NSArray *errors = [error code] == NSValidationMultipleErrorsError ?
  [[error userInfo] objectForKey:NSDetailedErrorsKey] : [NSArray arrayWithObject:error];

  // Iterate through the errors
  for (NSError *err in errors) {
    // Get the property that had a validation error
    NSString *propName = [[err userInfo] objectForKey:@"NSValidationErrorKey"];
    NSString *message;

    // Form an appropriate error message
    switch ([err code]) {
      case NSValidationNumberTooSmallError:
        message = [NSString stringWithFormat:@"%@ must be at least $15", propName];
        break;
      default:
        message = @"Unknown error. Press Home button to halt.";
      break;
    }

    // Separate the error messages with line feeds
    if ([errorText length] > 0) {
      [errorText appendString:@"\n"];
    }
    [errorText appendString:message];
  }
  return errorText;
}
```

Listing 4-34. Adding a Validation Error-Handling Routine (Swift)

```swift
func validationErrorText(error : NSError) -> String {
    // Create a string to hold all the error messages
    let errorText = NSMutableString(capacity: 100)
    // Determine whether we're dealing with a single error or multiples, and put them all
    // in an array
    let errors : NSArray = error.code == NSValidationMultipleErrorsError ? error.
    userInfo?[NSDetailedErrorsKey] as NSArray : NSArray(object: error)
```

```
        // Iterate through the errors
        for err in errors {
            // Get the property that had a validation error
            let e = err as NSError
            let info = e.userInfo
            let propName : AnyObject? = info!["NSValidationErrorKey"]
            var message : String?

            // Form an appropriate error message
            switch err.code {
            case NSValidationNumberTooSmallError:
                message = "\(propName!) must be at least $15"
            default:
                message = "Unknown error. Press Home button to halt."
            }

            // Separate the error messages with line feeds
            if errorText.length > 0 {
                errorText.appendString("\n")
            }

            errorText.appendString(message!)
        }

    return errorText
}
```

We now have a method that returns a more useful message to help the user. Let's hook it up to our test code. Since some of the books we insert in the `insertSomeData` method have a price lower than $15, the error should kick in.

Edit the saveContext method in the view controller to call the validationErrorText method, as Listing 4-35 (Objective-C) and Listing 4-36 (Swift) show.

Listing 4-35. Calling the Validation Error-Handling Routine (Objective-C)

```
- (void)saveContext {
  NSManagedObjectContext *managedObjectContext = self.managedObjectContext;
  if (managedObjectContext != nil) {
    NSError *error = nil;
    if ([managedObjectContext hasChanges] && ![managedObjectContext save:&error]) {
      NSString *message = [self validationErrorText:error];
      NSLog(@"Error: %@", message);
    }
  }
}
```

Listing 4-36. Calling the Validation Error-Handling Routine (Swift)

```swift
func saveContext() {
    var error: NSError? = nil
    if let managedObjectContext = self.managedObjectContext {
        if managedObjectContext.hasChanges && !managedObjectContext.save(&error) {
            let message = validationErrorText(error!)
            println("Error: \(message)")
        }
    }
}
```

Launch the BookStore app and you will see the validation errors in the logs where the books we tried to insert were invalid.

Summary

In this chapter, you have seen several techniques to help you manage the quality and the integrity of the data. You've learned how to help your users deal with unexpected failures and how to help manage a smooth landing instead of letting your application crash inexplicably. In the next chapter, you will learn how to delight your users by integrating the user interface with Core Data, how to smoothly migrate your data when upgrading your app, and many more advanced features all contributing to the quality of your applications.

Chapter 5

Integrating with the User Interface

The vaunted Model View Controller (MVC) pattern, which has spawned derivatives such as Model View Presenter (MVP) and Model View ViewModel (MVVM), separates an application's data (the model) from the display of that data (the view). Core Data, both by name and intent, covers the application data, or model, concerns of applications. Storing data usually doesn't suffice, however— applications usually must present that data onscreen. This chapter discusses some classes that take data from your Core Data stores and present that data onscreen efficiently and responsively. In this chapter, we cover the following:

- Using a fetched results controller (`NSFetchedResultsController`) to display data from a Core Data store in a table view

- Using Core Data's ability to store images outside the Core Data store for better performance

- Integrating a search display controller (`UISearchDisplayController`) with a table view

The application we build in this chapter is a bug tracker called CoreDump. The first screen, the Master view, shows a list of projects—each with a name and a uniform resource locator (URL). We group the displayed projects by their URLs' domain names, so that BitBucket projects are grouped together, GitHub projects are grouped together, and so on. We can then drill into any project to see a list of bugs associated with that project. We can add bugs to a project as well. By the end of this chapter, you'll have a bug tracker with some glaring deficiencies—you won't be able to delete or close bugs, for example—but you'll be more proficient at integrating Core Data with your user interfaces (UIs).

Displaying Table Data with NSFetchedResultController

From the iPhone's introduction, many (if not most) iOS applications displayed lists of data. Opting to call these single-column lists "tables," iOS offers a table view class (UITableView) and a controller (UITableViewController) that displays lists, allows fast scrolling through the data, and even provides mechanisms for tapping cells to drill further into a data hierarchy. This approach is so fundamental and essential to displaying data that all iOS developers know how to use this class and the classes that support it to display lists of data.

When using table views to display data from a Core Data store, you could simply fetch your data into an array and keep the table view ecosystem ignorant of the origin of your data, and indeed many applications do just that. The iOS SDK, however, provides a class called NSFetchedResultsController, which bridges table views and Core Data. NSFetchedResultsController pulls managed objects from the persistent store, from the entity you specify, caches them to improve performance, and gives them to the table view as necessary for display. It also manages adding, removing, and moving rows in the table in response to data changes.

Creating a Fetched Results Controller

You create a fetched results controller with four parameters.

- A fetch request (NSFetchRequest instance)
- A managed object context (NSManagedObjectContext instance)
- (Optional) A section name key path
- (Optional) A cache name

The following sections explain these parameters.

The Fetch Request

The fetch request that NSFetchedResultsController uses defines which data to fetch to display in the table. It is almost the same as any fetch request you've used throughout this book and in any of your Core Data development. It works with the entity in your data model that you specify and can optionally have a predicate (NSPredicate) to filter what it fetches. The one difference in this fetch request is that it must have at least one sort descriptor or your application will crash with the following message:

```
'NSInvalidArgumentException', reason: 'An instance of NSFetchedResultsController requires a fetch
request with sort descriptors.'
```

This is because the fetched results controller works within the constraints of a table, which displays cells in a predictable order, so the fetched results controller must also have the data in a predictable order. A sort descriptor provides the mechanism required to help sort the data.

The Managed Object Context

This is a normal managed object context that holds the managed objects. Saving the context saves all the objects in it. You typically use your application's managed object context for this parameter.

The Section Name Key Path

iOS divides table views into sections, with some number of rows in each section. This structure is fundamental to the operation of table views. A fetched results controller is optimized to work in that environment and can divide its data into sections that correspond to the table sections. The section name key path, set as the `sectionNameKeyPath` parameter, specifies a key path into your Core Data model that divides the managed objects for the fetch request's entity into these sections. Typically, you make this `sectionNameKeyPath` parameter point to one of the properties of the entity this table displays. Note that if you specify a value for the `sectionNameKeyPath` parameter, you also must sort your fetch by that value, or else your application will crash with an error. If your table view contains only one section, you can pass `nil` for the `sectionNameKeyPath` parameter.

The Cache Name

The cache name parameter specifies a name for the cache that the fetched results controller uses to cache the managed objects it fetches and feeds to the table. In the 3.x versions of iOS, you were encouraged to make this cache name unique across fetch results controllers, but your application would still work if you shared the cache name with other fetch results controllers. As of iOS 4.0, however, your application will not work correctly if you share cache names across fetched results controllers. Make sure your cache names are unique.

Note that this parameter is optional; you can set the cache to `nil` and the fetched results controller won't cache the data. This will slow down data display and application responsiveness, of course, so you usually won't set the cache to `nil`.

Creating the Fetched Results Controller Delegate

It's now time to create the fetched results controller delegate.

Building the CoreDump Application

To begin exploring fetched results controllers, create a new iOS Master-Detail Application project and call it CoreDump. Choose your language and check **Use Core Data**, as shown in Figure 5-1.

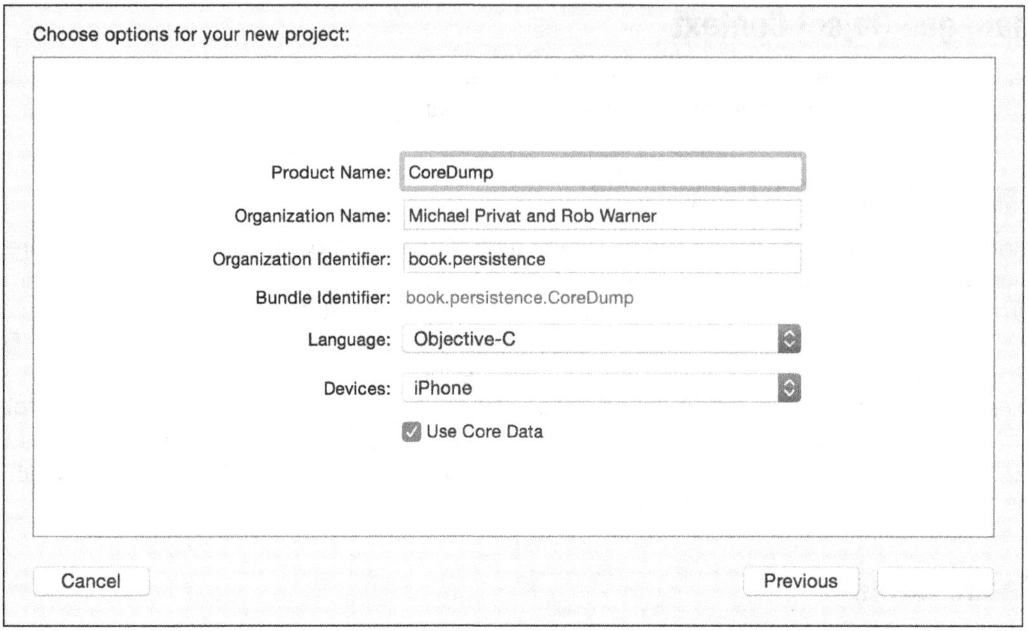

Figure 5-1. *Creating the CoreDump application*

Xcode creates a project with a storyboard tying together a master and a detail screen, a Core Data model containing a single entity (`Event`), and an `NSFetchedResultsController` to feed data from the Core Data store to the table view on the master screen. Go ahead and run the application, create a few events, drill down into them, and get a feel for how the generated application works. Also, poke around in the code to see what's going on. As usual, the Xcode-generated code provides both a good starting point for your applications and an excellent way to learn how to use Apple's technologies.

Examining the NSFetchedResultsController in the CoreDump Application

Let's make sure we understand how CoreDump implements the fetched results controller in the generated code. If you're building this project in Objective-C, open `MasterViewController.h` to see the declaration of the `MasterViewController` class, as shown in Listing 5-1.

Listing 5-1. MasterViewController.h

```
#import <UIKit/UIKit.h>
#import <CoreData/CoreData.h>

@interface MasterViewController : UITableViewController <NSFetchedResultsControllerDelegate>

@property (strong, nonatomic) NSFetchedResultsController *fetchedResultsController;
@property (strong, nonatomic) NSManagedObjectContext *managedObjectContext;

@end
```

You can see that the MasterViewController class subclasses UITableViewController and that it implements the NSFetchedResultsControllerDelegate protocol. It also has an NSFetchedResultsController property called fetchedResultsController, and an NSManagedObjectContext property called managedObjectContext.

If you're building CoreDump in Swift, you can find these same elements in MasterViewController. swift, although they're not all grouped together so you must search a little to find the elements that Listing 5-2 shows.

Listing 5-2. The Same Elements in MasterViewController.swift

```swift
import UIKit
import CoreData

class MasterViewController: UITableViewController, NSFetchedResultsControllerDelegate {

  var managedObjectContext: NSManagedObjectContext? = nil
...
  var _fetchedResultsController: NSFetchedResultsController? = nil
...
}
```

The implementation of MasterViewController references the fetchedResultsController several times. The next few sections examine these references.

Accessing fetchedResultsController

The MasterViewController implementation overrides the accessor for fetchedResultsController to create, initialize, and return it, as shown in Listing 5-3 (Objective-C) and Listing 5-4 (Swift).

Listing 5-3. The fetchedResultsController Accessor (Objective-C)

```objc
- (NSFetchedResultsController *)fetchedResultsController {
  if (_fetchedResultsController != nil) {
    return _fetchedResultsController;
  }

  NSFetchRequest *fetchRequest = [[NSFetchRequest alloc] init];
  // Edit the entity name as appropriate.
  NSEntityDescription *entity = [NSEntityDescription entityForName:@"Event"
inManagedObjectContext:self.managedObjectContext];
  [fetchRequest setEntity:entity];

  // Set the batch size to a suitable number.
  [fetchRequest setFetchBatchSize:20];

  // Edit the sort key as appropriate.
  NSSortDescriptor *sortDescriptor = [[NSSortDescriptor alloc] initWithKey:@"timeStamp"
ascending:NO];
  NSArray *sortDescriptors = @[sortDescriptor];

  [fetchRequest setSortDescriptors:sortDescriptors];
```

```
  // Edit the section name key path and cache name if appropriate.
  // nil for section name key path means "no sections".
  NSFetchedResultsController *aFetchedResultsController = [[NSFetchedResultsController alloc]
initWithFetchRequest:fetchRequest managedObjectContext:self.managedObjectContext
sectionNameKeyPath:nil cacheName:@"Master"];
  aFetchedResultsController.delegate = self;
  self.fetchedResultsController = aFetchedResultsController;

  NSError *error = nil;
  if (![self.fetchedResultsController performFetch:&error]) {
    // Replace this implementation with code to handle the error appropriately.
    // abort() causes the application to generate a crash log and terminate. You should not use this
       function in a shipping application, although it may be useful during development.
    NSLog(@"Unresolved error %@, %@", error, [error userInfo]);
    abort();
  }

  return _fetchedResultsController;
}
```

Listing 5-4. The fetchedResultsController Accessor (Swift)

```
var fetchedResultsController: NSFetchedResultsController {
    if _fetchedResultsController != nil {
        return _fetchedResultsController!
    }

    let fetchRequest = NSFetchRequest()
    // Edit the entity name as appropriate.
    let entity = NSEntityDescription.entityForName("Event", inManagedObjectContext:
    self.managedObjectContext!)
    fetchRequest.entity = entity

    // Set the batch size to a suitable number.
    fetchRequest.fetchBatchSize = 20

    // Edit the sort key as appropriate.
    let sortDescriptor = NSSortDescriptor(key: "timeStamp", ascending: false)
    let sortDescriptors = [sortDescriptor]

    fetchRequest.sortDescriptors = [sortDescriptor]

    // Edit the section name key path and cache name if appropriate.
    // nil for section name key path means "no sections".
    let aFetchedResultsController = NSFetchedResultsController(fetchRequest: fetchRequest,
    managedObjectContext: self.managedObjectContext!, sectionNameKeyPath: nil, cacheName: "Master")
    aFetchedResultsController.delegate = self
    _fetchedResultsController = aFetchedResultsController
```

```
var error: NSError? = nil
if !_fetchedResultsController!.performFetch(&error) {
    // Replace this implementation with code to handle the error appropriately.
    // abort() causes the application to generate a crash log and terminate. You should not use
    this function in a shipping application, although it may be useful during development.
      //println("Unresolved error \(error), \(error.userInfo)")
    abort()
}

  return _fetchedResultsController!
}
```

In the typical pattern, the code checks to see whether the `fetchedResultsController` property has been created and initialized. If it has, the code returns it. Otherwise, it creates the property and initializes it, doing the following:

- Sets the entity to retrieve to the `Event` entity.

- Adds a sort descriptor for the `timeStamp` attribute of `Event`.

- Creates the fetched results controller with the application's Core Data managed object context, no section name key path, and the cache name "Master."

- Sets the fetched result controller's delegate to its parent `MasterViewController` instance.

- Fetches the results it's configured to fetch.

Displaying Data in the Table

The data source and delegate for the table view owned by `MasterViewController` is the `MasterViewController` itself, which you can confirm by opening the storyboard, selecting the table view in the Master view, and clicking the Connections Inspector, as shown in Figure 5-2.

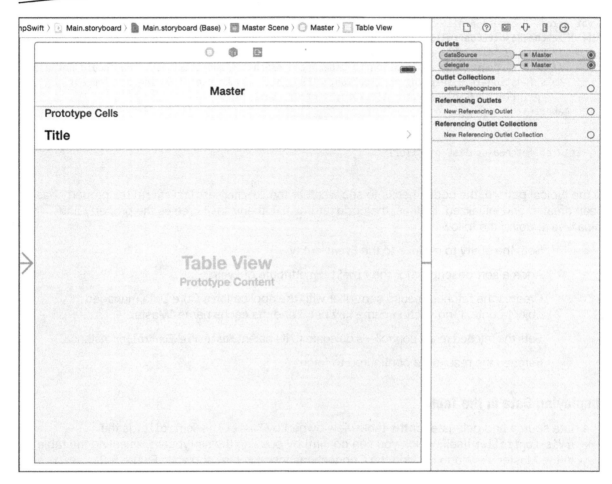

Figure 5-2. Verifying the data source and delegate for the table view

The implementations of the data source and delegate methods use `fetchedResultsController` extensively. For example, to calculate the number of sections in the table, the `numberOfSectionsInTableView:` method returns the count of `fetchedResultsController`'s section property, as shown in Listing 5-5 (Objective-C) and Listing 5-6 (Swift).

Listing 5-5. Calculating the Number of Table Sections (Objective-C)

```
- (NSInteger)numberOfSectionsInTableView:(UITableView *)tableView {
  return [[self.fetchedResultsController sections] count];
}
```

Listing 5-6. Calculating the Number of Table Sections (Swift)

```
override func numberOfSectionsInTableView(tableView: UITableView) -> Int {
  return self.fetchedResultsController.sections?.count ?? 0
}
```

The sections property is an NSArray containing NSFetchedResultsSectionInfo instances. The NSFetchedResultsSectionInfo protocol provides methods to retrieve information about the table section to which it corresponds.

- name—the name to display in the section header

- indexTitle—the title to use in the index that runs down the right side of the table, if shown

- numberOfObjects—the number of objects in the section

- objects—the actual objects in the section

To calculate the number of rows in a given section, the tableView:numberOfRowsInSection: method gets the NSFetchedResultsSectionInfo instance for the requested section and returns its numberOfObjects property, as shown in Listing 5-7 (Objective-C) and Listing 5-8 (Swift).

Listing 5-7. Calculating the Number of Rows in a Section (Objective-C)

```
- (NSInteger)tableView:(UITableView *)tableView numberOfRowsInSection:(NSInteger)section {
  id <NSFetchedResultsSectionInfo> sectionInfo = [self.fetchedResultsController sections][section];
  return [sectionInfo numberOfObjects];
}
```

Listing 5-8. Calculating the Number of Rows in a Section (Swift)

```
override func tableView(tableView: UITableView, numberOfRowsInSection section: Int) -> Int {
  let sectionInfo = self.fetchedResultsController.sections![section] as NSFetchedResultsSectionInfo
  return sectionInfo.numberOfObjects
}
```

The method for returning the actual cell to display in the table, tableView:cellForRowAtIndexPath:, creates a cell and calls a method named configureCell:atIndexPath: to configure it. This method retrieves the managed object, an Event instance, for the cell from fetchedResultsController. It then sets the managed object's timeStamp value as the cell's text. Listing 5-9 (Objective-C) and Listing 5-10 (Swift) show this code.

Listing 5-9. Configuring the Cell (Objective-C)

```
- (void)configureCell:(UITableViewCell *)cell atIndexPath:(NSIndexPath *)indexPath {
  NSManagedObject *object = [self.fetchedResultsController objectAtIndexPath:indexPath];
  cell.textLabel.text = [[object valueForKey:@"timeStamp"] description];
}
```

Listing 5-10. Configuring the Cell (Swift)

```
func configureCell(cell: UITableViewCell, atIndexPath indexPath: NSIndexPath) {
  let object = self.fetchedResultsController.objectAtIndexPath(indexPath) as NSManagedObject
  cell.textLabel.text = object.valueForKey("timeStamp")!.description
}
```

Adding an Event

When you click the + button on the right of the navigation bar, the `insertNewObject:` method is called (as configured in the `viewDidLoad`) method. The `insertNewObject` method, shown in Listing 5-11 (Objective-C) and Listing 5-12 (Swift), does the following:

1. Gets the managed object context from `fetchedResultsController`.

2. Gets the entity from `fetchedResultsController`.

3. Inserts a new managed object of the appropriate entity type into the managed object context.

4. Configures the managed object.

5. Saves the managed object context.

Listing 5-11. Inserting a New Object (Objective-C)

```objc
- (void)insertNewObject:(id)sender {
  NSManagedObjectContext *context = [self.fetchedResultsController managedObjectContext];
  NSEntityDescription *entity = [[self.fetchedResultsController fetchRequest] entity];
  NSManagedObject *newManagedObject = [NSEntityDescription insertNewObjectForEntityForName:
[entity name] inManagedObjectContext:context];

  // If appropriate, configure the new managed object.
  // Normally you should use accessor methods, but using KVC here avoids the need to add a custom
     class to the template.
  [newManagedObject setValue:[NSDate date] forKey:@"timeStamp"];

  // Save the context.
  NSError *error = nil;
  if (![context save:&error]) {
    // Replace this implementation with code to handle the error appropriately.
    // abort() causes the application to generate a crash log and terminate. You should not use this
       function in a shipping application, although it may be useful during development.
    NSLog(@"Unresolved error %@, %@", error, [error userInfo]);
    abort();
  }
}
```

Listing 5-12. Inserting a New Object (Swift)

```swift
func insertNewObject(sender: AnyObject) {
  let context = self.fetchedResultsController.managedObjectContext
  let entity = self.fetchedResultsController.fetchRequest.entity
  let newManagedObject = NSEntityDescription.insertNewObjectForEntityForName(entity.name,
  inManagedObjectContext: context) as NSManagedObject

  // If appropriate, configure the new managed object.
  // Normally you should use accessor methods, but using KVC here avoids the need to add a custom
  class to the template.
  newManagedObject.setValue(NSDate.date(), forKey: "timeStamp")
```

```
// Save the context.
var error: NSError? = nil
if !context.save(&error) {
    // Replace this implementation with code to handle the error appropriately.
    // abort() causes the application to generate a crash log and terminate. You should not use
    this function in a shipping application, although it may be useful during development.
    //println("Unresolved error \(error), \(error.userInfo)")
    abort()
    }
}
```

Note that inserting a new object causes the controllerWillChangeContent: method from the NSFetchedResultsControllerDelegate to be called. Remember that the delegate for fetchedResultsController is the MasterViewController instance, which implements that method to tell its table view that updates are about to begin, as shown in Listing 5-13 (Objective-C) and Listing 5-14 (Swift).

Listing 5-13. The controllerWillChangeContent: Method (Objective-C)

```
- (void)controllerWillChangeContent:(NSFetchedResultsController *)controller {
    [self.tableView beginUpdates];
}
```

Listing 5-14. The controllerWillChangeContent: Method (Swift)

```
func controllerWillChangeContent(controller: NSFetchedResultsController) {
    self.tableView.beginUpdates()
}
```

Next, another method from the NSFetchedResultsControllerDelegate protocol is called: controller: didChangeObject:atIndexPath:forChangeType:newIndexPath. MasterViewController implements that method to animate the insertion of the row in the table, as shown in Listing 5-15 (Objective-C) and Listing 5-16 (Swift). This method also handles animations for deleting or moving a row.

Listing 5-15. Method Called When an Object Changes (Objective-C)

```
- (void)controller:(NSFetchedResultsController *)controller didChangeObject:(id)anObject
        atIndexPath:(NSIndexPath *)indexPath forChangeType:(NSFetchedResultsChangeType)type
        newIndexPath:(NSIndexPath *)newIndexPath {
  UITableView *tableView = self.tableView;

  switch(type) {
    case NSFetchedResultsChangeInsert:
      [tableView insertRowsAtIndexPaths:@[newIndexPath] withRowAnimation:UITableViewRow
      AnimationFade];
      break;

    case NSFetchedResultsChangeDelete:
      [tableView deleteRowsAtIndexPaths:@[indexPath] withRowAnimation:UITableViewRowAnimationFade];
      break;
```

```
  case NSFetchedResultsChangeUpdate:
    [self configureCell:[tableView cellForRowAtIndexPath:indexPath] atIndexPath:indexPath];
    break;

  case NSFetchedResultsChangeMove:
    [tableView deleteRowsAtIndexPaths:@[indexPath] withRowAnimation:UITableViewRowAnimationFade];
    [tableView insertRowsAtIndexPaths:@[newIndexPath] withRowAnimation:UITableViewRowAnimationFade];
    break;
  }
}
```

Listing 5-16. Method Called When an Object Changes (Swift)

```
func controller(controller: NSFetchedResultsController, didChangeObject anObject: AnyObject, atIndexPath
indexPath: NSIndexPath, forChangeType type: NSFetchedResultsChangeType, newIndexPath: NSIndexPath) {
    switch type {
        case .Insert:
            tableView.insertRowsAtIndexPaths([newIndexPath], withRowAnimation: .Fade)
        case .Delete:
            tableView.deleteRowsAtIndexPaths([indexPath], withRowAnimation: .Fade)
        case .Update:
            self.configureCell(tableView.cellForRowAtIndexPath(indexPath)!, atIndexPath: indexPath)
        case .Move:
            tableView.deleteRowsAtIndexPaths([indexPath], withRowAnimation: .Fade)
            tableView.insertRowsAtIndexPaths([newIndexPath], withRowAnimation: .Fade)
        default:
            return
    }
}
```

In the insertion case, the NSFetchedResultsChangeInsert section of the switch statement is called. This is how the table view updates to display the new Event managed object.

Finally, the controllerDidChangeContent: method from the NSFetchedResultsControllerDelegate is called. MasterViewController's implementation tells the table view to end its updates, as shown in Listing 5-17 (Objective-C) and Listing 5-18 (Swift).

Listing 5-17. The controllerDidChangeContent: Method (Objective-C)

```
- (void)controllerDidChangeContent:(NSFetchedResultsController *)controller {
  [self.tableView endUpdates];
}
```

Listing 5-18. The controllerDidChangeContent: Method (Swift)

```
func controllerDidChangeContent(controller: NSFetchedResultsController) {
    self.tableView.endUpdates()
}
```

Deleting an Event

The generated application allows you to delete the Event instances from the Master table, either by swiping left on the table cell and tapping the Delete button that appears or by tapping the Edit link on the left of the navigation bar, tapping the Delete icon to the left of the table cell, and then tapping the Delete button. Don't forget to tap the Done link when you're done.

When you delete a row from the table, your tableView:commitEditingStyle:forRowAtIndexPath: method is called with the UITableViewCellEditingStyleDelete editing style. The implementation checks for that style, deletes the corresponding object from fetchedResultsController, and saves the managed object context. Listing 5-19 (Objective-C) and Listing 5-20 (Swift) show this code.

Listing 5-19. Deleting a Row from the Table and Core Data Store (Objective-C)

```
- (void)tableView:(UITableView *)tableView commitEditingStyle:(UITableViewCellEditingStyle)
  editingStyle forRowAtIndexPath:(NSIndexPath *)indexPath {
  if (editingStyle == UITableViewCellEditingStyleDelete) {
    NSManagedObjectContext *context = [self.fetchedResultsController managedObjectContext];
    [context deleteObject:[self.fetchedResultsController objectAtIndexPath:indexPath]];

    NSError *error = nil;
    if (![context save:&error]) {
      // Replace this implementation with code to handle the error appropriately.
      // abort() causes the application to generate a crash log and terminate. You should not use
         this function in a shipping application, although it may be useful during development.
      NSLog(@"Unresolved error %@, %@", error, [error userInfo]);
      abort();
    }
  }
}
```

Listing 5-20. Deleting a Row from the Table and Core Data Store (Swift)

```
override func tableView(tableView: UITableView, commitEditingStyle editingStyle:
UITableViewCellEditingStyle, forRowAtIndexPath indexPath: NSIndexPath) {
  if editingStyle == .Delete {
    let context = self.fetchedResultsController.managedObjectContext
    context.deleteObject(self.fetchedResultsController.objectAtIndexPath(indexPath) as
    NSManagedObject)

    var error: NSError? = nil
    if !context.save(&error) {
      // Replace this implementation with code to handle the error appropriately.
      // abort() causes the application to generate a crash log and terminate. You should not
      use this function in a shipping application, although it may be useful during development.
      //println("Unresolved error \(error), \(error.userInfo)")
      abort()
    }
  }
}
```

As with adding a row, deleting a row triggers calls to the three `NSFetchedResultsControllerDelegate` protocol methods discussed in a previous section, "Adding an Event."

Showing the Detail

You can find the last reference to `fetchedResultsController` in `MasterViewController` in the `prepareForSegue:sender:` method, which is called when you tap one of the rows in the Master view's table. This implementation extracts the managed object from `fetchedResultsController` for the tapped row and hands it to the Detail view controller for display, as shown in Listing 5-21 (Objective-C) and Listing 5-22 (Swift).

Listing 5-21. The prepareForSegue:sender: Method (Objective-C)

```
- (void)prepareForSegue:(UIStoryboardSegue *)segue sender:(id)sender {
  if ([[segue identifier] isEqualToString:@"showDetail"]) {
    NSIndexPath *indexPath = [self.tableView indexPathForSelectedRow];
    NSManagedObject *object = [[self fetchedResultsController] objectAtIndexPath:indexPath];
    [[segue destinationViewController] setDetailItem:object];
  }
}
```

Listing 5-22. The prepareForSegue:sender: Method (Swift)

```
override func prepareForSegue(segue: UIStoryboardSegue, sender: AnyObject?) {
  if segue.identifier == "showDetail" {
    if let indexPath = self.tableView.indexPathForSelectedRow() {
      let object = self.fetchedResultsController.objectAtIndexPath(indexPath) as NSManagedObject
      (segue.destinationViewController as DetailViewController).detailItem = object
    }
  }
}
```

Now we're ready to build the CoreDump application on top of the generated application's foundation.

Updating the Core Data Model

To build the CoreDump application, we must alter the Core Data model to store the data we want for our bug tracker. CoreDump will store a list of projects and a list of bugs for each project. For each project, we store

- Project name
- Project URL
- Hosting service

For each bug, we store

- Bug title
- Bug details

Delete the Event entity from the Core Data model and create two entities: Project and Bug. For Project, add the following properties:

- name—an attribute of type String
- url—an attribute of type String
- host—an attribute of type String
- bugs—an optional, to many relationship to Bug, with the Delete Rule set to Cascade

For the Bug entity, add the following properties:

- title—an attribute of type String
- details—an attribute of type String
- project—a Required, to one relationship to Project, with the Delete Rule set to Nullify. Don't forget to set the Inverse Relationship to bugs.

When you have finished updating your Core Data model, it should look like Figure 5-3.

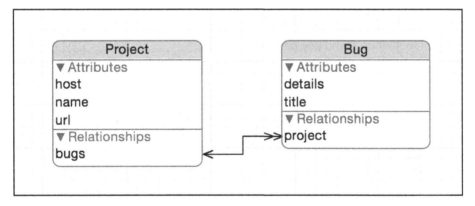

Figure 5-3. The updated Core Data model

Don't forget to delete the database generated by the old data model, or your application will crash when you try to run it.

Generating the Model Classes

Although we could use raw NSManagedObject instances throughout the CoreDump application, we instead will generate classes from the Core Data model. Create a new NSManagedObject subclass, select the CoreDump data model, and select both the Project and Bug entities to generate the Project and the Bug classes. If you're using Swift, remember to fix the namespaces in the generated classes. Your options are:

- Put the project name in the Core Data model, in the Class field of each entity (i.e., CoreDump.Project and CoreDump.Bug)

- Use the @objc keyword in the generated class files (i.e., @objc(Project) and @objc(Bug))

Updating the Fetched Results Controller

The fetched results controller currently tries to fetch using the Event entity, which no longer exists. Instead, you want to fetch the Project entity. Also, you want to display the projects in sections by hosting service. To do this, you must specify a section name key path corresponding to the host property. You must also sort by host, and then within each section sort by name. Locate the fetchedResultsController accessor and update it with the following changes:

- Change the entity to Project.

- Add a sort descriptor for host.

- Change the existing sort descriptor to use name.

- Change the section name key path to use host.

Listing 5-23 (Objective-C) and Listing 5-24 (Swift) show the updated fetchedResultsController accessor.

Listing 5-23. The Updated fetchedResultsController Accessor (Objective-C)

```objectivec
- (NSFetchedResultsController *)fetchedResultsController {
  if (_fetchedResultsController != nil) {
    return _fetchedResultsController;
  }

  NSFetchRequest *fetchRequest = [[NSFetchRequest alloc] init];
  // Edit the entity name as appropriate.
  NSEntityDescription *entity = [NSEntityDescription entityForName:@"Project"
inManagedObjectContext:self.managedObjectContext];
  [fetchRequest setEntity:entity];

  // Set the batch size to a suitable number.
  [fetchRequest setFetchBatchSize:20];

  // Edit the sort key as appropriate.
  NSSortDescriptor *hostSortDescriptor = [[NSSortDescriptor alloc] initWithKey:@"host"
ascending:YES];
```

```
  NSSortDescriptor *nameSortDescriptor = [[NSSortDescriptor alloc] initWithKey:@"name"
ascending:YES];
  NSArray *sortDescriptors = @[hostSortDescriptor, nameSortDescriptor];

  [fetchRequest setSortDescriptors:sortDescriptors];

  // Edit the section name key path and cache name if appropriate.
  // nil for section name key path means "no sections".
  NSFetchedResultsController *aFetchedResultsController = [[NSFetchedResultsController
alloc] initWithFetchRequest:fetchRequest managedObjectContext:self.managedObjectContext
sectionNameKeyPath:@"host" cacheName:@"Master"];
    aFetchedResultsController.delegate = self;
    self.fetchedResultsController = aFetchedResultsController;

    NSError *error = nil;
    if (![self.fetchedResultsController performFetch:&error]) {
    // Replace this implementation with code to handle the error appropriately.
    // abort() causes the application to generate a crash log and terminate. You should not use this
       function in a shipping application, although it may be useful during development.
    NSLog(@"Unresolved error %@, %@", error, [error userInfo]);
    abort();
    }

  return _fetchedResultsController;
}
```

Listing 5-24. The Updated fetchedResultsController Accessor (Swift)

```
var fetchedResultsController: NSFetchedResultsController {
    if _fetchedResultsController != nil {
       return _fetchedResultsController!
    }

    let fetchRequest = NSFetchRequest(entityName: "Project")

    // Set the batch size to a suitable number.
    fetchRequest.fetchBatchSize = 20

    // Edit the sort key as appropriate.
    let hostSortDescriptor = NSSortDescriptor(key: "host", ascending: true)
    let nameSortDescriptor = NSSortDescriptor(key: "name", ascending: true)
    let sortDescriptors = [hostSortDescriptor, nameSortDescriptor]

    fetchRequest.sortDescriptors = [sortDescriptors]

    // Edit the section name key path and cache name if appropriate.
    // nil for section name key path means "no sections".
    let aFetchedResultsController = NSFetchedResultsController(fetchRequest: fetchRequest,
    managedObjectContext: self.managedObjectContext!, sectionNameKeyPath: "host", cacheName: "Master")
    aFetchedResultsController.delegate = self
    _fetchedResultsController = aFetchedResultsController
```

```
    var error: NSError? = nil
    if !_fetchedResultsController!.performFetch(&error) {
        // Replace this implementation with code to handle the error appropriately.
        // abort() causes the application to generate a crash log and terminate. You should not use
        this function in a shipping application, although it may be useful during development.
          //println("Unresolved error \(error), \(error.userInfo)")
        abort()
    }

    return _fetchedResultsController!
}
```

Displaying a Project in the Table

The cells in the table are currently configured to show Event objects. You must change them to show Project objects instead. In each cell, you want to display the project's name and its URL. Tapping the project should drill down into its associated bugs, so you still want the disclosure indicator. You want to be able to edit the project's name and URL as well, so when the Master view is in editing mode, you want to show the detail disclosure accessory.

Additionally, you want to display the projects by hosting service, using the section names you configured in the fetched results controller. The following sections walk you through the changes.

Updating the Table View Cell to Show Projects

Open the storyboard file, Main.storyboard, and select the table view cell in the master screen. Select the Attributes inspector, and do the following:

- Change the Style to **Subtitle**.
- Change the Editing Acc. to **Detail Disclosure**.

See Figure 5-4 for the appropriate changes in the Attributes inspector.

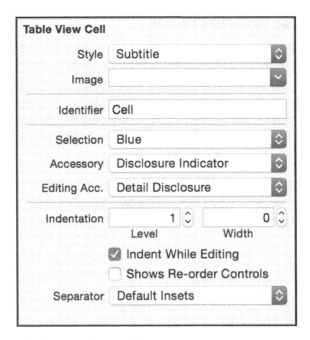

Figure 5-4. Configuring the attributes for the table view cell

Now you can update the configureCell:atIndexPath: method to use a Project object instead of an Event object. If you're building Objective-C, import the Project header file in MasterViewController.m.

```
#import "Project.h" // Objective-C
```

Now, update the cell to show the project's name and its URL, as shown in Listing 5-25 (Objective-C) and Listing 5-26 (Swift).

Listing 5-25. The Updated configureCell:atIndexPath: Method (Objective-C)

```
- (void)configureCell:(UITableViewCell *)cell atIndexPath:(NSIndexPath *)indexPath {
    Project *project = [self.fetchedResultsController objectAtIndexPath:indexPath];
    cell.textLabel.text = project.name;
    cell.detailTextLabel.text = project.url;
}
```

Listing 5-26. The Updated configureCell:atIndexPath: Function (Swift)

```
func configureCell(cell: UITableViewCell, atIndexPath indexPath: NSIndexPath) {
    let project = self.fetchedResultsController.objectAtIndexPath(indexPath) as Project
    cell.textLabel.text = project.name
    cell.detailTextLabel?.text = project.url
}
```

Updating the Table to Group by Hosting Service

Currently, the table style is **Plain**. To display sections, we must change it to **Grouped**, so open
Main.storyboard, select the table, and show the Attributes inspector. Change the style to **Grouped**.

Additionally, you must provide the names for the sections. Recall that the
NSFetchedResultsSectionInfo protocol provides a name property that corresponds to the
sectionNameKeyPath parameter used when creating a fetched results controller. We simply tell
our table to use that value for section names, as shown in Listing 5-27 (Objective-C) and
Listing 5-28 (Swift).

Listing 5-27. Displaying Section Names in the Table (Objective-C)

```
- (NSString *)tableView:(UITableView *)tableView titleForHeaderInSection:(NSInteger)section {
  id <NSFetchedResultsSectionInfo> sectionInfo = [self.fetchedResultsController sections][section];
  return [sectionInfo name];
}
```

Listing 5-28. Displaying Section Names in the Table (Swift)

```
override func tableView(tableView: UITableView, titleForHeaderInSection section: Int) -> String? {
  if tableView == self.tableView {
    var sectionInfo = self.fetchedResultsController.sections![section] as
NSFetchedResultsSectionInfo
    return sectionInfo.name
  }
  else {
    return nil
  }
}
```

Creating the Add and Edit Project Screen

The generated application didn't require a screen to accept input when adding a new Event object.
When you tapped to add an Event, the application just created the object, stuffed the current time
into its timeStamp attribute, and returned. We can't do that when creating a Project object, since
we must collect a name and a URL. In this section, we create a screen to add (and, later, edit) a
Project object.

Creating the View Controller for Adding and Editing a Project

We first create the view controller responsible for the Add/Edit Project screen. Create a new Cocoa
Touch Class file called ProjectViewController and make it a subclass of UIViewController. Check
the **Also create XIB file** check box, choose your language, and follow the steps to create the new
file. Open ProjectViewController.h (Objective-C) or ProjectViewController.swift (Swift) and add
the following:

- A property for the Project to edit (note: will be nil when adding a Project)
- A property for the fetched results controller
- An outlet for the project name text field

- An outlet for the project URL text field

- An initializer that takes a `Project` and a fetched results controller

- An action to save the `Project`

- An action to cancel adding or editing

Listing 5-29 (Objective-C) and Listing 5-30 (Swift) show the edited file.

Listing 5-29. `ProjectViewController.h`

```objc
#import <UIKit/UIKit.h>
#import <CoreData/CoreData.h>

@class Project;

@interface ProjectViewController : UIViewController

@property (strong, nonatomic) Project *project;
@property (strong, nonatomic) NSFetchedResultsController *fetchedResultsController;
@property (weak, nonatomic) IBOutlet UITextField *name;
@property (weak, nonatomic) IBOutlet UITextField *url;

- (id)initWithProject:(Project *)project fetchedResultsController:(NSFetchedResultsController *)
fetchedResultsController;
- (IBAction)save:(id)sender;
- (IBAction)cancel:(id)sender;

@end
```

Listing 5-30. `ProjectViewController.swift`

```swift
import UIKit
import CoreData

class ProjectViewController: UIViewController {

    var fetchedResultsController: NSFetchedResultsController? = nil
    var project: Project? = nil

    @IBOutlet weak var name: UITextField!
    @IBOutlet weak var url: UITextField!
    ...
}
```

Now edit `ProjectViewController.m` (Objective-C) or continue editing `ProjectViewController.`
`swift` (Swift) to implement the desired behaviors. If you're editing `ProjectViewController.m`,
import `Project.h` at the top of the file, and then in the new initializer method, shown in Listing 5-31
(Objective-C) and Listing 5-32 (Swift), store the `project` and `fetchedResultsController` parameters
in the properties.

Listing 5-31. The initWithProject:fetchedResultsController: Method (Objective-C)

```objective-c
- (id)initWithProject:(Project *)project fetchedResultsController:(NSFetchedResultsController *)
fetchedResultsController {
  self = [super init];
  if (self) {
        self.project = project;
    self.fetchedResultsController = fetchedResultsController;
  }
  return self;
}
```

Listing 5-32. The initWithProject:fetchedResultsController: Method (Swift)

```swift
convenience init(project: Project?, fetchedResultsController: NSFetchedResultsController) {
    self.init(nibName: "ProjectViewController", bundle: nil)

    self.fetchedResultsController = fetchedResultsController
    self.project = project
}
```

In the viewWillAppear: method, if the project property is non-nil, transfer the pertinent values from project to the appropriate text fields, as shown in Listing 5-33 (Objective-C) and Listing 5-34 (Swift).

Listing 5-33. The viewWillAppear: Method (Objective-C)

```objective-c
- (void)viewWillAppear:(BOOL)animated {
  [super viewWillAppear:animated];
  if (self.project != nil) {
    self.name.text = self.project.name;
    self.url.text = self.project.url;
  }
}
```

Listing 5-34. The viewWillAppear: Method (Swift)

```swift
override func viewWillAppear(animated: Bool) {
    super.viewWillAppear(animated)

    if let project = self.project {
        self.name.text = project.name
        self.url.text = project.url
    }
}
```

The cancel: method is simple: simply dismiss the modal window, as shown in Listing 5-35 (Objective-C) and Listing 5-36 (Swift).

Listing 5-35. The cancel: Method (Objective-C)

```objective-c
- (IBAction)cancel:(id)sender {
  [self dismissViewControllerAnimated:YES completion:nil];
}
```

Listing 5-36. The cancel: Method (Swift)

```swift
@IBAction func cancel(sender: AnyObject) {
  self.dismissViewControllerAnimated(true, completion: nil)
}
```

In the save: method, you determine whether we're adding a project (project is nil) or editing an existing project (project is non-nil). If we're adding a project, insert a new managed object into the Project entity. In both cases, transfer the name and URL from the text fields into the project object. Then, determine the name of the hosting service in a method called host that we will implement momentarily. Save the managed object context, and then dismiss the modal view. Listing 5-37 (Objective-C) and Listing 5-38 (Swift) show the save: method.

Listing 5-37. The save: Method (Objective-C)

```objc
- (IBAction)save:(id)sender {
  NSManagedObjectContext *context = [self.fetchedResultsController managedObjectContext];

  if (self.project == nil) {
    NSEntityDescription *entity = [[self.fetchedResultsController fetchRequest] entity];
    self.project = [NSEntityDescription insertNewObjectForEntityForName:[entity name]
inManagedObjectContext:context];
  }

  self.project.name = self.name.text;
  self.project.url = self.url.text;
  self.project.host = [self host];

  // Save the context.
  NSError *error = nil;
  if (![context save:&error]) {
    // Replace this implementation with code to handle the error appropriately.
    // abort() causes the application to generate a crash log and terminate. You should not use this
       function in a shipping application, although it may be useful during development.
    NSLog(@"Unresolved error %@, %@", error, [error userInfo]);
    abort();
  }

  [self dismissViewControllerAnimated:YES completion:nil];
}
```

Listing 5-38. The save: Method (Swift)

```swift
@IBAction func save(sender: AnyObject) {
  if let context = fetchedResultsController?.managedObjectContext {

    if self.project == nil {
      var entity = self.fetchedResultsController?.fetchRequest.entity
      self.project = NSEntityDescription.insertNewObjectForEntityForName(entity!.name!,
      inManagedObjectContext: context) as? Project
    }
```

```
    self.project?.name = self.name.text
    self.project?.url = self.url.text
    self.project?.host = self.host()

    var error: NSError? = nil
    if context.hasChanges && !context.save(&error) {
      // Replace this implementation with code to handle the error appropriately.
      // abort() causes the application to generate a crash log and terminate. You should not use
      this function in a shipping application, although it may be useful during development.
      NSLog("Unresolved error \(error), \(error!.userInfo)")
      abort()
    }

    self.dismissViewControllerAnimated(true, completion: nil)
  }
}
```

The host method uses a regular expression to pluck the host name from the URL. For example, if the URL were https://github.com/hoop33/wry, the method would return "github.com." If the regular expression finds no matches, it just returns the URL. Listing 5-39 (Objective-C) and Listing 5-40 (Swift) show the host method.

Listing 5-39. The host Method (Objective-C)

```
- (NSString *)host {
  NSRegularExpression *regex = [NSRegularExpression regularExpressionWithPattern:@".*?//(.*?)/.*"
                        options:0
                          error:nil];
  NSTextCheckingResult *match = [regex firstMatchInString:self.project.url
                                                  options:0
                                                    range:NSMakeRange(0, [self.project.url length])];
  if (match) {
    return [self.project.url substringWithRange:[match rangeAtIndex:1]];
  } else {
    return self.project.url;
  }
}
```

Listing 5-40. The host Function (Swift)

```
func host() -> String {
  let url : NSString = self.project!.url
  let regex = NSRegularExpression(pattern: ".*?//(.*?)/.*", options: nil, error: nil)
  let match =  regex!.firstMatchInString(url, options: NSMatchingOptions.ReportCompletion,
  range: NSMakeRange(0, url.length))
  if match != nil {
    let range = match?.rangeAtIndex(1)
    if let range = range {
      return url.substringWithRange(range)
    }
```

```
    else {
      return url
    }
  }
  else {
    return url
  }
}
```

The view controller is ready, but the corresponding XIB isn't. In the next section, we piece together the view in the XIB.

Creating the Screen for Adding and Editing a Project

Open `ProjectViewController.xib` and do the following:

- Drag a Navigation Bar from the Object Library to the top of the view, 20 pixels from the top.

- Change the bar's title to **Project**.

- Drag two Bar Button Items to the Navigation Bar, one in each corner, and change their titles to **Cancel** and **Save**, respectively.

- Wire the Bar Button Items to the `cancel:` and `save:` actions.

- Drag two Labels to the view and make one read **Name** and the other read **URL**.

- Drag two Text Fields to the view and wire them to the `name` and `url` properties.

- With the View selected, select the "Resolve Auto Layout Issues" button and select **Add Missing Constraints** in the **All Views in View** section.

Your view should match Figure 5-5.

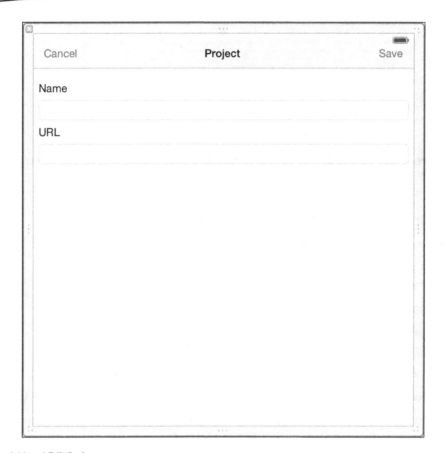

Figure 5-5. *The Add and Edit Project screen*

Showing the Project Screen for Adding a Project

When the user taps the + button to add a new project, the insertNewObject: method is called. You must change this method to show the Add/Edit Project screen, so add an import for ProjectViewController.h in MasterViewController.m, if you're doing Objective-C, and then update the method as shown in Listing 5-41 (Objective-C) and Listing 5-42 (Swift).

Listing 5-41. The updated insertNewObject: Method (Objective-C)

```objc
- (void)insertNewObject:(id)sender {
  ProjectViewController *projectViewController = [[ProjectViewController alloc] initWithProject:nil
  fetchedResultsController:self.fetchedResultsController];
  [self presentViewController:projectViewController animated:YES completion:nil];
}
```

Listing 5-42. The updated insertNewObject: Function (Swift)

```swift
func insertNewObject(sender: AnyObject) {
  let projectViewController = ProjectViewController(project: nil, fetchedResultsController:
self.fetchedResultsController)

  self.presentViewController(projectViewController, animated: true, completion: nil)
}
```

Showing the Project Screen for Editing a Project

When the user taps the Edit button on the master screen, the disclosure accessory for each cell changes to a detail disclosure accessory. If the user taps the detail disclosure accessory, the tableView:accessoryButtonTappedForRowWithIndexPath: method from UITableViewDelegate is called. In that method, we want to display the Project screen, but this time we pass the Project object for the tapped row. We do this only when the table is in editing mode; otherwise, we want the drill-down behavior to occur. Listing 5-43 (Objective-C) and Listing 5-44 (Swift) show the tableView:accessoryButtonTappedForRowWithIndexPath: implementation.

Listing 5-43. The tableView:accessoryButtonTappedForRowWithIndexPath: Method (Objective-C)

```objc
- (void)tableView:(UITableView *)tableView accessoryButtonTappedForRowWithIndexPath:(NSIndexPath *)
indexPath {
  if (tableView.editing) {
    Project *project = [self.fetchedResultsController objectAtIndexPath:indexPath];
    ProjectViewController *projectViewController = [[ProjectViewController alloc]
initWithProject:project fetchedResultsController:self.fetchedResultsController];
    [self presentViewController:projectViewController animated:YES completion:nil];
  }
}
```

Listing 5-44. The tableView:accessoryButtonTappedForRowWithIndexPath: Function (Swift)

```swift
override func tableView(tableView: UITableView, accessoryButtonTappedForRowWithIndexPath indexPath:
NSIndexPath) {
  if tableView.editing {
    let project = self.fetchedResultsController.objectAtIndexPath(indexPath) as? Project
    let projectViewController = ProjectViewController(project: project, fetchedResultsController:
self.fetchedResultsController)
    self.presentViewController(projectViewController, animated: true, completion: nil)
  }
}
```

Seeing the Projects in the Table

At this point, you can run the CoreDump application, as long as you promise not to try to drill down into a project to see its bugs. We haven't updated the Detail view yet, so drilling down will cause the application to crash.

Run the application and add a few projects. Tap the Edit button to go into editing mode, and then tap the detail disclosure accessory to edit projects. Delete projects. Rename projects. Change URLs to see how they're grouped into sections. Figure 5-6 shows the application after adding a few projects.

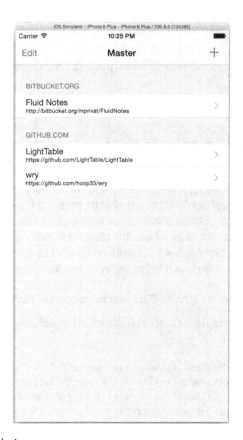

Figure 5-6. *The Master view with projects*

Updating the Detail View to Show Bugs in a Table

The current Detail view just shows a label: "Detail view content goes here." We want instead to show a table, similar to the Master view, but with Bug objects instead of Project objects. Start by updating the DetailViewController class header file to subclass UITableViewController instead of UIViewController. You can also get rid of the two properties, detailItem and detailDescriptionLabel, and add a property to store the parent Project object for the bugs. Listing 5-45 shows the updated header file for Objective-C, and Listing 5-46 shows the changes for Swift.

Listing 5-45. DetailViewController.h

```
#import <UIKit/UIKit.h>

@class Project;

@interface DetailViewController : UITableViewController

@property (strong, nonatomic) Project *project;

@end
```

Listing 5-46. `DetailViewController.swift`

```swift
import UIKit

class DetailViewController: UITableViewController {

  var project: Project? = nil
  ...
}
```

You also must update the implementation file to handle the table view. We don't have a fetched results controller this time—we have a `Project` object that the fetched results controller gave us. The `Project` object has a set of `Bug` objects that we can sort into an array. Using this array to populate a table is standard fare in iOS development. We also want to reload the table anytime the view will appear, and set the title in the navigation bar to the project name. Finally, we want to show a + button on the right of the navigation bar to insert a new bug, although we'll leave the implementation blank for now. Listing 5-47 shows the updated `DetailViewController.m` file, and Listing 5-48 shows the updated `DetailViewController.swift` file.

Listing 5-47. `DetailViewController.m`

```objc
#import "DetailViewController.h"
#import "Project.h"
#import "Bug.h"

@interface DetailViewController ()

@end

@implementation DetailViewController

- (void)viewDidLoad {
  [super viewDidLoad];

  UIBarButtonItem *addButton = [[UIBarButtonItem alloc] initWithBarButtonSystemItem:UIBarButton
SystemItemAdd target:self action:@selector(insertNewObject:)];
  self.navigationItem.rightBarButtonItem = addButton;
}

- (void)viewWillAppear:(BOOL)animated {
  [super viewWillAppear:animated];
  self.title = self.project.name;
  [self.tableView reloadData];
}

- (void)didReceiveMemoryWarning {
  [super didReceiveMemoryWarning];
  // Dispose of any resources that can be recreated.
}

- (void)insertNewObject:(id)sender {
}
```

```objc
#pragma mark - Table View

- (NSInteger)numberOfSectionsInTableView:(UITableView *)tableView {
  return 1;
}

- (NSInteger)tableView:(UITableView *)tableView numberOfRowsInSection:(NSInteger)section {
  return [self.project.bugs count];
}

- (UITableViewCell *)tableView:(UITableView *)tableView cellForRowAtIndexPath:(NSIndexPath *)
indexPath {
  UITableViewCell *cell = [tableView dequeueReusableCellWithIdentifier:@"DetailCell"
forIndexPath:indexPath];
  [self configureCell:cell atIndexPath:indexPath];
  return cell;
}

- (void)configureCell:(UITableViewCell *)cell atIndexPath:(NSIndexPath *)indexPath {
  Bug *bug = [self sortedBugs][indexPath.row];
  cell.textLabel.text = bug.title;
}

- (NSArray *)sortedBugs {
  NSSortDescriptor *sortDescriptor = [[NSSortDescriptor alloc] initWithKey:@"title" ascending:YES];
  return [self.project.bugs sortedArrayUsingDescriptors:@[sortDescriptor]];
}

@end
```

Listing 5-48. DetailViewController.swift

```swift
import UIKit

class DetailViewController: UITableViewController {

  var project: Project? = nil

  func configureView() {
    var addButton = UIBarButtonItem(barButtonSystemItem: .Add, target: self, action: "insertNewObject:")
    self.navigationItem.rightBarButtonItem = addButton
  }

  func insertNewObject(sender: AnyObject?) {
  }

  override func viewDidLoad() {
    super.viewDidLoad()
    // Do any additional setup after loading the view, typically from a nib.
    self.configureView()
  }
```

```swift
override func viewWillAppear(animated: Bool) {
  super.viewWillAppear(animated)
  self.title = self.project?.name
  self.tableView.reloadData()
}

override func didReceiveMemoryWarning() {
  super.didReceiveMemoryWarning()
  // Dispose of any resources that can be recreated.
}

//MARK: Table View

override func numberOfSectionsInTableView(tableView: UITableView) -> Int {
  return 1
}

override func tableView(tableView: UITableView, numberOfRowsInSection section: Int) -> Int {
  let result = self.project?.bugs.count
  return result!
}

override func tableView(tableView: UITableView, cellForRowAtIndexPath indexPath: NSIndexPath) ->
UITableViewCell {
    let cell = tableView.dequeueReusableCellWithIdentifier("DetailCell") as UITableViewCell
    self.configureCell(cell, atIndexPath: indexPath)
    return cell

}

func configureCell(cell: UITableViewCell, atIndexPath indexPath: NSIndexPath) {
  let bug = sortedBugs()?[indexPath.row]
  cell.textLabel.text = bug?.title
}

func sortedBugs() -> [Bug]? {
  let sortDescriptor = NSSortDescriptor(key: "title", ascending: true)
  let results = self.project?.bugs.sortedArrayUsingDescriptors([sortDescriptor])
  return results as [Bug]?
  }
}
```

We must also update the interface in the storyboard. Open the storyboard, Main.storyboard, and select the Detail view. Delete the existing View object and drag a Table View onto the view to replace it. Connect its dataSource and delegate properties to the Detail View Controller.

Next, drag a Table View Cell onto the Table View and set its style to **Basic** and its accessory to **Detail Disclosure** in the Attributes inspector. Also, set the identifier to **DetailCell**. Figure 5-7 shows the new layout.

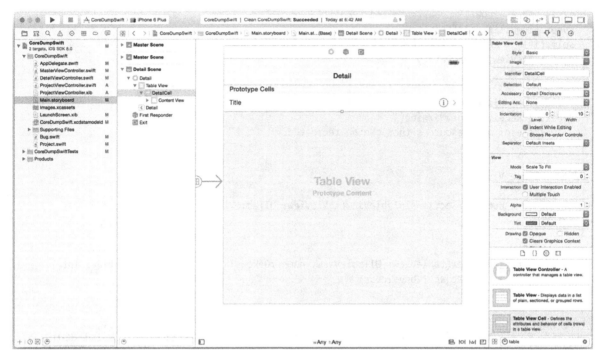

Figure 5-7. The Detail view with a table

Update the prepareForSegue:sender: method in MasterViewController.m or MasterViewController.swift to get the selected Project and set it on the Detail View Controller, as shown in Listing 5-49 (Objective-C) and Listing 5-50 (Swift).

Listing 5-49. Setting project Before the Segue (Objective-C)

```objc
- (void)prepareForSegue:(UIStoryboardSegue *)segue sender:(id)sender {
  if ([[segue identifier] isEqualToString:@"showDetail"]) {
    NSIndexPath *indexPath = [self.tableView indexPathForSelectedRow];
    Project *project = [[self fetchedResultsController] objectAtIndexPath:indexPath];
    [[segue destinationViewController] setProject:project];
  }
}
```

Listing 5-50. Setting project Before the Segue (Swift)

```swift
override func prepareForSegue(segue: UIStoryboardSegue, sender: AnyObject?) {
  var project : Project?
  if segue.identifier == "showDetail" {
    if let indexPath = self.tableView.indexPathForSelectedRow() {
      project = self.fetchedResultsController.objectAtIndexPath(indexPath) as? Project
      (segue.destinationViewController as DetailViewController).project = project
    }
  }
}
```

You can run the project now, and even drill down into a project without crashing. Without a way to add bugs, however, you can't see any bugs in the Detail view. In the next section, we create the screen to add and edit bugs. This screen will mimic the screen to add and edit projects created earlier in this chapter.

Creating the Add and Edit Bug Screen

As with the Add and Edit Project screen, you must create a screen that accepts input for adding a bug or editing an existing bug. The next few sections walk you through the steps for creating this screen.

Creating the View Controller for Adding and Editing a Bug

Create a new Cocoa Touch Class file called BugViewController and make it a subclass of UIViewController. Check the **Also create XIB file** check box, select your language, and follow the prompts to create the file. Open BugViewController.h or BugViewController.swift and add the following:

- ■ A property for the Bug to edit (note: will be nil when adding a Bug)

- ■ A property for the parent Project

- ■ An outlet for the bug title text field (note that we call it bugTitle to avoid clash with existing title property of UIViewController)

- ■ An outlet for the bug details text view

- ■ An initializer that takes a Bug and a parent Project

- ■ An action to save the Bug

- ■ An action to cancel adding or editing

Listing 5-51 shows the edited BugViewController.h file, and Listing 5-52 shows the edited BugViewController.swift file.

Listing 5-51. BugViewController.h

```objc
#import <UIKit/UIKit.h>

@class Bug;
@class Project;

@interface BugViewController : UIViewController

@property (strong, nonatomic) Bug *bug;
@property (strong, nonatomic) Project *project;
@property (weak, nonatomic) IBOutlet UITextField *bugTitle;
@property (weak, nonatomic) IBOutlet UITextView *details;

- (id)initWithBug:(Bug *)bug project:(Project *)project;
- (IBAction)save:(id)sender;
- (IBAction)cancel:(id)sender;

@end
```

Listing 5-52. BugViewController.swift

```swift
import UIKit

class BugViewController: UIViewController {
  var project: Project? = nil
  var bug: Bug? = nil

  @IBOutlet weak var bugTitle: UITextField!
  @IBOutlet weak var details: UITextView!
  ...
}
```

If you're working with Objective-C, open BugViewController.m and import the header files for Project and Bug, as Listing 5-53 shows. Then, add the new initializer to store the bug and project parameters, as shown in Listing 5-54. If you're working with Swift, add the initializer shown in Listing 5-55 to BugViewController.swift.

Listing 5-53. Adding the Imports

```objc
#import "Project.h"
#import "Bug.h"
```

Listing 5-54. The initWithBug:project: Method

```objc
- (id)initWithBug:(Bug *)bug project:(Project *)project {
  self = [super init];
  if (self) {
    self.bug = bug;
    self.project = project;
  }
  return self;
}
```

Listing 5-55. The init Function

```swift
convenience init(project: Project, andBug bug: Bug?) {
  self.init(nibName: "BugViewController", bundle: nil)

  self.project = project
  self.bug = bug
}
```

In the viewWillAppear: method, if the bug property is non-nil, transfer the values from bug to the appropriate text field and text view. Otherwise, clear out any text from the text view. See Listing 5-56 for the Objective-C version and Listing 5-57 for the Swift version.

Listing 5-56. The viewWillAppear: Method (Objective-C)

```objc
- (void)viewWillAppear:(BOOL)animated {
  [super viewWillAppear:animated];
  if (self.bug != nil) {
    self.bugTitle.text = self.bug.title;
    self.details.text = self.bug.details;
```

```
  } else {
    self.details.text = @"";
  }
}
```

Listing 5-57. The `viewWillAppear:` *Function (Swift)*

```swift
override func viewWillAppear(animated: Bool) {
  super.viewWillAppear(animated)

  if let bug = self.bug {
    self.bugTitle.text = bug.title
    self.details.text = bug.details
  }
  else {
    self.details.text = ""
  }
}
```

Again, the cancel: method simply dismisses the modal window, as shown in Listing 5-58 (Objective-C) and Listing 5-59 (Swift).

Listing 5-58. The `cancel:` *Method (Objective-C)*

```objc
- (IBAction)cancel:(id)sender {
  [self dismissViewControllerAnimated:YES completion:nil];
}
```

Listing 5-59. The `cancel:` *Function (Swift)*

```swift
@IBAction func cancel(sender: AnyObject) {
  self.dismissViewControllerAnimated(true, completion: nil)
}
```

In the save: method, you determine whether we're adding a bug (bug is nil) or editing an existing bug (bug is non-nil). Create a new Bug managed object if adding, and then update the properties appropriately. Also, if you're doing this project in Swift, be sure to import Core Data appropriately:

```
import CoreData // Swift
```

Listing 5-60 (Objective-C) and Listing 5-61 (Swift) show the save: method.

Listing 5-60. The `save:` *Method (Objective-C)*

```objc
- (IBAction)save:(id)sender {
  if (self.bug == nil) {
    self.bug = [NSEntityDescription insertNewObjectForEntityForName:@"Bug"
inManagedObjectContext:self.project.managedObjectContext];
  }

  self.bug.project = self.project;
  self.bug.title = self.bugTitle.text;
  self.bug.details = self.details.text;
```

```
    // Save the context.
    NSError *error = nil;
    if (![self.project.managedObjectContext save:&error]) {
        // Replace this implementation with code to handle the error appropriately.
        // abort() causes the application to generate a crash log and terminate. You should not use this
            function in a shipping application, although it may be useful during development.
        NSLog(@"Unresolved error %@, %@", error, [error userInfo]);
        abort();
    }


    [self dismissViewControllerAnimated:YES completion:nil];}
    }
```

Listing 5-61. The save: Function (Swift)

```
@IBAction func save(sender: AnyObject) {
    if let context = self.project?.managedObjectContext {
        if bug == nil {
            self.bug = NSEntityDescription.insertNewObjectForEntityForName("Bug", inManagedObjectContext:
            context) as? Bug
        }

        self.bug?.project = self.project!
        self.bug?.title = self.bugTitle.text
        self.bug?.details = self.details.text

        var error: NSError? = nil
        if context.hasChanges && !context.save(&error) {
            // Replace this implementation with code to handle the error appropriately.
            // abort() causes the application to generate a crash log and terminate. You should not use
            this function in a shipping application, although it may be useful during development.
            NSLog("Unresolved error \(error), \(error!.userInfo)")
            abort()
        }
    }

    self.dismissViewControllerAnimated(true, completion: nil)
}
```

Creating the Screen for Adding and Editing a Bug

Open BugViewController.xib and do the following:

- Drag a Navigation Bar from the Object Library to the top of the view, 20 pixels from the top.

- Change the bar's title to **Bug**.

- Drag two Bar Button Items to the Navigation Bar, one in each corner, and change their titles to **Cancel** and **Save**, respectively.

- Connect the Bar Button Items to the cancel: and save: actions.

- Drag two Labels to the view and make one read **Title** and the other read **Details**.

- Drag a Text Field to the view and connect it to the `bugTitle` property.

- Drag a Text View to the view and connect it to the `details` property.

- With the View selected, select the "Resolve Auto Layout Issues" button and select **Add Missing Constraints** in the **All Views in View** section.

Your view should match Figure 5-8.

Figure 5-8. *The Add and Edit Bug screen*

Showing the Bug Screen for Adding a Bug

When the user taps the + button to add a new bug, the `insertNewObject:` method in `DetailViewController.m` or `DetailViewController.swift` is called. We need to update insertNewObject: to display an instance of `BugViewController`. If you're using Objective-C, import `BugViewController.h` in `DetailViewController.m`.

```
#import "BugViewController.h"
```

Then, change `insertNewObject:` to show the Add/Edit Bug screen, as shown in Listing 5-62 (Objective-C) and Listing 5-63 (Swift).

Listing 5-62. The Updated insertNewObject: Method (Objective-C)

```objective-c
- (void)insertNewObject:(id)sender {
  BugViewController *bugViewController = [[BugViewController alloc] initWithBug:nil
project:self.project];
  [self presentViewController:bugViewController animated:YES completion:nil];
}
```

Listing 5-63. The Updated insertNewObject: Function (Swift)

```swift
func insertNewObject(sender: AnyObject?) {
  let bugViewController = BugViewController(project: self.project!, andBug: nil)
  self.presentViewController(bugViewController, animated: true, completion: nil)
}
```

Showing the Bug Screen for Editing a Bug

When the user taps the detail disclosure accessory for a row in the table, the tableView:accessory
ButtonTappedForRowWithIndexPath: method from UITableViewDelegate is called. In that method, we
want to display the Bug screen, but this time we pass the Bug object for the tapped row. Listing 5-64
(Objective-C) and Listing 5-65 (Swift) show the tableView:accessoryButtonTappedForRowWithIndex
Path: implementation.

Listing 5-64. The tableView:accessoryButtonTappedForRowWithIndexPath: Method (Objective-C)

```objective-c
- (void)tableView:(UITableView *)tableView accessoryButtonTappedForRowWithIndexPath:(NSIndexPath *)
indexPath {
  Bug *bug = [self sortedBugs][indexPath.row];
  BugViewController *bugViewController = [[BugViewController alloc] initWithBug:bug
project:self.project];
  [self presentViewController:bugViewController animated:YES completion:nil];
}
```

Listing 5-65. The tableView:accessoryButtonTappedForRowWithIndexPath: Function (Swift)

```swift
override func tableView(tableView: UITableView, accessoryButtonTappedForRowWithIndexPath indexPath:
NSIndexPath) {
  let bug = sortedBugs()?[indexPath.row]
  let bugViewController = BugViewController(project: self.project!, andBug: bug)
  self.presentViewController(bugViewController, animated: true, completion: nil)
}
```

Displaying and Adding Bugs

You should now be able to run CoreDump, drill down into a project, and add and edit bugs. Figure 5-9
shows the list of bugs for a project.

Figure 5-9. *A list of bugs*

Storing Images

Core Data offers a Binary Data type for attributes that stores binary data in any format, so it would seem a natural fit for storing images. This approach works, and in the case of small images, it probably works well. Storing larger images in Core Data, however, can create performance problems, as any access to those managed objects must load the image data, whether they're used or not.

To address the potential performance problems of storing images in Binary Data attributes in Core Data, many developers have instead opted to store the images in files in their applications' Documents directory, and then to store the path for each image in a String attribute in Core Data. This approach works as well, and it has the advantage that accessing a managed object doesn't load the entire image into memory. Instead, you load the image only when you explicitly want it. This two-step approach to loading images (get the image path from Core Data, then load that image from disk) has two disadvantages.

- Your code becomes a little more complicated, and

- Your application can run a little slower, especially in the case of loading several small images.

So, which approach should you use? Should you store your images in Binary Data attributes in Core Data? Or should you store your images on disk, and just store their paths in String attributes in Core Data? And why should you have to decide, anyway? Aren't iPhones and iPads computers? And aren't computers better at deciding these kinds of things?

As of iOS 5.0, you can indeed tell Core Data to make this decision for you. If your attribute type is Binary Data, a check box appears in the Xcode modeler with the label **Allows External Storage**, as shown in Figure 5-10. This check box corresponds to the `allowsExternalBinaryDataStorage` property of `NSAttributeDescription`. If you check that box, Core Data will decide whether to store your image (or any other type of binary data) in the data store or in an external file, and it will manage all access seamlessly.

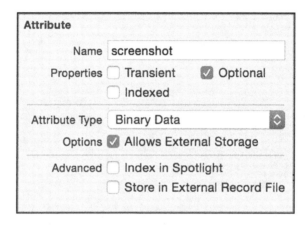

Figure 5-10. Setting an attribute to Allows External Storage in the Attributes inspector

Adding Screenshots to CoreDump

A textual description of a bug can help communicate to the developer what's going wrong and what must be fixed, but an actual screenshot displaying the bug and its consequences can really help. In the next few sections, we add the ability to store screenshots with the bugs in CoreDump.

Updating the Model to Store Images

We want to be able to store an optional screenshot with each Bug managed object in CoreDump. We also want to take advantage of Core Data's ability to seamlessly decide whether to store each image inside the Core Data store or in an external record. Open the Core Data model and add an attribute called `screenshot` to the Bug entity. Make it optional, and set the type to Binary Data. Check the Allows External Storage check box. Finally, regenerate the Bug class files. Note that, as of this writing, Xcode doesn't actually regenerate the files, even if you select to replace the existing files, so be sure to check the files for the inclusion of the new `screenshot` property. Listing 5-66 shows the updated header file, and Listing 5-67 (Objective-C) and Listing 5-68 (Swift) show the updated implementation files. You can see that the only difference is a new property called `screenshot` of type `NSData`. Nowhere in the class files does it refer to allowing external storage, or whether an object is in the Core Data store or in a separate file. That's all part of the Core Data model and runtime, and

you remain completely oblivious to those complexities. If you'd like, you can open the file CoreDump.
xcdatamodeld/CoreDump.xcdatamodel/contents, and you'll see that a line that looks like the following
has been added:

```
<attribute name="screenshot" optional="YES" attributeType="Binary" allowsExternalBinaryDataStorage="YES"
syncable="YES"/>
```

You can see that the allowsExternalBinaryDataStorage property of the screenshot attribute has
been set to YES.

Listing 5-66. Bug.h

```
#import <Foundation/Foundation.h>
#import <CoreData/CoreData.h>

@class Project;

@interface Bug : NSManagedObject

@property (nonatomic, retain) NSString * title;
@property (nonatomic, retain) NSString * details;
@property (nonatomic, retain) NSData * screenshot;
@property (nonatomic, retain) Project *project;

@end
```

Listing 5-67. Bug.m

```
#import "Bug.h"
#import "Project.h"

@implementation Bug

@dynamic title;
@dynamic details;
@dynamic screenshot;
@dynamic project;

@end
```

Listing 5-68. Bug.swift

```
import Foundation
import CoreData

@objc(Bug)
class Bug: NSManagedObject {

    @NSManaged var title: String
    @NSManaged var details: String
    @NSManaged var screenshot: NSData
    @NSManaged var project: Project

}
```

Adding Screenshots to the User Interface

Updating the UI for screenshots presents the following use cases:

- In the Bug view, I can add or replace a screenshot.
- In the Bug view, I can see the current screenshot.

To enable these user stories, we add a `UIImageView` instance to the Bug view screen that displays the image stored in the `screenshot` attribute. We also make the `UIImageView` tappable. When tapped, we allow selection of an image from the photo library to store in `screenshot`. Open `BugViewController.xib` in Interface Builder and adjust the width of the Details text view so that you can put an Image view beside it and both will be visible when the keyboard shows. Then, drag an image view into your view, as shown in Figure 5-11, and be sure to check the User Interaction Enabled checkbox.

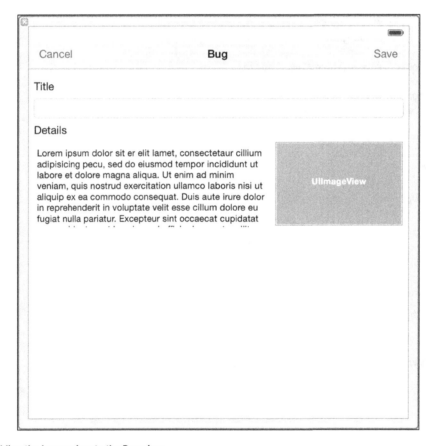

Figure 5-11. Adding the Image view to the Bug view

In BugViewController.h or BugViewController.swift, you do two things.

- Add an outlet (IBOutlet) to connect to the Image view you just added to the view.

- Declare that BugViewController adheres to the UINavigationControllerDelegate and UIUmagePickerControllerDelegate protocols, so that you can allow users to select images when they tap the Image view.

Your updated BugViewController.h should match Listing 5-69, and your updated BugViewController.swift should match Listing 5-70.

Listing 5-69. BugViewController.h with the Outlet and Protocol Declarations

```
#import <UIKit/UIKit.h>

@class Bug;
@class Project;

@interface CDBugViewController : UIViewController <UINavigationControllerDelegate,
UIImagePickerControllerDelegate>

@property (strong, nonatomic) Bug *bug;
@property (strong, nonatomic) Project *project;
@property (weak, nonatomic) IBOutlet UITextField *bugTitle;
@property (weak, nonatomic) IBOutlet UITextView *details;
@property (weak, nonatomic) IBOutlet UIImageView *screenshot;

...

@end
```

Listing 5-70. BugViewController.swift with the Outlet and Protocol Declarations

```
class BugViewController: UIViewController, UINavigationControllerDelegate,
UIImagePickerControllerDelegate {

  var project: Project? = nil
  var bug: Bug? = nil

  @IBOutlet weak var bugTitle: UITextField!
  @IBOutlet weak var details: UITextView!
  @IBOutlet weak var screenshot: UIImageView!
  ...
}
```

In Interface Builder, connect the screenshot outlet to the Image view. Then, open BugViewController.m or BugViewController.swift to implement the code for the images. You add code to do the following:

- Display a border around the Image view so that it's apparent when it's empty.

- Display the selected image in the Image view.

- Save the image to Core Data when the bug is saved.

■ Launch an image picker when the user taps the Image view.

■ Handle the save or cancel appropriately when the user dismisses the image picker.

Listing 5-71 shows the updates to BugViewController.m, and Listing 5-72 shows the updates to BugViewController.swift.

Listing 5-71. Handling Screenshots in BugViewController.m

```objc
#import "BugViewController.h"
#import "Project.h"
#import "Bug.h"

@interface BugViewController ()

@end

@implementation BugViewController

- (id)initWithBug:(Bug *)bug project:(Project *)project {
  self = [super init];
  if (self) {
    self.bug = bug;
    self.project = project;
  }
  return self;
}

- (void)viewWillAppear:(BOOL)animated {
  [super viewWillAppear:animated];
  if (self.bug != nil) {
    self.bugTitle.text = self.bug.title;
    self.details.text = self.bug.details;
    self.screenshot.image = [UIImage imageWithData:self.bug.screenshot];
  } else {
    self.details.text = @"";
  }
}

- (void)viewDidLoad {
  [super viewDidLoad];

  self.screenshot.layer.borderColor = [UIColor blackColor].CGColor;
  self.screenshot.layer.borderWidth = 1.0f;

  UITapGestureRecognizer *tapGestureRecognizer = [[UITapGestureRecognizer alloc] initWithTarget:self
action:@selector(screenshotTapped:)];
  [self.screenshot addGestureRecognizer:tapGestureRecognizer];
}
```

```objc
- (void)didReceiveMemoryWarning
{
  [super didReceiveMemoryWarning];
  // Dispose of any resources that can be recreated.
}

- (void)screenshotTapped:(id)sender {
  UIImagePickerController *imagePickerController = [[UIImagePickerController alloc] init];
  imagePickerController.delegate = self;
  imagePickerController.sourceType = UIImagePickerControllerSourceTypePhotoLibrary;
  imagePickerController.allowsEditing = YES;
  [self presentViewController:imagePickerController animated:YES completion:nil];
}

- (IBAction)cancel:(id)sender {
  [self dismissViewControllerAnimated:YES completion:nil];
}

- (IBAction)save:(id)sender {
  if (self.bug == nil) {
    self.bug = [NSEntityDescription insertNewObjectForEntityForName:@"Bug"
inManagedObjectContext:self.project.managedObjectContext];
  }

  self.bug.project = self.project;
  self.bug.title = self.bugTitle.text;
  self.bug.details = self.details.text;
  self.bug.screenshot = UIImagePNGRepresentation(self.screenshot.image);

  // Save the context.
  NSError *error = nil;
  if (![self.project.managedObjectContext save:&error]) {
    // Replace this implementation with code to handle the error appropriately.
    // abort() causes the application to generate a crash log and terminate. You should not use this
       function in a shipping application, although it may be useful during development.
    NSLog(@"Unresolved error %@, %@", error, [error userInfo]);
    abort();
  }

  [self dismissViewControllerAnimated:YES completion:nil];
}

#pragma mark - Image picker

- (void)imagePickerControllerDidCancel:(UIImagePickerController *)picker {
  [self dismissViewControllerAnimated:YES completion:nil];
}

- (void)imagePickerController:(UIImagePickerController *)picker didFinishPickingMediaWithInfo:
(NSDictionary *)info {
  [self dismissViewControllerAnimated:YES completion:nil];
  UIImage *image = info[UIImagePickerControllerEditedImage];
```

```
  dispatch_async(dispatch_get_main_queue(), ^{
    self.screenshot.image = image;
  });
}

@end
```

Listing 5-72. Handling Screenshots in BugViewController.swift

```swift
import UIKit
import CoreData

class BugViewController: UIViewController, UINavigationControllerDelegate,
UIImagePickerControllerDelegate {

  var project: Project? = nil
  var bug: Bug? = nil

  @IBOutlet weak var bugTitle: UITextField!
  @IBOutlet weak var details: UITextView!
  @IBOutlet weak var screenshot: UIImageView!

  convenience init(project: Project, andBug bug: Bug?) {
    self.init(nibName: "BugViewController", bundle: nil)

    self.project = project
    self.bug = bug
  }

  override func viewWillAppear(animated: Bool) {
    super.viewWillAppear(animated)

    if let bug = self.bug {
      self.bugTitle.text = bug.title
      self.details.text = bug.details
      self.screenshot.image = UIImage(data: bug.screenshot)
    }
    else {
      self.details.text = ""
    }
  }

  override func viewDidLoad() {
    super.viewDidLoad()

    self.screenshot.layer.borderColor = UIColor.blackColor().CGColor
    self.screenshot.layer.borderWidth = 1

    let tapGestureRecognizer = UITapGestureRecognizer(target: self, action:
Selector("screenshotTapped:"))
    self.screenshot.addGestureRecognizer(tapGestureRecognizer)
  }
```

```swift
override func didReceiveMemoryWarning() {
  super.didReceiveMemoryWarning()
  // Dispose of any resources that can be recreated.
}

func screenshotTapped(recognizer: UITapGestureRecognizer) {
  let imagePickerController = UIImagePickerController()
  imagePickerController.delegate = self
  imagePickerController.sourceType = .PhotoLibrary
  imagePickerController.allowsEditing = true
  self.presentViewController(imagePickerController, animated: true, completion: nil)
}

@IBAction func cancel(sender: AnyObject) {
  self.dismissViewControllerAnimated(true, completion: nil)
}

@IBAction func save(sender: AnyObject) {
  if let context = self.project?.managedObjectContext {
    if bug == nil {
      self.bug = NSEntityDescription.insertNewObjectForEntityForName("Bug",
inManagedObjectContext: context) as? Bug
    }

    self.bug?.project = self.project!
    self.bug?.title = self.bugTitle.text
    self.bug?.details = self.details.text
    if self.screenshot.image != nil {
      self.bug?.screenshot = UIImagePNGRepresentation(self.screenshot.image)
    }

    var error: NSError? = nil
    if context.hasChanges && !context.save(&error) {
      // Replace this implementation with code to handle the error appropriately.
      // abort() causes the application to generate a crash log and terminate. You should not use
      this function in a shipping application, although it may be useful during development.
      NSLog("Unresolved error \(error), \(error!.userInfo)")
      abort()
    }
  }

  self.dismissViewControllerAnimated(true, completion: nil)
}

func imagePickerControllerDidCancel(picker: UIImagePickerController) {
  self.dismissViewControllerAnimated(true, completion: nil)
}
```

```
func imagePickerController(picker: UIImagePickerController, didFinishPickingMediaWithInfo info:
[NSObject : AnyObject]) {
  self.dismissViewControllerAnimated(true, completion: nil)
  let image = info[UIImagePickerControllerEditedImage] as UIImage

  dispatch_async(dispatch_get_main_queue(), { () -> Void in
    self.screenshot.image = image
  })
}
}
```

Launch the CoreDump application, add a bug, and then add a screenshot to the bug using your new interface. Your Bug view should resemble Figure 5-12.

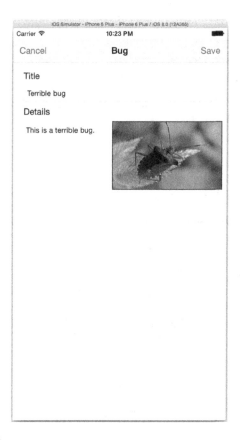

Figure 5-12. *A Bug with a screenshot*

Verifying the External Storage

Depending on the size of the image you've selected, Core Data may have stored the screenshot as an external record, with a unique identifier in the SQLite database. If the file has been stored externally, you can find it inside a subdirectory, in the same directory as your SQLite database file, called `.CoreDump_SUPPORT/_EXTERNAL_DATA`. For example, for the bug shown in the screenshot in Figure 5-12, we can see that Core Data has stored an identifier in SQLite that points to an external file.

```
sqlite> select * from zbug;1|1|5|1|This is a terrible bug|Terrible Bug|FC88541E-A362-40E2-8680-
5D4553764B86
```

We can see that file at `.CoreDump_SUPPORT/_EXTERNAL_DATA/FC88541E-A362-40E2-8680-5D4553764B86`, and can open it in Preview to see that it is, indeed, the image we stored.

Searching the Fetched Results in the Table

If you have a lot of projects in the Master view, you may have difficulty finding the project you're looking for. Users expect to be able to search through data and filter the results to narrow the result set and more quickly locate their targets. For searching in tables, iOS 8 deprecates the old Search Bar and Search Display Controller (UISearchDisplayController) and introduces a new class for searching: UISearchController. In the next few sections, we show you how to add searching capabilities using UISearchController to CoreDump's Master view.

Adding the Search Controller

Interface Builder hasn't yet added the new UISearchController, so you must add this form of search support via code. Start by declaring that MasterViewController conforms to the UISearchResultsUpdating protocol, either in MasterViewController.h or in MasterViewController.swift. While you're editing that file, add a property called searchController for the UISearchController instance. Also, for reasons we'll describe shortly, add a property to store an NSPredicate instance we'll call searchPredicate. Listing 5-73 (Objective-C) and Listing 5-74 (Swift) show these changes.

Listing 5-73. Updating MasterViewController.h for UISearchController (Objective-C)

```
@interface MasterViewController : UITableViewController <NSFetchedResultsControllerDelegate,
UISearchResultsUpdating>
...
@property (strong, nonatomic) UISearchController *searchController;
@property (strong, nonatomic) NSPredicate *searchPredicate;
...
@end
```

Listing 5-74. Updating MasterViewController.swift for UISearchController (Swift)

```
class MasterViewController: UITableViewController, NSFetchedResultsControllerDelegate,
UISearchResultsUpdating {
  ...
  var searchController: UISearchController!
  var searchPredicate: NSPredicate? = nil
  ...
}
```

In your viewDidLoad: method, create your UISearchController instance and assign it to searchController. The initializer takes a parameter for the view controller that displays the search results; passing nil will display results in the same view that you're searching, which in our case is the table view that displays the projects. We also do a few more things:

- Tell the background not to dim during search

- Set the search results updater (the class responsible for updating the search results) to our MasterViewController instance

- Size the search bar to fit

- Set the search bar as the header of our table

- Set the delegate of our table view to our MasterViewController instance, so we get taps whether we're searching or not

- Set ourselves as defining a presentation context

Listing 5-75 shows the Objective-C viewDidLoad: method, and Listing 5-76 shows the Swift viewDidLoad: function.

Listing 5-75. Creating the UISearchController (Objective-C)

```
- (void)viewDidLoad {
  [super viewDidLoad];

  self.navigationItem.leftBarButtonItem = self.editButtonItem;

    UIBarButtonItem *addButton = [[UIBarButtonItem alloc] initWithBarButtonSystemItem:UIBarButton
SystemItemAdd target:self action:@selector(insertNewObject:)];
  self.navigationItem.rightBarButtonItem = addButton;

  // Create the search controller with this controller displaying the search results
  self.searchController = [[UISearchController alloc] initWithSearchResultsController:nil];
  self.searchController.dimsBackgroundDuringPresentation = NO;
  self.searchController.searchResultsUpdater = self;
  [self.searchController.searchBar sizeToFit];
  self.tableView.tableHeaderView = self.searchController.searchBar;
  self.tableView.delegate = self;
  self.definesPresentationContext = YES;
}
```

Listing 5-76. Creating the UISearchController (Swift)

```
override func viewDidLoad() {
  super.viewDidLoad()

  self.navigationItem.leftBarButtonItem = self.editButtonItem()

  let addButton = UIBarButtonItem(barButtonSystemItem: .Add, target: self, action:
"insertNewObject:")
  self.navigationItem.rightBarButtonItem = addButton

  // Create the search controller with this controller displaying the search results
  self.searchController = UISearchController(searchResultsController: nil)
  self.searchController.dimsBackgroundDuringPresentation = false
  self.searchController.searchResultsUpdater = self
  self.searchController.searchBar.sizeToFit()
  self.tableView.tableHeaderView = self.searchController?.searchBar
  self.tableView.delegate = self
  self.definesPresentationContext = true
}
```

Retrieving the Search Results

Don't be tempted to scurry back to your Core Data store to get results for search queries. The Internet abounds with advice to create a second fetch results controller for retrieving search results, but this isn't necessary. You already have a fetched results controller with all the results you want to search. You just want to narrow down the result set from all objects to the ones that match the search query.

The fetched results controller has a property, fetchedObjects, that contains all the results. We can use that, along with our knowledge of predicates, to filter the fetched objects to just those that match the search query. For CoreDump, when users search, we want to display only the projects whose names or URLs contain the search text, case-insensitive. We create a new method on MasterViewController called updateSearchResultsForSearchController: to fulfill our promise to conform to the UISearchResultsUpdating protocol. This method, which is called when the search bar gains focus or the search text changes, creates the predicate that performs the filtering. It first grabs the search text, which is contained in self.searchController.searchBar.text, and if it finds any text, it creates an appropriate predicate and stores it in searchPredicate. Then, it reloads the table. Listing 5-77 (Objective-C) and Listing 5-78 (Swift) show the updateSearchResultsForSearchController: method.

Listing 5-77. Creating the Search Predicate in MasterViewController.m

```
- (void)updateSearchResultsForSearchController:(UISearchController *)searchController {
  NSString *searchText = self.searchController.searchBar.text;
  self.searchPredicate = searchText.length == 0 ? nil : [NSPredicate predicateWithFormat:@"name
contains[c] %@ or url contains[c] %@", searchText, searchText];

  [self.tableView reloadData];
}
```

Listing 5-78. Creating the Search Predicate in `MasterViewController.swift`

```swift
func updateSearchResultsForSearchController(searchController: UISearchController) {
  let searchText = self.searchController?.searchBar.text
  if let searchText = searchText {
    self.searchPredicate = searchText.isEmpty ? nil : NSPredicate(format: "name contains[c] %@ or
url contains[c] %@", searchText, searchText)

    self.tableView.reloadData()
  }
}
```

Displaying the Search Results

Since we use the same table for both the normal results and the search results, to toggle between them we update the methods in the table view datasource to check for a non-nil `searchPredicate`. If `searchPredicate` is non-nil, we apply it to the `fetchedObjects` property in the fetched results controller. Otherwise, we use the existing fetched results controller code.

For the search results, we don't section the results, so we want to have a single section with no section header. Listing 5-79 (Objective-C) and Listing 5-80 (Swift) show the updated `numberOfSectionsInTableView:` and `tableView:titleForHeaderInSection:` methods that return differing results, depending on whether we have a search predicate.

Listing 5-79. Setting Up the Sections for the Table View (Objective-C)

```objc
- (NSInteger)numberOfSectionsInTableView:(UITableView *)tableView {
  return self.searchPredicate == nil ? [[self.fetchedResultsController sections] count] : 1;
}


- (NSString *)tableView:(UITableView *)tableView titleForHeaderInSection:(NSInteger)section {
  if (self.searchPredicate == nil) {
    id <NSFetchedResultsSectionInfo> sectionInfo = [self.fetchedResultsController sections]
[section];
    return [sectionInfo name];
  } else {
    return nil;
  }
}
```

Listing 5-80. Setting Up the Sections for the Table View (Swift)

```swift
override func numberOfSectionsInTableView(tableView: UITableView) -> Int {
  return self.searchPredicate == nil ? self.fetchedResultsController.sections?.count ?? 0 : 1
}

override func tableView(tableView: UITableView, titleForHeaderInSection section: Int) -> String? {
  if self.searchPredicate == nil {
    let sectionInfo = self.fetchedResultsController.sections![section] as
NSFetchedResultsSectionInfo
    return sectionInfo.name
  } else {
    return nil
  }
}
```

For determining the number of rows for a section, we again check for a non-nil searchPredicate to determine whether to apply a predicate to the fetched results controller's fetched objects. Listing 5-81 (Objective-C) and Listing 5-82 (Swift) show the updated tableView:numberOfRowsInSection: method.

Listing 5-81. Returning the Number of Rows for a Section (Objective-C)

```objc
- (NSInteger)tableView:(UITableView *)tableView numberOfRowsInSection:(NSInteger)section {
  if (self.searchPredicate == nil) {
    id <NSFetchedResultsSectionInfo> sectionInfo = [self.fetchedResultsController sections]
[section];
    return [sectionInfo numberOfObjects];
  } else {
    return [[self.fetchedResultsController.fetchedObjects filteredArrayUsingPredicate:self.
searchPredicate] count];
  }
}
```

Listing 5-82. Returning the Number of Rows for a Section (Swift)

```swift
override func tableView(tableView: UITableView, numberOfRowsInSection section: Int) -> Int {
  if self.searchPredicate == nil {
    let sectionInfo = self.fetchedResultsController.sections![section] as
NSFetchedResultsSectionInfo
    return sectionInfo.numberOfObjects
  } else {
    let filteredObjects = self.fetchedResultsController.fetchedObjects?.filter() {
      return self.searchPredicate!.evaluateWithObject($0)
    }
    return filteredObjects == nil ? 0 : filteredObjects!.count
  }
}
```

For returning the cell to display in the table, we leave the existing tableView:cellForRowAtIndexPath: method intact, and simply update the configureCell:atIndexPath: method to determine whether to grab the project from the filtered or the unfiltered fetched objects, again depending on the presence of a search predicate. Listing 5-83 (Objective-C) and Listing 5-84 (Swift) show how to do that.

Listing 5-83. Configuring the Cell (Objective-C)

```
- (void)configureCell:(UITableViewCell *)cell atIndexPath:(NSIndexPath *)indexPath {
  Project *project = nil;
  if (self.searchPredicate == nil) {
    project = [self.fetchedResultsController objectAtIndexPath:indexPath];
  } else {
    project = [self.fetchedResultsController.fetchedObjects filteredArrayUsingPredicate:self.
searchPredicate][indexPath.row];
  }
  cell.textLabel.text = project.name;
  cell.detailTextLabel.text = project.url;
}
```

Listing 5-84. Configuring the Cell (Swift)

```
func configureCell(cell: UITableViewCell, atIndexPath indexPath: NSIndexPath) {
  let project = self.searchPredicate == nil ?
    self.fetchedResultsController.objectAtIndexPath(indexPath) as Project :
      self.fetchedResultsController.fetchedObjects?.filter() {
        return self.searchPredicate!.evaluateWithObject($0)
      }[indexPath.row] as Project

  cell.textLabel.text = project.name
  cell.detailTextLabel?.text = project.url
}
```

Since we don't allow editing of the search results, we update the tableView:canEditRowAtIndexPath: method to return YES or true only when the search predicate is nil, as Listing 5-85 (Objective-C) and Listing 5-86 (Swift) show.

Listing 5-85. Allowing Editing Only for the Unfiltered Results (Objective-C)

```
- (BOOL)tableView:(UITableView *)tableView canEditRowAtIndexPath:(NSIndexPath *)indexPath {
  return self.searchPredicate == nil;
}
```

Listing 5-86. Allowing Editing Only for the Unfiltered Results (Swift)

```
override func tableView(tableView: UITableView, canEditRowAtIndexPath indexPath: NSIndexPath) ->
Bool {
  return self.searchPredicate == nil
}
```

Since we don't allow editing in the search view, we can ignore all the methods that respond to a table view in edit mode.

The last change you must make is to the prepareForSegue:sender: method, to get the correct project to set into the detail controller. As with the configureCell:atIndexPath: method, you use the presence of a search predicate to determine whether to use the filtered objects. Listing 5-87 (Objective-C) and Listing 5-88 (Swift) show the updated prepareForSegue:sender: method.

Listing 5-87. Handling Filtered Results When a Project is Tapped (Objective-C)

```
- (void)prepareForSegue:(UIStoryboardSegue *)segue sender:(id)sender {
  if ([[segue identifier] isEqualToString:@"showDetail"]) {
    NSIndexPath *indexPath = [self.tableView indexPathForSelectedRow];
    Project *project = nil;
    if (self.searchPredicate == nil) {
      project = [self.fetchedResultsController objectAtIndexPath:indexPath];
    } else {
      project = [self.fetchedResultsController.fetchedObjects filteredArrayUsingPredicate:self.
searchPredicate][indexPath.row];
    }
    [[segue destinationViewController] setProject:project];
  }
}
```

Listing 5-88. Handling Filtered Results When a Project is Tapped (Swift)

```
override func prepareForSegue(segue: UIStoryboardSegue, sender: AnyObject?) {
  if segue.identifier == "showDetail" {
    if let indexPath = self.tableView.indexPathForSelectedRow() {

      let project = self.searchPredicate == nil ?
        self.fetchedResultsController.objectAtIndexPath(indexPath) as Project :
        self.fetchedResultsController.fetchedObjects?.filter() {
          return self.searchPredicate!.evaluateWithObject($0)
          }[indexPath.row] as Project

      (segue.destinationViewController as DetailViewController).project = project
    }
  }
}
```

You should be able to run CoreDump now and use the search bar to filter results, as shown in Figure 5-13.

Figure 5-13. Searching for "github"

Conclusion

The CoreDump application is woefully incomplete, but it demonstrates how to easily integrate data and images from a Core Data store into a table view–based application. Since most iOS applications use tables and images, you'll use fetched results controllers and external records many times in your application development to create applications that perform well.

Chapter 6

Versioning and Migrating Data

As you develop Core Data–based applications, you usually don't get your data model exactly right the first time. You start by creating a data model that seems to meet your application's data needs, but as you progress through the development of the application, you'll often find that your data model needs to change to serve your growing vision of what your application should do. During this stage of your application's life, changing your data model to match your new understanding of the application's data poses little cost: your application will no longer launch, crashing on startup with the following message:

The model used to open the store is incompatible with the one used to create the store.

You resolve this issue either by finding the database file on the file system and deleting it or by deleting your fledgling application from the iPhone Simulator or your device. Either way, the database file that uses your outdated schema disappears, along with data in the persistent store, and your application re-creates the database file the next time it launches. You'll probably do this several times during the development of your application.

Once you release your application, however, and people start using it, they will accumulate data they deem important in the persistent stores on their devices. Asking them to delete their data stores any time you want to release a new version of the application with a changed data model will drop your app instantly to one-star status, and the people commenting will decry Apple's rating system for not allowing ratings of zero or even negative stars.

Does that mean releasing your application freezes its data model? That the data model in the 1.0 version of your application is permanent? That you'd better get the first public version of the data model perfect, because you'll never be able to change it? Thankfully, no. Apple anticipated the need for improving Core Data models over the life of applications and built mechanisms for you to change data models and then migrate users' data to the new models, all without Apple's intervention or even awareness. This chapter goes through the process of versioning your data models and migrating data across those versions, however complex the changes you've made to the model.

Versioning

To take advantage of Core Data's support for versioning your data model and migrating data from version to version, you start by explicitly creating a new version of the data model. To illustrate how this works, let's bring back the BookStore application from Chapter 4. Make a copy of it, because you'll be changing its data model several times in this chapter. In the original version of BookStore, you created a data model that makes the model appear as shown in Figure 6-1.

Figure 6-1. *The single-version data model*

BookStore.xcdatamodeld contains the model and is actually a directory on your file system. It contains the files necessary to create the Core Data storage when your application runs. Since there is only one version of the object model, it is automatically the current version. To add a new version, from the Xcode menu, select Editor ➤ Add Model Version. A panel displays and allows you to enter a version name and select the model on which the new version is based, as shown in Figure 6-2.

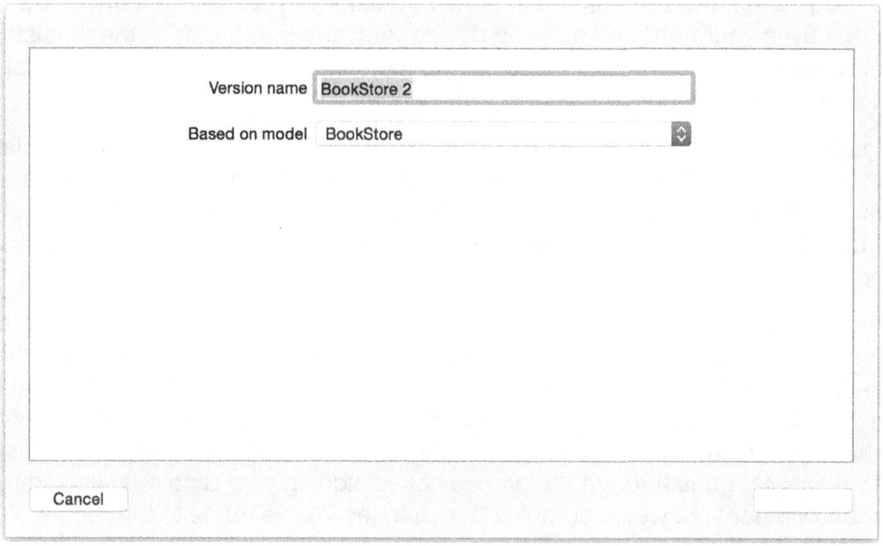

| Version name | BookStore 2 |
| Based on model | BookStore |

Cancel

Figure 6-2. *Creating a new model version*

Accept the defaults and select Finish. Xcode creates a new directory inside BookStore.xcdatamodeld called BookStore 2.xcdatamodel, as shown in Figure 6-3. Each listing below BookStore.xcdatamodeld represents a version of your data model; the green check mark denotes the version your application is currently using.

Figure 6-3. *The data model with two versions*

You can see that your original data model, BookStore.xcdatamodeld, is the current version. Before changing the current version from BookStore.xcdatamodeld to BookStore 2.xcdatamodel, run the BookStore application to create books so you have data to migrate across versions. You need data in your database to test that the data migrations throughout this chapter work properly.

Finally, we need to make a slight change to the BookStore application. In Chapter 4, we wanted to be able to have a clean data store for every run. Since we now want to test migrating existing data, we need to make sure the old data store isn't wiped out when the application starts. Open ViewController.m or ViewController.swift and edit the viewDidAppear: method by commenting the following lines:

```
// [self initStore];// [self insertSomeData];
```

or

```
// self.initStore()
// self.insertSomeData()
```

Launch the application again to make sure nothing is created. It should only display the output of the showExampleData method.

```
Book fetched: The second bookTitle: The second book, price: 15.00Book fetched: The third bookTitle: The third book, price: 10.00Book fetched: The first bookTitle: The first book, price: 10.00Book fetched: The fourth bookTitle: The fourth book, price: 12.00
```

Now, suppose you want to add a new author attribute to the Book entity. If you edit your current model and add an author attribute to the Book entity, you will have the unpleasant surprise of seeing your application crash on startup. That's because the data stored in the data store does not align with the new Core Data model. One option to alleviate this problem is to delete your existing data store. This is an acceptable option while you are developing your app, but if you already have customers using this app, this will trigger their wrath. For a smoother experience, we strongly recommend versioning your model and using Core Data's migrations to preserve your users' data by migrating it from the old model to the new. Any changes you make to your data model go into the new version of the model, not into any of the old ones. For you, this means that you'll add the name attribute to the Book entity in the BookStore 2 data model.

To make this change, select the BookStore 2 data model, and then add an `author` attribute of type `String` to the Book entity in the normal way. Figure 6-4 shows the Xcode window with the new version of the Core Data model and the `author` attribute added to the Book entity.

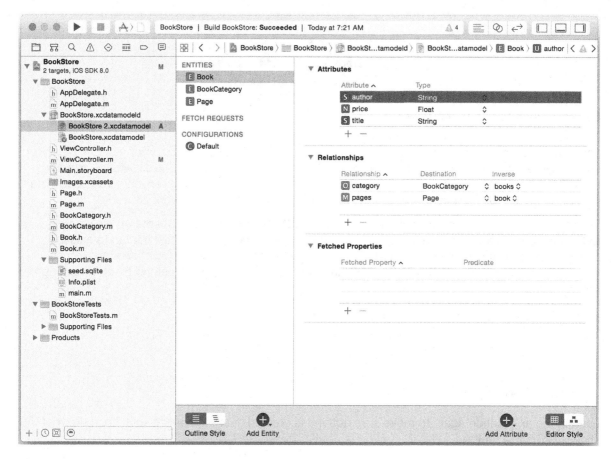

Figure 6-4. The Xcode window with a second version of the model

To change the current version of the model from BookStore to BookStore 2, select `BookStore.xcdatamodeld` and set the current version in the Utility panel to BookStore 2, as shown in Figure 6-5.

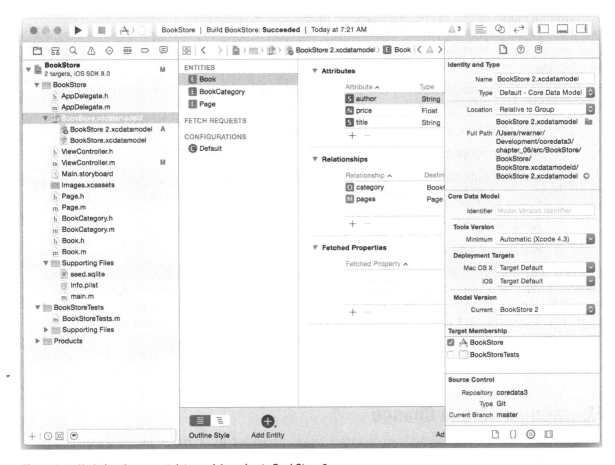

Figure 6-5. *Updating the current data model version to BookStore 2*

At this point, your application has a new current version of the data model, but it's not ready to run yet. You need to define a policy for migrating the data from the version of the model called BookStore to the one called BookStore 2. If you tried running the application now, you would get a crash because, just as if you had changed the first model, the data store does not match the current model. The application needs to be told how you want it to handle switching from the old model to the new one. The rest of this chapter discusses the various ways to do that.

Lightweight Migrations

Once you have a versioned data model, you can take advantage of Core Data's support for migrations as you evolve your data model. Each time you create a new data model version, users' application data must migrate from the old data model to the new. For the migration to occur, Core Data must have rules to follow to know how to properly migrate the data. You create these rules using a "mapping model." Support for creating mapping models is built in to Xcode. For certain straightforward cases, however, Core Data has enough smarts to figure out the mapping rules on its own without requiring you to create a mapping model. Called lightweight migrations, these cases represent the least work for you as a developer. Core Data does all the work and migrates the data. This section details the lightweight migration process and walks you through the list of changes the process supports and how to implement them.

For your migration to qualify as a lightweight migration, your changes must be confined to this narrow band.

- Add or remove a property (attribute or relationship).
- Make a nonoptional property optional.
- Make an optional attribute nonoptional, as long as you provide a default value.
- Add or remove an entity.
- Rename a property.
- Rename an entity.

In addition to requiring less work from you, a lightweight migration using a SQLite data store runs faster and uses less space than other migrations. Because Core Data can issue SQL statements to perform these migrations, it doesn't have to load all the data into memory in order to migrate them, and it doesn't have to move the data from one store to the other. Core Data simply uses SQL statements to alter the SQLite database in place. If feasible, you should aggressively try to confine your data model changes to those that lightweight migrations support. If not, the other sections in this chapter walk you through more complicated migrations.

Migrating a Simple Change

In a previous section, "Versioning," you created a new model version in the BookStore application called BookStore 2, and you added a new attribute called author to the Book entity in the BookStore 2 model. The final step to performing a lightweight migration with that change is to tell the persistent store coordinator two things.

- It should migrate the model automatically.
- It should infer the mapping model.

You do that by passing those instructions in the options parameter of the persistent store coordinator's addPersistentStoreWithType: method. You first set up options, an dictionary, as follows:

```
NSDictionary *options = @{
  NSMigratePersistentStoresAutomaticallyOption: @YES,
  NSInferMappingModelAutomaticallyOption: @YES
}; // Objective-C version

let options = [NSMigratePersistentStoresAutomaticallyOption: true,
NSInferMappingModelAutomaticallyOption: true] // Swift version
```

This code creates a dictionary with two entries.

- One with the key of NSMigratePersistentStoresAutomaticallyOption, value of YES or true, which tells the persistent store coordinator to automatically migrate the data.

- One with the key of NSInferMappingModelAutomaticallyOption, value of YES or true, which tells the persistent store coordinator to infer the mapping model.

You then pass this options object, instead of nil, for the options parameter in the call to addPersistentStoreWithType:. Open the AppDelegate.m file or the AppDelegate.swift file and change the persistentStoreCoordinator method to look like Listing 6-1 (Objective-C), or change the code to initialize persistentStoreCoordinator inside the managedObjectContext closure to look like Listing 6-2 (Swift).

Listing 6-1. Creating the Persistent Store Coordinator with Migration Options (Objective-C)

```objc
- (NSPersistentStoreCoordinator *)persistentStoreCoordinator {
    if (_persistentStoreCoordinator != nil) {
        return _persistentStoreCoordinator;
    }

    _persistentStoreCoordinator = [[NSPersistentStoreCoordinator alloc]
    initWithManagedObjectModel:[self managedObjectModel]];
    NSURL *storeURL = [[self applicationDocumentsDirectory]
    URLByAppendingPathComponent:@"BookStoreEnhanced.sqlite"];

    NSDictionary *options = @{
      NSMigratePersistentStoresAutomaticallyOption: @YES,
      NSInferMappingModelAutomaticallyOption: @YES
    };

    NSError *error = nil;
    if (![_persistentStoreCoordinator addPersistentStoreWithType:NSSQLiteStoreType
        configuration:nil URL:storeURL options:options error:&error]) {
      [self showCoreDataError];
    }

    return _persistentStoreCoordinator;
}
```

Listing 6-2. Creating the Persistent Store Coordinator with Migration Options (Swift)

```swift
// Initialize the persistent store coordinator
let storeURL = AppDelegate.applicationDocumentsDirectory.URLByAppendingPathComponent
("BookStoreEnhancedSwift.sqlite")
var error: NSError? = nil
let persistentStoreCoordinator = NSPersistentStoreCoordinator(managedObjectModel:
managedObjectModel!)
```

```
let options = [NSMigratePersistentStoresAutomaticallyOption: true,
NSInferMappingModelAutomaticallyOption: true]

if(persistentStoreCoordinator.addPersistentStoreWithType(NSSQLiteStoreType, configuration: nil,
URL: storeURL, options: options, error: &error) == nil) {
    self.showCoreDataError()
    return nil
}
```

That's all you have to do to migrate the data. Build and run the application, which no longer crashes but instead shows all the books you've created. Open a Terminal and navigate to the directory that contains the SQLite file for the BookStore application. Unlike early versions of iOS prior to iOS 5, which kept both the pre-migration and the post-migration versions of the database file, recent iOS versions keeps only the post-migration version. You'll find the post-migration file, BookStoreEnhanced.sqlite. Open it using the sqlite3 application and run the .schema command to see the definition for the ZBOOK table. You can see that the BookStoreEnhanced.sqlite file has added a column for the name attribute: ZAUTHOR VARCHAR, as shown.

```
sqlite> .schema ZBOOKCREATE TABLE ZBOOK ( Z_PK INTEGER PRIMARY KEY, Z_ENT INTEGER, Z_OPT
INTEGER, ZCATEGORY INTEGER, ZPRICE FLOAT, ZAUTHOR VARCHAR, ZTITLE VARCHAR );CREATE INDEX
ZBOOK_ZCATEGORY_INDEX ON ZBOOK (ZCATEGORY);
```

Renaming Entities and Properties

Lightweight migrations also support renaming entities and properties but require a little more effort from you. In addition to changing your model, you must specify the old name for the item whose name you changed. You can do this in one of two ways.

- In the Xcode data modeler

- In code

The Xcode data modeler is the simpler option. When you select an entity or property in the Xcode data modeler, general information about that entity or property shows in the Utilities panel to the right. With the Utilities panel displayed, open the Data Model inspector, and then the Versioning section. In the Renaming ID field, enter the old name of whatever you've changed (see Figure 6-6).

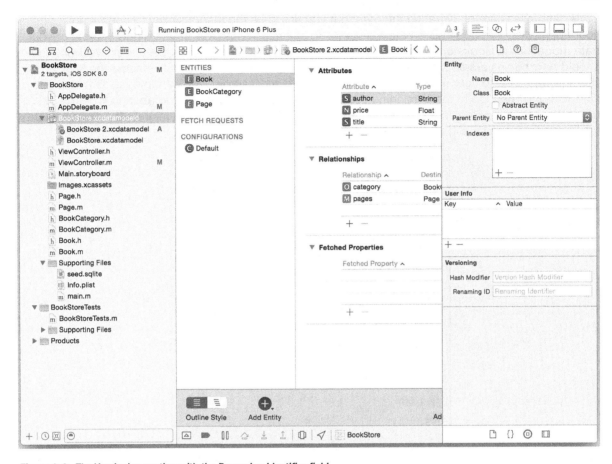

Figure 6-6. *The Versioning section with the Renaming Identifier field*

If you insist on specifying the old name in code, you'd make a call to the `setRenamingIdentifier:` method of `NSEntityDescription` or `NSPropertyDescription`, depending on what you've renamed, passing the old name for the entity or property. You do this after the model has loaded but before the call to open the persistent store (`addPersistentStoreWithType:`). If, for example, you want to change the name of the `Book` entity to `Publication`, you'd add the following code before the call to `addPersistentStoreWithType:`

```
// Objective-C
NSEntityDescription *publication = [[managedObjectModel entitiesByName]
objectForKey:@"Publication"];
[publication setRenamingIdentifier:@"Book"];

// Swift
if let publication: NSEntityDescription? = managedObjectModel.entitiesByName["Publication"] as?
NSEntityDescription {
  publication?.renamingIdentifier = "Book"
}
```

Core Data takes care of migrating the data, but you still have the responsibility to update any code in your application that depends on the old name. To see this in practice, create a new version of your data model called Bookstore 3, based on model Bookstore 2, and set it as the current version. You should now be on version 3 (BookStore 3). In this version of the model, you'll rename the Book entity to Publication. Go to your new model file, BookStore 3.xcdatamodel, and rename the Book entity to Publication. Then, go to the Versioning section in the Data Model inspector tab, and type the old name, Book, into the Renaming ID field so that Core Data will know how to migrate the existing data (as Figure 6-7 shows), and save this model.

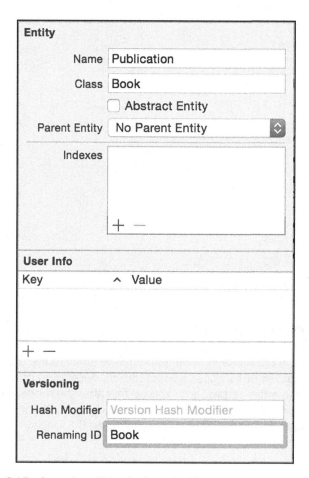

Figure 6-7. Renaming Book to Publication and specifying the Renaming ID

Wait! Before running the application, remember that you're responsible for changing any code that relies on the old name, Book. You could change the custom managed object class name from Book to Publication, change the relationship name in the Page entity from book to publication, and change any variable names appropriately. Let's keep it simple here and change the places the BookStore application refers to the Book entity name. You find them in ViewController.m or in ViewController.swift, in the calls to fetchRequestWithEntityName: and insertNewObjectForEntityForName:. In those calls, change the entity name string from Book to Publication.

You can now build and run the BookStore application; all existing books should still exist. You can open the SQLite database and confirm that the schema now has a ZPUBLICATION table.

```
CREATE TABLE ZPUBLICATION ( Z_PK INTEGER PRIMARY KEY, Z_ENT INTEGER, Z_OPT INTEGER, ZCATEGORY
INTEGER, ZPRICE FLOAT, ZAUTHOR VARCHAR, ZTITLE VARCHAR );
```

and no ZBOOK table.

As you've seen, lightweight migrations are nearly effortless, at least for you. Core Data handles the difficult work of figuring out how to map and migrate the data from the old model to new. However, if your model changes don't fit within what lightweight migrations can handle, you must specify your own mapping model.

Using a Mapping Model

When your data model changes exceed Core Data's ability to infer how to map data from the old model to the new, you can't use a lightweight migration to automatically migrate your data. Instead, you have to create "a mapping model" to tell Core Data how to execute the migration. This section walks you through the steps involved in creating a mapping model for your migration. A mapping model is roughly analogous to a data model—whereas a data model contains entities and properties, a mapping model, which is of type NSMappingModel, has entity mappings (of type NSEntityMapping) and property mappings (of type NSPropertyMapping). The entity mappings do just what you'd expect them to do: they map a source entity to a target entity. The property mappings, as well, do what you'd think: map source properties to target properties. The mapping model uses these mappings, along with their associated types and policies, to perform the migration.

> **Note** Apple's documentation and code use the terms "destination" and "target" interchangeably to refer to the new data model. In this chapter, we follow suit and use both "destination" and "target" interchangeably.

In a typical data migration, most entities and properties haven't changed from the old version to the new. For these cases, the entity mappings simply copy each entity from the source model to the target model. When you create a mapping model, you'll notice that Xcode generates these entity mappings, along with anything else it can infer from your model changes, and stores these mappings in the mapping model. These mappings represent how Core Data would have migrated your data in a lightweight migration. You have to create new mappings, or adjust the mappings Xcode generates, to change how your data migrate.

Understanding Entity Mappings

Each entity mapping, represented by an NSEntityMapping instance, contains three things.

- A source entity
- A destination entity
- A mapping type

When Core Data performs the migration, it uses the entity mapping to move the source to the destination, using the mapping type to determine how to do that. Table 6-1 lists the mapping types, their corresponding Core Data constants, and what they mean.

Table 6-1. The Entity Mapping Types

Type	Core Data Constant	Meaning
Add	NSAddEntityMappingType	The entity is new in the destination model—it doesn't exist in the source model—and should be added.
Remove	NSRemoveEntityMappingType	The entity doesn't exist in the destination model and should be removed.
Copy	NSCopyEntityMappingType	The entity exists in both the source and destination models unchanged and should be copied as is.
Transform	NSTransformEntityMappingType	The entity exists in both the source and destination models but with changes. The mapping tells Core Data how to migrate each source instance to a destination instance.
Custom	NSCustomEntityMappingType	The entity exists in both the source and destination models but with changes.

The mapping tells Core Data how to migrate each source instance to a destination instance. The Add, Remove, and Copy types don't generate much interest because lightweight migrations handle these types of entity mappings. The Transform and Custom types, however, are what make this section of the book necessary. They tell Core Data that each source entity instance must be transformed, according to any specified rules, into an instance of the destination entity. You'll see an example of both a Transform and a Custom entity mapping type in this chapter. If you specify a value expression for one of the entity's properties, the entity mapping is of a Transform type. If you specify a custom migration policy for the entity mapping, the entity mapping becomes a Custom type. As you work through this chapter, pay attention to the types the Core Data mapping modeler makes to your mapping model in response to changes you make. To specify the rules for a Custom entity mapping type, you create a migration policy, which is a class you write that derives from NSEntityMigrationPolicy. You then set the class you create as the custom policy for the entity mapping in the Xcode mapping modeler.

Core Data runs your migration in three stages.

1. It creates the objects in the destination model, including their attributes, based on the objects in the source model.

2. It creates the relationships among the objects in the destination model.

3. It validates the data in the destination model and saves them.

You can customize how Core Data performs these three steps through the Custom Policy. The NSEntityMigrationPolicy class has seven methods you can override to customize how Core Data will migrate data from the source entity to the target entity, though you'll rarely override all of them. These methods, listed in Apple's documentation for the NSEntityMigrationPolicy class, provide various places during the migration that you can override and change Core Data's migration behavior. You can override as few or as many of these methods as you'd like, though a custom migration policy that overrides none of the methods is pointless. Typically, you'll override `createDestinationInstancesForSourceInstance:` if you want to change how destination instances are created or how their attributes are populated with data. You'll override `createRelationshipsForDestinationInstance:` if you want to customize how relationships between the destination entity and other entities are created. Finally, you'll override `performCustomValidationForEntityMapping:` if you want to perform any custom validations during your migration.

The `createDestinationInstancesForSourceInstance:` method carries with it a caveat: if you don't call the superclass's implementation, which you probably won't because you're overriding this method to change the default behavior, you must call the migration manager's `associateSourceInstance:withDestinationInstance:forEntityMapping:` method to associate the source instance with the destination instance. Forgetting to do this will cause problems with your migration. You'll learn the proper way to call this method later in this chapter, with the BookStore application.

Understanding Property Mappings

A property mapping, like an entity mapping, tells Core Data how to migrate source to destination. A property mapping is an instance of `NSPropertyMapping` and contains the following three things:

- The name of the property in the source entity
- The name of the property in the destination entity
- A value expression that tells Core Data how to get from source to destination

To change the way a property mapping migrates data, you provide the value expression for the property mapping to use. Value expressions follow the same syntax as predicates and use the following six predefined keys to assist with retrieving values:

- `$manager`, which represents the migration manager
- `$source`, which represents the source entity
- `$destination`, which represents the destination entity
- `$entityMapping`, which represents the entity mapping
- `$propertyMapping`, which represents the property mapping
- `$entityPolicy`, which represents the entity migration policy

As you can see, these keys have names that make deducing their purposes easy. When you create a mapping model, you can explore the property mappings Xcode infers from your source and target data models to better understand what these keys mean and how they're used.

The simplest value expressions copy an attribute from the source entity to the destination entity. If you have a `Person` entity, for example, that has a `name` attribute and the `Person` entity hasn't changed between your old and your new model versions, the value expression for the name attribute in your `PersonToPerson` entity mapping would be as follows:

`$source.name`

You can also perform manipulations of source data using value expressions. Suppose, for example, that the same `Person` entity had an attribute called salary that stores each person's salary. In the new model, you want to give everyone 4% raises. Your value expression would look like the following:

```
$source.salary*1.04
```

Since properties represent both attributes and relationships, property mappings represent mappings for both attributes and relationships. The typical value expression for a relationship calls a function, passing the migration manager, the destination instances, the entity mapping, and the name of the source relationship. For example, if your old data model had a relationship called staff in the `Person` entity that represented everyone who reported to this person and your new model has renamed this relationship to reports, the value expression for the reports property would look like the following:

```
FUNCTION($manager, "destinationInstancesForEntityMappingNamed:sourceInstances:",
"PersonToPerson", $source.staff)
```

Note that you use the $manager key to pass the migration manager, that you get the destination instances from the entity mapping for the source instances, that you pass the appropriate entity mapping (`PersonToPerson`), and that you pass the old relationship that you get from the $source key.

Creating a New Model Version That Requires a Mapping Model

Lightweight migrations are often enough and you really don't need to get too far into the mechanics of Core Data migrations. There are times, however, when you need to get your hands a bit dirty and help the framework figure out what to do. This is the case, for example, when you realize you've been lazy and you have combined data into one field that should really be split into multiples. Think about the author field, for example, which is expected to contain the author's full name (e.g., John Doe). If you suddenly realized you wanted to split this into a *firstName* and a *lastName* field, you'd have to create a mapping model. This is exactly what we will do in this section.

Before we get to the migration, let's spend some time populating the author field in the `Publication` table so it gives us some data to migrate.

Open ViewController.m or ViewController.swift and add a new method called populateAuthors, as shown in Listing 6-3 (Objective-C) and Listing 6-4 (Swift).

Listing 6-3. Populating Authors (Objective-C)

```
- (void)populateAuthors {
  // 1. Create a list of author names to assign
  NSArray *authors = @[@"John Doe", @"Jane Doe", @"Bill Smith", @"Jack Brown"];

  // 2. Get all the publications from the data store
  NSFetchRequest *fetchRequest = [NSFetchRequest fetchRequestWithEntityName:@"Publication"];
  NSArray *books = [self.managedObjectContext executeFetchRequest:fetchRequest error:nil];
  for(int i=0; i<books.count; i++) {
    Book *book = books[i];
    book.price = 20+i;
```

```objc
    // 3. Set the author using one of the names in the array we created
    [book setValue:authors[i % authors.count] forKey:@"author"];
  }

  // 4. Commit everything to the store
  [self saveContext];
}
```

Listing 6-4. Populating Authors (Swift)

```swift
func populateAuthors() {
    // 1. Create a list of author names to assign
    let authors = ["John Doe", "Jane Doe", "Bill Smith", "Jack Brown"]

    // 2. Get all the publications from the data store
    let fetchRequest = NSFetchRequest(entityName: "Publication")
    let books = self.managedObjectContext?.executeFetchRequest(fetchRequest, error: nil)
    if let books = books {
        for var i = 0; i<books.count; i++ {
            var book = books[i] as Book
            book.price = 20 + Float(i)
            // 3. Set the author using one of the names in the array we created
            book.setValue(authors[i % authors.count], forKeyPath: "author")
        }
    }

    // 4. Commit everything to the store
    saveContext()
}
```

Note that we also change the price to make sure it is about $15 so that we don't trip the validation rules we had put in place in the original version of BookStore.

Finally, edit the `viewDidAppear:` method so it looks like Listing 6-5 (Objective-C) or Listing 6-6 (Swift).

Listing 6-5. Making the Call to Populate Authors (Objective-C)

```objc
- (void)viewDidAppear:(BOOL)animated {
  [super viewDidAppear:animated];
  [self populateAuthors];
  [self showExampleData];
}
```

Listing 6-6. Making the Call to Populate Authors (Swift)

```swift
override func viewDidAppear(animated: Bool) {
    super.viewDidAppear(animated)
    if let managedObjectContext = self.managedObjectContext {
        self.populateAuthors()
        self.showExampleData()
    }
}
```

Prior to running the app, you can see in the .sqlite database that the author is not populated.

```
sqlite> select ztitle,zauthor,zprice from zpublication;
```

```
ZTITLE              ZAUTHOR     ZPRICE
---------------     --------    ----------
The second book     NULL        20.0
The third book      NULL        21.0
The first book      NULL        22.0
The fourth book     NULL        23.0
```

Launch the application once and then run the same query again.

```
sqlite> select ztitle,zauthor,zprice from zpublication;
```

```
ZTITLE              ZAUTHOR      ZPRICE
---------------     --------     ----------
The second book     John Doe     20.0
The third book      Jane Doe     21.0
The first book      Bill Smith   22.0
The fourth book     Jack Brown   23.0
```

Now go back to viewDidAppear: and remove the call to populateAuthors:.

We are now ready to create the new version of the model. Go ahead and create the new version of your data model; you should be up to version 4. In the new model (BookStore 4.xcdatamodel), in the Publication entity, delete the author attribute and create two new attributes: firstName and lastName. Both should have the type String. Your model should look like the one shown in Figure 6-8.

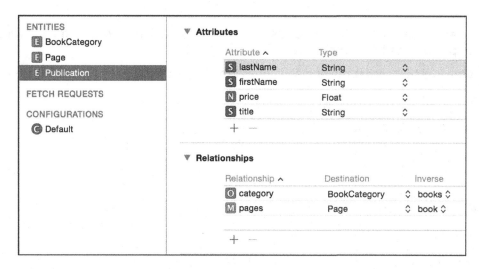

Figure 6-8. Splitting the two fields in the new model

Let's take the time to also make sure the entity class is up to date with the new fields. Open Book.h if you're doing this project in Objective-C and add declarations for the two new properties, firstName and lastName, as Listing 6-7 shows. Then add dynamic accessors for those properties in Book.m, as Listing 6-8 shows. If you're following along in Swift, add the code for firstName and lastName to Book.swift that Listing 6-9 shows.

Listing 6-7. Adding Properties for firstName and lastName to Book.h

```
@property (nonatomic, retain) NSString *firstName;
@property (nonatomic, retain) NSString *lastName;
```

Listing 6-8. Adding Dynamic Accessors to Book.m

```
@dynamic firstName;
@dynamic lastName;
```

Listing 6-9. Adding firstName and lastName to Book.swift

```
@NSManaged var firstName: String
@NSManaged var lastName: String
```

The model and entity class are both up to date. We now move on to the migration part.

Creating a Mapping Model

To create a mapping model, create a new file in Xcode. In the ensuing dialog box, select Core Data under iOS on the left, and select Mapping Model on the right, as shown in Figure 6-9. Click Next.

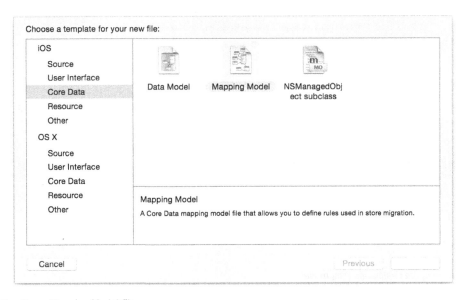

Figure 6-9. Creating a Mapping Model file

The next step is to select the source model. Select `BookStore 3.xcdatamodel`, as shown in Figure 6-10, and click Next. You are then asked to select the target model. Select `BookStore 4.xcdatamodel` for the destination, as shown in Figure 6-11, and click Next. The last step is to name the mapping model. Name it `Model3To4.xcmappingmodel` and click Create.

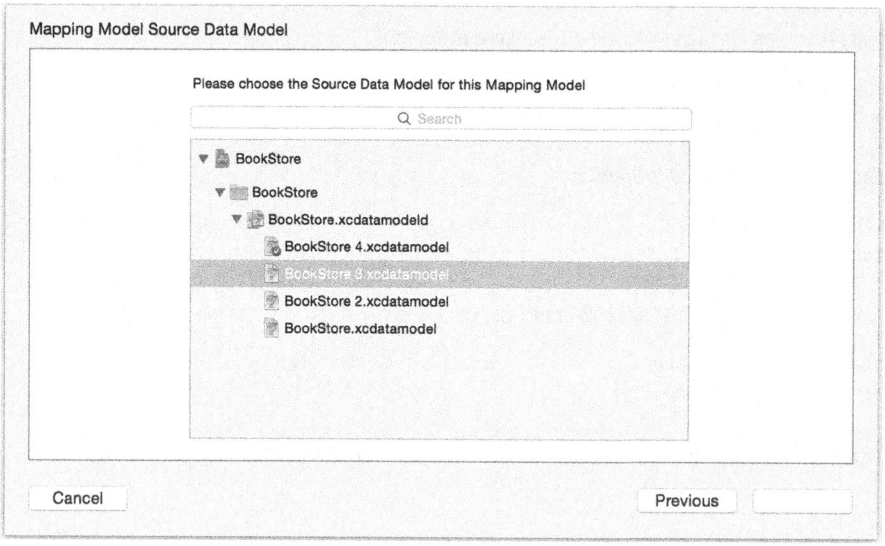

Figure 6-10. Selecting the source data model

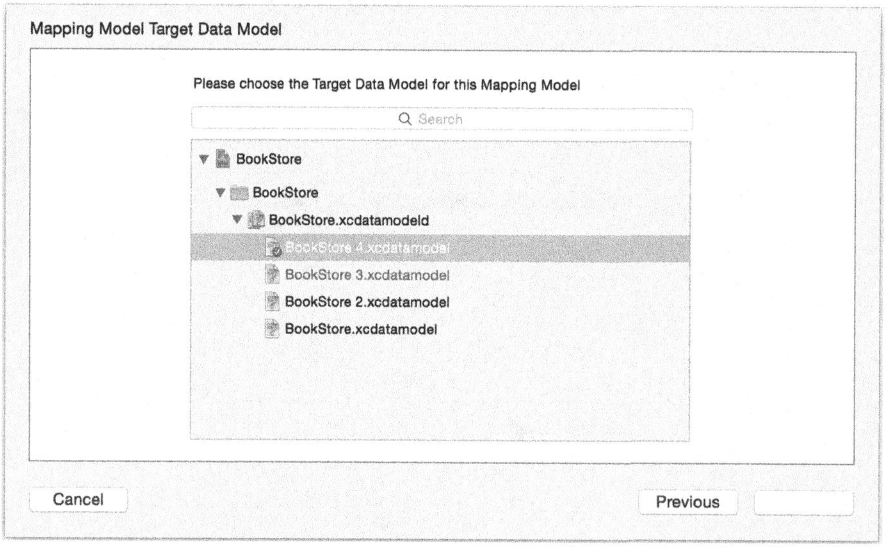

Figure 6-11. Selecting the destination data model

You should now see Xcode with your mapping model created, including all the entity mappings and property mappings that Core Data could infer, as shown in Figure 6-12.

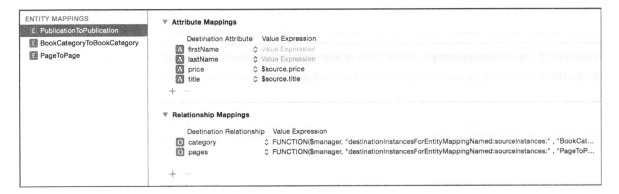

Figure 6-12. The new mapping model

Notice that Xcode has already done some work to help with the migration. Creating a mapping model puts you in the same place you'd be with a lightweight migration, with mappings that Core Data can infer from your source and target data models. Where it found entities to match up, it automatically set the new attribute value to be a copy of the source. Since we removed the `author` attribute and added two new ones, it doesn't quite know what to do. This is where you come in.

The next step is to customize the mapping model to migrate publications. Start by creating the custom policy you'll use, which is a subclass of `NSEntityMigrationPolicy`. Create a new Cocoa Touch class called `PublicationToPublicationMigrationPolicy` that subclasses `NSEntityMigrationPolicy`, as shown in Figure 6-13.

Choose options for your new file:

Class:	PublicationToPublicationMigrationPolicy
Subclass of:	NSEntityMigrationPolicy
	Also create XIB file
	iPhone
Language:	Objective-C

Cancel   Previous

Figure 6-13. Creating a new migration policy

In the implementation file, either PublicationToPublicationMigrationPolicy.m or
PublicationToPublicationMigrationPolicy.swift, you want to override the
createDestinationInstancesForSourceInstance: method. While performing the migration, Core
Data will call this method each time it goes to create a Publication instance from a source
Publication instance. In your implementation, you create a Publication instance, copy the price
and title, and separate the first name from the last name. Of course, our name splitting is a bit
rudimentary, but that is off topic here. This simple implementation will perfectly illustrate what we are
trying to do.

Finally, you tell the migration manager about the relationship between the source's Publication
instance and the target's new Publication instance, which is an important step for the migration to
occur properly. Listing 6-10 shows Objective-C version, and Listing 6-11 shows the Swift version.

Listing 6-10. Custom Migration Mapping (Objective-C)

```objc
- (BOOL)createDestinationInstancesForSourceInstance:(NSManagedObject *)sourceInstance
entityMapping:(NSEntityMapping *)mapping manager:(NSMigrationManager *)manager error:(NSError **)
error {
  // Create the book managed object
  NSManagedObject *book =
  [NSEntityDescription insertNewObjectForEntityForName:[mapping destinationEntityName]

                                inManagedObjectContext:[manager destinationContext]];
  [book setValue:[sourceInstance valueForKey:@"title"] forKey:@"title"];
  [book setValue:[sourceInstance valueForKey:@"price"] forKey:@"price"];

  // Get the author name from the source
  NSString *author = [sourceInstance valueForKey:@"author"];

  // Split the author name into first name and last name
  NSRange firstSpace = [author rangeOfString:@" "];
  NSString *firstName = [author substringToIndex:firstSpace.location];
  NSString *lastName = [author substringFromIndex:firstSpace.location+1];

  // Set the first and last names into the bbok
  [book setValue:firstName forKey:@"firstName"];
  [book setValue:lastName forKey:@"lastName"];

  // Set up the association between the old Publication and the new Publication for
  the migration manager
  [manager associateSourceInstance:sourceInstance withDestinationInstance:book
   forEntityMapping:mapping];
  return YES;
}
```

Listing 6-11. Custom Migration Mapping (Swift)

```
override func createDestinationInstancesForSourceInstance(sInstance: NSManagedObject!, entityMapping
mapping: NSEntityMapping!, manager: NSMigrationManager!, error: NSErrorPointer) -> Bool {
    // Create the book managed object

    var book = NSEntityDescription.insertNewObjectForEntityForName(mapping.destinationEntityName,
    inManagedObjectContext: manager.destinationContext) as NSManagedObject!

    book.setValue(sInstance.valueForKey("title"), forKey: "title")
    book.setValue(sInstance.valueForKey("price"), forKey: "price")

    // Get the author name from the source
    let author = sInstance.valueForKey("author") as String?

    // Split the author name into first name and last name
    let firstSpace = author?.rangeOfString(" ")
    if let firstSpace = firstSpace {
        let firstName = author?.substringToIndex(firstSpace.startIndex)
        let lastName = author?.substringFromIndex(firstSpace.endIndex)

        // Set the first and last names into the bbok
        book.setValue(firstName, forKeyPath: "firstName")
        book.setValue(lastName, forKeyPath: "lastName")
    }

    // Set up the association between the old Publication and the new Publication for
    the migration manager
    manager.associateSourceInstance(sInstance, withDestinationInstance: book,
    forEntityMapping: mapping)
    return true
}
```

Notice also that we didn't copy over the publication relationships. The relationships are copied over by default in NSEntityMigrationPolicy's createRelationshipsForDestinationInstance: method. By not overriding that method, we get Core Data to copy those over for us.

Now let's go back to the mapping model. Select the entity mapping called PublicationToPublication. In the panel to the right, set the custom policy to PublicationToPublicationMigrationPolicy (i.e., the one we just created), as Figure 6-14 shows.

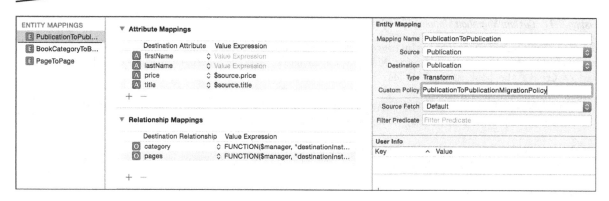

Figure 6-14. *Setting the new migration policy into the mapping model*

Your mapping model is ready to perform the migration. Just as with lightweight migrations, however, you need to add some code to the application delegate to tell Core Data to execute a migration.

Migrating Data

Creating the mapping model is essential to performing a migration that lightweight migrations can't handle, but you still must perform the actual migration. This section explains how to do this and then update the code for the BookStore application to actually run the migration. By the end of this section, you will have a BookStore application that includes all the books it had before, but now the first name and last name of the authors are correctly split.

Telling Core Data to migrate from the old model to the new one using a mapping model you create is similar to telling Core Data to use a lightweight migration. As you learned earlier, the way to tell Core Data to perform a lightweight migration is to pass an options dictionary that contains YES or true for two keys.

- NSMigratePersistentStoresAutomaticallyOption

- NSInferMappingModelAutomaticallyOption

The first key tells Core Data to automatically migrate the data, and the second tells Core Data to infer the mapping model.

For a migration using a mapping model you created, you clearly want Core Data to still automatically perform the migration, so you still set the NSMigratePersistentStoresAutomaticallyOption to YES or true. Since you've created the mapping model, however, you don't want Core Data to infer anything; you want it to use your mapping model. Therefore, you set NSInferMappingModelAutomaticallyOption to NO or false, or you leave it out of the options dictionary entirely.

How, then, do you specify the mapping model for Core Data to use to perform the migration? Do you set it in the options dictionary? Do you pass it somehow to the persistent store coordinator's addPersistentStoreWithType: method? Do you set it into the persistent store coordinator? Into the managed object model? Into the context?

The answer, which may seem a little shocking, is that you do nothing. Core Data will figure it out. It searches through your mapping models, finds one that's appropriate for migrating from the source to the destination, and uses it. This makes migrations almost criminally easy.

Running Your Migration

To run the migration of your BookStore data store, open the `AppDelegate.m` file or the `AppDelegate.swift` file and remove the `NSInferMappingModelAutomaticallyOption` key from the options dictionary. This is all you have to do to get Core Data to migrate your data using your mapping model, `Model3To4.xcmappingmodel`. Set your current model version to BookStore 4, if you haven't already, and then build and run the BookStore application; you should see all the books you had in the database before you ran the migration. Only this time, if you go look at the data store, you will see the names properly split:

```
sqlite> select ztitle,zfirstname,zlastname,zprice from zpublication;

ZTITLE            ZFIRSTNAME  ZLASTNAME   ZPRICE
----------------  ----------  ----------  ----------
The second book   John        Doe         20.0
The third book    Jane        Doe         21.0
The fourth book   Jack        Brown       23.0
The first book    Bill        Smith       22.0
```

Custom Migrations

In most data migration cases, using the default three-step migration process (create the destination objects, create the relationships, and validate and save) is sufficient. Data objects are created in the new data store from the previous version, then all relationships are created, and finally the data are validated and persisted. There are, however, some cases where you want to intervene in the middle of the migration. This is where you need custom migrations. Typically, you know you need to start thinking about custom migration when the data changes go beyond moving data from an old entity to a new one. This is the case, for example, when the order of migration matters or if you want the user to be made aware of the status of the migration progress.

Taking control of the migration process initialization means that you need to perform all the work that Core Data usually does for you. This means that you need to do the following:

- Make sure migration is actually needed.
- Set up the migration manager.
- Run your migration by splitting the model into independent parts.

This section goes through a custom migration example step by step to show you how to make a nontrivial migration work. As the migration occurs, we will display the progress in the console log.

To set the stage for this example. First create a new version of the data model. You should have `BookStore 5.xcdatamodel` at this point. In the new model, let's make some change to trigger the migration. Open the `Publication` entity and add a new property of type `String` called `synopsis`. Make `BookStore 5.xcdatamodel` the current model.

Making Sure Migration Is Needed

To validate that a model is compatible with the persistent store, you use the
isConfiguration:compatibleWithStoreMetadata: method of the NSManagedObjectModel class before
adding the persistent store to the coordinator. The data store metadata can be retrieved by querying
the coordinator using the metadataForPersistentStoreOfType:URL:error: method.

Open AppDelegate.m or AppDelegate.swift and edit the persistentStoreCoordinator getter, as
shown in Listing 6-12 (Objective-C) or Listing 6-13 (Swift).

Listing 6-12. Determining Whether Migration is Needed (Objective-C)

```objectivec
- (NSPersistentStoreCoordinator *)persistentStoreCoordinator {
  if (_persistentStoreCoordinator != nil) {
     return _persistentStoreCoordinator;
  }

  _persistentStoreCoordinator = [[NSPersistentStoreCoordinator alloc]
initWithManagedObjectModel:[self managedObjectModel]];
  NSURL *storeURL = [[self applicationDocumentsDirectory]
URLByAppendingPathComponent:@"BookStoreEnhanced.sqlite"];

  NSError *error = nil;
  NSDictionary *sourceMetadata = [NSPersistentStoreCoordinator
  metadataForPersistentStoreOfType:NSSQLiteStoreType URL:storeURL error:&error];

  NSManagedObjectModel *destinationModel = [_persistentStoreCoordinator managedObjectModel];

  BOOL pscCompatible = [destinationModel isConfiguration:nil
  compatibleWithStoreMetadata:sourceMetadata];

  if (!pscCompatible) {
    // Migration is needed

    // ... perform the migration here
  }

  if (![_persistentStoreCoordinator addPersistentStoreWithType:NSSQLiteStoreType
  configuration:nil URL:storeURL options:nil error:&error]) {
    [self showCoreDataError];
  }

  return _persistentStoreCoordinator;
}
```

Listing 6-13. Determining Whether Migration is Needed (Swift)

```swift
lazy var managedObjectContext: NSManagedObjectContext? = {
    // Initialize the managed object model
    let modelURL = NSBundle.mainBundle().URLForResource("BookStoreSwift", withExtension: "momd")
    let managedObjectModel = NSManagedObjectModel(contentsOfURL: modelURL!)

    // Initialize the persistent store coordinator
    let storeURL = AppDelegate.applicationDocumentsDirectory.URLByAppendingPathComponent
("BookStoreEnhancedSwift.sqlite")

    var error: NSError? = nil
    let persistentStoreCoordinator = NSPersistentStoreCoordinator(managedObjectModel:
managedObjectModel)

    let sourceMetadata = NSPersistentStoreCoordinator.metadataForPersistentStoreOfType
    (NSSQLiteStoreType, URL: storeURL, error: nil)

    let destinationModel = persistentStoreCoordinator.managedObjectModel
    let pscCompatible = destinationModel.isConfiguration(nil, compatibleWithStoreMetadata:
    sourceMetadata)

    if(!pscCompatible) {
        // Custom migration is needed

        // ... perform the migration here
    }

    if(persistentStoreCoordinator.addPersistentStoreWithType(NSSQLiteStoreType, configuration:
nil, URL: storeURL, options: nil, error: &error) == nil) {
        self.showCoreDataError()
        return nil
    }

    var managedObjectContext = NSManagedObjectContext()
    managedObjectContext.persistentStoreCoordinator = persistentStoreCoordinator

    // Add the undo manager
    managedObjectContext.undoManager = NSUndoManager()

    return managedObjectContext
}()
```

If migration is not needed, then the persistent store can be registered with the coordinator as usual.

Setting Up the Migration Manager

Once it has been determined that migration is indeed needed, the next step is to set up the migration manager, which is a subclass of NSMigrationManager. To do that, you need to retrieve the model that matches the current persistent store: the previous version of the model. This is the model you use as the source model of your migration process. The source model can be obtained using the mergedModelFromBundles:forStoreMetadata: method, which looks for a model in the application main bundle that matches the given metadata.

Start with creating your custom migration manager by creating a new class that extends NSMigrationManager. In this example we will call it MyMigrationManager. Listing 6-14 shows the Objective-C header file for this new class, and Listing 6-15 shows the Objective-C implementation file. Listing 6-16 shows the Swift implementation. The implementation of the migration overrides the associateSourceInstance:withDestinationInstance:forEntityMapping: method, which is called during the execution of the migration policy when destination instances are created for source instances. Your implementation creates an instance that is being migrated and assigns the synopsis attribute during the migration by simply copying the title attribute.

Listing 6-14. MyMigrationManager.h

```
#import <CoreData/CoreData.h>

@interface MyMigrationManager : NSMigrationManager

@end
```

Listing 6-15. MyMigrationManager.m

```
#import "MyMigrationManager.h"@implementation MyMigrationManager- (void)associateSourceInstance:
(NSManagedObject*)sourceInstance withDestinationInstance:(NSManagedObject *)destinationInstance
forEntityMapping:(NSEntityMapping *)entityMapping {
    [super associateSourceInstance:sourceInstance withDestinationInstance:destinationInstance
forEntityMapping:entityMapping];

    NSString *name = [entityMapping destinationEntityName];
    if([name isEqualToString:@"Publication"]) { NSString *title =
    [sourceInstance valueForKey:@"title"];
        [destinationInstance setValue:title forKey:@"synopsis"];
    }
}@end
```

Listing 6-16. MyMigrationManager.swift

```
import Foundation
import CoreData

class MyMigrationManager : NSMigrationManager {
    override func associateSourceInstance(sourceInstance: NSManagedObject, withDestinationInstance
destinationInstance: NSManagedObject, forEntityMapping entityMapping: NSEntityMapping) {
        super.associateSourceInstance(sourceInstance, withDestinationInstance: destinationInstance,
forEntityMapping: entityMapping)

        let name = entityMapping.destinationEntityName
        if name == "Publication" {
            let title = sourceInstance.valueForKey("title") as? String
            destinationInstance.setValue(title, forKeyPath: "synopsis")
        }
    }
}
```

Running the Migration

In this last step, you need to set your own class as the manager in charge of performing this migration. For the Objective-C version of BookStore, add an import for `MyMigrationManager.h` at the top of the `AppDelegate.h` file. For both Objective-C and Swift, add a new `migrationManager` property, like this:

```
@property (readonly, strong, nonatomic) MyMigrationManager *migrationManager; // Objective-C
var migrationManager: MyMigrationManager? // Swift
```

Finally, where we placed the comments that the migration was needed and to "perform the migration here," add the code to actually perform the migration. Listing 6-17 shows the Objective-C code, and Listing 6-18 shows the Swift code.

Listing 6-17. Performing the migration (Objective-C)

```objc
if (!pscCompatible) {
  // Migration is needed
  NSManagedObjectModel *sourceModel = [NSManagedObjectModel mergedModelFromBundles:nil
  forStoreMetadata:sourceMetadata];
  _migrationManager = [[MyMigrationManager alloc] initWithSourceModel:sourceModel
  destinationModel:[self managedObjectModel]];
  [_migrationManager addObserver:self forKeyPath:@"migrationProgress"
  options:NSKeyValueObservingOptionNew context:NULL];
  NSMappingModel *mappingModel = [NSMappingModel inferredMappingModelForSourceModel:sourceModel
  destinationModel:[self managedObjectModel] error:nil];

  NSURL *tempURL = [[self applicationDocumentsDirectory] URLByAppendingPathComponent:
  @"BookStoreEnhanced-temp.sqlite"];


  if(![_migrationManager migrateStoreFromURL:storeURL
                                type:NSSQLiteStoreType
                                options:nil
                      withMappingModel:mappingModel
                      toDestinationURL:tempURL
                      destinationType:NSSQLiteStoreType
                      destinationOptions:nil
                                error:&error]) {
    // Deal with error
    NSLog(@"%@", error);
  }
  else {
    // Delete the old store, rename the new one
    NSFileManager *fm = [NSFileManager defaultManager];
    [fm removeItemAtPath:[storeURL path] error:nil];
    [fm moveItemAtPath:[tempURL path] toPath:[storeURL path] error:nil];
  }
}
```

Listing 6-18. Performing the migration (Swift)

```swift
if(!pscCompatible) {
    // Custom migration is needed
    let sourceModel = NSManagedObjectModel.mergedModelFromBundles([NSBundle.mainBundle()],
    forStoreMetadata: sourceMetadata!)

    var appDelegate = UIApplication.sharedApplication().delegate as? AppDelegate

    let migrationManager = MyMigrationManager(sourceModel: sourceModel!, destinationModel:
    managedObjectModel!)

    migrationManager.addObserver(self, forKeyPath: "migrationProgress", options: .New, context: nil)

    appDelegate?.migrationManager = migrationManager

    let mappingModel = NSMappingModel.inferredMappingModelForSourceModel(sourceModel!,
    destinationModel:managedObjectModel!, error: nil)

    let tempURL = AppDelegate.applicationDocumentsDirectory.URLByAppendingPathComponent
    ("BookStoreEnhancedSwift-temp.sqlite")

    if !migrationManager.migrateStoreFromURL(storeURL, type: NSSQLiteStoreType, options:nil,
    withMappingModel:mappingModel, toDestinationURL:tempURL, destinationType:NSSQLiteStoreType,
    destinationOptions:nil, error:&error) {
        self.showCoreDataError()
        abort()
        //return nil
    }
    else {
        let fm = NSFileManager()

        fm.removeItemAtPath(storeURL.path!, error: nil)
        fm.moveItemAtPath(tempURL.path!, toPath: storeURL.path!, error: nil)
    }
}
```

Note that the source and destination store URLs (uniform resource locators) are the same since we are migrating data for the same persistent store.

We also added a key/value observer to the NSMigrationManager to monitor the progress. Update the existing method to observe the value and log it. Listing 6-19 shows the Objective-C method, and Listing 6-20 shows the Swift function.

Listing 6-19. Monitoring the Progress of the Migration (Objective-C)

```objectivec
- (void)observeValueForKeyPath:(NSString *)keyPath
                      ofObject:(id)object
                        change:(NSDictionary *)change
                       context:(void *)context {
  if ([keyPath isEqualToString:@"migrationProgress"]) {
    NSMigrationManager *manager = (NSMigrationManager*)object;
    NSLog(@"Migration progress: %d%%", (int)(manager.migrationProgress * 100.0));
  }
}
```

Listing 6-20. Monitoring the Progress of the Migration (Swift)

```swift
override func observeValueForKeyPath(keyPath: String!,
  ofObject object: AnyObject,
  change: [NSObject : AnyObject],
  context: UnsafeMutablePointer<()>) {
  if keyPath == "migrationProgress" {
    let manager = object as NSMigrationManager
    println(String(format: "Migration progress: %d%%",manager.migrationProgress * 100.0))
  }
}
```

Run the application to execute the custom migration and you will see the migration progress in the console:

```
BookStore[21313:70b] Migration progress: 11%BookStore[21313:70b] Migration progress:
22%BookStore[21313:70b] Migration progress: 33%BookStore[21313:70b] Migration progress:
44%BookStore[21313:70b] Migration progress: 55%BookStore[21313:70b] Migration progress:
66%BookStore[21313:70b] Migration progress: 77%BookStore[21313:70b] Migration progress:
88%BookStore[21313:70b] Migration progress: 100%
```

Summary

Although changing data models can be painful in other programming environments, Core Data makes changing your data models nearly painless. With its support for model versions, lightweight migrations, and mapping models for migrations that aren't lightweight, you can change your data models with impunity and let Core Data make sure your users' data stay intact. As with any part of your application, however, make sure you test your migrations. Test them extensively. Test them even more than you test your application code. Users can handle an occasional application crash, but if they upgrade to the latest version of your application and lose their data in the process, your application and reputation may never recover.

Chapter 7

Transforming and Encrypting Data

Although Core Data offers a reasonable array of supported data types, not all data fit neatly into strings, Booleans, numbers, and so on. Core Data offers a catch-all data type, Binary Data, that can store any type of binary data. We used a Binary Data type in Chapter 5, for example, to store images. Core Data marshals any data stored in a Binary Data type to and from an NSData instance. While this means that Core Data can store any kind of arbitrary data in a Binary Data column, it also means that your applications must transform NSData instances into representations useful to your application, and vice versa. While sometimes this may be trivial—with images, for example, creating an image from an NSData instance is as easy as calling UIImage imageWithData: and UIImagePNGRepresentation—in other cases, you may find your code sprinkled with logic to transform raw data to usable data in various places. Wouldn't it be nice to have Core Data do this transformation work for you?

In this chapter, we explore the Transformable Core Data type, which allows you to hand the transformation reins to Core Data. We also explore how you can use Transformable in a specific, topical use case: encryption. Using the techniques in this chapter, you can keep user data safe in this social media age.

Using Transformable

In this section, we build an application that displays a dot on the screen, in a random color, for each time the user taps the screen. Figure 7-1 shows the finished application, with many dots.

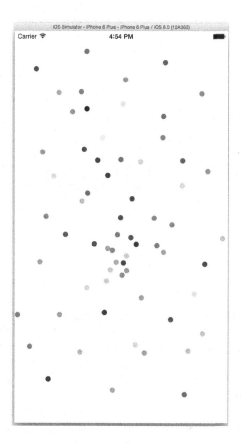

Figure 7-1. *The TapOut application*

For each tap, Core Data stores three pieces of data.

- The x value of the tap, using `Float`
- The y value of the tap, using `Float`
- A random color, using `Transformable`

Creating the Project and Adding Core Data

Create an Xcode project using the Single View Application template. Set the Product Name to TapOut and leave the User Core Data checkbox unchecked. After creating the project, add Core Data support, as we have before, using the following steps:

1.   Add the TapOut data model, `TapOut.xcdatamodeld`.

2.   Add the `Persistence` class, which encapsulates TapOut's Core Data interaction.

Listing 7-1 shows the Objective-C header file for the `Persistence` class., and Listing 7-2 shows the Objective-C implementation file. Listing 7-3 shows the Swift version of `Persistence`.

Listing 7-1. Persistence.h

```objc
#import <Foundation/Foundation.h>
@import CoreData;

@interface Persistence : NSObject

@property (readonly, strong, nonatomic) NSManagedObjectContext *managedObjectContext;
@property (readonly, strong, nonatomic) NSManagedObjectModel *managedObjectModel;
@property (readonly, strong, nonatomic) NSPersistentStoreCoordinator *persistentStoreCoordinator;

- (void)saveContext;
- (NSURL *)applicationDocumentsDirectory;

@end
```

Listing 7-2. Persistence.m

```objc
#import "Persistence.h"

@implementation Persistence

- (id)init {
  self = [super init];
  if (self != nil) {
    // Initialize the managed object model
    NSURL *modelURL = [[NSBundle mainBundle] URLForResource:@"TapOut" withExtension:@"momd"];
    _managedObjectModel = [[NSManagedObjectModel alloc] initWithContentsOfURL:modelURL];

    // Initialize the persistent store coordinator
    NSURL *storeURL = [[self applicationDocumentsDirectory] URLByAppendingPathComponent:
    @"TapOut.sqlite"];

    NSError *error = nil;
    _persistentStoreCoordinator = [[NSPersistentStoreCoordinator alloc]
    initWithManagedObjectModel:self.managedObjectModel];
    if (![_persistentStoreCoordinator addPersistentStoreWithType:NSSQLiteStoreType
                                      configuration:nil
                                                URL:storeURL
                                            options:nil
                                              error:&error]) {
      NSLog(@"Unresolved error %@, %@", error, [error userInfo]);
      abort();
    }

    // Initialize the managed object context
    _managedObjectContext = [[NSManagedObjectContext alloc] init];
    [_managedObjectContext setPersistentStoreCoordinator:self.persistentStoreCoordinator];
  }
  return self;
}
```

```objc
#pragma mark - Helper Methods

- (void)saveContext {
  NSError *error = nil;
  if ([self.managedObjectContext hasChanges] && ![self.managedObjectContext save:&error]) {
    NSLog(@"Unresolved error %@, %@", error, [error userInfo]);
    abort();
  }
}


- (NSURL *)applicationDocumentsDirectory {
  return [[[NSFileManager defaultManager] URLsForDirectory:NSDocumentDirectory
inDomains:NSUserDomainMask] lastObject];
}

@end
```

Listing 7-3. Persistence.swift

```swift
import Foundation
import CoreData

class Persistence {
    // MARK: - Core Data stack

    lazy var applicationDocumentsDirectory: NSURL = {
        // The directory the application uses to store the Core Data store file. This code uses a
        // directory named "book.persistence.TapOutSwift" in the application's documents Application
        // Support directory.
        let urls = NSFileManager.defaultManager().URLsForDirectory(.DocumentDirectory,
        inDomains: .UserDomainMask)
        return urls[urls.count-1] as NSURL
        }()

    lazy var managedObjectModel: NSManagedObjectModel = {
        // The managed object model for the application. This property is not optional. It is a
        // fatal error for the application not to be able to find and load its model.
        let modelURL = NSBundle.mainBundle().URLForResource("TapOutSwift", withExtension: "momd")!
        return NSManagedObjectModel(contentsOfURL: modelURL)!
        }()

    lazy var persistentStoreCoordinator: NSPersistentStoreCoordinator? = {
        // The persistent store coordinator for the application. This implementation creates and
        // return a coordinator, having added the store for the application to it. This property is
        // optional since there are legitimate error conditions that could cause the creation of the
        // store to fail.
        // Create the coordinator and store
        var coordinator: NSPersistentStoreCoordinator? = NSPersistentStoreCoordinator
        (managedObjectModel: self.managedObjectModel)
        let url = self.applicationDocumentsDirectory.URLByAppendingPathComponent("TapOutSwift.sqlite")
        var error: NSError? = nil
```

```
        var failureReason = "There was an error creating or loading the application's saved data."
        if coordinator!.addPersistentStoreWithType(NSSQLiteStoreType, configuration: nil, URL: url,
        options: nil, error: &error) == nil {
            coordinator = nil
            // Report any error we got.
            let dict = NSMutableDictionary()
            dict[NSLocalizedDescriptionKey] = "Failed to initialize the application's saved data"
            dict[NSLocalizedFailureReasonErrorKey] = failureReason
            dict[NSUnderlyingErrorKey] = error
            error = NSError(domain: "YOUR_ERROR_DOMAIN", code: 9999, userInfo: dict)
            // Replace this with code to handle the error appropriately.
            // abort() causes the application to generate a crash log and terminate. You should
            not use this function in a shipping application, although it may be useful during
            development.
            NSLog("Unresolved error \(error), \(error!.userInfo)")
            abort()
        }

        return coordinator
        }()

lazy var managedObjectContext: NSManagedObjectContext? = {
        // Returns the managed object context for the application (which is already bound to the
        persistent store coordinator for the application.) This property is optional since there are
        legitimate error conditions that could cause the creation of the context to fail.
        let coordinator = self.persistentStoreCoordinator
        if coordinator == nil {
            return nil
        }
        var managedObjectContext = NSManagedObjectContext()
        managedObjectContext.persistentStoreCoordinator = coordinator
        return managedObjectContext
        }()

// MARK: - Core Data Saving support

func saveContext () {
        if let moc = self.managedObjectContext {
            var error: NSError? = nil
            if moc.hasChanges && !moc.save(&error) {
                // Replace this implementation with code to handle the error appropriately.
                // abort() causes the application to generate a crash log and terminate. You should
                not use this function in a shipping application, although it may be useful during
                development.
                NSLog("Unresolved error \(error), \(error!.userInfo)")
                abort()
            }
        }
    }
}


}
```

Then, add a property for a `Persistence` instance to `AppDelegate`, as shown in Listing 7-4 (Objective-C) and Listing 7-5 (Swift), and initialize it when the application launches, as shown in Listing 7-6 (Objective-C) and Listing 7-7 (Swift).

Listing 7-4. Adding a Persistence Property to AppDelegate.h

```
@class Persistence;
...
@property (strong, nonatomic) Persistence *persistence;
```

Listing 7-5. Adding a Persistence Property to AppDelegate.swift

```
var persistence : Persistence?
```

Listing 7-6. Initializing the Core Data Stack in AppDelegate.m

```
#import "Persistence.h"


...


- (BOOL)application:(UIApplication *)application didFinishLaunchingWithOptions:(NSDictionary *)
launchOptions {
    self.persistence = [[Persistence alloc] init];
    return YES;
}
```

Listing 7-7. Initializing the Core Data Stack in AppDelegate.swift

```
func application(application: UIApplication, didFinishLaunchingWithOptions launchOptions:
[NSObject: AnyObject]?) -> Bool {
    persistence = Persistence()
    return true
}
```

To wrap up adding Core Data, open your Core Data model, `TapOut.xcdatamodeld`, and add an entity called Tap. Give it three attributes.

- x, of type `Float`
- y, of type `Float`
- color, of type `Transformable`

Generate a class for it in Xcode, making sure to check the checkbox to use scalar properties for primitive types. If you look in the Objective-C header file, `Tap.h`, or in the Swift file, `Tap.swift`, you'll notice that Core Data has set the type of `color` to `id`, if you're using Objective-C, or AnyObject, if you're using Swift. This is the default, as Core Data has no idea what type you plan to transform from and to. You can safely update this type to the type you plan to use, `UIColor *` (Objective-C) or `UIColor` (Swift), so that `Tap.h` now matches Listing 7-8 and `Tap.swift` matches Listing 7-9.

Listing 7-8. Tap.h

```
#import <Foundation/Foundation.h>
#import <CoreData/CoreData.h>
#import <UIKit/UIKit.h>

@interface Tap : NSManagedObject

@property (nonatomic) float x;
@property (nonatomic) float y;
@property (nonatomic, retain) UIColor *color;

@end
```

Listing 7-9. Tap.swift

```
import Foundation
import CoreData
import UIKit

@objc(Tap)
class Tap: NSManagedObject {

    @NSManaged var color: UIColor
    @NSManaged var x: Float
    @NSManaged var y: Float

}
```

Creating Taps

Anytime the user taps the screen, we create a Tap object in the Core Data store. We'll handle the tap in the view controller, ViewController, and add a method to Persistence to actually add the Tap. We start in Persistence. Open Persistence.h, if you're doing this in Objective-C, and add a method declaration for adding a Tap, as shown in Listing 7-10.

Listing 7-10. Declaration of a Method in Persistence.h to Add a Tap

```
#import <UIKit/UIKit.h>

...

- (void)addTap:(CGPoint)point;
```

In Persistence.m or Persistence.swift, add the definition of addTap:. This method creates a Tap instance in the managed object context, sets its x and y values to the corresponding values in the specified point, sets color to a random color using a helper function, and then saves the managed object context. Listing 7-11 shows the Objective-C version of this method and the random-color-generating helper, and Listing 7-12 shows the Swift version.

Listing 7-11. Adding a Tap in Persistence.m

```objc
#import "Tap.h"

...

- (void)addTap:(CGPoint)point {
  Tap *tap = [NSEntityDescription insertNewObjectForEntityForName:@"Tap"
inManagedObjectContext:self.managedObjectContext];
  tap.x = point.x;
  tap.y = point.y;
  tap.color = [self randomColor];
  [self saveContext];
}

- (UIColor *)randomColor {
  float red = (arc4random() % 256) / 255.0f;
  float green = (arc4random() % 256) / 255.0f;
  float blue = (arc4random() % 256) / 255.0f;

  return [UIColor colorWithRed:red green:green blue:blue alpha:1.0];
}
```

Listing 7-12. Adding a Tap in Persistence.swift

```swift
func addTap(point: CGPoint) {
    var tap = NSEntityDescription.insertNewObjectForEntityForName("Tap", inManagedObjectContext:
    self.managedObjectContext!) as? Tap

    tap?.x = Float(point.x)
    tap?.y = Float(point.y)
    tap?.color = self.randomColor()
    self.saveContext()
}

func randomColor() -> UIColor {
    let red = CGFloat(arc4random() % UInt32(256)) / 255.0
    let green = CGFloat(arc4random() % UInt32(256)) / 255.0
    let blue = CGFloat(arc4random() % UInt32(256)) / 255.0

    return UIColor(red: red, green: green, blue: blue, alpha: 1.0)
}
```

Now add a tap gesture recognizer to the view controller that ultimately calls the addTap: method when you tap the view. Listing 7-13 shows the updated ViewController.m file, and Listing 7-14 shows the updated ViewController.swift file.

Listing 7-13. ViewController.m with a Tap Gesture Recognizer

```objc
#import "ViewController.h"
#import "AppDelegate.h"
#import "Persistence.h"

@implementation ViewController

- (void)viewDidLoad {
  [super viewDidLoad];
  UITapGestureRecognizer *tapGestureRecognizer = [[UITapGestureRecognizer alloc]
initWithTarget:self action:@selector(viewWasTapped:)];
  [self.view addGestureRecognizer:tapGestureRecognizer];
}

- (void)viewWasTapped:(UIGestureRecognizer *)sender {
  if (sender.state == UIGestureRecognizerStateEnded) {
    AppDelegate *appDelegate = (AppDelegate *)[[UIApplication sharedApplication] delegate];
    Persistence *persistence = appDelegate.persistence;
    CGPoint point = [sender locationInView:sender.view];
    [persistence addTap:point];
    [self.view setNeedsDisplay];
  }
}

@end
```

Listing 7-14. ViewController.swift with a Tap Gesture Recognizer

```swift
import UIKit

class ViewController: UIViewController {

    override func viewDidLoad() {
        super.viewDidLoad()
        let tapGestureRecognizer = UITapGestureRecognizer(target: self, action: "viewWasTapped:")
        self.view.addGestureRecognizer(tapGestureRecognizer)
    }

    func viewWasTapped(sender: UIGestureRecognizer) {
        if sender.state == .Ended {
            let appDelegate = UIApplication.sharedApplication().delegate as AppDelegate
            let point = sender.locationInView(sender.view)
            appDelegate.persistence?.addTap(point)
            self.view.setNeedsDisplay()
        }
    }
}
```

You should be able to build and run TapOut now and tap the screen to create Tap instances. You can verify that the Tap instances are created by looking in the SQLite database, but nothing displays yet on the screen. In the next section, we add code to actually display the Tap instances that Core Data is storing.

Creating the View and Displaying the Taps

To display the Tap instances, we first fetch them from Core Data. Then, we iterate through them, drawing them on the view using standard drawing primitives. Add a method called taps to Persistence that fetches all the Tap instances from the Core Data store. This code should be familiar, as it's standard code for fetching objects from Core Data. Listing 7-15 shows the method declaration in Persistence.h, Listing 7-16 shows the Objective-C definition in Persistence.m, and Listing 7-17 shows the Swift definition in Persistence.swift.

Listing 7-15. Declaring the taps Method in Persistence.h

```
- (NSArray *)taps;
```

Listing 7-16. Fetching All the Tap Instances in Persistence.m

```
- (NSArray *)taps {
  NSError *error = nil;
  NSFetchRequest *fetchRequest = [NSFetchRequest fetchRequestWithEntityName:@"Tap"];
  NSArray *taps = [self.managedObjectContext executeFetchRequest:fetchRequest error:&error];
  if (taps == nil) {
    NSLog(@"Error fetching taps %@, %@", error, [error userInfo]);
  }
  return taps;
}
```

Listing 7-17. Fetching All the Tap Instances in Persistence.swift

```
func taps() -> [Tap] {
    var error: NSError? = nil
    let fetchRequest = NSFetchRequest(entityName: "Tap")
    let taps = self.managedObjectContext?.executeFetchRequest(fetchRequest, error: &error)

    return taps as [Tap]
}
```

Now create a class called TapView that extends UIView. In the drawRect: method, fetch the Tap instances using the method you just created, and then iterate through them to draw them on the screen as circles, centered on their x and y values, in the color stored in Core Data. Listing 7-18 shows TapView.h, Listing 7-19 shows the Objective-C TapView.m, and Listing 7-20 shows the Swift TapView.swift.

Listing 7-18. TapView.h

```
@interface TapView : UIView

@end
```

Listing 7-19. TapView.m

```objc
#import "TapView.h"
#import "AppDelegate.h"
#import "Persistence.h"
#import "Tap.h"

@implementation TapView

- (void)drawRect:(CGRect)rect {
static float DIAMETER = 10.0f;

  CGContextRef context = UIGraphicsGetCurrentContext();

  AppDelegate *appDelegate = (AppDelegate *)[[UIApplication sharedApplication] delegate];
  NSArray *taps = [appDelegate.persistence taps];
  for (Tap *tap in taps) {
    const CGFloat *rgb = CGColorGetComponents(tap.color.CGColor);
    CGContextSetRGBFillColor(context, rgb[0], rgb[1], rgb[2], 1.0f);
    CGContextFillEllipseInRect(context, CGRectMake(tap.x - DIAMETER/2, tap.y - DIAMETER/2,
DIAMETER, DIAMETER));
  }
}

@end
```

Listing 7-20. TapView.swift

```swift
import Foundation
import UIKit

class TapView : UIView {
    override func drawRect(rect: CGRect) {
        let DIAMETER = CGFloat(10.0)

        let context = UIGraphicsGetCurrentContext()

        let appDelegate = UIApplication.sharedApplication().delegate as? AppDelegate
        let taps = appDelegate?.persistence?.taps()
        if let taps = taps {
            for tap : Tap in taps {
                let rgb = CGColorGetComponents(tap.color.CGColor)
                CGContextSetRGBFillColor(context, rgb[0], rgb[1], rgb[2], 1.0)
                CGContextFillEllipseInRect(context, CGRectMake(CGFloat(tap.x - Float(DIAMETER/2)),
                CGFloat(tap.y - Float(DIAMETER/2)), DIAMETER, DIAMETER))
            }
        }
    }
}
```

Update the application's view to use this new view class.

1.   Open Main.storyboard.

2.   Select the View.

3.   In the Identity Inspector, change the Class dropdown to TapView.

Now, run the application, and all the Tap instances you've added should be displayed. You can also tap the screen to add more dots. You can tap until your iPhone looks like it's contracted measles!

Hey, Wait a Minute! How Did My Color Transform?

You might notice that we didn't write any transformation code to transform our UIColor instance into or out of the Core Data store. How did Core Data know how to transform it?

In pre-iOS 5 days, we would have had to write a custom transformer class to perform transformations for UIColor instances. As of iOS 5, however, UIColor adheres to the NSCoding protocol, so it's automatically encoded and decoded properly. It's so easy, it almost feels like cheating.

We won't be so lucky with our encryption transformation, however, and will have to write a custom transformation class to encrypt and decrypt our data. We do this in the next section.

Encrypting Data

In this age of social media, identity theft, and NSA (National Security Agency) snooping, people increasingly value privacy. Keeping your device physically secure can protect your data—until you leave your iPhone in a bar or a thief steals it. In the event that someone else gains control of your iPhone or iPad, that person can siphon off the SQLite databases that Core Data uses in various applications and, using tools like the ones we're using in this book, read all your data—including the private, sensitive bits that can make you blush, or can even destroy your life.

One way to safeguard that data is to encrypt them using known, industry-strength encryption algorithms. In the rest of this chapter, we create a secure note-taking application called SecureNote that stores all notes in encrypted format. We use Core Data's Transformable data type and a custom transformation class to manage the encryption and decryption of the data. The finished application will resemble Figure 7-2.

Figure 7-2. *The SecureNote application*

Creating the Project and Setting Up the Core Data Model

Create a new project in Xcode using the Master-Detail Application. Call it SecureNote and make sure the Use Core Data check box is checked. Once Xcode creates your project, open the Core Data model, SecureNote.xcdatamodeld, and delete the Event entity that Xcode created for you. Then, add an entity called Note and give it three attributes.

- timeStamp (Date)
- title (Transformable)
- body (Transformable)

We leave timeStamp unencrypted, but we will encrypt title and body using a custom transformer class. The next section discusses encryption and decryption and then builds a custom transformer class that Core Data will use for encrypting and decrypting title and body.

Before we move on to encryption and decryption, however, update the NSFetchedResultsController that Xcode generated for you to fetch Note instances. You'll find this code in MasterViewController.m or MasterViewController.swift in the fetchedResultsController accessor. Change it to match Listing 7-21.

Listing 7-21. Fetching Note Instances

```
NSEntityDescription *entity = [NSEntityDescription entityForName:@"Note"
inManagedObjectContext:self.managedObjectContext]; // Objective-C

let entity = NSEntityDescription.entityForName("Note", inManagedObjectContext:
self.managedObjectContext!) // Swift
```

Generate an NSManagedObject subclass for the Note entity. The generated class will set the type of body and title to id (Objective-C) or AnyObject (Swift), because it doesn't know what else to set it to, but you can change the type for both to NSString * (Objective-C) or String (Swift). Listing 7-22 shows the Note.h header file, Listing 7-23 shows the Note.m Objective-C implementation file, and Listing 7-24 shows the Note.swift Swift implementation file.

Listing 7-22. Note.h

```
#import <Foundation/Foundation.h>
#import <CoreData/CoreData.h>

@interface Note : NSManagedObject

@property (nonatomic, retain) NSString *body;
@property (nonatomic, retain) NSDate *timeStamp;
@property (nonatomic, retain) NSString *title;

@end
```

Listing 7-23. Note.m

```
#import "Note.h"

@implementation Note

@dynamic body;
@dynamic timeStamp;
@dynamic title;

@end
```

Listing 7-24. Note.swift

```
import Foundation
import CoreData

@objc(Note)
class Note: NSManagedObject {

    @NSManaged var timeStamp: NSDate
    @NSManaged var title: String
    @NSManaged var body: String

}
```

We want the master view to show the note's title, with the timestamp displayed below it, so open the storyboard (`Main.storyboard`), select the prototype cell in the master view, and change its style in the Attributes inspector from Basic to Subtitle, as shown in Figure 7-3.

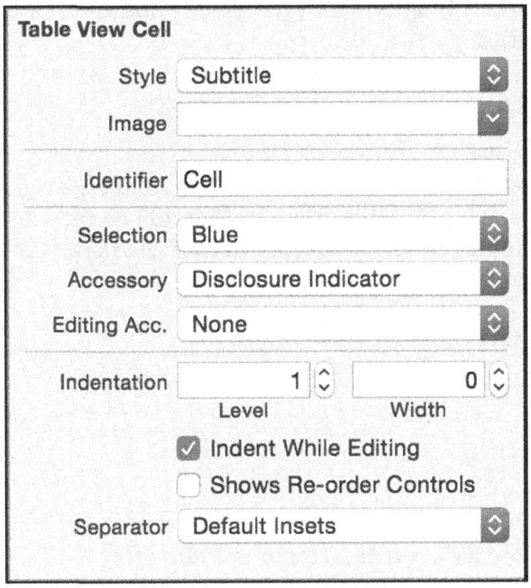

Figure 7-3. Setting the table view cell to Subtitle

Now, update the `configureCell:atIndexPath:` method in `MasterViewController.m` or `MasterViewController.swift` to show the title of the note in the main text label, with the timestamp in the detail text label, as shown in Listing 7-25 (Objective-C) and Listing 7-26 (Swift).

Listing 7-25. Showing the Note Title and the Timestamp in the Cell (Objective-C)

```
#import "Note.h"

...

- (void)configureCell:(UITableViewCell *)cell atIndexPath:(NSIndexPath *)indexPath {
  Note *note = [self.fetchedResultsController objectAtIndexPath:indexPath];
  cell.textLabel.text = note.title;
  cell.detailTextLabel.text = [note.timeStamp description];
}
```

Listing 7-26. Showing the Note Title and the Timestamp in the Cell (Swift)

```
func configureCell(cell: UITableViewCell, atIndexPath indexPath: NSIndexPath) {
    let note = self.fetchedResultsController.objectAtIndexPath(indexPath) as Note
    cell.textLabel.text = note.title
    cell.detailTextLabel?.text = note.timeStamp.description
}
```

You should update the insertNewObject: method in MasterViewController.m or
MasterViewController.swift as well to use the new Note class, as shown in Listing 7-27
(Objective-C) and Listing 7-28 (Swift). In that method, we create a new Note instance, and we set the
timestamp to the current date and time, the title to "New Note," and the body to an empty string.
We also select the new note and transition to its detail view, so that, once we update the detail view,
we'll be able to edit the new note.

Listing 7-27. Using the Note Class When Creating a New Object (Objective-C)

```objc
- (void)insertNewObject:(id)sender {
NSManagedObjectContext *context = [self.fetchedResultsController managedObjectContext];
  NSEntityDescription *entity = [[self.fetchedResultsController fetchRequest] entity];
  Note *note = [NSEntityDescription insertNewObjectForEntityForName:[entity name]
  inManagedObjectContext:context];

  note.timeStamp = [NSDate date];
  note.title = @"New Note";
  note.body = @"";

  // Save the context.
  NSError *error = nil;
  if (![context save:&error]) {
    NSLog(@"Unresolved error %@, %@", error, [error userInfo]);
    abort();
  }

  // Select the new note and segue to its detail view
  NSIndexPath *indexPath = [NSIndexPath indexPathForRow:0 inSection:0];
  [self.tableView selectRowAtIndexPath:indexPath animated:YES
  scrollPosition:UITableViewScrollPositionTop];
  [self performSegueWithIdentifier:@"showDetail" sender:self];
}
```

Listing 7-28. Using the Note Class When Creating a New Object (Swift)

```swift
func insertNewObject(sender: AnyObject) {
    let context = self.fetchedResultsController.managedObjectContext
    let entity = self.fetchedResultsController.fetchRequest.entity
    let note = NSEntityDescription.insertNewObjectForEntityForName(entity!.name!,
    inManagedObjectContext: context) as Note

    note.timeStamp = NSDate()
    note.title = "New Note"
    note.body = ""

    // Save the context.
    var error: NSError? = nil
    if !context.save(&error) {
      abort()
    }
```

```
// Select the new note and segue to its detail view
let indexPath = NSIndexPath(forRow: 0, inSection: 0)
self.tableView.selectRowAtIndexPath(indexPath, animated: true, scrollPosition: .Top)
self.performSegueWithIdentifier("showDetail", sender: self)
}
```

Performing the Encryption and Decryption

To do the actual encryption and decryption, we use the Common Crypto library supplied by iOS. This isn't a book on encryption, so we don't delve into details on how the encryption works. We encourage you to do your own research on encryption if you want to know more. Some iOS cryptography resources include

- ▦ Apple's Cryptographics Services Guide at `https://developer.apple.com/library/mac/documentation/security/conceptual/cryptoservices/Introduction/Introduction.html`

- ▦ Rob Napier's blog post: "Properly Encrypting With AES With CommonCrypto" at `http://robnapier.net/aes-commoncrypto/`

For the purposes of this chapter, you should understand the following:

- ▦ We use symmetrical encryption using a user-supplied password as the key.

- ▦ For each string we encrypt, we create a random salt that we combine with the password and hash using SHA1.

- ▦ We use the AES algorithm for encryption.

We use a user-supplied password that we store in a member of the application delegate called, appropriately, password. Add it to AppDelegate.h or AppDelegate.swift, as shown in Listing 7-29 (Objective-C) and Listing 7-30 (Swift).

Listing 7-29. Adding Password to the Application Delegate (Objective-C)

```
@property (copy, nonatomic) NSString *password;
```

Listing 7-30. Adding Password to the Application Delegate (Swift)

```
var password: String?
```

Before we discuss how to prompt the user for the password and how to verify it's correct, and how to generate and store the salts for each string, we build the actual value transformer. Before building it, we must understand the value transformer methods and what they do.

Understanding the NSValueTransformer Methods

NSValueTransformer has four interesting methods: two are static, and two are instance methods. Table 7-1 lists these methods and what they do.

Table 7-1. The NSValueTransformer *Methods*

Method	Description
+ (BOOL)allowsReverseTransformation	Static method that returns YES if this value transformer supports reverse transformations, NO if it doesn't. The default is YES.
+ (Class)transformedValueClass	The class of the value returned by a forward transformation.
- (id)transformedValue:(id)value	Called to transform value into the new value.
- (id)reverseTransformedValue:(id)value	Called to transform in reverse, transforming value to the new value. Your value transformer must support reverse transformations. Override this method if you can't reverse a transformation simply by reapplying transformedValue;.

Implementing the Encryption/Decryption Value Transformer

For our encryption/decryption value transformer, we must support both forward and reverse transformations—we encrypt on a forward transformation into the Core Data data store and decrypt on a reverse transformation into memory and onto the screen. Thus, we override transformedValue: and reverseTransformedValue: to encrypt and decrypt, respectively. We don't bother to override allowsReverseTransformation, as the default return value is YES. We return the NSData class for transformedValueClass, since that is the type of the object we return from transformedValue:.

An interesting problem is how to store two pieces of data for each string we encrypt: the salt and the initialization vector (IV), each of which is random data. These bits of data combine with the password to prevent rainbow table attacks across your data. We create these when we encrypt a string, and then use them to decrypt the string. Since we must have the salt and IV for each string to decrypt it, we must store both the salt and the IV for each encrypted string.

You might think we could create attributes in the Note entity in the Core Data model to store the salt and the IV for each managed object, but remember that we're giving Core Data an NSTransformer-derived class to read and write our Transformable attributes. Core Data code, not our code, will be instantiating and calling our transformers. Further, our transformer class knows nothing about the context in which it's called—it doesn't know anything about the managed object that it's being used for. All it knows is that it receives a value and returns a value. We can't read from or write to other attributes in the model in our transformer because we don't know which managed object we're working with, or even which attribute we're encrypting or decrypting.

The solution, then, is to mash together the salt, IV, and encrypted string into a single attribute when we write the data, and parse the salt, IV, and encrypted string back from the data when we read so we can perform the decryption. We'll store the data as follows:

- Salt (8 bytes)
- IV (16 bytes)
- Encrypted string (the rest of the bytes)

For the actual encryption and decryption, we create a parameterized helper method called transform:, which allows us to specify whether to encrypt or decrypt, since the code for doing each operation is so similar. This method takes the password, salt, and IV as parameters.

As we said before, we don't discuss the details of the actual encryption and decryption but have added comments to the code that you can follow.

To add the security framework to the Objective-C version of the project, you simply add this statement to any file that must reference any security code:

```
@import SystemConfiguration;
```

Adding frameworks to a Swift project isn't so easy, at least as of this writing. To add the security framework to your Swift project, do the following:

1. Create a dummy Objective-C file in your project.

2. Xcode will ask you if you want to create a bridge header file. Say yes.

3. Delete the dummy Objective-C file.

4. Open the bridge header, SecureNoteSwift-Bridging-Header.h, and add these imports:

   ```
   #import <CommonCrypto/CommonCryptor.h>
   #import <CommonCrypto/CommonDigest.h>

   #import "SSKeychain.h"
   ```

Listing 7-31 shows the header file for our value transformer, EncryptionTransformer, Listing 7-32 shows the Objective-C implementation file, and Listing 7-33 shows the Swift implementation file.

Listing 7-31. EncryptionTransformer.h

```
#import <Foundation/Foundation.h>

@interface EncryptionTransformer : NSValueTransformer

@end
```

Listing 7-32. EncryptionTransformer.m

```
@import SystemConfiguration;

#import <CommonCrypto/CommonCryptor.h>
#import <CommonCrypto/CommonDigest.h>
#import "EncryptionTransformer.h"
#import "AppDelegate.h"

#define kSaltLength 8

@implementation EncryptionTransformer

+ (Class)transformedValueClass {
  return [NSData class];
}
```

```objc
- (id)transformedValue:(id)value {
  // We're passed in a string (NSString) that we're going to encrypt.
  // The format of the bytes we return is:
  // salt (16 bytes) | IV (16 bytes) | encrypted string
  NSData *salt = [self randomDataOfLength:kSaltLength];
  NSData *iv = [self randomDataOfLength:kCCBlockSizeAES128];
  NSData *data = [(NSString *)value dataUsingEncoding:NSUTF8StringEncoding];

  // Do the actual encryption
  NSData *result = [self transform:data
                          password:[self password]
                              salt:salt
                                iv:iv
                         operation:kCCEncrypt];

  // Build the response data
  NSMutableData *response = [[NSMutableData alloc] init];
  [response appendData:salt];
  [response appendData:iv];
  [response appendData:result];
  return response;
}

- (id)reverseTransformedValue:(id)value {
  // We're passed in bytes (NSData) from Core Data that we're going to transform
  // into a string (NSString) and return to the application.

  // The bytes are in the format:
  // salt (16 bytes) | IV (16 bytes) | encrypted data
  NSData *data = (NSData *)value;
  NSData *salt = [data subdataWithRange:NSMakeRange(0, kSaltLength)];
  NSData *iv = [data subdataWithRange:NSMakeRange(kSaltLength, kCCBlockSizeAES128)];
  NSData *text = [data subdataWithRange:NSMakeRange(kSaltLength + kCCBlockSizeAES128,
  [data length] - kSaltLength - kCCBlockSizeAES128)];

  // Get the decrypted data
  NSData *decrypted = [self transform:text password:[self password] salt:salt iv:iv
  operation:kCCDecrypt];

  // Return only the decrypted string
  return [[NSString alloc] initWithData:decrypted encoding:NSUTF8StringEncoding];
}

- (NSData *)transform:(NSData *)value
             password:(NSString *)password
                 salt:(NSData *)salt
                   iv:(NSData *)iv
            operation:(CCOperation)operation {
  // Get the key by salting the password
  NSData *key = [self keyForPassword:password salt:salt];
```

```objc
    // Perform the operation (encryption or decryption)
    size_t outputSize = 0;
    NSMutableData *outputData = [NSMutableData dataWithLength:value.length + kCCBlockSizeAES128];
    CCCryptorStatus status = CCCrypt(operation,
                                     kCCAlgorithmAES128,
                                     kCCOptionPKCS7Padding,
                                     key.bytes,
                                     key.length,
                                     iv.bytes,
                                     value.bytes,
                                     value.length,
                                     outputData.mutableBytes,
                                     outputData.length,
                                     &outputSize);

    // On success, set the size and return the data
    // On failure, return nil
    if (status == kCCSuccess) {
      outputData.length = outputSize;
      return outputData;
    } else {
      return nil;
    }
}

- (NSData *)keyForPassword:(NSString *)password
                      salt:(NSData *)salt {
    // Append the salt to the password
    NSMutableData *passwordAndSalt = [[password dataUsingEncoding:NSUTF8StringEncoding] mutableCopy];
    [passwordAndSalt appendData:salt];

    // Hash it
    NSData *hash = [self sha1:passwordAndSalt];

    // Create the key by using the hashed password and salt, making
    // it the proper size for AES128 (0-padding if necessary)
    NSRange range = NSMakeRange(0, MIN(hash.length, kCCBlockSizeAES128));
    NSMutableData *key = [NSMutableData dataWithLength:kCCBlockSizeAES128];
    [key replaceBytesInRange:range withBytes:hash.bytes];
    return key;
}

- (NSData *)sha1:(NSData *)data {
    // Get the SHA1 into an array
    uint8_t digest[CC_SHA1_DIGEST_LENGTH];
    CC_SHA1(data.bytes, (CC_LONG) data.length, digest);
```

```objc
  // Create a formatted string with the SHA1
  NSMutableString* sha1 = [NSMutableString stringWithCapacity:CC_SHA1_DIGEST_LENGTH * 2];
  for (int i = 0; i < CC_SHA1_DIGEST_LENGTH; i++) {
    [sha1 appendFormat:@"%02x", digest[i]];
  }
  return [sha1 dataUsingEncoding:NSUTF8StringEncoding];
}

- (NSString *)password {
  return ((AppDelegate *)[[UIApplication sharedApplication] delegate]).password;
}

- (NSData *)randomDataOfLength:(size_t)length {
  // SecRandomCopyBytes returns 0 on success, non-zero on failure
  // If the call fails, the buffer will be full of zeros left over
  // from NSMutableData dataWithLength:, which is less secure!
  // A shipping app may choose to fail if this step fails
  NSMutableData *randomData = [NSMutableData dataWithLength:length];
  SecRandomCopyBytes(kSecRandomDefault, length, randomData.mutableBytes);
  return randomData;
}

@end
```

Listing 7-33. EncryptionTransformer.swift

```swift
import Foundation

import UIKit
import Security

@objc(EncryptionTransformer)
class EncryptionTransformer : NSValueTransformer {
    let saltLength : UInt = 8

    override class func transformedValueClass() -> AnyClass {
        return NSData.self
    }

    override func transformedValue(value: AnyObject?) -> AnyObject? {
        // We're passed in a string (NSString) that we're going to encrypt.
        // The format of the bytes we return is:
        // salt (16 bytes) | IV (16 bytes) | encrypted string

        let salt = self.randomDataOfLength(saltLength)
        let iv = self.randomDataOfLength(UInt(kCCBlockSizeAES128))

        let data = value?.dataUsingEncoding(NSUTF8StringEncoding)
```

```
        // Do the actual encryption
        let result = self.transform(data!, password: self.password()!, salt: salt, iv: iv,
        operation: UInt32(kCCEncrypt))

        // Build the response data
        var response = NSMutableData()
        response.appendData(salt)
        response.appendData(iv)
        response.appendData(result!)
        return response
    }

    override func reverseTransformedValue(value: AnyObject?) -> AnyObject? {
        // We're passed in bytes (NSData) from Core Data that we're going to transform
        // into a string (NSString) and return to the application.
        let data = value as NSData?
        if let data = data {
            let salt = data.subdataWithRange(NSMakeRange(0, Int(saltLength)))
            let iv = data.subdataWithRange(NSMakeRange(Int(saltLength), kCCBlockSizeAES128))
            let text = data.subdataWithRange(NSMakeRange(Int(saltLength) + kCCBlockSizeAES128,
            data.length - Int(saltLength) - kCCBlockSizeAES128))

            // Get the decrypted data
            let decrypted = self.transform(text, password: self.password()!, salt: salt, iv: iv,
            operation: UInt32(kCCDecrypt))

            // Return only the decrypted data
            return NSString(data: decrypted!, encoding: NSUTF8StringEncoding)
        }
        else {
            return nil
        }
    }

    func transform(value: NSData, password: String, salt: NSData, iv: NSData, operation:
    CCOperation) -> NSData? {
        // Get the key by salting the password
        let key = self.keyForPassword(password, salt: salt)

        var outputSize :UInt = 0

        // Perform the operation (encryption or decryption)
        let outputData = NSMutableData(length: value.length + kCCBlockSizeAES128)
        let status = CCCrypt(operation, UInt32(kCCAlgorithmAES128), UInt32(kCCOptionPKCS7Padding),
        key.bytes, UInt(key.length), iv.bytes, value.bytes, UInt(value.length), outputData!.
        mutableBytes, UInt(outputData!.length), &outputSize)

        // On success, set the size and return the data
        // On failure, return nil
        if UInt32(status) == UInt32(kCCSuccess)  {
            outputData!.length = Int(outputSize)
            return outputData
        }
```

```
        else {
            return nil
        }
    }

    func sha1(data: NSData) -> NSData {
        // Get the SHA1 into an array
        var digest = [UInt8](count:Int(CC_SHA1_DIGEST_LENGTH), repeatedValue: 0)
        CC_SHA1(data.bytes, CC_LONG(data.length), &digest)

        // Create a formatted string with the SHA1
        let sha1 = NSMutableString(capacity: Int(CC_SHA1_DIGEST_LENGTH))
        for byte in digest {
            sha1.appendFormat("%02x", byte)
        }

        return sha1.dataUsingEncoding(NSUTF8StringEncoding, allowLossyConversion: false)!
    }

    func keyForPassword(password: String, salt: NSData) -> NSData {
        // Append the salt to the password
        let passwordAndSalt = password.dataUsingEncoding(NSUTF8StringEncoding,
        allowLossyConversion: false)?.mutableCopy() as? NSMutableData
        passwordAndSalt?.appendData(salt)

        // Hash it
        let hash = self.sha1(passwordAndSalt!)

        // Create the key by using the hashed password and salt, making
        // it the proper size for AES128 (0-padding if necessary)
        let range = NSMakeRange(0, min(hash.length, kCCBlockSizeAES128));
        let key = NSMutableData(length: kCCBlockSizeAES128)
        key.replaceBytesInRange(range, withBytes: hash.bytes)
        return key
    }

    func randomDataOfLength(length: UInt) -> NSData {
        let data = NSMutableData(length: Int(length))
        var dataPointer = UnsafeMutablePointer<UInt8>(data.mutableBytes)
        SecRandomCopyBytes(kSecRandomDefault, length, dataPointer);
        return data
    }

    func password() -> NSString? {
        let appDelegate = UIApplication.sharedApplication().delegate as AppDelegate
        return appDelegate.password
    }
}
```

Although you'll find code to cover the encryption details, you can also see the NSValueTransformer methods as you'd expect: transformedValue: receives a string to encrypt and returns the data structure we discussed earlier—the salt, IV, and encrypted string. The reverseTransformedValue: method, as expected, receives that same data structure, parses the salt, IV, and encrypted string, and returns the decrypted string.

Open the Core Data model, SecureNote.xcdatamodeld, and set both the title and body attributes of Note to use this transformer. You do this by selecting the attribute, opening the Data Model inspector, and typing the transformer's class name, EncryptionTransformer, in the Name field below the Attribute Type dropdown, as shown in Figure 7-4.

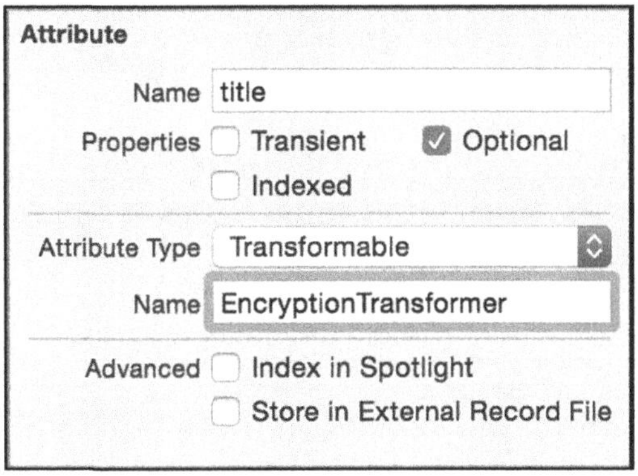

Figure 7-4. Setting title to use EncryptionTransformer

Setting Up the Detail View to Edit a Note

The existing SecureNote detail view shows the timestamp of the selected entity. Instead, we want to show the selected note's title and body in editable fields. When the user taps the back button, we save the data from the fields into the Note entity and then save the managed object context.

In DetailViewController.h, change the detailItem property to note, of type Note*. Delete the existing UILabel and create the text field and text view for the note's title and body, respectively. Listing 7-34 shows the updated header file.

Listing 7-34. DetailViewController.h with the Fields for the Note

```
#import <UIKit/UIKit.h>

@class Note;

@interface SNDetailViewController : UIViewController

@property (strong, nonatomic) Note *note;
@property (weak, nonatomic) IBOutlet UITextField *noteTitle;
@property (weak, nonatomic) IBOutlet UITextView *noteBody;

@end
```

Update DetailViewController.m to use the note instance and the noteTitle and noteBody controls instead of detailItem and detailDescriptionLabel. Also, in viewWillDisappear:, update note's body and title and save the managed object context. Listing 7-35 shows the updated implementation file for Objective-C. Listing 7-36 shows the updated DetailViewController.swift that implements the corresponding changes.

Listing 7-35. DetailViewController.m with the Fields for the Note

```objc
#import "DetailViewController.h"
#import "Note.h"

@implementation DetailViewController

#pragma mark - Managing the note

- (void)setNote:(Note *)note {
  if (_note != note) {
    _note = note;
    [self configureView];
  }
}

- (void)configureView {
  if (self.note) {
    self.noteTitle.text = self.note.title;
    self.noteBody.text = self.note.body;
  } else {
    self.noteTitle.text = @"";
    self.noteBody.text = @"";
  }
}

- (void)viewDidLoad {
  [super viewDidLoad];
  [self configureView];
}

- (void)viewWillDisappear:(BOOL)animated {
  self.note.title = self.noteTitle.text;
  self.note.body = self.noteBody.text;

  NSError *error;
  if (![[self.note managedObjectContext] save:&error]) {
    NSLog(@"Error saving note %@ -- %@ %@", self.noteTitle.text, error, [error userInfo]);
  }
}

@end
```

Listing 7-36. DetailViewController.swift with the Fields for the Note

```swift
import UIKit

class DetailViewController: UIViewController {
    @IBOutlet weak var noteTitle: UITextField!
    @IBOutlet weak var noteBody: UITextView!

    var note: Note? {
        didSet {
            self.configureView()
        }
    }

    func configureView() {
        if self.noteTitle != nil {
            if let note = self.note {
                self.noteTitle.text = note.title
                self.noteBody.text = note.body
            }
            else {
                self.noteTitle.text = ""
                self.noteBody.text = ""
            }
        }
    }

    override func viewDidLoad() {
        super.viewDidLoad()
        self.configureView()
    }

    override func viewWillDisappear(animated: Bool) {
        self.note?.title = self.noteTitle.text
        self.note?.body = self.noteBody.text

        if let managedObjectContext = self.note?.managedObjectContext {
            var error: NSError? = nil
            if !managedObjectContext.save(&error) {
              NSLog("Error saving note \(self.noteTitle.text) -- \(error) \(error!.userInfo)")
            }
        }
    }

    func setNote(note: Note) {
        if(self.note != note) {
            self.note = note
            self.configureView()
        }
    }
}
```

Update the prepareForSegue:sender: method in MasterViewController.m or
MasterViewController.swift to call setNote: instead of setDetailItem:, as shown in Listing 7-37
(Objective-C) or Listing 7-38 (Swift).

Listing 7-37. Calling setNote: Instead of setDetailItem: in MasterViewController.m

```
- (void)prepareForSegue:(UIStoryboardSegue *)segue sender:(id)sender {
  if ([[segue identifier] isEqualToString:@"showDetail"]) {
    NSIndexPath *indexPath = [self.tableView indexPathForSelectedRow];
    Note *note = [[self fetchedResultsController] objectAtIndexPath:indexPath];
    [[segue destinationViewController] setNote:note];
  }
}
```

Listing 7-38. Calling setNote: Instead of setDetailItem: in MasterViewController.swift

```
override func prepareForSegue(segue: UIStoryboardSegue, sender: AnyObject?) {
    if segue.identifier == "showDetail" {
        if let indexPath = self.tableView.indexPathForSelectedRow() {
            let note = self.fetchedResultsController.objectAtIndexPath(indexPath) as Note
            (segue.destinationViewController as DetailViewController).note = note
        }
    }
}
```

Open the storyboard, Main.storyboard, to update the user interface. In the detail view, delete the
existing label. Add a borderless text field to the top of the view with the placeholder text **Note Title**,
bump its font size to 18, and make it span the width of the view. Below that, add a text view that fills
the rest of the space. Connect these two controls to noteTitle and noteBody, respectively. Use the
Resolve Autolayout Issues popup menu to add missing constraints. Figure 7-5 shows the updated
detail view.

Figure 7-5. The detail view with the note details

Prompting For and Verifying the Password

We've been ignoring the need for the user to enter a password that SecureNote uses to encrypt and decrypt the notes, so let's address that now. To address password entry, we do the following:

1. Insert a new view and view controller in front of the master view controller that displays a password entry field and a Log In button.

2. When the user attempts to log in, set the `password` field we created in the application delegate to the entered password.

3. If the user has not yet entered a password, accept any input as the official password, store it in the iOS keychain, and segue to the master view.

4. If the user already has a password in the iOS keychain, compare the entered password to the stored password and, only if they match, segue to the master view.

Since we must interface with the iOS keychain, and the keychain API is a nasty mess of C code, we're going to cheat a little and download Sam Soffes's excellent library SSKeychain from `https://github.com/soffes/sskeychain`. Add this library to your project, either through CocoaPods or by cloning the repository and adding the source files. Since we already added the security framework to the project, you should be ready to use SSKeychain once you add the source files.

Adding the Password View Controller

Create a new `UIViewController` class (with no XIB file) called `PasswordViewController` that will control the password view, accept the password input, verify the password entered, and determine whether to segue to the master view. This controller will also be responsible for setting the managed object context in the master view controller to the application's managed object context. The header file, `PasswordViewController.h`, should have an outlet for the password text field so we can extract the password that the user enters, as shown in Listing 7-39.

Listing 7-39. `PasswordViewController.h` with an Outlet for the Password Field

```
#import <UIKit/UIKit.h>

@interface PasswordViewController : UIViewController

@property (weak, nonatomic) IBOutlet UITextField *passwordField;

@end
```

The implementation file, either `PasswordViewController.m` or `PasswordViewController.swift`, overrides two methods.

- `prepareForSegue:sender:`, which allows us to do any preparation before the segue is performed.

- `shouldPerformSegueWithIdentifier:sender:`, which gives us the opportunity to either allow or disallow the segue to be performed.

In `prepareForSegue:sender:`, we grab the managed object context from the application delegate and set it on the Master View Controller.

In `shouldPerformSegueWithIdentifier:sender:`, we make sure the user has actually entered something in the password field. We set whatever the user has entered into the application delegate. Then, we grab the SecureNote password stored in the iOS keychain. If the password from the keychain is blank, we store the password the user entered into the keychain and then allow the segue to be performed by returning YES. If we find a SecureNote password in the keychain, however, we verify it against the password that the user entered and allow the segue to be performed only if they match. Listing 7-40 shows `PasswordViewController.m` and Listing 7-41 shows `PasswordViewController.swift`.

Listing 7-40. PasswordViewController.m

```objc
#import "PasswordViewController.h"
#import "AppDelegate.h"
#import "MasterViewController.h"
#import "SSKeychain.h"

@implementation PasswordViewController

#pragma mark - Navigation

- (void)prepareForSegue:(UIStoryboardSegue *)segue sender:(id)sender {
  if ([segue.identifier isEqualToString:@"logIn"]) {
    // Set the managed object context in the master view controller
    AppDelegate *appDelegate = (AppDelegate *)[[UIApplication sharedApplication] delegate];
    MasterViewController *controller = (MasterViewController *)[segue destinationViewController];
    controller.managedObjectContext = appDelegate.managedObjectContext;
  }
}

- (BOOL)shouldPerformSegueWithIdentifier:(NSString *)identifier sender:(id)sender {
  // Make sure they've entered something in the password field
  NSString *enteredPassword = self.passwordField.text;
  if ([identifier isEqualToString:@"logIn"] && enteredPassword.length > 0) {

    // Store whatever they've entered in the application delegate
    AppDelegate *appDelegate = (AppDelegate *)[[UIApplication sharedApplication] delegate];
    appDelegate.password = enteredPassword;

    // Retrieve the password from the keychain
    NSString *password = [SSKeychain passwordForService:@"SecureNote" account:@"default"];

    // If they've never entered a password, they're creating a new one
    if (password == nil) {
      // Store the password in the keychain and allow segue to be performed
      [SSKeychain setPassword:enteredPassword forService:@"SecureNote" account:@"default"];
      return YES;
    } else {
      // Verify password and allow segue only if verified
      return [password isEqualToString:enteredPassword];
    }
  } else {
    return NO;
  }
}

@end
```

Listing 7-41. PasswordViewController.swift

```swift
import Foundation
import UIKit

class PasswordViewController : UIViewController {
    @IBOutlet weak var passwordField: UITextField!

    override func prepareForSegue(segue: UIStoryboardSegue, sender: AnyObject?) {
        if segue.identifier == "logIn" {
            // Set the managed object context in the master view controller
            let appDelegate = UIApplication.sharedApplication().delegate as AppDelegate
            let controller = segue.destinationViewController as MasterViewController
            controller.managedObjectContext = appDelegate.managedObjectContext
        }
    }

    override func shouldPerformSegueWithIdentifier(identifier: String?, sender:
    AnyObject?) -> Bool {
        // Make sure they've entered something in the password field
        let enteredPassword = self.passwordField.text
        if identifier == "logIn" {
            // Store whatever they've entered in the application delegate
            let appDelegate = UIApplication.sharedApplication().delegate as AppDelegate
            appDelegate.password = enteredPassword

            // Retrieve the password from the keychain
            let password = SSKeychain.passwordForService("SecureNote", account: "default")

            // If they've never entered a password, they're creating a new one
            if password == nil {
                // Store the password in the keychain and allow segue to be performed
                SSKeychain.setPassword(enteredPassword, forService: "SecureNote", account: "default")
                return true
            } else {
                // Verify password and allow segue only if verified
                return password == enteredPassword
            }
        }
        else {
            return false;
        }
    }
}
```

Adding the Password View to the Storyboard

After some fiddling with the storyboard and a tweak to the application delegate code, we'll finally be ready to run SecureNote.

1. First, edit the `application:didFinishLaunchingWithOptions:` method in `AppDelegate.m` or `AppDelegate.swift` to do nothing but return `YES` or `true`, as shown in Listing 7-42 (Objective-C) or Listing 7-43 (Swift).

   Listing 7-42. Removing the Code That Sets the Managed Object Context (Objective-C)

   ```objc
   - (BOOL)application:(UIApplication *)application
   didFinishLaunchingWithOptions:(NSDictionary *)launchOptions {
     return YES;
   }
   ```

   Listing 7-43. Removing the Code That Sets the Managed Object Context (Swift)

   ```swift
   func application(application: UIApplication, didFinishLaunchingWithOptions
   launchOptions: [NSObject: AnyObject]?) -> Bool {
       return true
   }
   ```

2. Now open the storyboard, `Main.storyboard`, and drag a new View Controller between the Navigation Controller and the Master View Controller. You may have to move the Master View Controller and the Detail View Controller to the right to make room.

3. Set the Custom Class in the Identity inspector of your new View Controller to `PasswordViewController`.

4. In the Attributes inspector, set the Title field to Password. Drag a label onto the view and set its text to **Password:**. Drag a Text Field below the label, size it to the width of the view, and connect it to the `passwordField` outlet. Also, in the Attributes inspector, check the **Secure Text Entry** checkbox so that the password is masked as the user types it. Finally, drag a button onto the view, below the password field, and set its text to **Log In**. Add missing constraints from the popup menu.

5. Control+drag from the button to the Master View Controller and, in the pop-up that appears, select **show**, so that tapping this button will initiate the segue to the Master View Controller. Also, with the arrow representing the segue selected, open the Attributes inspector and set the Identifier to **logIn**. Figure 7-6 shows the Password View Controller.

Figure 7-6. The Password View Controller

6. Your last task is to change the segue from the Navigation Controller to point to the Password View Controller. Select the Navigation Controller, open the Connections inspector, and break the connection to the Master View Controller. Then, drag from the circle at the end of the **root view controller** line to the Password View Controller, and the segue will update properly. Your finished storyboard should resemble Figure 7-7.

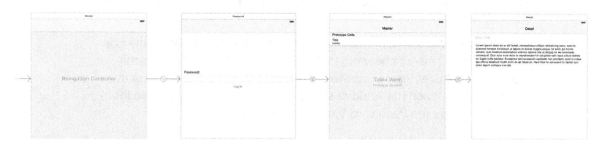

Figure 7-7. The finished storyboard

Running SecureNote

You should now be able to build and run SecureNote. When you run it, you should see the password view. Enter anything to set your password, and then click Log In. You should then be able to tap the + button to add notes or tap existing notes to edit them.

If you rerun the application, you should see the password view again. Entering an incorrect password and tapping Log In should do nothing. Entering the correct password and tapping Log In should take you to the master view with your list of notes.

If you open your SQLite database and look at the data, you should find that the data in the ZBODY and ZTITLE columns in the ZNOTE table contain incomprehensible gobbledygook—the fruits of our encryption transformer.

An Alternative to Transformable: Data Protection

In the previous section, we encrypted data on a field-by-field basis using value transformers and the Common Crypto library. Apple offers another way to encrypt data on an iPhone or iPad using what's called data protection. If you enable data protection on your device, iOS encrypts a portion of its data storage when the device is locked and decrypts it when it's unlocked. To enable data protection, set your device to require a passcode in Settings ➤ Touch ID & Passcode or Settings ➤ Passcode, depending on your device and iOS version. At the very bottom of that settings screen, you should see the following message: "Data protection is enabled." Note that this is available on a device only and not on the iOS Simulator.

Turning on data protection doesn't automatically encrypt all the storage on the device. If you want to encrypt a Core Data data store, you must turn it on by setting an attribute on the persistent store. You do this by passing a dictionary with the value NSFileProtectionComplete for the key NSFileProtectionKey to the setAttributes:ofItemAtPath:error method of NSFileManager. This would look something like Listing 7-44 (Objective-C) or Listing 7-45 (Swift).

Listing 7-44. Setting the Core Data Persistent Store to Use Data Protection (Objective-C)

```
- (NSPersistentStoreCoordinator *)persistentStoreCoordinator {
  if (_persistentStoreCoordinator != nil) {
    return _persistentStoreCoordinator;
  }

  NSURL *storeURL = [[self applicationDocumentsDirectory] URLByAppendingPathComponent:
  @"SecureNote.sqlite"];

  NSError *error = nil;
  _persistentStoreCoordinator = [[NSPersistentStoreCoordinator alloc]
  initWithManagedObjectModel:[self managedObjectModel]];
  if (![_persistentStoreCoordinator addPersistentStoreWithType:NSSQLiteStoreType
  configuration:nil URL:storeURL options:nil error:&error]) {
    NSLog(@"Unresolved error %@, %@", error, [error userInfo]);
    abort();
  }
```

```objc
// Encrypt the persistent store
NSDictionary *fileAttributes = @{ NSFileProtectionKey : NSFileProtectionComplete };
if (![[NSFileManager defaultManager] setAttributes: fileAttributes
                                    ofItemAtPath:[storeURL path]
                                         error:&error]) {
  NSLog(@"Unresolved error with persistent store encryption %@, %@", error, [error userInfo]);
  abort();
}

return _persistentStoreCoordinator;
}
```

Listing 7-45. Setting the Core Data Persistent Store to Use Data Protection (Swift)

```swift
lazy var persistentStoreCoordinator: NSPersistentStoreCoordinator? = {
    var coordinator: NSPersistentStoreCoordinator? =
    NSPersistentStoreCoordinator(managedObjectModel: self.managedObjectModel)
    let url = self.applicationDocumentsDirectory.URLByAppendingPathComponent("SecureNoteSwift.sqlite")
    var error: NSError? = nil
    var failureReason = "There was an error creating or loading the application's saved data."
    if coordinator!.addPersistentStoreWithType(NSSQLiteStoreType, configuration: nil, URL: url,
    options: nil, error: &error) == nil {
        coordinator = nil
        // Report any error we got.
        let dict = NSMutableDictionary()
        dict[NSLocalizedDescriptionKey] = "Failed to initialize the application's saved data"
        dict[NSLocalizedFailureReasonErrorKey] = failureReason
        dict[NSUnderlyingErrorKey] = error
        error = NSError.errorWithDomain("YOUR_ERROR_DOMAIN", code: 9999, userInfo: dict)
        NSLog("Unresolved error \(error), \(error!.userInfo)")
        abort()
    }

    // Encrypt the persistent store
    let fileAttributes = [NSFileProtectionKey : NSFileProtectionComplete]
    if !NSFileManager.defaultManager().setAttributes(fileAttributes, ofItemAtPath: url.path!,
    error: &error) {
      NSLog("Unresolved error with persistent store encryption \(error), \(error!.userInfo)")
      abort()
    }

    return coordinator
}()
```

When you run your application on a device that has data protection enabled, the persistent store's database file will be automatically encrypted when the device is locked. This method is cheap to implement, but understand that once the device is unlocked, the file is automatically decrypted so the database is as secure as the device. If someone can guess the passcode, the database will be accessible, especially if the device is jail broken (i.e., root access is available). Another inconvenience with this encryption method is that for very large databases, the time required to unlock and start your application might be rather large since a huge file will need to be decrypted before it can be used.

Summary

In this chapter we saw value transformers and how to use them to extend Core Data to be able to store any data type. If our data type supports the NSCoding protocol, as UIColor does, we saw that we don't even need to provide a customer value transformer class. Even when our data type doesn't support the NSCoding protocol, we see how simple adding a custom value transformer can be to allow us to simply read and write any data type into and out of a Core Data store.

We also saw how to use the data protection built in to iOS by setting attributes on our Core Data store file.

With this knowledge, we can protect our applications' data from prying eyes, and perhaps even the NSA!

Chapter 8

Talking to Services: iCloud and Dropbox

With iOS 5, Apple introduced iCloud sync for Core Data. iOS developers rejoiced at the prospect of a drop-in solution for synching data among iPhone apps, iPad apps, and Mac OS X apps. Then they started using iCloud to sync Core Data data stores . . . and tears replaced the joy. Sync, as it turns out, is a hard problem to solve, and Apple hasn't nailed it yet—at least for Core Data. As Apple iterates through the sync technology, however, it will likely get Core Data sync over iCloud working correctly in a future release of the SDK. So that you can have the information, we present the information for using iCloud Core Data sync in this chapter.

Other Core Data synching solutions have emerged, including libraries like ParcelKit (`https://github.com/overcommitted/ParcelKit`), Ensembles (`www.ensembles.io/`), and TICoreDataSync (`http://timisted.github.io/TICoreDataSync/`). We encourage you to investigate these solutions and refer to their respective documentation on their web sites, to see whether these are a better fit for you and your apps. We don't replicate that documentation or cover all these libraries in this book. We do, however, explore the sync solution offered by Dropbox, as well as the aforementioned ParcelKit, which syncs Core Data over Dropbox.

Integrating with iCloud

While early versions of iCloud Core Data sync required some cerebral contortions to get anything to somewhat work, iOS 7 makes iCloud sync a lot simpler to manage. In this section, we build a simple app using one of Xcode's templates and we use iCloud to sync data to the cloud. To get started, create a new project in Xcode using the Master-Detail Application template as shown in Figure 8-1.

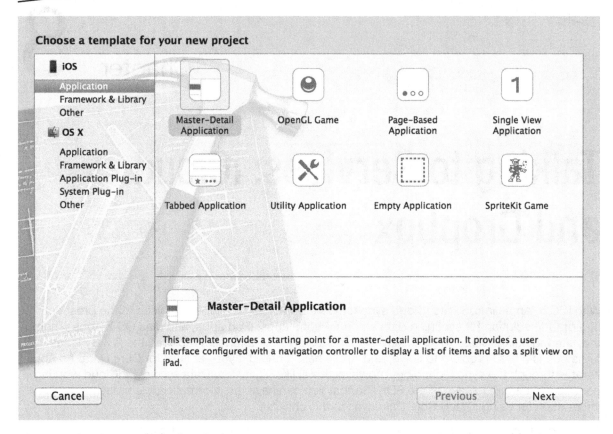

Figure 8-1. Creating a master-detail application

On the next screen, name your app **iCloudApp**, select iPhone for the device and be sure to check the Use Core Data checkbox. At this point, we have a very simple app that uses a local Core Data store. You can launch the app to try it out.

TIP   If you haven't already done so, now is a good time to enable iCloud in the iOS simulator. In the iOS simulator, launch the Settings app and select the iCloud option. Enter your credentials and sign in.

Using iCloud's Ubiquity Container

In this subsection, we tell iOS that the data store file needs to be saved in iCloud, in what's called a ubiquity container. Open AppDelegate.m or AppDelegate.swift and look at the persistentStoreCoordinator method shown in Listing 8-1 (Objective-C) and Listing 8-2 (Swift).

Listing 8-1. The Default persistentStoreCoordinator *Method (Objective-C)*

```objc
- (NSPersistentStoreCoordinator *)persistentStoreCoordinator {
    // The persistent store coordinator for the application. This implementation creates and return
    a coordinator, having added the store for the application to it.
    if (_persistentStoreCoordinator != nil) {
        return _persistentStoreCoordinator;
    }

    // Create the coordinator and store

    _persistentStoreCoordinator = [[NSPersistentStoreCoordinator alloc] initWithManagedObjectModel:[
    self managedObjectModel]];
    NSURL *storeURL = [[self applicationDocumentsDirectory] URLByAppendingPathComponent:@"iCloudApp.sqlite"];
    NSError *error = nil;
    NSString *failureReason = @"There was an error creating or loading the application's saved data.";
    if (![_persistentStoreCoordinator addPersistentStoreWithType:NSSQLiteStoreType
    configuration:nil URL:storeURL options:nil error:&error]) {
        // Report any error we got.
        NSMutableDictionary *dict = [NSMutableDictionary dictionary];
        dict[NSLocalizedDescriptionKey] = @"Failed to initialize the application's saved data";
        dict[NSLocalizedFailureReasonErrorKey] = failureReason;
        dict[NSUnderlyingErrorKey] = error;
        error = [NSError errorWithDomain:@"YOUR_ERROR_DOMAIN" code:9999 userInfo:dict];
        // Replace this with code to handle the error appropriately.
        // abort() causes the application to generate a crash log and terminate. You should not use
        this function in a shipping application, although it may be useful during development.
        NSLog(@"Unresolved error %@, %@", error, [error userInfo]);
        abort();
    }

    return _persistentStoreCoordinator;
}
```

Listing 8-2. The Default persistentStoreCoordinator *Method (Swift)*

```swift
lazy var persistentStoreCoordinator: NSPersistentStoreCoordinator? = {
    // The persistent store coordinator for the application. This implementation creates and return
    a coordinator, having added the store for the application to it. This property is optional since
    there are legitimate error conditions that could cause the creation of the store to fail.
    // Create the coordinator and store
    var coordinator: NSPersistentStoreCoordinator? = NSPersistentStoreCoordinator(managedObjectModel:
    self.managedObjectModel)
    let url = self.applicationDocumentsDirectory.URLByAppendingPathComponent("iCloudAppSwift.sqlite")
    var error: NSError? = nil
    var failureReason = "There was an error creating or loading the application's saved data."
    if coordinator!.addPersistentStoreWithType(NSSQLiteStoreType, configuration: nil, URL: url,
    options: nil, error: &error) == nil {
        coordinator = nil
```

```
        // Report any error we got.
        let dict = NSMutableDictionary()
        dict[NSLocalizedDescriptionKey] = "Failed to initialize the application's saved data"
        dict[NSLocalizedFailureReasonErrorKey] = failureReason
        dict[NSUnderlyingErrorKey] = error
        error = NSError(domain: "YOUR_ERROR_DOMAIN", code: 9999, userInfo: dict)
        // Replace this with code to handle the error appropriately.
        // abort() causes the application to generate a crash log and terminate. You should not use
        this function in a shipping application, although it may be useful during development.
        NSLog("Unresolved error \(error), \(error!.userInfo)")
        abort()
    }

    return coordinator
}()
```

In order to add the integration with iCloud, we need tell Core Data that the store file needs to be synced. Update the method to pass an options dictionary to the addPersistentStoreWithType call, as shown in Listing 8-3 (Objective-C) or Listing 8-4 (Swift).

Listing 8-3. *The* persistentStoreCoordinator *Method Updated for iCloud Sync (Objective-C)*

```
if (![_persistentStoreCoordinator addPersistentStoreWithType:NSSQLiteStoreType configuration:nil
URL:storeURL options:@{ NSPersistentStoreUbiquitousContentNameKey : @"iCloudApp" } error:&error]) {
```

Listing 8-4. *The persistentStoreCoordinator Method Updated for iCloud Sync (Swift)*

```
let options = [NSPersistentStoreUbiquitousContentNameKey: "iCloudAppSwift"]
if coordinator!.addPersistentStoreWithType(NSSQLiteStoreType, configuration: nil, URL: url, options:
options, error: &error) == nil {
```

The only change is to set the NSPersistentStoreUbiquitousContentNameKey as an option of the persistent store coordinator. A ubiquity container is a component that automatically manages syncing files with iCloud. It's a local representation of the iCloud data and sits on the file system outside your app's sandbox. By setting this option, you tell Core Data that the persistent store file resides in a ubiquity container and is therefore synced with iCloud.

If you launched iCloudApp before, delete it from the iPhone Simulator so that any SQLite database files are removed. Then, launch the app. You'll notice that not much has changed—it starts just normally. What is different, however, is the location of the data store file. If you open the Terminal application and navigate to the Documents folder of the app, you will notice that there is no iCloudApp.sqlite file.

Instead, there is a CoreDataUbiquitySupport directory that was created by iOS to attach your file to the ubiquity container. If you navigate through this directory, you will find your SQLite file buried deep in the file structure.

```
find "$HOME/Library/Developer/CoreSimulator" -name "iCloudApp.sqlite"
```

Synching Content

At this point, we have an application that saves its data store in iCloud. This is a great solution for keeping a backup of the data, but not so good if you are using your app on multiple devices. Unfortunately, the cloud will retain only the data saved by the last device you used, possibly overwriting what was saved by other devices you used.

In order for your code to synchronize data across devices, you subscribe to the notifications that Core Data sends for iCloud synching. Table 8-1 lists these notifications.

Table 8-1. Available Notification Types

Notification type	Description
NSPersistentStoreUbiquitousTransition TypeAccountAdded	Sent when a new iCloud account was added while the app was running. This is useful to transition a store to the new account.
NSPersistentStoreUbiquitousTransition TypeAccountRemoved	Sent when the existing iCloud account was removed from the device while the app was running. This tells you that the persistent store is transitioning to local storage.
NSPersistentStoreUbiquitousTransition TypeContentRemoved	Sent when the user clears the contents of the iCloud account, usually using Delete All from Documents & Data in Settings. The Core Data integration will transition to an empty store file as a result of this event.
NSPersistentStoreUbiquitousTransition TypeInitialImportCompleted	Sent when Core Data has finished building a store file that is consistent with the contents of the iCloud account.

You can make sure your app reacts to changes in iCloud in order to merge everything correctly by using the store notifications.

Open AppDelegate.m or AppDelegate.swift and add the appropriate notifications to the persistentStoreCoordinator method right after creating the persistent store, but right before adding it to the coordinator. The method should look like Listing 8-5 (Objective-C) or Listing 8-6 (Swift).

Listing 8-5. Adding the iCloud Notifications to the persistentStoreCoordinator Method (Objective-C)

```
...
_persistentStoreCoordinator = [[NSPersistentStoreCoordinator alloc]
initWithManagedObjectModel:[self managedObjectModel]];
NSURL *storeURL = [[self applicationDocumentsDirectory]
URLByAppendingPathComponent:@"iCloudApp.sqlite"];
NSError *error = nil;
NSString *failureReason = @"There was an error creating or loading the application's saved data.";
```

```objc
// iCloud notification subscriptions
NSNotificationCenter *notificationCenter = [NSNotificationCenter defaultCenter];
[notificationCenter addObserver:self selector:@selector(storeWillChange:) name:NSPersistentStoreCoor
dinatorStoresWillChangeNotification object:_persistentStoreCoordinator];
[notificationCenter addObserver:self selector:@selector(storeDidChange:) name:NSPersistentStoreCoord
inatorStoresDidChangeNotification object:_persistentStoreCoordinator];
[notificationCenter addObserver:self selector:@selector(storeDidImportUbiquitousContentChanges:)
name:NSPersistentStoreDidImportUbiquitousContentChangesNotification
object:_persistentStoreCoordinator];

if (![_persistentStoreCoordinator addPersistentStoreWithType:NSSQLiteStoreType configuration:nil
URL:storeURL options:@{ NSPersistentStoreUbiquitousContentNameKey : @"iCloudApp" } error:&error])
{
...
```

Listing 8-6. Adding the iCloud Notifications to the persistentStoreCoordinator Function (Swift)

```swift
...
var coordinator: NSPersistentStoreCoordinator? = NSPersistentStoreCoordinator(managedObjectModel:
self.managedObjectModel)
let url = self.applicationDocumentsDirectory.URLByAppendingPathComponent("iCloudAppSwift.sqlite")
var error: NSError? = nil
var failureReason = "There was an error creating or loading the application's saved data."

let notificationCenter = NSNotificationCenter.defaultCenter()
notificationCenter.addObserver(self, selector: "storeWillChange:",
    name: NSPersistentStoreCoordinatorStoresWillChangeNotification,
    object: coordinator!)
notificationCenter.addObserver(self, selector: "storeDidChange:",
    name: NSPersistentStoreCoordinatorStoresDidChangeNotification,
    object: coordinator!)
notificationCenter.addObserver(self, selector: "storeDidImportUbiquitousContentChanges:",
    name: NSPersistentStoreDidImportUbiquitousContentChangesNotification,
    object: coordinator!)

let options = [NSPersistentStoreUbiquitousContentNameKey: "iCloudAppSwift"]
if coordinator!.addPersistentStoreWithType(NSSQLiteStoreType, configuration: nil, URL: url, options:
options, error: &error) == nil {
...
```

Of course, you must create the three new methods referred to by the notification selectors in order to remove compilation warnings (and ultimately runtime exceptions). Still in AppDelegate.m or AppDelegate.swift, add the methods shown in Listing 8-7 (Objective-C) or Listing 8-8 (Swift).

Listing 8-7. Handling iCloud Notifications (Objective-C)

```objc
- (void)storeDidImportUbiquitousContentChanges:(NSNotification*)notification {
}

- (void)storeWillChange:(NSNotification*)notification {
}

- (void)storeDidChange:(NSNotification*)notification {
}
```

Listing 8-8. Handling iCloud Notifications (Swift)

```swift
func storeDidImportUbiquitousContentChanges(notification: NSNotification) {
}

func storeWillChange(notification: NSNotification) {
}

func storeDidChange(notification: NSNotification) {
}
```

Leaving these methods empty won't do much, of course. In the next section we fill out these methods to merge content from iCloud.

Merging Content from iCloud

When data change on another device that uses the same iCloud account as the device you are currently using, the app needs to know and be able to incorporate the new content from the cloud with its current content. Its current content might also include newly created content that iCloud doesn't even know about yet. You merge changes between a device and iCloud in your handler for the NSPersistentStoreDidImportUbiquitousContentChangesNotification notification. Modify the storeDidImportUbiquitousContentChanges method as shown in Listing 8-9 (Objective-C) or Listing 8-10 (Swift) to do the merges.

Listing 8-9. The storeDidImportUbiquitousContentChanges Method Updated for iCloud Sync (Objective-C)

```objc
- (void)storeDidImportUbiquitousContentChanges:(NSNotification*)notification {
  NSLog(@"%@", notification.userInfo.description);

  NSManagedObjectContext *moc = self.managedObjectContext;
  [moc performBlock:^{
    // Merge the content
    [moc mergeChangesFromContextDidSaveNotification:notification];
  }];

  dispatch_async(dispatch_get_main_queue(), ^{
    // Refresh the UI here
  });
}
```

Listing 8-10. The storeDidImportUbiquitousContentChanges Function Updated for iCloud Sync (Swift)

```swift
func storeDidImportUbiquitousContentChanges(notification: NSNotification) {
    print("did import: \(notification.userInfo?.description)")

    if let moc = self.managedObjectContext {
        moc.performBlock({ () -> Void in
            // Merge the content
            moc.mergeChangesFromContextDidSaveNotification(notification)
        })
```

```
        dispatch_async(dispatch_get_main_queue()) {
            // Refresh UI here
        }
    }
}
```

In this method, we simply call mergeChangesFromContextDidSaveNotification: on the managed object context and let Core Data deal with merging. We do this using the performBlock: method so that the change is done asynchronously on the context's queue rather than on the main queue so as to not degrade the user interface responsiveness.

Finally, if necessary, we can refresh the user interface (UI). If your application is showing views that need to be modified because the data they are showing depends on the data that were changed, this is a good place to invoke a UI refresh.

Dealing with iCloud Account Changes

If your application is running while changes are made to the iCloud configuration—for example, if you enable iCloud—then you should handle the potential changes that the configuration changes may cause. To handle such changes, react to notifications indicating persistent store changes inside both storeWillChange: and storeDidChange:. Update the code in these methods as shown in Listing 8-11 (Objective-C) or Listing 8-12 (Swift).

Listing 8-11. Handling Changes to the iCloud Account (Objective-C)

```objc
- (void)storeWillChange:(NSNotification *)notification {
  NSLog(@"%@", notification.userInfo.description);
  NSManagedObjectContext *moc = self.managedObjectContext;
  [moc performBlockAndWait:^{
    NSError *error = nil;
    if ([moc hasChanges]) {
      [moc save:&error];
    }

    [moc reset];
  }];

  // This is a good place to let your UI know it needs to get ready
  // to adjust to the change and deal with new data. This might include
  // invalidating UI caches, reloading data, resetting views, etc...
}

- (void)storeDidChange:(NSNotification *)notification {
  NSLog(@"%@", notification.userInfo.description);
  // At this point it's official, the change has happened. Tell your
  // user interface to refresh itself
  dispatch_async(dispatch_get_main_queue(), ^{
    // Refresh the UI here
  });
}
```

Listing 8-12. Handling Changes to the iCloud Account (Swift)

```swift
func storeWillChange(notification: NSNotification) {
    print("will change: \(notification.userInfo?.description)")

    if let moc = self.managedObjectContext {
        moc.performBlockAndWait({ () -> Void in
            var error: NSError? = nil
            if moc.hasChanges {
                moc.save(&error)
            }

            moc.reset()
        })
    }
}

func storeDidChange(notification: NSNotification) {
    print("did change: \(notification.userInfo?.description)")
    // At this point it's official, the change has happened. Tell your
    // user interface to refresh itself
    dispatch_async(dispatch_get_main_queue()) {
        NSFetchedResultsController.deleteCacheWithName("Master")
        // Refresh UI here
    }
}
```

It's often better to prepare the UI for the change as early as possible to reduce the time it takes to actually apply the refresh. For this reason, the notifications are broken down into two phases you are probably already familiar with (change will happen and change did happen).

In our `storeWillChange:` implementation, we save the managed object context (if it has changes) and then reset its state, which discards all its managed objects. This is the point at which you'd prepare your UI to change.

In our `storeDidChange:` implementation, we asynchronously update the UI.

Your code is now ready to deal with iCloud integration. Before you can submit your application to Apple, you will need to add the iCloud entitlement to your app. You do this from within Xcode by selecting the project and going to the Capabilities tab. In that tab, you see a section for iCloud with a switch beside it. Turn on that switch, as shown in Figure 8-2, to add the iCloud entitlement to your app.

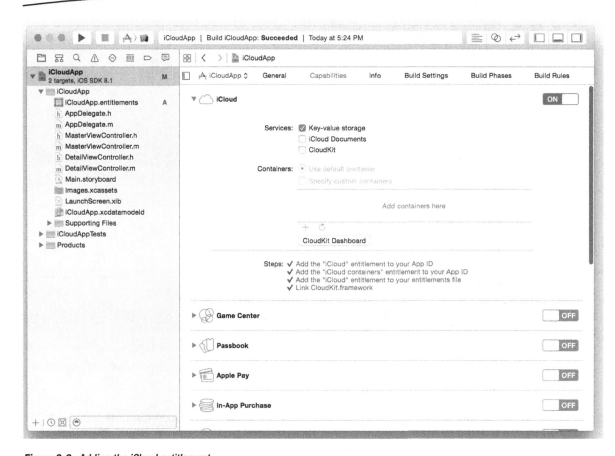

Figure 8-2. Adding the iCloud entitlement

Integrating with Dropbox Datastore API

With iOS, a lot of attention is often given to integrating with iCloud for persistence. Other solutions, however, might make sense for you depending on your app and your target audience. Dropbox has released its Datastore application programming interface (API), which allows you to use its cloud service as a ubiquitous data store. One of the obvious advantages of using Dropbox, rather than iCloud, is that Dropbox has APIs for multiple platforms. The Dropbox Datastore API doesn't function like Core Data. It is not meant to act as a relational database where you create links between resources. Instead, it is a simple key/value pair store much like NoSQL databases such as MongoDB or Cassandra. One essential particularity is that is allows you to work without a schema, and therefore you need not worry so much about schema updates and migrations.

Setting Up the API Access

For iOS, the setup instructions are located at www.dropbox.com/developers/datastore/sdks/ios. The first step in setting up Dropbox with your app is to create a Dropbox app on the Dropbox web site. Log in to your Dropbox account and go to www.dropbox.com/developers/apps to create a new app. Select **Dropbox API app** and **Datastores only**, and choose a name for your app. For the name, be sure to not infringe on the Dropbox branding guidelines. In particular, don't use "Dropbox" or something like it in the name of the app. The name must be unique across all Dropbox apps, so you'll have to choose something other than "iOSPersistenceApp," which is what we chose (see Figure 8-3).

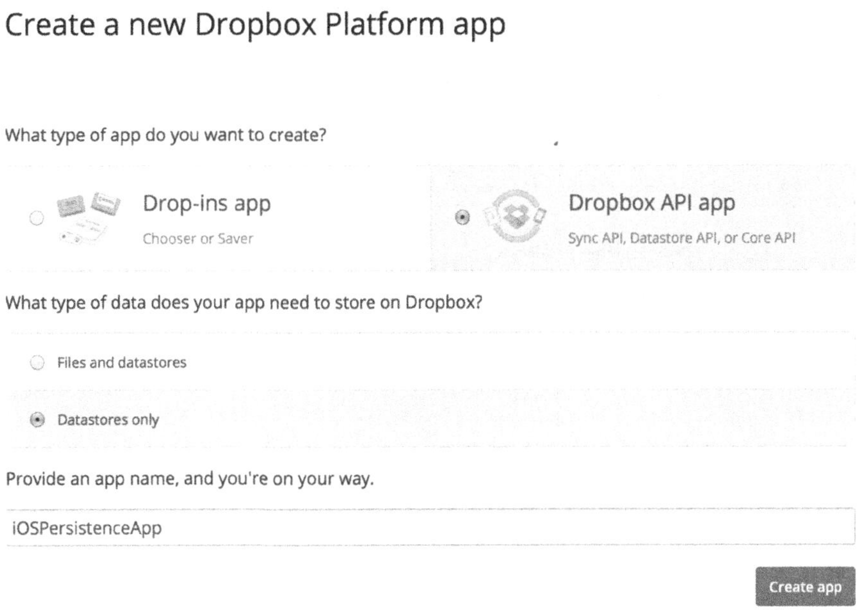

Create a new Dropbox Platform app

What type of app do you want to create?

○ Drop-ins app
Chooser or Saver

◉ Dropbox API app
Sync API, Datastore API, or Core API

What type of data does your app need to store on Dropbox?

○ Files and datastores

◉ Datastores only

Provide an app name, and you're on your way.

iOSPersistenceApp

Create app

Figure 8-3. *Creating a Dropbox application*

Once you create the app, the next screen shows you your app key and app secret, which you'll need in the code for your app to be able to communicate with Dropbox. The app secret, as its name implies, should be kept secret.

We're now ready to create our new application.

Creating a Blank App to Use with Dropbox

Since we're now trying to use Dropbox as our persistence framework, we will leave Core Data alone for a while.

1. In Xcode, create a new Single View Application called DropboxPersistenceApp and don't select the Core Data check box.

2. Once Xcode has created your app, add the Dropbox framework to the app. To do so, download it from Dropbox's site (www.dropbox.com/developers/datastore/sdks/ios) and unzip the downloaded file to a temporary directory. Then, drag and drop Dropbox.framework onto your Xcode project, below the Products folder.

3.   In the sheet that appears, be sure to check **Copy items if needed** before clicking Finish.

4.   Then, add to your project the other frameworks that the Dropbox SDK requires: CFNetwork.framework, Security.framework, SystemConfiguration. framework, QuartzCore.framework, libc++.dylib, and libz.dylib.

Your project structure should look like Figure 8-4.

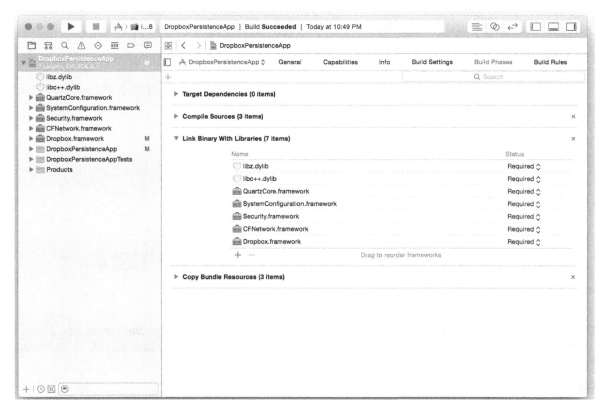

Figure 8-4. *Adding the Dropbox framework to the app*

Configuring the Callback URL

For your app to authenticate against Dropbox, your app cedes control to the Dropbox authentication controller that the Dropbox SDK provides. This authentication controller shows the Dropbox login screen and, on successfully authenticating a user, returns control to your application by calling back via uniform resource locator (URL). Your app must register itself as a handler for that URL's scheme, so that iOS can properly hand control back to your app.

To register your app as a handler for the URL scheme, go to Xcode, select your project under TARGETS, and go to the Info tab. Expand the URL Types section and press the + button to create a new URL type. In the URL Schemes field, enter **db-APP_KEY**, but replace APP_KEY with the app key Dropbox gave you when you created the app. It should look something like **db-vp4jwudouxvhzz9**. Leave the other fields as they are. When your app is installed, whether in the simulator or on an actual device, it will properly register itself.

Linking to Dropbox Using the Datastore API

For your code to use the Dropbox Datastore API, it must initialize the store manager, a DBStoreManager instance. A good place to perform this initialization is in your app delegate. Open AppDelegate.m if you're building this project in Objective-C and add two import directives:

```
#import "TargetConditionals.h"
#import <Dropbox/Dropbox.h>
```

Then edit the application: didFinishLaunchingWithOptions: method to add the Dropbox Datastore initialization. Listing 8-13 shows the Objective-C version, and Listing 8-14 shows the Swift version.

Listing 8-13. Initializing the Dropbox Datastore API (Objective-C)

```
DBAccountManager *accountManager = [[DBAccountManager alloc]
                          initWithAppKey:@"APP_KEY" secret:@"APP_SECRET"];
[DBAccountManager setSharedManager:accountManager];
```

Listing 8-14. Initializing the Dropbox Datastore API (Swift)

```
let accountManager = DBAccountManager(appKey: "APP_KEY", secret: "APP_SECRET")
DBAccountManager.setSharedManager(accountManager)
```

Be sure to replace APP_KEY and APP_SECRET with the values given to you by Dropbox when you created your app on the Dropbox web site.

Once this configuration is done, we need to worry about letting the user link their Dropbox account through the app. We provide the mechanism for the user to link to Dropbox in the view controller to our app by doing the following:

1. In ViewController.h, (if you're doing this in Objective-C) add the declaration of the method that will handle a tap to launch the Dropbox login window, as shown in Listing 8-15.

2. Implement that method in ViewController.m, as shown in Listing 8-16, or in ViewController.swift, as shown in Listing 8-17. Also, for the Objective-C version, add import statement in ViewController.m for "TargetConditionals.h" and <Dropbox/Dropbox.h>.

3. In Interface Builder, add a button with the label "Link to Dropbox" to the application's view in Main.storyboard and connect it, through the Touch Up Inside event, to the didPressLink method.

Listing 8-15. Declaring the Event Handler in `ViewController.h`

```
- (IBAction)didPressLink;
```

Listing 8-16: Handling the Button Tap to Log In to Dropbox (Objective-C)

```
- (IBAction)didPressLink {
  DBAccount *linkedAccount = [[DBAccountManager sharedManager] linkedAccount];
  if (linkedAccount) {
    NSLog(@"App already linked");
  }
  else {
    [[DBAccountManager sharedManager] linkFromController:self];
  }
}
```

Listing 8-17: Handling the Button Tap to Log In to Dropbox (Swift)

```
@IBAction func didPressLink(sender: AnyObject) {
    if let linkedAccount = DBAccountManager.sharedManager().linkedAccount {
        println("App already linked")
    }
    else {
        DBAccountManager.sharedManager().linkFromController(self)
    }
}
```

Now you are ready to launch the app. Once you do, you can tap the Link to Dropbox button and the Dropbox login screen appears. You can sign in with your own Dropbox credentials (note that this screen also handles two-factor authentication if you have that set in Dropbox), and control will return to our app. Unfortunately, our app doesn't know quite what to do when control comes back from the Dropbox login screen. That is because the Dropbox login screen is performing a callback to our application, and that callback is done through the URL we set up earlier. We must instruct our app to handle the callback and open from that URL. In order to do this, implement `application: openURL: sourceApplication:annotation:` in AppDelegate.m or `AppDelegate.swift`, as shown in Listing 8-18 (Objective-C) or Listing 8-19 (Swift).

Listing 8-18. Handling the URL Callback in `AppDelegate.m`

```
- (BOOL)application:(UIApplication *)application openURL:(NSURL *)url sourceApplication:(NSString *)
sourceApplication annotation:(id)annotation {
  DBAccount *account = [[DBAccountManager sharedManager] handleOpenURL:url];
  if (account) {
    NSLog(@"App linked successfully from %@", sourceApplication);
    return YES;
  }
  return NO;
}
```

Listing 8-19. Handling the URL Callback in `AppDelegate.swift`

```swift
func application(application: UIApplication, openURL url: NSURL, sourceApplication: String,
annotation: AnyObject?) -> Bool {
    let account = DBAccountManager.sharedManager().handleOpenURL(url)
    if let account = account {
        println("App linked successfully from \(sourceApplication)")
        return true
    }
    return false
}
```

This is where you will want to update your UI to show that the Dropbox account is now linked and prepare the application to continue with Dropbox connectivity enabled. We do this in the next section.

Creating and Synching Data with the Dropbox API

Now that we've got our application linked to Dropbox, let's do something with the Dropbox Persistence API. Declare a button property in ViewController.h for the Objective-C version, as shown in Listing 8-20, and then connect it in Interface Builder to the Link to Dropbox button. This way, we can alter its text appropriately to reflect the connection status to Dropbox.

Listing 8-20. Declaring the Button in `ViewController.h`

```objectivec
@property (weak, nonatomic) IBOutlet UIButton *theButton;
```

In AppDelegate.m or AppDelegate.swift, change the application: openURL:sourceApplication:ann otation: method to look like Listing 8-21 (Objective-C) or Listing 8-22 (Swift) to set the button's text to "Store" after successfully linking to Dropbox. For the Objective-C AppDelegate.m, add an import for ViewController.h.

Listing 8-21 Setting the Button's Title to "Store" in `AppDelegate.m`

```objectivec
- (BOOL)application:(UIApplication *)application openURL:(NSURL *)url sourceApplication:(NSString *)
sourceApplication annotation:(id)annotation {
  DBAccount *account = [[DBAccountManager sharedManager] handleOpenURL:url];
  if (account) {
    NSLog(@"App linked successfully from %@", sourceApplication);

    ViewController *rvc = (ViewController*)self.window.rootViewController;
    [rvc.theButton setTitle:@"Store" forState:UIControlStateNormal];

    return YES;
  }
  return NO;
}
```

Listing 8-22. Setting the Button's Title to "Store" in AppDelegate.swift

```swift
func application(application: UIApplication, openURL url: NSURL, sourceApplication: String,
annotation: AnyObject?) -> Bool {
    let account = DBAccountManager.sharedManager().handleOpenURL(url)
    if let account = account {
        println("App linked successfully from \(sourceApplication)")

        let controller = self.window?.rootViewController as? ViewController
        controller?.theButton?.setTitle("Store", forState: .Normal)

        return true
    }
    return false
}
```

Then, for consistency, edit the viewDidLoad method in ViewController.m or ViewController.swift
to set the label of the button to the current link state, as shown in Listing 8-23 (Objective-C) or
Listing 8-24 (Swift).

Listing 8-23. Setting the Button Text in ViewController.m

```objc
- (void)viewDidLoad {
  [super viewDidLoad];

  if ([[DBAccountManager sharedManager] linkedAccount]) {
    [self.theButton setTitle:@"Store" forState:UIControlStateNormal];
  }
  else {
    [self.theButton setTitle:@"Link Dropbox" forState:UIControlStateNormal];
  }
}
```

Listing 8-24. Setting the Button Text in ViewController.swift

```swift
override func viewDidLoad() {
    super.viewDidLoad()

    if let linkedAccount = DBAccountManager.sharedManager().linkedAccount {
        self.theButton?.setTitle("Store", forState: .Normal)
    }
    else {
        self.theButton?.setTitle("Link Dropbox", forState: .Normal)
    }
}
```

Of course, at this point we haven't stored anything and if you run the app, link to Dropbox, and then
press the "Store" button, all you will get is a message in the log saying the account is already linked.
That is because in our event handling of the button touches, we don't do anything else but try to link
to Dropbox. So let's change that.

In ViewController.m or ViewController.swift, add a private property that will contain a reference to our Dropbox data store, as shown in Listing 8-25 (Objective-C) or Listing 8-26 (Swift).

Listing 8-25. A Private Property for the Dropbox Data Store in ViewController.m

```
@interface ViewController ()
@property (nonatomic, strong) DBDatastore* datastore;
@end
```

Listing 8-26. A Property for the Dropbox Data Store in ViewController.swift

```
var datastore: DBDatastore?
```

The DBDatastore property represents the data container that will automatically be synced with Dropbox. As long as you keep an instance of it in your app, the data store will sync automatically.

Now you can edit the didPressLink: method to behave differently if the account is already linked, as shown in Listing 8-27 (Objective-C) or Listing 8-28 (Swift). As its comments describe, this updated method does the following:

- Creates a data store in Dropbox if one doesn't already exist

- Gets a handle to the Notes table, creating it if necessary

- Creates a new note with the current date as its text and stores it in Dropbox

- Syncs the data store

Listing 8-27. Create a Note in Dropbox (Objective-C)

```
- (IBAction)didPressLink {
  DBAccount *linkedAccount = [[DBAccountManager sharedManager] linkedAccount];
  if (linkedAccount) {
    // If there isn't a store yet, make one
    if (!self.datastore) self.datastore = [DBDatastore openDefaultStoreForAccount:linkedAccount
    error:nil];

    // Create or get a handle to the Notes table if it already exists
    DBTable *notes = [self.datastore getTable:@"Notes"];

    // Make a new note to store. In a normal app, this comes from typed text. To keep things
    // simple, we just manufacture the text with a timestamp
    NSDate *now = [NSDate date];
    NSString *noteText = [NSDateFormatter localizedStringFromDate:now
dateStyle:NSDateFormatterShortStyle
timeStyle:NSDateFormatterFullStyle];

    // Insert the new note into the table
    [notes insert:@{ @"details": noteText, @"createDate": now, @"encrypted": @NO }];

    NSLog(@"Inserted new note: %@", noteText);
```

```
    // Make sure to tell Dropbox to sync the store
    [self.datastore sync:nil];
  }
  else {
    [[DBAccountManager sharedManager] linkFromController:self];
  }
}
```

Listing 8-28. Create a Note in Dropbox (Swift)

```swift
@IBAction func didPressLink(sender: AnyObject) {
    if let linkedAccount = DBAccountManager.sharedManager().linkedAccount {
        // if there isn't a store yet, make one
        if self.datastore == nil {
            self.datastore = DBDatastore.openDefaultStoreForAccount(linkedAccount, error: nil)
        }

        // Create or get a handle to the Notes table if it already exists
        let notes = datastore?.getTable("Notes")

        // Make a new note to store. In a normal app, this comes from typed text. To keep things
        // simple, we just manufacture the text with a timestamp
        let now = NSDate()
        let noteText = NSDateFormatter.localizedStringFromDate(now, dateStyle: .ShortStyle,
        timeStyle: .FullStyle)

        // Insert the new note into the table
        notes?.insert(["details": noteText, "createDate": now, "encrypted": false])

        println("Inserted new note \(noteText)")

        // Make sure to tell Dropbox to sync the store
        datastore?.sync(nil)
    }
    else {
        DBAccountManager.sharedManager().linkFromController(self)
    }
}
```

At this point, you can run the app and after you've linked to Dropbox, every time you press the "Store" button, a new note is added into your data store. You can even verify that everything went well using Dropbox's web view at www.dropbox.com/developers/apps/datastores. You should see the app you created with a link to browse the data store. If you click the Browse link, you should see a listing of the notes you've created from the app.

Of course, you can always query the data store in your application code to get your records back. For example, to get all the notes in the Notes table, you'd write code like that shown in Listing 8-29 (Objective-C) or Listing 8-30 (Swift).

Listing 8-29. Retrieving All the Notes (Objective-C)

```
NSError *error;
DBTable *notes = [self.datastore getTable:@"Notes"];
NSArray *myNotes = [notes query:nil error:&error];
```

Listing 8-30. Retrieving All the Notes (Swift)

```
var error: DBError?
let notes = datastore?.getTable("Notes")
let myNotes = notes?.query(nil, error: &error)
```

Notice that the parameter we passed for query is nil, so the data store will return all records in the Notes table. The query parameter takes an NSDictionary (Objective-C) or AnyObject (Swift) instance to filter the result set it returns. We can filter the results by passing a dictionary object with the fields specified that we want to filter on. Suppose, for example, that some of the records we put into the Notes table are encrypted—that is, the dictionary passed to insert: has @"encrypted" set to @YES. To retrieve only those records, we'd use code like that shown in Listing 8-31 (Objective-C) or Listing 8-32 (Swift).

Listing 8-31. Filtering the Result Set (Objective-C)

```
NSError *error;
DBTable *notes = [self.datastore getTable:@"Notes"];
NSArray *myNotes = [notes query:@{ @"encrypted": @YES } error:&error];
```

Listing 8-32. Filtering the Result Set (Swift)

```
var error: DBError?
let notes = datastore?.getTable("Notes")
let myNotes = notes?.query([ "encrypted": true ], error: &error)
```

You could, of course, set multiple values in the dictionary to filter on multiple keys.

Using Core Data with the Dropbox Datastore API: ParcelKit

We've seen how iCloud can be used to back up and sync Core Data stores. We've also seen how Dropbox's Datastore API can be used as a schema-less store. In this section, we look at how the Datastore API can be used as a substitute for iCloud with your Core Data store. For this, we use the ParcelKit library (https://github.com/overcommitted/ParcelKit).

In order to illustrate the complete process, we start with a fresh application. In Xcode, create a new project using the Master-Detail Application template. Name the project DropboxEvents, and, this time, be sure to check the Use Core Data check box.

Of course, you may launch the application and get the regular Master-Detail sample application where you can hit the + button to create new events.

Adding the Required Frameworks for Dropbox and ParcelKit

You can add ParcelKit by using Cocoapods (`http://cocoapods.org`), or you can download the source from `https://github.com/overcommitted/ParcelKit` and follow the instructions on that page to build the framework. If you use cocoapods, you can skip the rest of this section.

In the previous section, we've seen how to integrate with Dropbox and add the frameworks it requires. For the DropboxEvents app, repeat those steps to add `Dropbox.framework` and the other required standard frameworks to the project.

- ▦ `CFNetwork.framework`

- ▦ `Security.framework`

- ▦ `SystemConfiguration.framework`

- ▦ `QuartzCore.framework`

- ▦ `libc++.dylib`

- ▦ `libz.dylib`

Next, add the ParcelKit library itself to your project. The dependencies should look as shown in Figure 8-5.

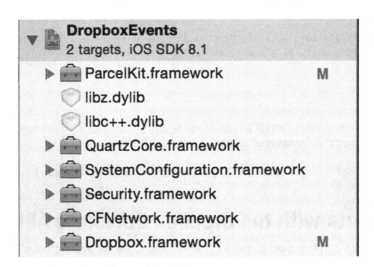

Figure 8-5. *The dependencies of the Dropbox/ParcelKit application*

As part of the ParcelKit configuration, go to the Build Settings of your project and add the –ObjC flag to the Other Linker Flags entry, as shown in Figure 8-6. Note that you do this for both the Objective-C and the Swift versions.

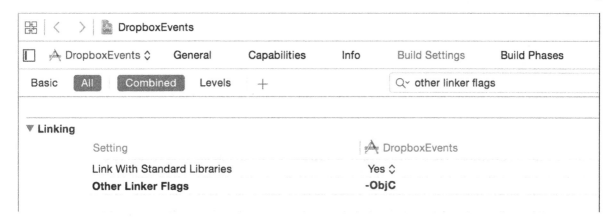

Figure 8-6. Other Linker Flags entry

Integrating DropboxEvents with Dropbox

As with the DropboxPersistenceApp application we built in the Dropbox Datastore API section, we must integrate DropboxEvents with Dropbox. Let's go through it once more.

1. Open AppDelegate.m or AppDelegate.swift and edit the application:
   didFinishLaunchingWithOptions: method as shown in Listing 8-33
   (Objective-C) or Listing 8-34 (Swift) to initialize the Dropbox SDK.

Listing 8-33. Initializing the Dropbox SDK (Objective-C)

```
- (BOOL)application:(UIApplication *)application didFinishLaunchingWithOptions:(NSDictionary *)
launchOptions {

  DBAccountManager *accountManager = [[DBAccountManager alloc]
                                    initWithAppKey:@"APP_KEY" secret:@"APP_SECRET"];
  [DBAccountManager setSharedManager:accountManager];

  UINavigationController *navigationController = (UINavigationController *)self.window.
  rootViewController;
  MasterViewController *controller = (MasterViewController *)navigationController.topViewController;
  controller.managedObjectContext = self.managedObjectContext;
  return YES;
}
```

Listing 8-34. Initializing the Dropbox SDK (Swift)

```
func application(application: UIApplication, didFinishLaunchingWithOptions launchOptions: [NSObject:
AnyObject]?) -> Bool {
    let accountManager = DBAccountManager(appKey: "APP_KEY", secret: "APP_SECRET")
    DBAccountManager.setSharedManager(accountManager)
```

```
  // Override point for customization after application launch.
  let navigationController = self.window!.rootViewController as UINavigationController
  let controller = navigationController.topViewController as MasterViewController
  controller.managedObjectContext = self.managedObjectContext
  return true
}
```

2. Be sure to import "TargetConditionals.h" and <Dropbox/Dropbox.h> at the top of the AppDelegate.m, if applicable, and replace the app key and secret with the one you got from Dropbox. You can reuse the app key and secret you used for the DropboxPersistenceApp, or you can create a new app on Dropbox and get a new app key and secret.

3. You also must add, again in AppDelegate.m or AppDelegate.swift, the method necessary to handle the return from the Dropbox authentication controller, as shown in Listing 8-35 (Objective-C) or Listing 8-36 (Swift).

Listing 8-35. Handling the URL Callback (Objective-C)

```objc
- (BOOL)application:(UIApplication *)application openURL:(NSURL *)url sourceApplication:(NSString *)
sourceApplication annotation:(id)annotation {
  DBAccount *account = [[DBAccountManager sharedManager] handleOpenURL:url];
  if (account) {
    NSLog(@"App linked successfully from %@", sourceApplication);

    return YES;
  }
  return NO;
}
```

Listing 8-36. Handling the URL Callback (Swift)

```swift
func application(application: UIApplication, openURL url: NSURL, sourceApplication: String,
annotation: AnyObject?) -> Bool {
    let account = DBAccountManager.sharedManager().handleOpenURL(url)
    if let account = account {
        println("App linked successfully from \(sourceApplication)")

        return true
    }
    return false
}
```

4. To make sure the app is able to receive the callback from the Dropbox authentication controller, edit DropboxEvents-Info.plist and add the Dropbox URL type, as we did in the previous section and as illustrated in Figure 8-7. Again, use your actual app key from Dropbox, not "APP_KEY."

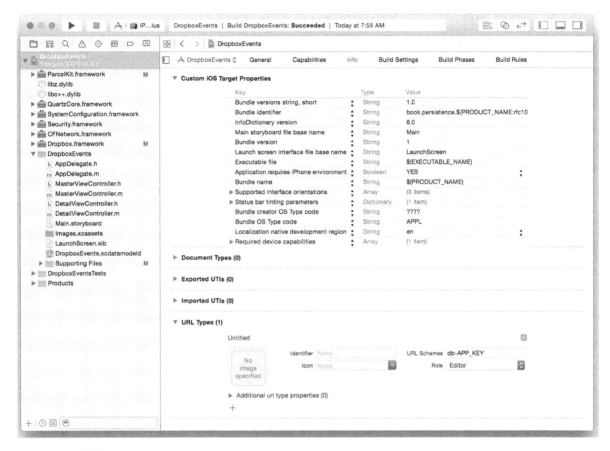

Figure 8-7. *The URL types*

Once the setup work is done, we can start worrying about actually coding the app's persistence with ParcelKit. Fortunately, ParcelKit does most of the hard work for us, and all we have to do is configure it through code.

1. The remainder of the work resides in `MasterViewController.m` or `MasterViewController.swift`, so let's pop the appropriate file open. The first thing we need to do is disable the `NSFetchedResultsController`'s cache in order to prevent cache inconsistencies when receiving data from the cloud. This may feel a little weird, since normally you are supposed to provide a cache for `NSFetchedResultsController` for performance reasons, but data consistency trumps performance. Go to the `fetchedResultsController` method and change the cache name from `"Master"` to `nil`, as shown in Listing 8-37 (Objective-C) or Listing 8-38 (Swift).

Listing 8-37. Removing the Cache from fetchedResultsController (Objective-C)

```
NSFetchedResultsController *aFetchedResultsController = [[NSFetchedResultsController alloc] initWi
thFetchRequest:fetchRequest managedObjectContext:self.managedObjectContext sectionNameKeyPath:nil
cacheName:nil];
```

Listing 8-38. Removing the Cache from fetchedResultsController (Swift)

```
let aFetchedResultsController = NSFetchedResultsController(fetchRequest: fetchRequest,
managedObjectContext: self.managedObjectContext!, sectionNameKeyPath: nil, cacheName: nil)
```

2. Since we're going to use Dropbox and ParcelKit, add the appropriate import statements at the top of the file for the Objective-C version, as shown in Listing 8-39.

Listing 8-39. Adding the Dropbox and ParcelKit Import Statements

```
#import "TargetConditionals.h"
#import <Dropbox/Dropbox.h>
#import <ParcelKit/ParcelKit.h>
```

3. Still in MasterViewController.m or MasterViewController.swift, add two properties to the private interface as shown in Listing 8-40 (Objective-C) or Listing 8-41 (Swift).

Listing 8-40. Adding Private Properties for the Data Store and Sync Manager (Objective-C)

```
@interface MasterViewController ()
@property (nonatomic, strong) DBDatastore *datastore;
@property (nonatomic, strong) PKSyncManager *syncManager;
@end
```

Listing 8-41. Adding Private Properties for the Data Store and Sync Manager (Swift)

```
var datastore: DBDatastore?
var syncManager: PKSyncManager?
```

4. Next we need to worry about the linking process. In our case, since everything relies on Dropbox being linked, we check for the link status when the master view appears—in the viewDidAppear: method. Add the code shown in Listing 8-42 (Objective-C) or Listing 8-43 (Swift) to MasterViewController.m or MasterViewController.swift.

Listing 8-42. Checking the Dropbox Link Status When the View Appears (Objective-C)

```
- (void)viewDidAppear:(BOOL)animated {
  [super viewDidAppear:animated];

  DBAccount *linkedAccount = [[DBAccountManager sharedManager] linkedAccount];
  if (linkedAccount) {
    if (!self.datastore) {
      NSLog(@"Initializing datastore with ParcelKit sync");
      self.datastore = [DBDatastore openDefaultStoreForAccount:linkedAccount error:nil];
```

```
    PKSyncManager *syncManager = [[PKSyncManager alloc] initWithManagedObjectContext:self.
    managedObjectContext datastore:self.datastore];

    [syncManager setTable:@"Events" forEntityName:@"Event"];
    [syncManager startObserving];
    self.syncManager = syncManager;
  }
}
else {
  NSLog(@"Needs link");
  [[DBAccountManager sharedManager] linkFromController:self];
}
}
```

Listing 8-43. Checking the Dropbox Link Status When the View Appears (Swift)

```
override func viewDidAppear(animated: Bool) {
    super.viewDidAppear()
    if let linkedAccount = DBAccountManager.sharedManager().linkedAccount {
        if datastore == nil {
            println("Initializing datastore with ParcelKit sync")

            self.datastore = DBDatastore.openDefaultStoreForAccount(linkedAccount, error: nil)

            self.syncManager = PKSyncManager(managedObjectContext: self.managedObjectContext,
            datastore: datastore)

            syncManager?.setTable("Events", forEntityName: "Event")
            syncManager?.startObserving()
        }
    }
    else {
        println("Needs link")
        DBAccountManager.sharedManager().linkFromController(self)
    }
}
```

Let's take a moment to examine the method's logic. First, we grab the Dropbox linked account. If there isn't any (i.e., it is nil), then we create one and we launch the linking process.

If the app already has a linked account, then we use it. We set up the Dropbox Datastore exactly in the same manner as we explained in the previous section. We then create an instance of ParcelKit's PKSyncManager, which is in charge of observing changes to Core Data's managed objects and synching them with Dropbox, and also observing changes to object in Dropbox and synching them with Core Data's managed objects. To perform this magic, ParcelKit requires us to tell it which Core Data entities we want to observe. In this case, there is only one: the Event entity, which we want to link with the Events table in the Dropbox Datastore. Note that though we've chosen to match the name of the Core Data entity with the Dropbox Datastore table name, they don't have to match. PKSyncManager's setTable:forEntityName: allows you to map the two using whatever names you choose.

Once the PKSyncManager instance is fully set up, we must assign it to the syncManager property in order to keep it alive. Otherwise, it would fall out of scope and be destroyed.

That's it for all the code we need to write. See, we told you that ParcelKit does all the hard work! There is, however, one last bit we need to put in place in order to make all this work. ParcelKit requires an additional attribute called syncID to be set on each entity it observes. This is the key it uses to compare the different instances of the entity and ensure that it keeps everything synced correctly. Open DropboxEvents.xcdatamodeld and add a syncID attribute of type String to the Event entity, as shown in Figure 8-8.

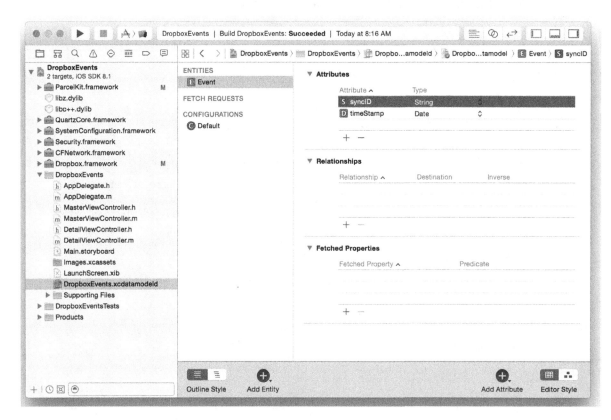

Figure 8-8. The syncID *attribute set for ParcelKit*

Since we've modified the Core Data model, you will need to delete the existing Core Data data store from the simulator to avoid Core Data model collision. In the iPhone simulator, press and hold on the app's icon. Once it wiggles, press the delete button to uninstall it. Then press the home button to exit this mode.

This time, we're all set. Launch the application and notice how nothing different seems to be happening. Go ahead and add a couple more events. They add without any problem. To notice a difference, we need to log into Dropbox's web view at www.dropbox.com/developers/apps/datastores. Browse to your data store and you should see the events you just created, as illustrated by Figure 8-9.

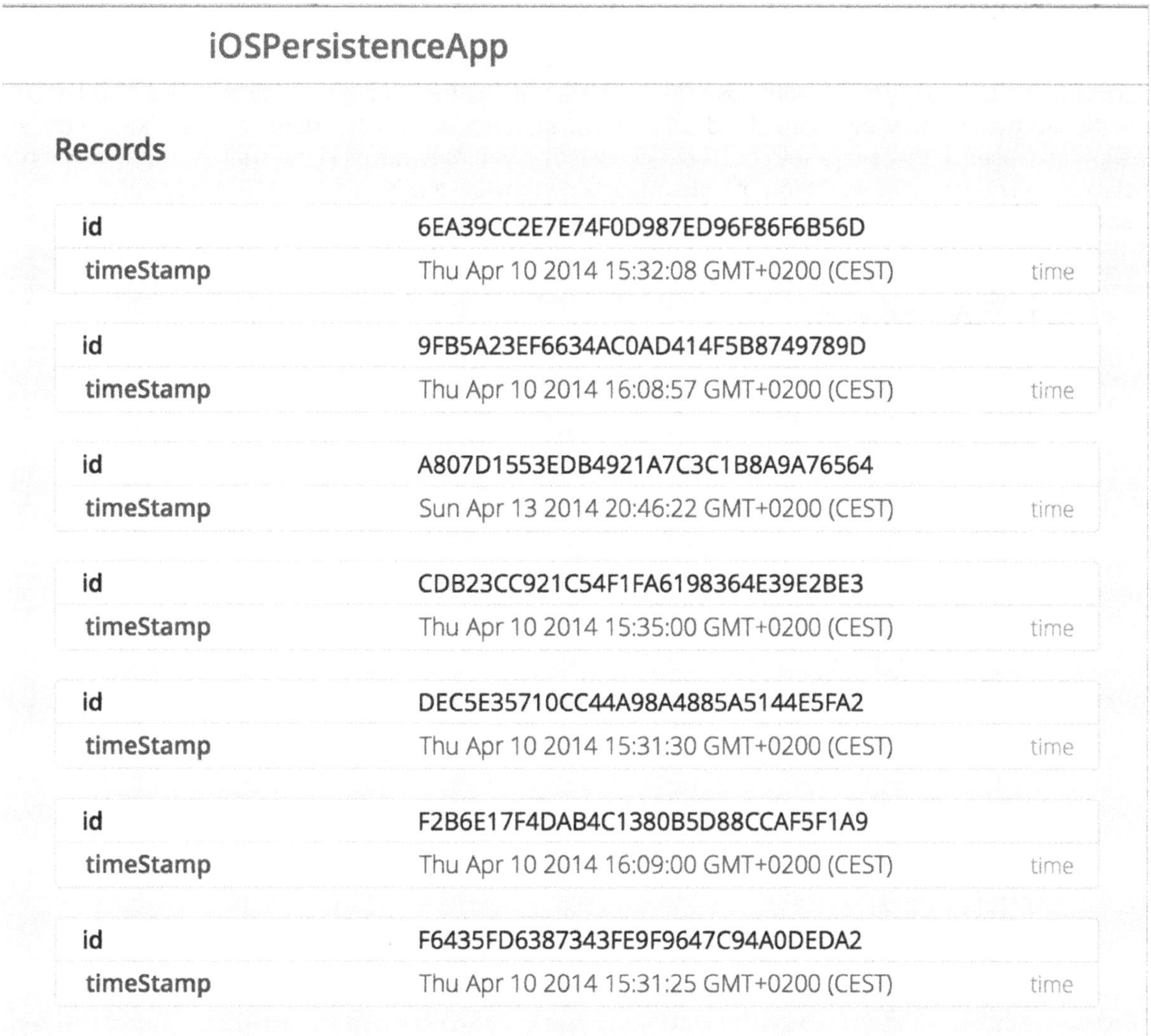

iOSPersistenceApp

Records

id	6EA39CC2E7E74F0D987ED96F86F6B56D	
timeStamp	Thu Apr 10 2014 15:32:08 GMT+0200 (CEST)	time

id	9FB5A23EF6634AC0AD414F5B8749789D	
timeStamp	Thu Apr 10 2014 16:08:57 GMT+0200 (CEST)	time

id	A807D1553EDB4921A7C3C1B8A9A76564	
timeStamp	Sun Apr 13 2014 20:46:22 GMT+0200 (CEST)	time

id	CDB23CC921C54F1FA6198364E39E2BE3	
timeStamp	Thu Apr 10 2014 15:35:00 GMT+0200 (CEST)	time

id	DEC5E35710CC44A98A4885A5144E5FA2	
timeStamp	Thu Apr 10 2014 15:31:30 GMT+0200 (CEST)	time

id	F2B6E17F4DAB4C1380B5D88CCAF5F1A9	
timeStamp	Thu Apr 10 2014 16:09:00 GMT+0200 (CEST)	time

id	F6435FD6387343FE9F9647C94A0DEDA2	
timeStamp	Thu Apr 10 2014 15:31:25 GMT+0200 (CEST)	time

Figure 8-9. Dropbox's Datastore web view

As you add new events in your app, new records appear in the data store. Now that you've created a few events, stop the application. Following the same procedure as before, uninstall the app from the iPhone simulator. This will erase the local Core Data store. With a regular Core Data application, if you launched the app again you'd have no events. Go ahead and launch the app and notice how all the events are still there. That is because they have been synced with Dropbox's Datastore API.

Conclusion

Nowadays, most consumers own multiple devices and they expect their data to be omnipresent across those devices. We've seen examples of three options for storing your data on the cloud and mentioned two more. Many more cloud solutions exist, ranging from standard services like the ones we've discussed in this chapter to custom services that you may develop yourself. No matter which solution you choose, the evolution of data storage undeniably leads to a need for cloud storage. People will be more likely to download and use your apps if you take care of syncing across devices. The decision between iCloud, Dropbox, or other is one that you need to make based on your target users, the characteristics specific to your app, and whether or not you want to sync data with apps running on non-Apple devices.

Chapter 9

Tuning Performance, Memory Usage, and Multithreading

People want answers. Now. They expect their devices to provide those answers quickly. If they believe the applications on their devices are locked up or even just slow, they'll abandon or perhaps even delete them. You can show spinners to indicate that your applications are working hard on providing those results, which will mollify users somewhat. Giving a visual clue that the device is working beats giving no such clue and letting customers think their devices have locked up; better still would be to never have episodes of slowness that make users wait. You may not always be able to achieve that goal, but you should always try.

Fetching and storing data in a persistent store can take a long time, especially when mounds of data are involved. This chapter will make sure that you understand how Core Data helps you—and how you must help yourself—to ensure that you don't pepper your users with "Please Wait" spinners or, worse, an unresponsive application that appears locked up while it retrieves or saves large object graphs. You will learn how to utilize the various tools and strategies, such as caching, faulting, multiple threads, and the Instruments application that comes with Xcode.

Tuning Performance

The phrase "tuning performance" conjures an image of a mechanic with a set of wrenches, huddled over an engine on his workbench, turning bolts and tweaking valves and measuring the effects of his adjustments on the performance of the engine. When tuning the performance of your applications, you must have the same discipline to make adjustments and measure their effects on overall performance. In this chapter, we cover various approaches to improving the performance of your applications. You should try out these approaches on the applications you write and measure their effects, both in the simulator and on actual iDevices.

Building the Application for Testing

You need a way to perform all this performance testing so that you can verify results. This section walks you through building an application that will allow you to run various tests and see the results. The application, shown in Figure 9-1, presents a list of tests you can run in a standard picker view. To run a test, select it in the picker, click the Run Selected Test button, and wait for the results. After the test runs, you'll see the start time, the stop time, the number of elapsed seconds for the test, and some text describing the results of the test.

Figure 9-1. The PerformanceTuning application

Creating the Project

In Xcode, create a new single-view application for iPhone called **PerformanceTuning** with the User Core Data check box unchecked. Add a Core Data data model called PerformanceTuning. xcdatamodeld and a class called Persistence to manage the Core Data stack. Listings 9-1 and 9-2 show Persistence.h and Persistence.m, respectively. Listing 9-3 shows Persistence.swift.

Listing 9-1. Persistence.h

```
@import CoreData;

@interface Persistence : NSObject

@property (readonly, strong, nonatomic) NSManagedObjectContext *managedObjectContext;
@property (readonly, strong, nonatomic) NSManagedObjectModel *managedObjectModel;
@property (readonly, strong, nonatomic) NSPersistentStoreCoordinator *persistentStoreCoordinator;

- (void)saveContext;
- (NSURL *)applicationDocumentsDirectory;

@end
```

Listing 9-2. Persistence.m

```
#import "Persistence.h"

@implementation Persistence

- (instancetype)init {
  self = [super init];
  if (self != nil) {
    // Initialize the managed object model
    NSURL *modelURL = [[NSBundle mainBundle] URLForResource:@"PerformanceTuning"
    withExtension:@"momd"];
    _managedObjectModel = [[NSManagedObjectModel alloc] initWithContentsOfURL:modelURL];

    // Initialize the persistent store coordinator
    NSURL *storeURL = [[self applicationDocumentsDirectory] URLByAppendingPathComponent:
    @"PerformanceTuning.sqlite"];

    NSError *error = nil;
    _persistentStoreCoordinator = [[NSPersistentStoreCoordinator alloc]
    initWithManagedObjectModel:self.managedObjectModel];
    if (![_persistentStoreCoordinator addPersistentStoreWithType:NSSQLiteStoreType
                                      configuration:nil
                                                URL:storeURL
                                            options:nil
                                              error:&error]) {
      NSLog(@"Unresolved error %@, %@", error, [error userInfo]);
      abort();
    }

    // Initialize the managed object context
    _managedObjectContext = [[NSManagedObjectContext alloc] init];
    [_managedObjectContext setPersistentStoreCoordinator:self.persistentStoreCoordinator];
  }
  return self;
}
```

```objc
#pragma mark - Helper Methods

- (void)saveContext {
  NSError *error = nil;
  if ([self.managedObjectContext hasChanges] && ![self.managedObjectContext save:&error]) {
    NSLog(@"Unresolved error %@, %@", error, [error userInfo]);
    abort();
  }
}

- (NSURL *)applicationDocumentsDirectory {
  return [[[NSFileManager defaultManager] URLsForDirectory:NSDocumentDirectory
inDomains:NSUserDomainMask] lastObject];
}

@end
```

Listing 9-3. Persistence.swift

```swift
import Foundation
import CoreData

class Persistence {
    // MARK: - Core Data stack

    lazy var applicationDocumentsDirectory: NSURL = {
        // The directory the application uses to store the Core Data store file. This code uses a
            directory named "book.persistence.PerformanceTuningSwift" in the application's documents
            Application Support directory.
        let urls = NSFileManager.defaultManager().URLsForDirectory(.DocumentDirectory,
        inDomains: .UserDomainMask)
        return urls[urls.count-1] as NSURL
        }()

    lazy var managedObjectModel: NSManagedObjectModel = {
        // The managed object model for the application. This property is not optional. It is a
            fatal error for the application not to be able to find and load its model.
        let modelURL = NSBundle.mainBundle().URLForResource("PerformanceTuningSwift", withExtension:
        "momd")!
        return NSManagedObjectModel(contentsOfURL: modelURL)!
        }()

    lazy var persistentStoreCoordinator: NSPersistentStoreCoordinator? = {
        // The persistent store coordinator for the application. This implementation creates and
            return a coordinator, having added the store for the application to it. This property is
            optional since there are legitimate error conditions that could cause the creation of the
            store to fail.
        // Create the coordinator and store
        var coordinator: NSPersistentStoreCoordinator? = NSPersistentStoreCoordinator(managedObjectM
        odel: self.managedObjectModel)
        let url = self.applicationDocumentsDirectory.URLByAppendingPathComponent("PerformanceTuning
        Swift.sqlite")
```

```
        var error: NSError? = nil
        var failureReason = "There was an error creating or loading the application's saved data."
        if coordinator!.addPersistentStoreWithType(NSSQLiteStoreType, configuration: nil, URL: url,
        options: nil, error: &error) == nil {
            coordinator = nil
            // Report any error we got.
            let dict = NSMutableDictionary()
            dict[NSLocalizedDescriptionKey] = "Failed to initialize the application's saved data"
            dict[NSLocalizedFailureReasonErrorKey] = failureReason
            dict[NSUnderlyingErrorKey] = error
            error = NSError(domain: "YOUR_ERROR_DOMAIN", code: 9999, userInfo: dict)
            // Replace this with code to handle the error appropriately.
            // abort() causes the application to generate a crash log and terminate. You should
                not use this function in a shipping application, although it may be useful during
                development.
            NSLog("Unresolved error \(error), \(error!.userInfo)")
            abort()
        }

        return coordinator
        }()

    lazy var managedObjectContext: NSManagedObjectContext? = {
        // Returns the managed object context for the application (which is already bound to the
        persistent store coordinator for the application.) This property is optional since there are
        legitimate error conditions that could cause the creation of the context to fail.
        let coordinator = self.persistentStoreCoordinator
        if coordinator == nil {
            return nil
        }
        var managedObjectContext = NSManagedObjectContext()
        managedObjectContext.persistentStoreCoordinator = coordinator
        return managedObjectContext
        }()

    // MARK: - Core Data Saving support

    func saveContext () {
        if let moc = self.managedObjectContext {
            var error: NSError? = nil
            if moc.hasChanges && !moc.save(&error) {
                // Replace this implementation with code to handle the error appropriately.
                // abort() causes the application to generate a crash log and terminate. You should
                    not use this function in a shipping application, although it may be useful during
                    development.
                NSLog("Unresolved error \(error), \(error!.userInfo)")
                abort()
            }
        }
    }
}
```

For the Objective-C version, add a Persistence property to AppDelegate.h, as shown in Listing 9-4. For both Swift and Objective-C, initialize the Persistence property in AppDelegate's application:di dFinishLaunchingWithOptions: method, as shown in Listing 9-5 (Objective-C) or Listing 9-6 (Swift). Make sure to import Persistence.h in AppDelegate.m if you're doing this in Objective-C

Listing 9-4. AppDelegate.h with the Persistence Property

```
#import <UIKit/UIKit.h>

@class Persistence;

@interface AppDelegate : UIResponder <UIApplicationDelegate>

@property (strong, nonatomic) UIWindow *window;
@property (strong, nonatomic) Persistence *persistence;

@end
```

Listing 9-5. Initializing the Core Data Stack in AppDelegate.m (Objective-C)

```
- (BOOL)application:(UIApplication *)application didFinishLaunchingWithOptions:(NSDictionary *)
launchOptions {
  self.persistence = [[Persistence alloc] init];
  return YES;
}
```

Listing 9-6. Initializing the Core Data Stack in AppDelegate.swift (Swift)

```
var persistence: Persistence?

func application(application: UIApplication, didFinishLaunchingWithOptions launchOptions: [NSObject:
AnyObject]?) -> Bool {
    self.persistence = Persistence()
    return true
}
```

Creating the Data Model and Data

The data model for this application tracks people and selfies (photographs taken of oneself, optionally including other people) across social networks and consists of three entities: Person, Selfie, and SocialNetwork. Each person can appear in multiple selfies, and each selfie can tag multiple people. Also, each selfie can be posted to multiple social networks, and each social network can display multiple selfies. This means that Person and Selfie have an optional many-to-many relationship, and Selfie and SocialNetwork have an optional many-to-many relationship.

We also want some attributes on each entity, and to simplify the model we'll give each a name attribute of the type String and a rating attribute of the type Integer 16. Go ahead and create this model, which should match Figure 9-2.

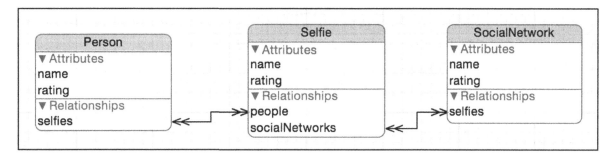

Figure 9-2. *The Core Data model*

We'll next push enough data into the data model so we can run performance tests and differentiate results. It should be sufficient to create 500 people, selfies, and social networks and relate them all to each other—that will give us three tables with 500 rows each (Person, Selfie, and SocialNetwork) and two join tables with 250,000 rows each (Person-to-Selfie and Selfie-to-SocialNetwork).

To insert the data, open Persistence.h (for Objective-C) and declare a method to load the data.

```
- (void)loadData;
```

Implement the method in Persistence.m or Persistence.swift. The implementation should check the persistent store to determine whether the data have already been loaded so that subsequent invocations of the program don't compound the data store. If the data have not been inserted, the loadData method creates 500 people with names like Person 1, Person 2, and so on; 500 selfies with names like Selfie 1; and 500 social networks with names like SocialNetwork 1. It uses a helper method called insertObjectForName:index: to actually create the object. After creating all the objects, the code loops through all the selfies and adds relationships to all the people and all the social networks. Finally, loadData saves the object graph to the persistent data store. Listing 9-7 shows the Objective-C code, and Listing 9-8 shows the Swift code.

Listing 9-7. Loading the Data in Persistence.m *(Objective-C)*

```
- (void)loadData {
  static int NumberOfRows = 500;

  // Fetch the people. If we have NumberOfRows, assume our data is loaded.
  NSFetchRequest *peopleFetchRequest = [NSFetchRequest fetchRequestWithEntityName:@"Person"];
  NSArray *people = [self.managedObjectContext executeFetchRequest:peopleFetchRequest
                                                  error:nil];
  if ([people count] != NumberOfRows) {
    NSLog(@"Creating objects");
    // Load the objects
    for (int i = 1; i <= NumberOfRows; i++) {
      [self insertObjectForName:@"Person" index:i];
      [self insertObjectForName:@"Selfie" index:i];
      [self insertObjectForName:@"SocialNetwork" index:i];
    }
  }
```

```objc
    // Get all the people, selfies, and social networks
    people = [self.managedObjectContext executeFetchRequest:peopleFetchRequest
                                                      error:nil];

    NSFetchRequest *selfiesFetchRequest = [NSFetchRequest fetchRequestWithEntityName:@"Selfie"];
    NSArray *selfies = [self.managedObjectContext executeFetchRequest:selfiesFetchRequest
                                                                error:nil];

    NSFetchRequest *socialNetworksFetchRequest = [NSFetchRequest fetchRequestWithEntityName:@"Socia
    lNetwork"];
    NSArray *socialNetworks = [self.managedObjectContext executeFetchRequest:socialNetworksFetchReq
    uest error:nil];

    // Set up all the relationships
    NSLog(@"Creating relationships");
    for (NSManagedObject *selfie in selfies) {
      NSMutableSet *peopleSet = [selfie mutableSetValueForKey:@"people"];
      [peopleSet addObjectsFromArray:people];

      NSMutableSet *socialNetworksSet = [selfie mutableSetValueForKey:@"socialNetworks"];
      [socialNetworksSet addObjectsFromArray:socialNetworks];
    }

    [self saveContext];
  }
}

- (NSManagedObject *)insertObjectForName:(NSString *)name index:(NSInteger)index {
  NSManagedObject *object = [NSEntityDescription insertNewObjectForEntityForName:name
                                                         inManagedObjectContext:self.
                                                         managedObjectContext];
  [object setValue:[NSString stringWithFormat:@"%@ %ld", name, (long)index]
            forKey:@"name"];
  [object setValue:[NSNumber numberWithInt:((arc4random() % 10) + 1)]
            forKey:@"rating"];
  return object;
}
```

Listing 9-8. Loading the Data in `Persistence.swift` *(Swift)*

```swift
func loadData() {
    let NumberOfRows = 500

    // Fetch the people. If we have NumberOfRows, assume our data is loaded.
    let peopleFetchRequest = NSFetchRequest(entityName: "Person")
    var people = self.managedObjectContext?.executeFetchRequest(peopleFetchRequest, error: nil)
    if people?.count != NumberOfRows {
        println("Creating objects")
```

```swift
        // Load the objects
        for var i=1; i<=NumberOfRows; i++ {
            self.insertObjectForName("Person", index: i)
            self.insertObjectForName("Selfie", index: i)
            self.insertObjectForName("SocialNetwork", index: i)
        }

        // Get all the people, selfies, and social networks
        people = self.managedObjectContext?.executeFetchRequest(peopleFetchRequest, error: nil)

        let selfiesFetchRequest = NSFetchRequest(entityName: "Selfie")
        var selfies = self.managedObjectContext?.executeFetchRequest(selfiesFetchRequest,
        error: nil)

        let socialNetworksFetchRequest = NSFetchRequest(entityName: "SocialNetwork")
        var socialNetworks = self.managedObjectContext?.executeFetchRequest
        (socialNetworksFetchRequest, error: nil)

        // Set up all the relationships
        println("Creating relationships")
        for selfie in selfies as [NSManagedObject] {
            var peopleSet = selfie.mutableSetValueForKey("people")
            peopleSet.addObjectsFromArray(people!)

            var socialNetworksSet = selfie.mutableSetValueForKey("socialNetworks")
            socialNetworksSet.addObjectsFromArray(socialNetworks!)
        }

        self.saveContext()
    }
}

func insertObjectForName(name: String, index: Int) -> NSManagedObject! {
    var object = NSEntityDescription.insertNewObjectForEntityForName(name, inManagedObjectContext:
    self.managedObjectContext!) as NSManagedObject

    object.setValue(NSString(format: "%@ %ld", name, index), forKey: "name")
    object.setValue(NSNumber(int: Int(arc4random() % 10) + 1), forKey: "rating")

    return object
}
```

Each time the application launches, we call loadData to load if the data are necessary. Add this call in AppDelegate.m or AppDelegate.swift, as shown in Listing 9-9 (Objective-C) or Listing 9-10 (Swift).

Listing 9-9. Calling loadData in AppDelegate.m (Objective-C)

```objc
- (BOOL)application:(UIApplication *)application didFinishLaunchingWithOptions:(NSDictionary *)
launchOptions {
  self.persistence = [[Persistence alloc] init];
  [self.persistence loadData];
  return YES;
}
```

Listing 9-10. Calling loadData in AppDelegate.swift (Swift)

```swift
func application(application: UIApplication, didFinishLaunchingWithOptions launchOptions: [NSObject:
AnyObject]?) -> Bool {
    // Override point for customization after application launch.
    self.persistence = Persistence()
    self.persistence?.loadData()
    return true
}
```

Build and run the program to create your persistent data store. You should see the log messages in the Xcode console that your program is creating the objects and relationships. If you quit the program and run it again, you shouldn't see any such log messages.

Creating the Testing View

The PerformanceTuning application presents a picker with the list of tests you can run and buttons to launch the selected test. When you run a test, the application lists the start time, stop time, and elapsed time for the test, as well as a description of the test's results. Open ViewController.h, declare that it implements the protocols for your picker, add properties for the user interface (UI) elements, and add a method declaration for running a test, as Listing 9-11 shows.

Listing 9-11. ViewController.h

```objc
@interface ViewController : UIViewController <UIPickerViewDataSource, UIPickerViewDelegate>

@property (nonatomic, weak) IBOutlet UILabel *startTime;
@property (nonatomic, weak) IBOutlet UILabel *stopTime;
@property (nonatomic, weak) IBOutlet UILabel *elapsedTime;
@property (nonatomic, weak) IBOutlet UITextView *results;
@property (nonatomic, weak) IBOutlet UIPickerView *testPicker;

- (IBAction)runTest:(id)sender;

@end
```

Open ViewController.m and add stub implementations for the picker view protocols and the runTest: method, as Listing 9-12 shows.

Listing 9-12. ViewController.m

```objc
#import "ViewController.h"

@implementation ViewController

#pragma mark - UIPickerViewDataSource methods

- (NSInteger)numberOfComponentsInPickerView:(UIPickerView *)pickerView {
    return 0;
}
```

```objc
- (NSInteger)pickerView:(UIPickerView *)pickerView numberOfRowsInComponent:(NSInteger)component {
  return 0;
}

#pragma mark - UIPickerViewDelegate methods

- (NSString *)pickerView:(UIPickerView *)pickerView titleForRow:(NSInteger)row
forComponent:(NSInteger)component {
  return nil;
}

#pragma mark - Handlers

- (IBAction)runTest:(id)sender {
}

@end
```

If you're using Swift, make the corresponding changes, shown in Listing 9-13, in ViewController. swift.

Listing 9-13. ViewController.swift

```swift
class ViewController: UIViewController, UIPickerViewDelegate, UIPickerViewDataSource {

    @IBOutlet weak var startTime: UILabel!
    @IBOutlet weak var stopTime: UILabel!
    @IBOutlet weak var elapsedTime: UILabel!
    @IBOutlet weak var results: UITextView!
    @IBOutlet weak var testPicker: UIPickerView!

...

    func numberOfComponentsInPickerView(pickerView: UIPickerView) -> Int {
        return 1
    }

    func pickerView(pickerView: UIPickerView, numberOfRowsInComponent component: Int) -> Int {
        return self.tests.count
    }

    func pickerView(pickerView: UIPickerView, titleForRow row: Int, forComponent component: Int) ->
    String! {
        let test = self.tests[row]
        let fullName = _stdlib_getDemangledTypeName(test)
        let tokens = split(fullName, { $0 == "." })
        return tokens.last
    }

    @IBAction func runTest(sender: AnyObject) {
    }
}
```

Open `Main.storyboard` and build the UI. Add labels for Start Time, Stop Time, and Elapsed Time, as well as right-aligned labels with Autoshrink set to "Minimum Font Size" of 9, to show the actual start time, stop time, and elapsed time when running a test. Add a text view to display the results of a test, a button for launching a test, and finally a picker view to show the available tests. Drag all those items to the view and arrange them to mimic Figure 9-3. Connect the view's controls to the corresponding properties in the code and the button to the `runTest:` method. Also, connect the picker view's data source and delegate to the view controller.

Figure 9-3. Building the view for PerformanceTuning

Building the Testing Framework

The picker view will contain a list of tests that we can run. To create that list, we create a protocol called `PerfTest` and then create several classes that implement that protocol. Then, we'll create an array to store instances of our test classes. The application will display the names of those test classes in the picker view and execute the selected test when the user taps the Run Selected Test button.

To begin, create a new protocol called PerfTest and declare a required method called runTestWithContext:. Listing 9-14 shows the Objective-C version, PerfTest.h, and Listing 9-15 shows the Swift version, PerfTest.swift.

Listing 9-14. PerfTest.h

```
#import <Foundation/Foundation.h>
@import CoreData;

@protocol PerfTest <NSObject>

- (NSString *)runTestWithContext:(NSManagedObjectContext *)context;

@end
```

Listing 9-15. PerfTest.swift

```
import Foundation
import CoreData

protocol PerfTest {
    func runTestWithContext(context: NSManagedObjectContext) -> String!
}
```

Before integrating the testing framework into the application, create a test—a "test" test, if you will—so that you have something both to see in the picker view and to run. The first test you create will fetch all the objects—the people, selfies, and social networks—from the persistent store. Create a new class called FetchAll as a subclass of NSObject, and make it implement the PerfTest protocol. Then, in the implementation of runWithContext:, simply fetch all the objects and return a string describing the number of objects of each entity fetched. Listing 9-16 shows FetchAll.h, Listing 9-17 shows FetchAll.m, and Listing 9-18 shows FetchAll.swift.

Listing 9-16. FetchAll.h

```
#import "PerfTest.h"

@interface FetchAll : NSObject <PerfTest>

@end
```

Listing 9-17. FetchAll.m

```
#import "FetchAll.h"

@implementation FetchAll

- (NSString *)runTestWithContext:(NSManagedObjectContext *)context {
  NSFetchRequest *peopleFetchRequest = [NSFetchRequest fetchRequestWithEntityName:@"Person"];
  NSFetchRequest *selfiesFetchRequest = [NSFetchRequest fetchRequestWithEntityName:@"Selfie"];
  NSFetchRequest *socialNetworksFetchRequest = [NSFetchRequest fetchRequestWithEntityName:@"Social
Network"];
```

```
    NSArray *people = [context executeFetchRequest:peopleFetchRequest
                                 error:nil];
    NSArray *selfies = [context executeFetchRequest:selfiesFetchRequest
                                 error:nil];
    NSArray *socialNetworks = [context executeFetchRequest:socialNetworksFetchRequest
                                       error:nil];

    return [NSString stringWithFormat:@"Fetched %ld people, %ld selfies, and %ld social networks",
    [people count], [selfies count], [socialNetworks count]];
}

@end
```

Listing 9-18. FetchAll.swift

```
import Foundation
import CoreData

class FetchAll : PerfTest {
    func runTestWithContext(context: NSManagedObjectContext) -> String! {
        let peopleFetchRequest = NSFetchRequest(entityName: "Person")
        let selfiesFetchRequest = NSFetchRequest(entityName: "Selfie")
        let socialNetworkFetchRequest = NSFetchRequest(entityName: "SocialNetwork")

        let people = context.executeFetchRequest(peopleFetchRequest, error: nil)!
        let selfies = context.executeFetchRequest(selfiesFetchRequest, error: nil)!
        let socialNetworks = context.executeFetchRequest(socialNetworkFetchRequest, error: nil)!

        return NSString(format: "Fetched %ld people, %ld selfies, and %ld social networks",
        people.count, selfies.count, socialNetworks.count)
    }
}
```

Adding the Testing Framework to the Application

Now you must modify the view controller to use the testing framework. Add a property to
ViewController.h to hold all the test instances.

```
@property (nonatomic, strong) NSArray *tests; // Objective-C
var tests = [PerfTest]() // Swift
```

In ViewController.m or ViewController.swift, you'll do the following:

- ■ Add necessary imports.

- ■ Implement viewDidLoad to blank out fields and create your tests array.

- ■ Update the UIPickerViewDataSource and UIPickerViewDelegate methods to
  populate the picker view.

- ■ Update the runTest: method to run the selected test.

Listing 9-19 shows the updated ViewController.m file, and Listing 9-20 shows the updated ViewController.swift file. You can see that in the runTest: method, we determine which test is selected in the picker view. We grab a pointer to the application's managed object context and we reset it so our test times are consistent. We mark the start time, run the selected test, and then mark the stop time. Finally, we update the UI to show the times and results.

Listing 9-19. ViewController.m Updated with the Testing Framework

```objc
#import "ViewController.h"
#import "FetchAll.h"
#import "AppDelegate.h"
#import "Persistence.h"

@implementation ViewController

- (void)viewDidLoad {
  [super viewDidLoad];

  self.startTime.text = @"";
  self.stopTime.text = @"";
  self.elapsedTime.text = @"";
  self.results.text = @"";

  self.tests = @[[[FetchAll alloc] init]];
}

#pragma mark - UIPickerViewDataSource methods

- (NSInteger)numberOfComponentsInPickerView:(UIPickerView *)pickerView {
  return 1;
}

- (NSInteger)pickerView:(UIPickerView *)pickerView numberOfRowsInComponent:(NSInteger)component {
  return [self.tests count];
}

#pragma mark - UIPickerViewDelegate methods

- (NSString *)pickerView:(UIPickerView *)pickerView titleForRow:(NSInteger)row
forComponent:(NSInteger)component {
  id <PerfTest> test = self.tests[row];
  return [[test class] description];
}

#pragma mark - Handlers

- (IBAction)runTest:(id)sender {
  // Get the selected test
  id <PerfTest> test = self.tests[[self.testPicker selectedRowInComponent:0]];
  AppDelegate *delegate = (AppDelegate *)[[UIApplication sharedApplication] delegate];
  NSManagedObjectContext *context = delegate.persistence.managedObjectContext;
```

```
// Clear out any objects so we get clean test results
[context reset];

// Mark the start time, run the test, and mark the stop time
NSDate *start = [NSDate date];
NSString *results = [test runTestWithContext:delegate.persistence.managedObjectContext];
NSDate *stop = [NSDate date];

// Update the UI with the test results
self.startTime.text = [start description];
self.stopTime.text = [stop description];
self.elapsedTime.text = [NSString stringWithFormat:@"%.03f seconds", [stop
timeIntervalSinceDate:start]];
self.results.text = results;
}

@end
```

Listing 9-20. *ViewController.swift Updated with the Testing Framework*

```
import UIKit

class ViewController: UIViewController, UIPickerViewDelegate, UIPickerViewDataSource {

    @IBOutlet weak var startTime: UILabel!
    @IBOutlet weak var stopTime: UILabel!
    @IBOutlet weak var elapsedTime: UILabel!
    @IBOutlet weak var results: UITextView!
    @IBOutlet weak var testPicker: UIPickerView!

    var tests = [PerfTest]()

    func numberOfComponentsInPickerView(pickerView: UIPickerView) -> Int {
        return 1
    }

    func pickerView(pickerView: UIPickerView, numberOfRowsInComponent component: Int) -> Int {
        return self.tests.count
    }

    func pickerView(pickerView: UIPickerView, titleForRow row: Int, forComponent component: Int) ->
    String! {
        let test = self.tests[row]
        let fullName = _stdlib_getDemangledTypeName(test)
        let tokens = split(fullName, { $0 == "." })
        return tokens.last
    }

    @IBAction func runTest(sender: AnyObject) {
        // Get the selected test
        let test = self.tests[self.testPicker.selectedRowInComponent(0)]
```

```
        let appDelegate = UIApplication.sharedApplication().delegate as AppDelegate
        let context = appDelegate.persistence?.managedObjectContext
        if let context = context {
            // Clear out any objects so we get clean test results
            context.reset()

            // Mark the start time, run the test, and mark the stop time
            let start = NSDate()
            let testResults = test.runTestWithContext(context)
            let stop = NSDate()

            let formatter = NSDateFormatter()
            formatter.timeStyle = .MediumStyle

            // Update the UI with the test results
            self.startTime.text = formatter.stringFromDate(start)
            self.stopTime.text = formatter.stringFromDate(stop)
            self.elapsedTime.text = NSString(format: "%.03f seconds", stop.
            timeIntervalSinceDate(start))
            self.results.text = testResults
        }
    }

    override func viewDidLoad() {
        super.viewDidLoad()

        self.startTime.text = ""
        self.stopTime.text = ""
        self.elapsedTime.text = ""
        self.results.text = ""

        self.tests.append(FetchAll())
    }
}
```

You have completed the application—for now. As you work through this chapter, you will add tests to cover the scenarios you read about.

Running Your First Test

Build and run the application. When you run the application, you should see the iOS Simulator with a single test, "FetchAll," in the picker view. If the picker view is blank, you likely neglected to connect the picker view's dataSource and delegate properties to the view controller. Once you have everything working, and with "FetchAll" selected, tap on Run Selected Test. The application will fetch all the objects and display the results, as shown in Figure 9-4.

Figure 9-4. The results of fetching all the objects

The rest of this chapter explains the various performance considerations imposed by Core Data on iOS and the devices it runs on. As you learn about these performance considerations, you'll add tests to the PerformanceTuning application. Feel free to add your own tests as well so that you always give the users of your applications the best possible experience.

Faulting

When you run SQL queries against a database, you know the depth and range of the data you're pulling. You know if you're joining tables, you know the columns you're pulling back, and, if you're careful, you can limit the number of rows you yank from the database into working memory. You may have to work harder to get data than you do with Core Data, but you have more control. You know about how much memory you're using to hold the data you fetch.

With Core Data, however, you've given up some amount of control in exchange for ease of use. In the PerformanceTuning model, for example, each Selfie instance has a relationship to a collection of Person instances, which you access in an object-oriented, not a data-oriented, way. You don't have to care whether Core Data pulls the Person data from the database when the application starts, when the Selfie loads, or when you first access the Person objects. Core Data cares, however, and attempts to delay loading data from the persistent store into the object graph until necessary, reducing both fetch time and memory usage. It does this using what's termed "faults."

Think of a fault like a symlink on a Unix file system, which is not the actual file it points to nor does it contain the file's data. The symlink represents the file, though, and when called upon can get to the file and its data, just as if it were the file itself. Like a symlink, a fault is a placeholder that can get to the persistent store's data. A fault can represent either a managed object or, when it represents a to-many relationship, a collection of managed objects. As a link to or a shadow of the data, a fault occupies much less memory than the actual data do. See Figure 9-5 for a depiction of a managed object and a fault. In this case, the managed object is an instance of Selfie, and the fault points to the related collection of Person objects. The Selfie is boldly depicted, representing the fact that it has been fetched from the persistent store and resides in memory. The Person objects, represented on the "to-many" side of the relationship, are faint and grayed out, because they haven't been fetched from the persistent store and do not reside in memory.

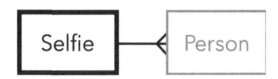

Figure 9-5. *A selfie and its faulted people*

Firing Faults

Core Data uses the term "firing faults" when it must pull the data from the persistent store that a fault points to and then put that data into memory. Core Data has "fired" off a request to fetch data from the data store, and the fault has been "fired" from its job to represent the actual data. You cause a fault to fire any time you request a managed object's persistent data, whether through valueForKey: or through methods of a custom class that either return or access the object's persistent data. Methods that access a managed object's metadata and not any of the data stored in the persistent store don't fire a fault. This means you can query a managed object's class, hash, description, entity, and object ID, among other things, and not cause a fault to fire. For the complete list of which methods don't fire a fault, see Apple's documentation at http://developer.apple.com/library/ios/#documentation/Cocoa/Conceptual/CoreData/Articles/cdPerformance.html under the section "Faulting Behavior."

Explicitly asking a managed object for its persistent data causes a fault to fire, but so does calling any methods or constructs that access persistent data from a managed object. You can, for example, access a collection through a managed object's relationships without causing a fault to fire. Sorting the collection, however, will fire a fault because any logical sorting will sort by some of the object's persistent data. The test you build later in this section demonstrates this behavior.

Faulting and Caching

We fibbed a bit when we said that firing faults fetches data from the persistent store. That's often true, but before Core Data treks all the way to the persistent store to retrieve data, it first checks its cache for the data it seeks. If Core Data finds its intended data in the cache, it pulls the data from cache and skips the longer trip to the persistent store. The sections "Caching" and "Expiring the Cache" discuss caching in more detail.

Refaulting

One way to take control of your application's persistent data and memory use is to turn managed objects back into faults, thereby relinquishing the memory their data were occupying. You turn objects back into faults by calling the managed object context's `refreshObject:mergeChanges:` method, passing the object you want to fault and NO for the `mergeChanges:` parameter. If, for example, I had a managed object called `foo` that I wanted to turn back into a fault, I would use code similar to the following:

```
[context refreshObject:foo mergeChanges:NO]; // Objective-C
context.refreshObject(foo, mergeChanges:false) // Swift
```

After this call, `foo` is now a fault, and `[foo isFault]` (or `foo.fault` for Swift) returns YES (or `true` for Swift). Understanding the `mergeChanges` parameter is important. Passing NO or `false`, as the previous code does, throws away any changed data that has not yet been saved to the persistent store. Take care when doing this because you lose all data changes in this object you're faulting, and all the objects to which the faulted object relates are released. If any of the relationships have changed and the context is then saved, your faulted object is out of sync with its relationships, and you have created data integrity issues in your persistent store.

Passing YES or `true` for `mergeChanges` doesn't fault the object. Instead, it reloads all the object's persistent data from the persistent store (or the last cached state) and then reapplies any changes that existed before the call to `refreshObject:mergeChanges:` that have not yet been saved.

When you turn a managed object into a fault, Core Data sends two messages to the managed object.

- `willTurnIntoFault:` before the object faults
- `didTurnIntoFault:` after the object faults

If you have implemented custom classes for your managed objects, you can implement either or both of these methods in your classes to perform some action on the object. Suppose, for example, that your custom managed object performs an expensive calculation on some persistent values and caches the result, and you want to nullify that cached result if the values it depends on aren't present. You could nullify the calculation in `didTurnIntoFault:`.

Building the Faulting Test

To test what you've learned about faulting in this section, build a test that will do the following:

1. Retrieve the first selfie from the persistent store.

2. Grab a social network from that selfie.

3. Check whether the social network is a fault.

4. Get the name of the social network.

5. Check whether the social network is a fault.

6. Turn the social network back into a fault.

7. Check whether the social network is a fault.

To start, generate NSManagedObject classes for all your Core Data entities. Open SocialNetwork.m or SocialNetwork.swift and implement the methods willTurnIntoFault and didTurnIntoFault. We won't do anything special in these methods, but rather we will simply log that they've been called, so that we can verify that they're being called appropriately. Listing 9-21 (Objective-C) and Listing 9-22 (Swift) show the implementations of these methods.

Listing 9-21. Handling Fault Status Changes in SocialNetwork.m

```
- (void)willTurnIntoFault {
  NSLog(@"%@ named %@ will turn into fault", [[self class] description], self.name);
}

- (void)didTurnIntoFault {
  NSLog(@"%@ did turn into fault", [[self class] description]);
}
```

Listing 9-22. Handling Fault Status Changes in SocialNetwork.swift

```
override func willTurnIntoFault() {
    println(NSString(format: "%@ named %@ will turn into fault", self, self.name))
}

override func didTurnIntoFault() {
    println(NSString(format: "%@ did turn into fault", self))
}
```

Notice that we log the social network's name in the willTurnIntoFault method. In the didTurnIntoFault method, however, we don't log the name. Why? Because we don't have the name to log. The object is a fault, remember? We don't have its attributes, including its name, in memory.

Now, create a test called DidFault that conforms to the PerfTest protocol, and then implement its runWithContext: method to perform the seven steps outlined previously. Listing 9-23 shows DidFault.h, Listing 9-24 shows DidFault.m, and Listing 9-25 shows DidFault.swift.

Listing 9-23. DidFault.h

```
#import "PerfTest.h"

@interface DidFault : NSObject <PerfTest>

@end
```

Listing 9-24. DidFault.m with the Faulting Test Implemented

```
#import "DidFault.h"
#import "Selfie.h"
#import "SocialNetwork.h"

@implementation DidFault

-(NSString *)runTestWithContext:(NSManagedObjectContext *)context {
  NSString *result = nil;
```

```
// 1) Fetch the first selfie
NSFetchRequest *fetchRequest = [NSFetchRequest fetchRequestWithEntityName:@"Selfie"];
fetchRequest.predicate = [NSPredicate predicateWithFormat:@"name = %@", @"Selfie 1"];
NSArray *selfies = [context executeFetchRequest:fetchRequest error:nil];
if ([selfies count] == 1) {
  Selfie *selfie = selfies[0];

  // 2) Grab a social network from the selfie
  SocialNetwork *socialNetwork = [selfie.socialNetworks anyObject];
  if (socialNetwork != nil) {
    // 3) Check if it's a fault
    result = [NSString stringWithFormat:@"Social Network %@ a fault\n",
              [socialNetwork isFault] ? @"is" : @"is not"];

    // 4) Get the name
    result = [result stringByAppendingFormat:@"Social Network is named '%@'\n",
              socialNetwork.name];

    // 5) Check if it's a fault
    result = [result stringByAppendingFormat:@"Social Network %@ a fault\n",
              [socialNetwork isFault] ? @"is" : @"is not"];

    // 6) Turn it back into a fault
    [context refreshObject:socialNetwork mergeChanges:NO];
    result = [result stringByAppendingFormat:@"Turning Social Network into a fault\n"];

    // 7) Check if it's a fault
    result = [result stringByAppendingFormat:@"Social Network %@ a fault\n",
              [socialNetwork isFault] ? @"is" : @"is not"];
  } else {
    result = @"Couldn't find social networks for selfie";
  }
} else {
  result = @"Failed to fetch first selfie";
}
  return result;
}

@end
```

Listing 9-25. DidFault.swift with the Faulting Test Implemented

```swift
import Foundation
import CoreData

class DidFault : PerfTest {
    func runTestWithContext(context: NSManagedObjectContext) -> String! {
        var result : String?

        // 1) Fetch the first selfie
        let fetchRequest = NSFetchRequest(entityName: "Selfie")
        fetchRequest.predicate = NSPredicate(format: "name = %@", "Selfie 1")
```

```
        let selfies = context.executeFetchRequest(fetchRequest, error: nil)
        if selfies?.count == 1 {
            let selfie = selfies?[0] as Selfie

            // 2) Grab a social network from the selfie
            let socialNetwork = selfie.socialNetworks.anyObject() as SocialNetwork?
            if let socialNetwork = socialNetwork {
                // 3) Check if it's a fault
                result = NSString(format: "Social Network %@ a fault\n", socialNetwork.fault ?
                "is" : "is not")

                // 4) Get the name
                result = result?.stringByAppendingFormat("Social Network is named '%@'\n",
                socialNetwork.name)

                // 5) Check if it's a fault
                result = result?.stringByAppendingFormat("Social Network %@ a fault\n",
                socialNetwork.fault ? "is" : "is not")

                // 6) Turn it back into a fault
                context.refreshObject(socialNetwork, mergeChanges: false)
                result = result?.stringByAppendingFormat("Turning Social Network into a fault\n")

                // 7) Check if it's a fault
                result = result?.stringByAppendingFormat("Social Network %@ a fault\n",
                socialNetwork.fault ? "is" : "is not")
            }
            else {
                result = "Couldn't find social networks for selfie"
            }
        }
        else {
            result = "Failed to fetch first selfie"
        }

        return result!
    }
}
```

This code follows the seven steps, as promised. Accessing the social network's name in step 4 is what fires the fault, so that in step 5 the social network is not a fault. Step 6, of course, turns the social network back into a fault.

To add this new test to the picker view, so we can select it and run it, open ViewController.m, add an import for DidFault.h, and add an instance of DidFault to the tests array, as Listing 9-26 shows.

Listing 9-26. Adding an Instance of DidFault in the viewDidLoad Method of ViewController.m

```objc
- (void)viewDidLoad {
  [super viewDidLoad];

  self.startTime.text = @"";
  self.stopTime.text = @"";
  self.elapsedTime.text = @"";
  self.results.text = @"";

  self.tests = @[[[FetchAll alloc] init],
                 [[DidFault alloc] init]];
}
```

For Swift, add the instance in `ViewController.swift`, as Listing 9-27 shows.

Listing 9-27. Adding an Instance of DidFault in the viewDidLoad Method of ViewController.swift

```swift
override func viewDidLoad() {
    super.viewDidLoad()

    self.startTime.text = ""
    self.stopTime.text = ""
    self.elapsedTime.text = ""
    self.results.text = ""

    self.tests.append(FetchAll())
    self.tests.append(DidFault())
}
```

Build and run the application. You should see `DidFault` in the picker. Select it and tap Run Selected Test. You should see output similar to the following:

```
Social Network is a fault
Social Network is named 'SocialNetwork 117'
Social Network is not a fault
Turning Social Network into a fault
Social Network is a fault
```

You should also see output in the logs from when `willTurnIntoFault` and `didTurnIntoFault` were called, like the following:

```
2014-11-04 07:25:57.149 PerformanceTuning[38171:2069648] SocialNetwork named SocialNetwork 387 will
turn into fault
2014-11-04 07:25:57.151 PerformanceTuning[38171:2069648] SocialNetwork did turn into fault
```

Taking Control: Firing Faults on Purpose

This section on faulting began by explaining that you have more control over memory usage when you run SQL queries yourself than you do by allowing Core Data to manage data fetches. Although true, you can exert some amount of control over Core Data's fault management by firing faults yourself. By firing faults yourself, you can avoid inefficient scenarios in which Core Data must fire several small faults to fetch your data, incurring several trips to the persistent store.

Core Data provides two means for optimizing the firing of faults.

- Batch faulting
- Prefetching

We are going to test both batch faulting and prefetching. Before we do that, though, we create a test for firing single faults, so that we understand the performance gains of batch faulting and prefetching. Add a class called `SingleFault` that conforms to the `PerfTest` protocol. This test should fetch all the selfies and loop through them one at a time while doing the following:

- Access the name attribute so that a fault fires for this selfie only.
- Loop through all the related social networks and access their name attributes, one at a time, so that each access fires a fault.
- Reset each social network so that the next selfie will have to fire faults for each social network.
- Do the same for all the related people.

Listing 9-28 shows the header file, `SingleFault.h`, and Listing 9-29 shows `SingleFault.m`. Listing 9-30 shows the Swift implementation, `SingleFault.swift`.

Listing 9-28. SingleFault.h

```
#import "PerfTest.h"

@interface SingleFault : NSObject <PerfTest>

@end
```

Listing 9-29. SingleFault.m

```
#import "SingleFault.h"
#import "Selfie.h"
#import "SocialNetwork.h"
#import "Person.h"

@implementation SingleFault

- (NSString *)runTestWithContext:(NSManagedObjectContext *)context {
  // Fetch all the selfies
  NSFetchRequest *fetchRequest = [NSFetchRequest fetchRequestWithEntityName:@"Selfie"];
  NSArray *selfies = [context executeFetchRequest:fetchRequest error:nil];

  // Loop through all the selfies
  for (Selfie *selfie in selfies) {
    // Fire a fault just for this selfie
    [selfie valueForKey:@"name"];
```

```objectivec
        // Loop through the social networks for this selfie
        for (SocialNetwork *socialNetwork in selfie.socialNetworks) {
          // Fire a fault just for this social network
          [socialNetwork valueForKey:@"name"];

          // Put this social network back in a fault
          [context refreshObject:socialNetwork mergeChanges:NO];
        }

        // Loop through the people for this selfie
        for (Person *person in selfie.people) {
          // Fire a fault for this person
          [person valueForKey:@"name"];

          // Put this person back in a fault
          [context refreshObject:person mergeChanges:NO];
        }
      }
    }
    return @"Test complete";
}

@end
```

Listing 9-30. SingleFault.swift

```swift
import Foundation
import CoreData

class SingleFault : PerfTest {
    func runTestWithContext(context: NSManagedObjectContext) -> String! {
        // Fetch all the selfies
        let fetchRequest = NSFetchRequest(entityName: "Selfie")
        let selfies = context.executeFetchRequest(fetchRequest, error: nil)

        // Loop through all the selfies
        for selfie in selfies as [Selfie] {
            // Fire a fault just for this selfie
            selfie.valueForKey("name")

            // Loop through the social networks for this selfie
            for obj in selfie.socialNetworks {
                let socialNetwork = obj as SocialNetwork

                // Fire a fault just for this social network
                socialNetwork.valueForKey("name")

                // Put this social network back in a fault
                context.refreshObject(socialNetwork, mergeChanges: false)
            }
```

```
            // Loop through the people for this selfie
            for obj in selfie.people {
                let person = obj as Person

                // Fire a fault for this person
                person.valueForKey("name")

                // Put this person back in a fault
                context.refreshObject(person, mergeChanges: false)
            }
        }

        return "Test complete"
    }
}
```

As with the DidFault class, add an instance of SingleFault to the tests array in ViewController.m, as well as an import for SingleFault.h. The tests array should now match Listing 9-31 for Objective-C or Listing 9-32 for Swift.

Listing 9-31. Adding SingleFault to the Tests Array (Objective-C)

```
self.tests = @[[[FetchAll alloc] init],
               [[DidFault alloc] init],
               [[SingleFault alloc] init]];
```

Listing 9-32. Adding SingleFault to the Tests Array (Swift)

```
self.tests.append(FetchAll())
self.tests.append(DidFault())
self.tests.append(SingleFault())
```

Before you build and run the application, comment out the willTurnIntoFault and didTurnIntoFault methods of SocialNetwork, so that we don't fill the logs or skew the timing results. Then, build and run the application and run the SingleFault test. Running this on an iPhone 6 Plus takes just under 30 seconds. Let's see if we can improve on these results!

Batch Faulting

When you execute a fetch request, you can tell Core Data to return the objects as faults or non-faults by calling NSFetchRequest's setReturnsObjectsAsFaults: method before executing the fetch request. This method takes a Boolean parameter: pass YES or true to this method to return the fetched objects as faults, or NO or false to return the objects as non-faults. By passing NO or false, you get the objects with all their associated attributes loaded (but, of course, not all the attributes of their relationships).

In this section, we create a test that mirrors the SingleFault test, but instead of firing the faults one by one, it fires them in batches. Create a class called BatchFault that conforms to the PerfTest protocol. By now, you should be able to determine what the header file looks like (it follows the same pattern as DidFault.h and SingleFault.h), so we don't list it, or any of the other test header files we write in this chapter, here. The implementation file resembles SingleFault.m or SingleFault.swift—it loops through the selfies and, for each selfie, loops through the social networks and people. The difference, however, is that BatchFault uses batch faulting to fault all the objects at once. That is, it faults all the selfies as once, and then for each selfie, it faults all its social networks and people at once. It does this by creating fetch request and calling setReturnsObjectsAsFaults: on them, passing NO or false each time. Listing 9-33 shows the code for BatchFault.m, and Listing 9-34 shows the code for BatchFault.swift.

Listing 9-33. BatchFault.m

```
#import "BatchFault.h"
#import "Selfie.h"
#import "SocialNetwork.h"
#import "Person.h"

@implementation BatchFault

- (NSString *)runTestWithContext:(NSManagedObjectContext *)context {
  // Fetch all the selfies
  NSFetchRequest *fetchRequest = [NSFetchRequest fetchRequestWithEntityName:@"Selfie"];

  // Return the selfies as non-faults
  [fetchRequest setReturnsObjectsAsFaults:NO];
  NSArray *selfies = [context executeFetchRequest:fetchRequest error:nil];

  // Loop through all the selfies
  for (Selfie *selfie in selfies) {
    // Doesn't fire a fault, the data are already in memory
    [selfie valueForKey:@"name"];

    // For this selfie, fire faults for all the social networks
    NSFetchRequest *snFetchRequest = [NSFetchRequest fetchRequestWithEntityName:@"SocialNetwork"];
    [snFetchRequest setReturnsObjectsAsFaults:NO];
    [context executeFetchRequest:snFetchRequest error:nil];

    // For this selfie, fire faults for all the social networks
    NSFetchRequest *pFetchRequest = [NSFetchRequest fetchRequestWithEntityName:@"Person"];
    [pFetchRequest setReturnsObjectsAsFaults:NO];
    [context executeFetchRequest:pFetchRequest error:nil];

    // Loop through the social networks for this selfie
    for (SocialNetwork *socialNetwork in selfie.socialNetworks) {
      // Doesn't fire a fault, the data are already in memory
      [socialNetwork valueForKey:@"name"];

      // Put this social network back in a fault
      [context refreshObject:socialNetwork mergeChanges:NO];
    }
```

```
    // Loop through the people for this selfie
    for (Person *person in selfie.people) {
      // Doesn't fire a fault, the data are already in memory
      [person valueForKey:@"name"];

      // Put this person back in a fault
      [context refreshObject:person mergeChanges:NO];
    }
  }
  return @"Test complete";
}

@end
```

Listing 9-34. BatchFault.swift

```swift
import Foundation
import CoreData

class BatchFault : PerfTest {
    func runTestWithContext(context: NSManagedObjectContext) -> String! {
        // Fetch all the selfies
        let fetchRequest = NSFetchRequest(entityName: "Selfie")

        // Return the selfies as non-faults
        fetchRequest.returnsObjectsAsFaults = true
        let selfies = context.executeFetchRequest(fetchRequest, error: nil) as [Selfie]

        // Loop through all the selfies
        for selfie in selfies {
            // Doesn't fire a fault, the data are already in memory
            selfie.valueForKey("name")

            // For this selfie, fire faults for all the social networks
            let snFetchRequest = NSFetchRequest(entityName: "SocialNetwork")
            snFetchRequest.returnsObjectsAsFaults = false
            context.executeFetchRequest(snFetchRequest, error: nil)

            // For this selfie, fire faults for all the people
            let pFetchRequest = NSFetchRequest(entityName: "Person")
            pFetchRequest.returnsObjectsAsFaults = false
            context.executeFetchRequest(pFetchRequest, error: nil)

            // Loop through the social networks for this selfie
            for obj in selfie.socialNetworks {
                let socialNetwork = obj as SocialNetwork

                // Doesn't fire a fault, the data are already in memory
                socialNetwork.valueForKey("name")

                // Put this social network back in a fault
                context.refreshObject(socialNetwork, mergeChanges: false)
            }
```

```
            // Loop through the people for this selfie
            for obj in selfie.people {
                let person = obj as Person

                // Doesn't fire a fault, the data are already in memory
                person.valueForKey("name")

                // Put this person back in a fault
                context.refreshObject(person, mergeChanges: false)
            }
        }

        return "Test complete"
    }
}
```

Add an instance of BatchFault to the tests array in ViewController.m (with an import for BatchFault.h) or ViewController.swift, as we did for the other tests, and build and run the program. Run the BatchFault test and check the elapsed time. On our iPhone 6 Plus it takes . . . a little over 30 seconds. That's slower than the SingleFault test. That's disappointing, but it shows the importance of practice over theory. Theoretically, firing the faults in batches should be much faster than firing them singly. In practice, however, we haven't gained any performance—in fact, we've lost some—and have made the code a little less readable. Let's see if prefetching works any better.

Prefetching

Similar to batch faulting, prefetching minimizes the number of times that Core Data has to fire faults and go fetch data. With prefetching, though, you tell Core Data when you perform a fetch to also fetch the related objects you specify. For example, using this chapter's data model, when you fetch the selfies, you can tell Core Data to prefetch the related social networks, people, or both.

To prefetch related objects, call NSFetchRequest's setRelationshipKeyPathsForPrefetching: method, passing an array that contains the names of the relationships that you want Core Data to prefetch. To prefetch the related social networks and people when you fetch the selfies, for example, use the following Objective-C code:

```
NSFetchRequest *fetchRequest = [NSFetchRequest fetchRequestWithEntityName:@"Selfie"];
[fetchRequest setRelationshipKeyPathsForPrefetching:@[@"socialNetworks", @"people"]];
NSArray *selfies = [context executeFetchRequest:fetchRequest error:nil];
```

In Swift, it looks like the following:

```
let fetchRequest = NSFetchRequest(entityName: "Selfie")
fetchRequest.relationshipKeyPathsForPrefetching = ["socialNetwork", "people"]
let selfies = context.executeFetchRequest(fetchRequest, error: nil) as [Selfie]
```

The lines in bold instruct Core Data to prefetch all the related social networks and people when it fetches the selfies. Note that you'll get no error if the strings you pass don't match any existing relationship names, so check your spelling carefully. You may think you're prefetching relationships, but an errant misspelling may be denying your performance gains.

To test prefetching, create a class called Prefetch that conforms to the PerfTest protocol. In the implementation of runTestWithContext:, use essentially the same code as SingleFault, but this time add a call to setRelationshipKeyPathsForPrefetching:, passing an array containing the names of the relationships. Listing 9-35 shows the code for Prefetch.m, and Listing 9-36 shows the code for Prefetch.swift.

Listing 9-35. Prefetch.m

```objc
#import "Prefetch.h"
#import "Selfie.h"
#import "SocialNetwork.h"
#import "Person.h"

@implementation Prefetch

- (NSString *)runTestWithContext:(NSManagedObjectContext *)context {
  // Set up the fetch request for all the selfies
  NSFetchRequest *fetchRequest = [NSFetchRequest fetchRequestWithEntityName:@"Selfie"];

  // Prefetch the social networks and people
  [fetchRequest setRelationshipKeyPathsForPrefetching:@[@"socialNetworks", @"people"]];

  // Perform the fetch
  NSArray *selfies = [context executeFetchRequest:fetchRequest error:nil];

  // Loop through the selfies
  for (Selfie *selfie in selfies) {
    // Fire a fault just for this selfie
    [selfie valueForKey:@"name"];

    // Loop through the social networks for this selfie
    for (SocialNetwork *socialNetwork in selfie.socialNetworks) {
      // Fire a fault just for this social network
      [socialNetwork valueForKey:@"name"];

      // Put this social network back in a fault
      [context refreshObject:socialNetwork mergeChanges:NO];
    }

    // Loop through the people for this selfie
    for (Person *person in selfie.people) {
      // Fire a fault for this person
      [person valueForKey:@"name"];

      // Put this person back in a fault
      [context refreshObject:person mergeChanges:NO];
    }
  }
  return @"Test complete";
}

@end
```

Listing 9-36. Prefetch.swift

```swift
import Foundation
import CoreData

class Prefetch : PerfTest {
    func runTestWithContext(context: NSManagedObjectContext) -> String! {
        // Set up the fetch request for all the selfies
        let fetchRequest = NSFetchRequest(entityName: "Selfie")

        // Prefetch the social networks and people
        fetchRequest.relationshipKeyPathsForPrefetching = ["socialNetwork", "people"]

        // Perform the fetch
        let selfies = context.executeFetchRequest(fetchRequest, error: nil) as [Selfie]

        // Loop through the selfies
        for selfie in selfies {
            // For a fault just for the selfie
            selfie.valueForKey("name")

            // Loop through the social networks for this selfie
            for obj in selfie.socialNetworks {
                let socialNetwork = obj as SocialNetwork

                // Fire a fault for this social network
                socialNetwork.valueForKey("name")

                // Put this social network back in a fault
                context.refreshObject(socialNetwork, mergeChanges: false)
            }

            // Loop through the people for this selfie
            for obj in selfie.people {
                let person = obj as Person

                // Fire a fault for this person
                person.valueForKey("name")

                // Put this person back in a fault
                context.refreshObject(person, mergeChanges: false)
            }
        }

        return "Test complete"
    }
}
```

Add a Prefetch instance to the tests array in ViewController.m or ViewController.swift, as well as an import for Prefetch.h (if you're doing Objective-C), and build and run the application. Run the Prefetch test. On our iPhone 6 Plus, it takes just under 3 seconds—about a 90% improvement!

As with batch faulting you should test prefetching with your own data model instead of coming to absolute conclusions, but prefetching is obviously a candidate for improving fetch speed for large data models with relationships.

Caching

Regardless of target language or platform, most data persistence frameworks and libraries have an internal caching mechanism. Properly implemented caches provide opportunities for significant performance gains, especially for applications that need to retrieve the same data repeatedly. Core Data is no exception. The NSManagedObjectContext class serves as a built-in cache for the Core Data framework. When you retrieve an object from the backing persistent store, the context keeps a reference to it to track its changes. If you retrieve the object again, the context can give the caller the same object reference as it did in the first invocation.

The obvious trade-off that results from the use of caching is that, while improving performance, caching uses more memory. If no cache management scheme were in place to limit the memory usage of the cache, the cache could fill up with objects until the whole system collapses from lack of memory. To manage memory, the Core Data context has weak references to the managed objects it pulls out of the persistent store. This means that if the retain count of a managed object reaches zero because no other object has a reference to it, the managed object will be discarded. The exception to this rule is if the object has been modified in any way. In this case, the context keeps a strong reference (i.e., sends a retain signal to the managed object) and keeps it until the context is either committed or rolled back, at which point it becomes a weak reference again.

> **Note**   The default retain behavior can be changed by setting the returnsObjectsAsFaults property of NSManagedObjectContext to YES or true. Setting it to YES or true will cause the context to retain all registered objects. The default behavior retains registered objects only when they are inserted, updated, deleted, or locked.

In this section, you will examine the difference between fetching objects from the persistent store or from the cache. You will build a test that does the following:

1. Retrieves all selfies.

2. Retrieves all social networks for each selfie.

3. Displays the time it took to perform both retrievals.

4. Retrieves all selfies (this time the objects will be cached).

5. Retrieves all social networks for each selfie.

6. Displays the time it took to perform both retrievals.

Create a test class, conforming to the PerfTest protocol, called Cache. Listing 9-37 shows the code for Cache.m, and Listing 9-38 shows the code for Cache.swift.

Listing 9-37. Cache.m

```objc
#import "Cache.h"
#import "Selfie.h"
#import "SocialNetwork.h"
#import "Person.h"

@implementation Cache

- (NSString *)runTestWithContext:(NSManagedObjectContext *)context {
  NSMutableString *result = [NSMutableString string];

  // Load the data while it's not cached
  NSDate *start1 = [NSDate date];
  [self loadDataWithContext:context];
  NSDate *end1 = [NSDate date];

  // Record the results
  [result appendFormat:@"Without cache: %.3f s\n", [end1 timeIntervalSinceDate:start1]];

  // Load the data while it's cached
  NSDate *start2 = [NSDate date];
  [self loadDataWithContext:context];
  NSDate *end2 = [NSDate date];

  // Record the results
  [result appendFormat:@"With cache: %.3f s\n", [end2 timeIntervalSinceDate:start2]];

  return result;
}

- (void)loadDataWithContext:(NSManagedObjectContext *)context {
  // Load the selfies
  NSFetchRequest *fetchRequest = [NSFetchRequest fetchRequestWithEntityName:@"Selfie"];
  NSArray *selfies = [context executeFetchRequest:fetchRequest error:nil];

  // Loop through the selfies
  for (Selfie *selfie in selfies) {
    // Load the selfie's data
    [selfie valueForKey:@"name"];

    // Loop through the social networks
    for (SocialNetwork *socialNetwork in selfie.socialNetworks) {
      // Load the social network's data
      [socialNetwork valueForKey:@"name"];
    }
  }
}

@end
```

Listing 9-38. Cache.swift

```swift
import Foundation
import CoreData

class Cache : PerfTest {
    func runTestWithContext(context: NSManagedObjectContext) -> String! {
        let result = NSMutableString()

        // Load the data while it's not cached
        let start1 = NSDate()
        self.loadDataWithContext(context)
        let end1 = NSDate()

        // Record the results
        result.appendFormat("Without cache: %.3f s\n", end1.timeIntervalSinceDate(start1))

        // Load the data while it's cached
        let start2 = NSDate()
        self.loadDataWithContext(context)
        let end2 = NSDate()

        // Record the results
        result.appendFormat("With cache: %.3f s\n", end2.timeIntervalSinceDate(start2))

        return result
    }

    func loadDataWithContext(context: NSManagedObjectContext) {
        // Load the selfies
        let fetchRequest = NSFetchRequest(entityName: "Selfie")
        let selfies = context.executeFetchRequest(fetchRequest, error: nil) as [Selfie]

        // Loop through the selfies
        for selfie in selfies {
            // Load the selfie's data
            selfie.valueForKey("name")

            // Loop through the social networks
            for obj in selfie.socialNetworks {
                let socialNetwork = obj as SocialNetwork

                // Load the social network's data
                socialNetwork.valueForKey("name")
            }
        }
    }
}
```

Let's examine the `runWithContext:` method. It does the same thing twice: fetches all the selfies and all the social networks. The first time, the cache is explicitly cleared, as it is before each test, by calling `[context reset]` or `context.reset()` in the `runTest:` handler in `ViewController`.

The second time, the objects will be in the cache, and therefore the data will come back much faster. The `loadDataWithContext:` method does the actual fetches. You explicitly get the `name` property of the selfies and social networks in order to force Core Data to load the attributes for the objects, firing a fault if necessary.

Add an instance of `Cache` to the `tests` array in `ViewController.m` or `ViewController.swift`, and also an import for `Cache.h` if using Objective-C. Build the application and run the `Cache` test. On our iPhone 5s, the test takes about 0.6 seconds without a cache, and about 0.09 seconds with the cache, which is about an 85% improvement. The lesson, then, is to be judicious about expiring your cache by calling `reset` on your managed object context, as its caching can improve performance significantly. The next section discusses cache expiration strategies.

Expiring the Cache

Any time an application uses a cache, the question of cache expiration arises: when should objects in the cache expire and be reloaded from the persistent store? The difficulty in determining the expiration interval comes from juggling the performance gain obtained by caching objects for long intervals versus the extra memory consumption this entails and the potential staleness of the cached data. This section examines the trade-offs of the two possibilities for expiring the cache and freeing some memory.

Memory Consumption

As more and more objects are put into the cache, memory usage increases. Even if a managed object is entirely faulted, you can determine the minimum amount of memory an `NSManagedObject` instance uses by calling the following:

```
NSLog(@"%zu", class_getInstanceSize(NSManagedObject.class)); // Objective-C
println(String(format: "%zu", class_getInstanceSize(NSManagedObject.self))) // Swift
```

Note that, for the `class_getInstanceSize()` function, you must import `<objc/objc-runtime.h>` in Objective-C. If you're running on a 32-bit system, you'll see that the allocated size of an unpopulated managed object is 48 bytes. On a 64-bit system, the size is 96 bytes. This is because it holds references (i.e., 4-byte or 8-byte pointers, depending on the bitness of the operating system) to other objects such as the entity description, the context, and the object ID. Even without any actual data, a managed object occupies a minimum of 48 bytes (32-bit OS) or 96 bytes (64-bit OS). This is a best-case scenario because this approximation does not include the memory occupied by the unique object ID, which is populated. This means that if you have 100,000 managed objects in the cache, even faulted, you are using at least 5MB (32-bit OS) or 10MB (64-bit OS) of memory for things other than your data. If you start fetching data without faulting, you can run into memory issues quickly.

The trick to this balancing act is to remove data from the cache when it's no longer needed or if you can afford to pay the price of retrieving the objects from the persistent store when you need them again.

Brute-Force Cache Expiration

If you don't care about losing all the managed objects, you can reset the context entirely. This is rarely the option you want to choose, but it is extremely efficient. `NSManagedObjectContext`, as we've seen, has a `reset` method that will wipe the cache out in one swoop. Once you call `[context reset]` or `context.reset()`, your memory footprint will be dramatically smaller, but you will have to pay the price of going to the persistent store if you want to retrieve any objects again. Please also understand that, as with any other kind of mass destruction mechanism, resetting the cache in the middle of a running application has serious side effects and collateral damage. For example, any managed objects that you were using prior to the reset are now invalid. If you try to do anything with them, your efforts will be met with runtime errors.

Expiring the Cache Through Faulting

Faulting is a more subtle option, as the section on faulting explains. You can fault any managed object by calling `[context refreshObject:managedObject mergeChanges:NO]` (or the Swift equivalent). After this method call, the object is faulted, and therefore the memory it occupies in the cache is minimized, although not zero. A non-negligible advantage of this strategy, however, is that when the managed object is turned into a fault, any managed object it has a reference to (through relationships) is released. If those related managed objects have no other references to them, then they will be removed from the cache, further reducing the memory footprint. Faulting managed objects in this manner helps prune the entire object graph.

Uniquing

Both business and technology like to turn nouns into verbs, and the pseudoword "uniquing" testifies to this weakness. It attempts to define the action of making something unique or ensuring uniqueness. Usage suggests not only that Apple didn't invent the term but also that it predates Core Data. Apple embraces the term in its Core Data documentation, however, raising fears that one day Apple will call the action of listening to music *iPodding*.

The technology industry uses the term "uniquing" in conjunction with memory objects versus their representation in a data store. In *Core Java Data Objects* by Sameer Tyagi and Michael Vorburger (Prentice Hall, 2003), it says that uniquing "ensures that no matter how many times a persistent object is found, it has only one in-memory representation. All references to the same persistent object within the scope of the same PersistenceManager instance reference the same in-memory object."

Martin Fowler, in *Patterns of Enterprise Application Architecture* (Addison-Wesley Professional, 2005), gives it a less colorful, more descriptive, and more English-compliant name: *identity map*. He explains that an identity map "ensures that each object gets loaded only once by keeping every loaded object in a map." Whatever you call it or however you describe it, *uniquing* means that Core Data conserves memory use by ensuring the uniqueness of each object in memory and that no two memory instances of an object point to the same instance in the persistent store.

Consider, for example, the Core Data model in the application in this chapter. Each `Selfie` instance has a relationship with 500 `Person` instances. When you run the application and reference the `Person` instances through any `Selfie` instances, you always get the same `Person` instances, as Figure 9-6 depicts. If Core Data didn't use uniquing, you could find yourself in the scenario shown in Figure 9-7, where each Person instance is represented in memory several times, once for each Selfie instance, and each Selfie instance is represented in memory several times, once for each Person instance.

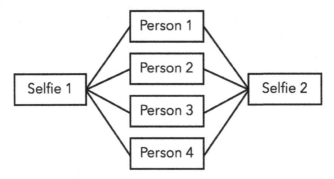

Figure 9-6. Uniquing selfies and people

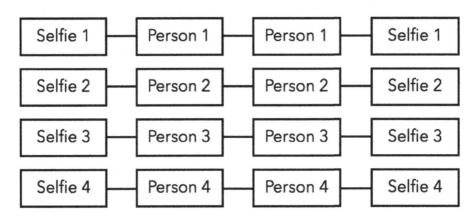

Figure 9-7. Nonuniquing selfies and people

Uniquing not only conserves memory but also eliminates data inconsistency issues. Think what could happen, for example, if Core Data didn't employ uniquing and the PerformanceTuning application had 500 memory instances of each selfie (one for each person). Suppose that Person 1 changed the rating of a selfie to 5 and Person 2 changed the rating of the same selfie to 7. What rating should the selfie really have? When the application stores the selfie in the persistent store, what rating should it save? You can imagine the data inconsistency bugs you'd have to track down if Core Data maintained more than one instance of each data object in memory.

Note that uniquing occurs within a single managed object context only, not across managed object contexts. The good news, however, is that Core Data's default behavior, which you can't change, is to unique. Uniquing comes free with Core Data.

To test uniquing, create a test called Uniquing (again, make it conform to PerfTest) that fetches all the selfies from the persistent store and then compares each of their related people to each other selfie's related people. For the test to pass, the code must verify that only 500 Person instances live in memory and that each selfie points to the same 500 Person instances. To make these comparisons easier, the code sorts the people into a determined order so you can predictably compare instances. The first time through the loop for the first selfie, the code stores the people in a reference array so that all subsequent loops have something to compare the people against. In each subsequent loop, the code pulls the people for the selfie and compares them to the reference array. If just one person doesn't match, the test fails. Listing 9-39 shows the code for Uniquing.m, and Listing 9-40 shows the code for Uniquing.swift.

Listing 9-39. Uniquing.m

```
#import "Uniquing.h"
#import "Selfie.h"
#import "Person.h"

@implementation Uniquing

- (NSString *)runTestWithContext:(NSManagedObjectContext *)context {
  // Array to hold the people for comparison purposes
  NSArray *referencePeople = nil;

  // Sorting for the people
  NSSortDescriptor *sortDescriptor  = [[NSSortDescriptor alloc] initWithKey:@"name"
                                                                  ascending:YES];

  // Fetch all the selfies
  NSFetchRequest *fetchRequest = [NSFetchRequest fetchRequestWithEntityName:@"Selfie"];
  NSArray *selfies = [context executeFetchRequest:fetchRequest error:nil];

  // Loop through the selfies
  for (Selfie *selfie in selfies) {
    // Get the sorted people
    NSArray *people = [selfie.people sortedArrayUsingDescriptors:@[sortDescriptor]];

    // Store the first selfie's people for comparison purposes
    if (referencePeople == nil) {
      referencePeople = people;
    } else {
      // Do the comparison
      for (int i = 0, n = (int)[people count]; i < n; i++) {
        if (people[i] != referencePeople[i]) {
          return [NSString stringWithFormat:@"Uniquing test failed; %@ != %@",
                  people[i], referencePeople[i]];
        }
      }
    }
  }
  return @"Test complete";
}

@end
```

Listing 9-40. Uniquing.swift

```swift
import Foundation
import CoreData

class Uniquing : PerfTest {
    func runTestWithContext(context: NSManagedObjectContext) -> String! {
        // Array to hold the people for comparison purposes
        var referencePeople : [Person]?

        // Sorting for the people
        let sortDescriptor = NSSortDescriptor(key: "name", ascending: true)

        // Fetch all the selfies
        let fetchRequest = NSFetchRequest(entityName: "Selfie")
        let selfies = context.executeFetchRequest(fetchRequest, error: nil) as [Selfie]

        // Loop through the selfies
        for selfie in selfies {
            // Get the sorted people
            let people = selfie.people.sortedArrayUsingDescriptors([sortDescriptor]) as [Person]

            // Store the first selfie's people for comparison purposes
            if let referencePeople = referencePeople {
                // Do the comparison
                for var i=0, n = people.count; i<n; i++ {
                    if people[i] != referencePeople[i] {
                        return NSString(format: "Uniquing test failed; %@ != %@", people[i],
                            referencePeople[i])
                    }
                }
            }
            else {
                referencePeople = people
            }
        }

        return "Test complete"
    }
}
```

Add an instance of Uniquing to the tests array in ViewController.m or ViewController.swift, add an import for Uniquing.h if necessary, build and run the application, and run the new test. You'll eventually see the "Test complete" message, indicating that the test passed and uniquing worked.

Improve Performance with Better Predicates

Despite the year in the movie title *2001: A Space Odyssey*, we are still far away from our machines having the intelligence to respond with things like "I'm sorry, Dave. I'm afraid I can't do that." As of the time of writing this book, programmers still have to do a lot of hand-holding to walk their machines through the process of doing what they are asked to do. This means that how you write your code determines how efficient it will be. There are often multiple ways to retrieve the same data, but the solution you use can significantly alter the performance of your application.

Using Faster Comparators

Generally speaking, string comparators perform more slowly than primitive comparators. When predicates are compounded using an OR operator, it is always more efficient to put the primitive comparators first because if they resolve to TRUE, then the rest of the comparators don't need to be evaluated. This is because "TRUE OR anything" is always true. A similar strategy can be used with AND-compounded predicates. In this case, if the first predicate fails, then the second will not be evaluated, because "FALSE AND anything" is always false.

To validate this, add a new test to your performance test application called Predicate and make it conform to the PerfTest protocol. This test consists of two fetch requests, which retrieve the same objects using an OR-compounded predicate. In the first test, the string comparator LIKE is used before the primitive comparator. In the second test, the comparators are permuted. Run each test 1,000 times in order to get significant timings; each time through the loop, the cache is reset to keep a clean context. Listing 9-41 shows Predicate.m and Listing 9-42 shows Predicate.swift.

Listing 9-41. Predicate.m

```objc
#import "Predicate.h"

@implementation Predicate

- (NSString *)runTestWithContext:(NSManagedObjectContext *)context {
  NSMutableString *result = [NSMutableString string];

  // Set up the first fetch request
  NSFetchRequest *fetchRequest1 = [NSFetchRequest fetchRequestWithEntityName:@"Selfie"];
  fetchRequest1.predicate = [NSPredicate predicateWithFormat:@"(name LIKE %@) OR (rating < %d)",
  @"*e*ie*", 5];

  // Run the first fetch request and measure
  NSDate *start1 = [NSDate date];
  for (int i = 0; i < 1000; i++) {
    [context reset];
    [context executeFetchRequest:fetchRequest1 error:nil];
  }
  NSDate *end1 = [NSDate date];
  [result appendFormat:@"Slow predicate: %.3f s\n", [end1 timeIntervalSinceDate:start1]];

  // Set up the second fetch request
  NSFetchRequest *fetchRequest2 = [NSFetchRequest fetchRequestWithEntityName:@"Selfie"];
  fetchRequest1.predicate = [NSPredicate predicateWithFormat:@"(rating < %d) OR (name LIKE %@)",
  5, @"*e*ie*"];
```

```objc
  // Run the first fetch request and measure
  NSDate *start2 = [NSDate date];
  for (int i = 0; i < 1000; i++) {
    [context reset];
    [context executeFetchRequest:fetchRequest2 error:nil];
  }
  NSDate *end2 = [NSDate date];
  [result appendFormat:@"Fast predicate: %.3f s\n", [end2 timeIntervalSinceDate:start2]];

  return result;
}

@end
```

Listing 9-42. Predicate.swift

```swift
import Foundation
import CoreData

class Predicate : PerfTest {
    func runTestWithContext(context: NSManagedObjectContext) -> String! {
        let result = NSMutableString()

        // Set up the first fetch request
        let fetchRequest1 = NSFetchRequest(entityName: "Selfie")
        fetchRequest1.predicate = NSPredicate(format: "(name LIKE %@) OR (rating < %d)", "*e*ie*", 5)

        // Run the first fetch request and measure
        let start1 = NSDate()
        for var i=0; i<1000; i++ {
            context.reset()
            context.executeFetchRequest(fetchRequest1, error: nil)
        }
        let end1 = NSDate()
        result.appendFormat("Slow predicate: %.3f s\n", end1.timeIntervalSinceDate(start1))

        // Set up the second fetch request
        let fetchRequest2 = NSFetchRequest(entityName: "Selfie")
        fetchRequest2.predicate = NSPredicate(format: "(rating < %d) OR (name LIKE %@)", 5, "*e*ie*")

        // Run the first fetch request and measure
        let start2 = NSDate()
        for var i=0; i<1000; i++ {
            context.reset()
            context.executeFetchRequest(fetchRequest2, error: nil)
        }
        let end2 = NSDate()
        result.appendFormat("Fast predicate: %.3f s\n", end2.timeIntervalSinceDate(start2))

        return result
    }
}
```

After importing `Predicate.h` into `ViewController.m` and adding a `Predicate` instance to the `tests` array, build and run the application, run the `Predicate` test, and note the times for the slow predicate versus the fast predicate. On our iPhone 6 Plus, the slow predicate takes about 6.3 seconds, while the fast predicate takes about a third of the time: about 2.3 seconds.

Using Subqueries

You saw in Chapter 3 how to use subqueries to help simplify the code. In this section, you add a test to show the difference between using subqueries and retrieving related data manually. Consider an example in which you want to find all people from a selfie who match certain criteria. To do this without using a subquery, you have to first fetch all the selfies that match the criteria. You then have to iterate through each selfie and extract the people. You then go through the people and add them to your result set, making sure you don't duplicate people if they appear in multiple selfies. Listing 9-43 shows the manual subquery code in Objective-C, and Listing 9-44 shows the Swift version.

Listing 9-43. Doing a Subquery the Hard Way (Objective-C)

```
NSMutableDictionary *people = [NSMutableDictionary dictionary];

NSFetchRequest *fetchRequest = [NSFetchRequest fetchRequestWithEntityName:@"Selfie"];
fetchRequest.predicate = [NSPredicate predicateWithFormat:@"(rating < %d) OR (name LIKE %@)", 5,
@"*e*ie*"];
NSArray *selfies = [context executeFetchRequest:fetchRequest error:nil];

for (Selfie *selfie in selfies) {
  for (Person *person in selfie.people) {
    [people setObject:person forKey:[[[person objectID] URIRepresentation] description]];
  }
}
```

Listing 9-44. Doing a Subquery the Hard Way (Swift)

```
var people = [String: Person]()

let fetchRequest = NSFetchRequest(entityName: "Selfie")
fetchRequest.predicate = NSPredicate(format: "(rating < %d) OR (name LIKE %@)", 5, "*e*ie*")
let selfies = context.executeFetchRequest(fetchRequest, error: nil) as [Selfie]

for selfie in selfies {
    for obj in selfie.people {
        let person = obj as Person
        let key : String = person.objectID.URIRepresentation().description
        people[key] = person
    }
}
```

In this implementation, the people dictionary contains all the matching people. You keyed them by objectID to eliminate duplicates. The alternative to this approach is to let Core Data do the matching for you by using subqueries. Listing 9-45 (Objective-C) or Listing 9-46 (Swift) shows the same result set using a subquery.

Listing 9-45. Doing a Subquery the Right Way (Objective-C)

```objc
NSFetchRequest *fetchRequest = [NSFetchRequest fetchRequestWithEntityName:@"Person"];
fetchRequest.predicate = [NSPredicate predicateWithFormat:@"(SUBQUERY(selfies, $x, ($x.rating < %d)
OR ($x.name LIKE %@)).@count > 0)", 5, @"*e*ie*"];
NSArray *people = [context executeFetchRequest:fetchRequest error:nil];
```

Listing 9-46. Doing a Subquery the Right Way (Swift)

```swift
let fetchRequest = NSFetchRequest(entityName: "Person")
fetchRequest.predicate = NSPredicate(format: "(SUBQUERY(selfies, $x, ($x.rating < %d) OR ($x.name
LIKE %@)).@count > 0)", 5, "*e*ie*")
let people = context.executeFetchRequest(fetchRequest2, error: nil) as [Selfie]
```

One of the major differences here is that you let the persistent store do all the work of retrieving the matching people, which means that most of the results don't land in the context layer of Core Data for you to post-process. With the subquery, you don't actually retrieve the selfies, as you did in the manual approach, and the fetched request is set up to fetch people directly. Also, the manual option has to fire faults to retrieve the people after retrieving the selfies.

To demonstrate the improved efficiency of the subquery approach, create a new PerfTest-conforming class called Subquery. Listing 9-47 shows Subquery.m, and Listing 9-48 shows Subquery.swift.

Listing 9-47. Subquery.m

```objc
#import "Subquery.h"
#import "Selfie.h"
#import "Person.h"


@implementation Subquery

- (NSString *)runTestWithContext:(NSManagedObjectContext *)context {
  NSMutableString *result = [NSMutableString string];

  // Set up the first fetch request, with no subquery
  NSFetchRequest *fetchRequest1 = [NSFetchRequest fetchRequestWithEntityName:@"Selfie"];
  fetchRequest1.predicate = [NSPredicate predicateWithFormat:@"(rating < %d) OR (name LIKE %@)", 5,
  @"*e*ie*"];

  // Mark the time and get the results
  NSDate *start1 = [NSDate date];
  NSArray *selfies = [context executeFetchRequest:fetchRequest1 error:nil];
  NSMutableDictionary *people1 = [NSMutableDictionary dictionary];
  for (Selfie *selfie in selfies) {
    for (Person *person in selfie.people) {
      [people1 setObject:person forKey:[[[person objectID] URIRepresentation] description]];
    }
  }
  NSDate *end1 = [NSDate date];

  // Record the results of the manual request
  [result appendFormat:@"No subquery: %.3f s\n", [end1 timeIntervalSinceDate:start1]];
  [result appendFormat:@"People retrieved: %ld\n", [people1 count]];
```

```objc
  // Reset the context so we get clean results
  [context reset];

  // Set up the second fetch request, with subquery
  NSFetchRequest *fetchRequest2 = [NSFetchRequest fetchRequestWithEntityName:@"Person"];
  fetchRequest2.predicate = [NSPredicate predicateWithFormat:@"(SUBQUERY(selfies, $x,
  ($x.rating < %d) OR ($x.name LIKE %@)).@count > 0)", 5, @"*e*ie*"];

  // Mark the time and get the results
  NSDate *start2 = [NSDate date];
  NSArray *people2 = [context executeFetchRequest:fetchRequest2 error:nil];
  NSDate *end2 = [NSDate date];

  // Record the results of the subquery request
  [result appendFormat:@"Subquery: %.3f s\n", [end2 timeIntervalSinceDate:start2]];
  [result appendFormat:@"People retrieved: %ld\n", [people2 count]];

  return result;
}

@end
```

Listing 9-48. Subquery.swift

```objc
#import "Subquery.h"
#import "Selfie.h"
#import "Person.h"

@implementation Subquery

- (NSString *)runTestWithContext:(NSManagedObjectContext *)context {
  NSMutableString *result = [NSMutableString string];

  // Set up the first fetch request, with no subquery
  NSFetchRequest *fetchRequest1 = [NSFetchRequest fetchRequestWithEntityName:@"Selfie"];
  fetchRequest1.predicate = [NSPredicate predicateWithFormat:@"(rating < %d) OR (name LIKE %@)",
  5, @"*e*ie*"];

  // Mark the time and get the results
  NSDate *start1 = [NSDate date];
  NSArray *selfies = [context executeFetchRequest:fetchRequest1 error:nil];
  NSMutableDictionary *people1 = [NSMutableDictionary dictionary];
  for (Selfie *selfie in selfies) {
    for (Person *person in selfie.people) {
      [people1 setObject:person forKey:[[[person objectID] URIRepresentation] description]];
    }
  }
  NSDate *end1 = [NSDate date];

  // Record the results of the manual request
  [result appendFormat:@"No subquery: %.3f s\n", [end1 timeIntervalSinceDate:start1]];
  [result appendFormat:@"People retrieved: %ld\n", [people1 count]];
```

```
// Reset the context so we get clean results
[context reset];

// Set up the second fetch request, with subquery
NSFetchRequest *fetchRequest2 = [NSFetchRequest fetchRequestWithEntityName:@"Person"];
fetchRequest2.predicate = [NSPredicate predicateWithFormat:@"(SUBQUERY(selfies, $x,
($x.rating < %d) OR ($x.name LIKE %@)).@count > 0)", 5, @"*e*ie*"];

// Mark the time and get the results
NSDate *start2 = [NSDate date];
NSArray *people2 = [context executeFetchRequest:fetchRequest2 error:nil];
NSDate *end2 = [NSDate date];

// Record the results of the subquery request
[result appendFormat:@"Subquery: %.3f s\n", [end2 timeIntervalSinceDate:start2]];
[result appendFormat:@"People retrieved: %ld\n", [people2 count]];

    return result;
}

@end
```

Add your import (Subquery.h) and your Subquery instance to ViewController, and then run the test. On our iPhone 6 Plus, the no-subquery version takes just over 30 seconds, while the subquery version takes about 1.5 seconds—over 20 times faster!

How you write your predicates can have a profound effect on the performance of your application. You should always be mindful of what you are asking Core Data to do and how you can accomplish the same results with more efficient predicates.

Batch Updates

In the pre-iOS Core Data world, if you wanted to update a raft of Core Data objects, you had to fetch all the objects you wanted to update, iterate through them, set the new value or values, and then save the managed object context. Depending on the save of the data set you wish to update, this can be a slow and memory-intensive operation, as all the objects had to be fetched into memory and then written to in an iterative loop. For large updates—updates too large to fit in memory, perhaps—developers had to create custom solutions to break the updates into smaller batches.

iOS 8 (and OS X Yosemite) introduced batch updates for Core Data to address this gap in the form of a class called NSBatchUpdateRequest. Surprisingly, the Apple documentation (as of Xcode 6.1 and iOS 8.1) omit any documentation for this class except to show that it inherits from NSPersistentStoreRequest. The header file, NSBatchUpdateRequest.h, gives us a little info, though. Here are two important points we learn from the header file's comments.

- NSBatchUpdateRequest talks directly to the underlying persistent store without loading data into memory. Not all persistent stores support this approach, but since you're most likely using a SQLite persistent store, you should be OK.

- Because it talks directly to the underlying persistent store, it doesn't go through the validation that the managed object model and managed object context provide. You are responsible for enforcing the validation rules yourself.

To execute a batch update request, you create an NSBatchUpdateRequest instance, specifying the entity from your model that the request will update. Optionally, you set a predicate on the request to filter the objects to update. You set the properties to update and the values to update them to. You also set the type of result you want returned. Finally, you run the update.

You specify the properties to update in a dictionary, with the name of the property to update as the key and the desired value as the value. This necessarily means that you are specifying a single value for a given property that all matching objects will be updated to—you can't specify different values for each object. This makes sense; Core Data is going to generate and execute a SQL statement that looks something like the following:

```
UPDATE ZMYENTITY SET ZNAME = ?
```

You can, of course, set multiple properties to update.

For the type of result you want returned from running the batch update, you can specify one of three values.

- NSStatusOnlyResultType—return nothing. This is the default.
- NSUpdateObjectIDsResultType—return the object IDs of the updated objects.
- NSUpdatedObjectsCountResultType—return the number of objects that were updated.

The return type you'll want to specify depends on your application's needs, of course. The NSUpdateObjectIDsResultType can be useful, though, so that you can fault the updated objects in your managed object context. Remember that the batch update bypasses the managed object context, so if you have the objects in your managed object context, they're sitting there with the old value or values. You can fault them and then refetch them to get the updated objects.

Whatever type you specify, executing the batch update sets the result member of the NSBatchUpdateResult to the appropriate value.

To test batch updates, create a PerfTest-conforming class called BatchUpdate. In the test this method implements, we update the rating for all the selfies twice. The first time we perform the update, we do it the pre-iOS 8 way: one at a time. We fetch all the selfies, then iterate through them to set their rating values to 5. Finally, we save the managed object context. The second time we perform the update, we use a batch update to set the rating values to 7. Listing 9-49 shows the Objective-C version, and Listing 9-50 shows the Swift version.

Listing 9-49. BatchUpdate.m

```
#import "BatchUpdate.h"

@implementation BatchUpdate

- (NSString *)runTestWithContext:(NSManagedObjectContext *)context {
  NSMutableString *result = [NSMutableString string];

  // Update all the selfies one at a time
  NSFetchRequest *fetchRequest = [NSFetchRequest fetchRequestWithEntityName:@"Selfie"];
  NSDate *start1 = [NSDate date];
```

```objc
  NSArray *selfies = [context executeFetchRequest:fetchRequest error:nil];
  for (NSManagedObject *selfie in selfies) {
    [selfie setValue:@5 forKey:@"rating"];
  }
  [context save:nil];
  NSDate *end1 = [NSDate date];
  [result appendFormat:@"One-at-a-time update: %.3f s\n", [end1 timeIntervalSinceDate:start1]];

  // Update the selfies as a batch

  // Create the batch update request for the Selfie entity
  NSBatchUpdateRequest *batchUpdateRequest = [NSBatchUpdateRequest batchUpdateRequestWithEntityName
  :@"Selfie"];

  // Set the desired result type to be the count of updated objects
  batchUpdateRequest.resultType = NSUpdatedObjectsCountResultType;

  // Update the rating property to 7
  batchUpdateRequest.propertiesToUpdate = @{ @"rating" : @7 };

  // Mark the time and run the update
  NSDate *start2 = [NSDate date];
  NSBatchUpdateResult *batchUpdateResult = (NSBatchUpdateResult *)[context executeRequest:
  batchUpdateRequest error:nil];
  NSDate *end2 = [NSDate date];

  // Record the results
  [result appendFormat:@"Batch update (%@ rows): %.3f s\n", batchUpdateResult.result,
  [end2 timeIntervalSinceDate:start2]];

  return result;
}

@end
```

Listing 9-50. BatchUpdate.swift

```swift
import Foundation
import CoreData

class BatchUpdate : PerfTest {
    func runTestWithContext(context: NSManagedObjectContext) -> String! {
        let result = NSMutableString()

        // Update all the selfies one at a time
        let fetchRequest = NSFetchRequest(entityName: "Selfie")
        let start1 = NSDate()
        let selfies = context.executeFetchRequest(fetchRequest, error: nil) as [Selfie]
        for selfie in selfies {
            selfie.setValue(5, forKey:"rating")
        }
```

```
        context.save(nil)
        let end1 = NSDate()
        result.appendFormat("One-at-a-time update: %.3f s\n", end1.timeIntervalSinceDate(start1))

        // Update the selfies as a batch

        // Create the batch update request for the Selfie entity
        let batchUpdateRequest = NSBatchUpdateRequest(entityName: "Selfie")

        // Set the desired result type to be the count of updated objects
        batchUpdateRequest.resultType = .UpdatedObjectsCountResultType;

        // Update the rating property to 7
        batchUpdateRequest.propertiesToUpdate = [ "rating" : 7 ];

        // Mark the time and run the update
        let start2 = NSDate()
        let batchUpdateResult = context.executeRequest(batchUpdateRequest, error: nil) as
        NSBatchUpdateResult
        let end2 = NSDate()

        // Record the results
        result.appendFormat("Batch update (\(batchUpdateResult.result!) rows): %.3f s\n", end2.
        timeIntervalSinceDate(start2))

        return result
    }
}
```

Add a BatchUpdate to your tests array, build and run the application, and run the BatchUpdate test. On our iPhone 6 Plus, the one-at-a-time update takes about 0.07 seconds, while the batch update takes about 0.007 seconds. There are two things to notice.

- The batch update is about 10 times faster.

- The one-at-a-time update is still pretty fast.

We updated only 500 objects in our test, which the pre-iOS 8 approach handled in a few hundredths of a second. This tells us that we probably shouldn't do all updates through the batch route, since we're forsaking the validation that Core Data gives us to squeeze out a little performance. Instead, we should save batch updates for when we truly need them: when we must update tens of thousands (or more) of objects.

Analyzing Performance

Although thinking things through before writing code and understanding the implications of things such as faulting, prefetching, and memory usage usually nets you solid code that performs well, you often need a nonbiased, objective opinion on how your application is performing. The least biased and most objective opinion on your application's performance comes from the computer it's running on, so asking your computer to measure the results of your application's Core Data interaction provides essential insight for optimizing performance.

Apple provides a tool called Instruments that allows you to measure several facets of an application, including Core Data–related items. This section shows how to use Instruments to measure the Core Data aspects of your application. We encourage you to explore the other measurements Instruments offers as well.

Launching Instruments

To launch Instruments and begin profiling your application, select Product ➤ Profile from the Xcode menu. This launches Instruments and displays a dialog asking you what you want to profile, as Figure 9-8 shows.

Figure 9-8.   Instruments asking you to choose a template

Select the Core Data template and click the Choose button. That opens the main Instruments window with the Core Data instruments in the left sidebar, as Figure 9-9 shows.

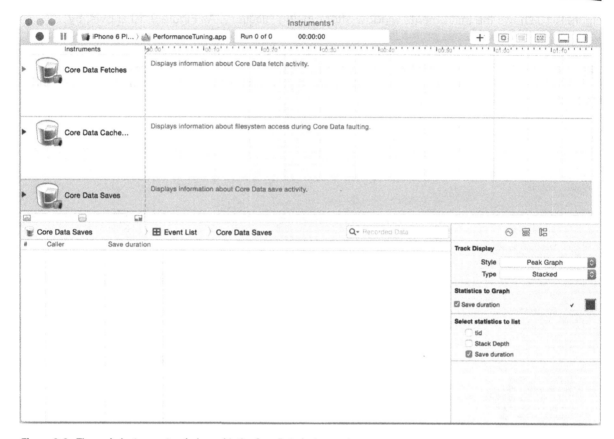

Figure 9-9. The main Instruments window with the Core Data instruments

Click the Record button at the top left of the Instruments window to launch the iOS Simulator (Instruments does not support profiling Core Data instruments on the device) and the PerformanceTuning application.

Understanding the Results

The Instruments window shows the Core Data measurements it's tracking, which include the following:

- Core Data fetches
- Core Data cache misses
- Core Data saves

Run any of the tests in the PerformanceTuning application—say, Subquery—and wait for the test to complete. When the test finishes, click the Stop button in the upper left of Instruments to stop the application and stop recording Core Data measurements. You can then review the results from your test to see information about saves, fetches, faults, and cache misses. You can save the results to the file system for further review by selecting File ➤ Save As from the menu. You reopen them in Instruments using the standard File ➤ Open menu item.

Figure 9-10 shows the Instruments window after running Subquery. As Figure 9-10 shows, by selecting Core Data Fetches on the left, you can see the fetch counts and fetch durations, which are in microseconds, for the Core Data fetches. The code ran three fetch requests (Instruments lists the call for a fetch twice: once when the call starts and once when it finishes). The first request, which took 1,192 microseconds, fetched 500 people, which you can tell from the fetch entity, Person, and the fetch count, 500.

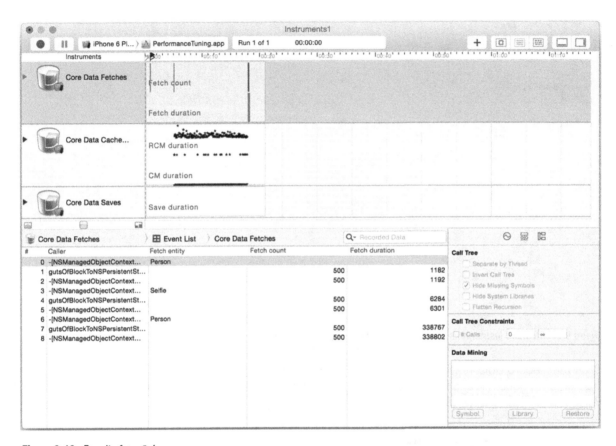

Figure 9-10. Results from Subquery

You can see the call tree for the fetch request by changing the drop-down in the middle of the window from Event List to Call Tree. You can reduce the navigation depth required to see the calls in your application's code by checking the box next to Hide System Libraries on the right of the window. Figure 9-11 shows the call tree for the fetch request. Using the call tree, you can determine which parts of your code are fetching data from your Core Data store.

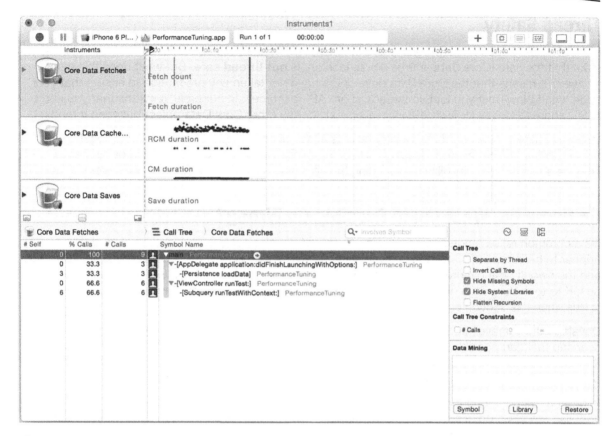

Figure 9-11. The call tree for the fetch requests

This is just a taste of what Instruments can do for you to help you determine how your application is using Core Data and how it can lead you to places where Core Data performance is slow enough to warrant optimization efforts. We encourage you to investigate the Instruments tool further, trying out the other Core Data instruments to see things like cache misses and saves so you can determine your application's hot spots.

Dealing with Multiple Threads

There inevitably comes a time, when writing a non-trivial app, that you consider using multiple threads. Usually it is done for performance reasons—to offload tasks to the background—but the performance gains come at the expense of some complexity. This section shows you how to recognize some common problems that arise when using multiple threads with Core Data and how to solve them.

Thread Safety

Most of Apple's application programming interfaces (APIs) aren't thread safe unless they explicitly state that they are. Core Data, in true Apple fashion, is **not thread safe**. But what does this mean anyway? It means that the Core Data developers have not taken any precaution to ensure that your code won't blow up if you let two threads share API resources. In our case, it means that you can't safely share NSManagedObject, NSManagedContext, or any other Core Data object between threads.

Instead of thinking the non-thread safety reflects a lack of care or quality, look at it as delegating responsibility. Apple preferred focusing on keeping things simple and on maximizing performance. They delegate the responsibility of managing thread safety to you, the developer, whenever you need it.

Oh Come On, What Could Possibly Go Wrong?

It's a common reflex among some developers to just dismiss complexity if the damage doesn't appear to be immediate. Maybe you're thinking that your threads are well behaved and well trained, and they won't fight over resources. Maybe you're thinking your app is not very complex so it should be OK to toss Core Data objects across threads. Or, maybe you're simply feeling lucky. If any of this is true, then this section is for you.

Developers who have had to deal with live production applications over time often say that any scenario that can possibly happen will happen when the app is in the hands of real users. If two threads could potentially collide, they will. If you are not careful, you will have these concurrency problems. This section will show you how to recognize some of these problems.

In order to demonstrate thread concurrency issues, we build a simple app that writes a lot of data and also reports progress. One thought you might have is that we could write some data, report status, write some more, report more status, and so on. It's true, we could perform writing and reading in serial chunks, but this would significantly increase the amount of time it takes to write your data and therefore deteriorate the user experience. By using threads, we can perform these tasks in parallel and keep the UI responsive.

Open Xcode and create a new application using the single-view application template. Call the application MultiThread. Our first step is to set up and initialize a Core Data stack. Create a new data model called MultiThread.xcdatamodeld. Add a single entity called MyData and give it a single attribute called myValue of type Integer 16. Your data model should match Figure 9-12.

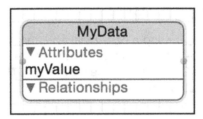

Figure 9-12. The MultiThread data model

For clarity, we create a class that contains the Core Data setup. Create a new class called Persistence (a subclass of NSObject) and make Persistence.h look as shown in Listing 9-51.

Listing 9-51. Persistence.h

```
#import <Foundation/Foundation.h>
@import CoreData;

@interface Persistence : NSObject

@property (readonly, strong, nonatomic) NSManagedObjectModel *managedObjectModel;
@property (readonly, strong, nonatomic) NSPersistentStoreCoordinator *persistentStoreCoordinator;

- (NSManagedObjectContext*)createManagedObjectContext;

@end
```

This header file should look familiar, although you might notice that, instead of a managed object context property, we have a method that creates a managed object context. We do this for threading purposes, which we explain later in this chapter.

Next, open Persistence.m or Persistence.swift and implement the initialization in a manner similar to what we have done in previous chapters. Listing 9-52 shows the Objective-C version and Listing 9-53 shows the Swift version.

Listing 9-52. Persistence.m

```
- (instancetype)init {
  self = [super init];
  if (self != nil) {
    // Initialize the managed object model
    NSURL *modelURL = [[NSBundle mainBundle]
            URLForResource:@"MultiThread" withExtension:@"momd"];
    _managedObjectModel = [[NSManagedObjectModel alloc]
            initWithContentsOfURL:modelURL];

    // Initialize the persistent store coordinator
    NSURL *storeURL = [[self applicationDocumentsDirectory]
            URLByAppendingPathComponent:@"MultiThread.sqlite"];

    // Delete the existing store if it exists so we can also start fresh
    NSFileManager *fm = [NSFileManager defaultManager];
    [fm removeItemAtURL:storeURL error:nil];

    NSError *error = nil;
    _persistentStoreCoordinator = [[NSPersistentStoreCoordinator alloc]
            initWithManagedObjectModel:self.managedObjectModel];
    if (![_persistentStoreCoordinator addPersistentStoreWithType:NSSQLiteStoreType
                                          configuration:nil
                                                    URL:storeURL
                                                options:nil
```

```objc
                                                    error:&error]) {
        NSLog(@"Unresolved error %@, %@", error, [error userInfo]);
        abort();
      }
    }
    return self;
}

- (NSURL *)applicationDocumentsDirectory {
    return [[[NSFileManager defaultManager]
          URLsForDirectory:NSDocumentDirectory
          inDomains:NSUserDomainMask] lastObject];
}

- (NSManagedObjectContext*)createManagedObjectContext {
    NSManagedObjectContext *managedObjectContext =
          [[NSManagedObjectContext alloc] init];
    [managedObjectContext
          setPersistentStoreCoordinator:self.persistentStoreCoordinator];

    return managedObjectContext;
}

@end
```

Listing 9-53. Persistence.swift

```swift
import Foundation
import CoreData

class Persistence {
    init() {
        println("Pretending to do a migration");
        NSThread.sleepForTimeInterval(10)
        println("Done with pretending...");
    }

    // MARK: - Core Data stack

    lazy var applicationDocumentsDirectory: NSURL = {
        // The directory the application uses to store the Core Data store file. This code uses
            a directory named "book.persistence.MultiThreadSwift" in the application's documents
            Application Support directory.
        let urls = NSFileManager.defaultManager().URLsForDirectory(.DocumentDirectory, inDomains:
        .UserDomainMask)
        return urls[urls.count-1] as NSURL
        }()
```

```swift
lazy var managedObjectModel: NSManagedObjectModel = {
    // The managed object model for the application. This property is not optional. It is a
    fatal error for the application not to be able to find and load its model.
    let modelURL = NSBundle.mainBundle().URLForResource("MultiThreadSwift", withExtension:
    "momd")!
    return NSManagedObjectModel(contentsOfURL: modelURL)!
}()

lazy var persistentStoreCoordinator: NSPersistentStoreCoordinator? = {
    // The persistent store coordinator for the application. This implementation creates and
        return a coordinator, having added the store for the application to it. This property is
        optional since there are legitimate error conditions that could cause the creation of the
        store to fail.
    // Create the coordinator and store
    var coordinator: NSPersistentStoreCoordinator? = NSPersistentStoreCoordinator(managedObjectM
    odel: self.managedObjectModel)
    let url = self.applicationDocumentsDirectory.URLByAppendingPathComponent("MultiThreadSwift.
    sqlite")

    // Delete the existing store if it exists so we can also start fresh
    let fm = NSFileManager.defaultManager()
    fm.removeItemAtURL(url, error: nil)

    var error: NSError? = nil
    var failureReason = "There was an error creating or loading the application's saved data."
    if coordinator!.addPersistentStoreWithType(NSSQLiteStoreType, configuration: nil, URL: url,
    options: nil, error: &error) == nil {
        coordinator = nil
        // Report any error we got.
        let dict = NSMutableDictionary()
        dict[NSLocalizedDescriptionKey] = "Failed to initialize the application's saved data"
        dict[NSLocalizedFailureReasonErrorKey] = failureReason
        dict[NSUnderlyingErrorKey] = error
        error = NSError(domain: "YOUR_ERROR_DOMAIN", code: 9999, userInfo: dict)
        // Replace this with code to handle the error appropriately.
        // abort() causes the application to generate a crash log and terminate. You should
            not use this function in a shipping application, although it may be useful during
            development.
        NSLog("Unresolved error \(error), \(error!.userInfo)")
        abort()
    }

    return coordinator
}()

lazy var managedObjectContext: NSManagedObjectContext? = {
    return self.createManagedObjectContext()
}()
```

```swift
func createManagedObjectContext() -> NSManagedObjectContext? {
    // Returns the managed object context for the application (which is already bound to the
        persistent store coordinator for the application.) This property is optional since there
        are legitimate error conditions that could cause the creation of the context to fail.
    let coordinator = self.persistentStoreCoordinator
    if coordinator == nil {
        return nil
    }

    var managedObjectContext = NSManagedObjectContext()
    managedObjectContext.persistentStoreCoordinator = coordinator
    return managedObjectContext
}

// MARK: - Core Data Saving support

func saveContext () {
    if let moc = self.managedObjectContext {
        var error: NSError? = nil
        if moc.hasChanges && !moc.save(&error) {
            // Replace this implementation with code to handle the error appropriately.
            // abort() causes the application to generate a crash log and terminate. You should
                not use this function in a shipping application, although it may be useful during
                development.
            NSLog("Unresolved error \(error), \(error!.userInfo)")
            abort()
        }
    }
}
```

> **Important**   Notice how the code deletes the SQLite file if it exists by calling NSFileManager's
> removeItemAtURL:error: method. In a real-world app, this is obviously a bad practice as it removes all
> of the persisted data. In our case, it is very handy as it allows us to launch the app multiple times without
> having to worry about residual data.

Now that we are done with the Core Data setup code, we can move on to ViewController and experiment with the code to see what we can do with threads.

For the Objective-C version, edit ViewController.m, to add the appropriate import statements, private properties for Persistence and NSManagedObjectContext instances, and an initializer to run the setup code, as Listing 9-54 shows. For Swift, make similar edits to ViewController.swift, as Listing 9-55 shows.

Listing 9-54. ViewController.m

```objc
@import CoreData;
#import "ViewController.h"
#import "Persistence.h"

@interface ViewController ()
@property (nonatomic, strong) Persistence *persistence;
@property (nonatomic, strong) NSManagedObjectContext *managedObjectContext;
@end

@implementation ViewController

- (instancetype)initWithCoder:(NSCoder *)aDecoder {
    self = [super initWithCoder:aDecoder];
    if(self) {
        self.persistence = [[Persistence alloc] init];
        self.managedObjectContext = [self.persistence createManagedObjectContext];
    }

    return self;
}

- (void)viewDidLoad {
    [super viewDidLoad];
    // Do any additional setup after loading the view, typically from a nib.
}

- (void)didReceiveMemoryWarning {
    [super didReceiveMemoryWarning];
    // Dispose of any resources that can be recreated.
}

@end
```

Listing 9-55. ViewController.swift

```swift
import UIKit
import CoreData

class ViewController: UIViewController {

    var persistence: Persistence?
    var managedObjectContext: NSManagedObjectContext?

    required init(coder aDecoder: NSCoder) {
        super.init(coder: aDecoder)

        self.persistence = Persistence()
        self.managedObjectContext = self.persistence?.managedObjectContext
    }
```

```swift
    override func viewDidLoad() {
        super.viewDidLoad()
    }

    override func didReceiveMemoryWarning() {
        super.didReceiveMemoryWarning()
        // Dispose of any resources that can be recreated.
    }
}
```

At this point, you should be able to launch the app and see nothing but a blank screen.

Still in ViewController, we now create a new method for writing the data. In this method, we write 10,000 objects to the store. We save the context when we're done writing so all the objects will be in the persistent store, so that any other managed object context will see them. Listing 9-56 shows the Objective-C version and Listing 9-57 shows the Swift version.

Listing 9-56. Writing 10,000 Objects (Objective-C)

```objectivec
- (void)writeData {
  NSManagedObjectContext *context = self.managedObjectContext;

  NSLog(@"Writing");
  for(int i=0; i<10000; i++) {
    NSManagedObject *obj = [NSEntityDescription
            insertNewObjectForEntityForName:@"MyData"
            inManagedObjectContext:context];
    [obj setValue:[NSNumber numberWithInt:i] forKey:@"myValue"];
  }

  NSError *error;
  [context save:&error];
  if(error) {
    NSLog(@"Boom while writing! %@", error);
  }

  NSLog(@"Done");
}
```

Listing 9-57. Writing 10,000 Objects (Swift)

```swift
func writeData() {
    if let context = self.managedObjectContext {
        println("Writing")
        for var i=0; i<10000; i++ {
            let obj = NSEntityDescription.insertNewObjectForEntityForName("MyData",
inManagedObjectContext: context) as NSManagedObject
            obj.setValue(Int(i), forKey: "myValue")
        }

        persistence?.saveContext()
```

```
        println("Done")
    }
    else {
        println("Missing context. Cannot write.")
    }
}
```

Next, we add a method to report status—a method to read what we've written. It returns the fraction of the 10,000 objects that have been written. Listing 9-58 shows the Objective-C method and Listing 9-59 shows the Swift function.

Listing 9-58. Reading 10,000 Objects (Objective-C)

```objectivec
- (CGFloat)reportStatus {
  NSManagedObjectContext *context = self.managedObjectContext;

  NSFetchRequest *request = [[NSFetchRequest alloc] init];
  request.entity = [NSEntityDescription entityForName:@"MyData"
                inManagedObjectContext:context];

  NSError *error;
  NSUInteger count = [context countForFetchRequest:request error:&error];

  if(error) {
    NSLog(@"Boom while reading! %@", error);
  }

  return (CGFloat)count / 10000.0f;
}
```

Listing 9-59. Reading 10,000 Objects (Swift)

```swift
func reportStatus() -> Float {
    if let context = self.managedObjectContext {
        let request = NSFetchRequest(entityName: "MyData")
        var error: NSError? = nil
        let count = context.countForFetchRequest(request, error: &error)
        if error != nil {
            println("Error while reading")
        }

        return Float(count) / 10000.0
    }
    else {
        println("Missing context. Cannot report status")
        return 0
    }
}
```

Now that we can read and write objects, we just have to call the code to do that. We will do this in the viewDidAppear: method as shown in Listing 9-60 (Objective-C) and Listing 9-61 (Swift).

Listing 9-60. Calling the Writing and Reading Methods (Objective-C)

```objectivec
- (void)viewDidAppear:(BOOL)animated {
    [super viewDidAppear:animated];

    [self writeData];

    CGFloat status = 0;
    while(status < 1.0) {
        status = [self reportStatus];
        NSLog(@"Status: %lu%%", (unsigned long)(status * 100));
    }

    NSLog(@"All done");
}
```

Listing 9-61. Calling the Writing and Reading Methods (Swift)

```swift
override func viewDidAppear(animated: Bool) {
    super.viewDidAppear(animated)

    self.writeData()

    var status : Float = 0
    while (status < 1) {
        status = self.reportStatus()
        println(NSString(format: "Status: %lu%%", Int(status * 100)))
    }
    println("All done")
}
```

Obviously, if you launch the app at this point, all the writing will occur before any progress can be reported. Once status is reported, the only one you will see is 100%. Try it.

```
09:35:11.586 MultiThread[3246:60b] Writing
09:35:11.738 MultiThread[3246:60b] Done
09:35:11.753 MultiThread[3246:60b] Status: 100%
09:35:11.754 MultiThread[3246:60b] All done
```

Surely you already know what happened. Since we're running everything on the same thread, writing the data happens first, and only after the write completes do we start reporting status. We could flip this around and start reporting status before writing the data, but then the writing section would never happen since the status loop would iterate forever.

This is a case for multiple threads. The solution is to dispatch each of the two actions (writing and reporting progress) to their own threads. Edit viewDidAppear: to use multiple threads using Grand Central Dispatch. One thread will write the data, and the other thread will report status by reading the data. Both threads will run asynchronously, allowing us to write the data while reporting on the progress of those writes. Listing 9-62 shows the Objective-C version, and Listing 9-63 shows the Swift version.

Listing 9-62. Writing and Reading on Separate Threads (Objective-C)

```objc
- (void)viewDidAppear:(BOOL)animated {
  [super viewDidAppear:animated];

  dispatch_async(dispatch_get_global_queue(DISPATCH_QUEUE_PRIORITY_DEFAULT, 0), ^{
    [self writeData];
  });

  dispatch_async(dispatch_get_global_queue(DISPATCH_QUEUE_PRIORITY_DEFAULT, 0), ^{
    CGFloat status = 0;
    while(status < 1.0) {
      status = [self reportStatus];
      NSLog(@"Status: %lu%%", (unsigned long)(status * 100));
    }

    NSLog(@"All done");
  });
}
```

Listing 9-63. Writing and Reading on Separate Threads (Swift)

```swift
override func viewDidAppear(animated: Bool) {
    super.viewDidAppear(animated)

    dispatch_async(dispatch_get_global_queue(DISPATCH_QUEUE_PRIORITY_DEFAULT, 0), { () -> Void in
        self.writeData()
    })

    dispatch_async(dispatch_get_global_queue(DISPATCH_QUEUE_PRIORITY_DEFAULT, 0), { () -> Void in
        var status : Float = 0
        while (status < 1) {
            status = self.reportStatus()
            println(NSString(format: "Status: %lu%%", Int(status * 100)))
        }
        println("All done")
    })
}
```

Now, when the app runs, both tasks will happen simultaneously. So you were feeling lucky, huh? Go ahead and try your luck by launching the app.

Odds are, you got something like the following (if you didn't, we'd like you to help us pick lottery numbers):

```
09:40:03.120 MultiThread[3282:1303] Writing
09:40:03.122 MultiThread[3282:3603] Status: 0%
09:40:03.124 MultiThread[3282:3603] *** Terminating app due to uncaught exception
'NSGenericException', reason: '*** Collection <__NSCFSet: 0x1096122b0> was mutated while being
enumerated.'
```

```
*** First throw call stack:
(
    0   CoreFoundation              0x000000010194a495 __exceptionPreprocess + 165
    1   libobjc.A.dylib             0x00000001016a999e objc_exception_throw + 43
    2   CoreFoundation              0x00000001019ce68e __NSFastEnumerationMutationHandler +
                                    126
    3   CoreData                    0x0000000101c2666b -[NSManagedObjectContext
                                    (_NSInternalAdditions) _countWithNoChangesForRequest:
                                    error:] + 1675
    4   CoreData                    0x0000000101c25d5b -[NSManagedObjectContext
                                    countForFetchRequest:error:] + 1211
    5   MultiThread                 0x00000001000022ae -[ViewController reportStatus] + 286
    6   MultiThread                 0x0000000100001ed9 __32-[ViewController viewDidAppear:]_
                                    block_invoke17 + 89
    7   libdispatch.dylib           0x00000001020e7851 _dispatch_call_block_and_release + 12
    8   libdispatch.dylib           0x00000001020fa72d _dispatch_client_callout + 8
    9   libdispatch.dylib           0x00000001020eab27 _dispatch_root_queue_drain + 380
   10   libdispatch.dylib           0x00000001020ead12 _dispatch_worker_thread2 + 40
   11   libsystem_pthread.dylib     0x0000000102447ef8 _pthread_wqthread + 314
   12   libsystem_pthread.dylib     0x000000010244afb9 start_wqthread + 13
)
libc++abi.dylib: terminating with uncaught exception of type NSException
```

The problem here is that we're peeking at the context's cache while it's writing to it. This isn't necessarily a Core Data issue. You cannot iterate through a collection and peek into it at the same time from two different threads. So it's definitely a thread safety issue. This experiment exposes the cardinal rule when using multiple threads with Core Data: give each thread its own managed object context. Remember the createManagedObjectContext method we created? We use that to give the writeData method its own managed object context, rather than using the managed object context that the reportStatus method uses.

When inmates fight, they go into confinement. They are stripped from their reason to fight because they have nothing to fight over and nobody to fight with. Thread confinement is a common strategy to deal with threads not "playing nice" with each other.

Things go wrong pretty fast when using Core Data with multiple threads. Managing concurrency is done simply by avoiding sharing the resources threads fight over. It bears repeating: the most common solution is to create a context for each thread.

Important   Each context must be created by the thread that is going to use it.

Another change we make to this code is to save the managed object context after we add each object. We do this so that the context's cache is written through to the persistent store, so that the managed object context used in the reportStatus method sees the objects. If we waited until all

10,000 objects were written before saving the context, the reportStatus method would report a 0% status until the writeData thread finishes writing, and then reportStatus would jump directly to 100%.

Listing 9-64 shows the updated Objective-C version, and Listing 9-65 shows the updated Swift version.

Listing 9-64. Saving the Context After Every Write (Objective-C)

```objc
- (void)writeData {
  NSManagedObjectContext *context = [self.persistence createManagedObjectContext];

  NSLog(@"Writing");
  for(int i=0; i<10000; i++) {
    NSManagedObject *obj = [NSEntityDescription insertNewObjectForEntityForName:@"MyData" inManagedO
bjectContext:context];
    [obj setValue:[NSNumber numberWithInt:i] forKey:@"myValue"];

    NSError *error;
    [context save:&error];
    if(error) {
      NSLog(@"Boom while writing! %@", error);
    }
  }

  NSLog(@"Done");
}
```

Listing 9-65. Saving the Context After Every Write (Swift)

```swift
func writeData () {
    if let context = self.persistence?.createManagedObjectContext() {
        println("Writing");
        for var i=0; i<10000; i++ {
            let obj = NSEntityDescription.insertNewObjectForEntityForName("MyData",
inManagedObjectContext: context) as NSManagedObject
            obj.setValue(Int(i), forKey: "myValue")

            context.save(nil)
        }

        println("Done")
    }
    else {
        println("Missing context. Cannot write.")
    }
}
```

If you build and run the application now, you'll see the status percentage in the console steadily climb until it reaches 100% and then the "All done" message appears.

Gratuitous User Interface

Since we've managed to make our app multithreaded, let's finish the work and put a progress bar on our UI so we can examine how to display progress in a way that users can see.

Open Main.storyboard and add a progress bar and a label to the view, as Figure 9-13 shows. The label will display a textual message indicating the progress, and the progress bar will graphically reflect the same progress.

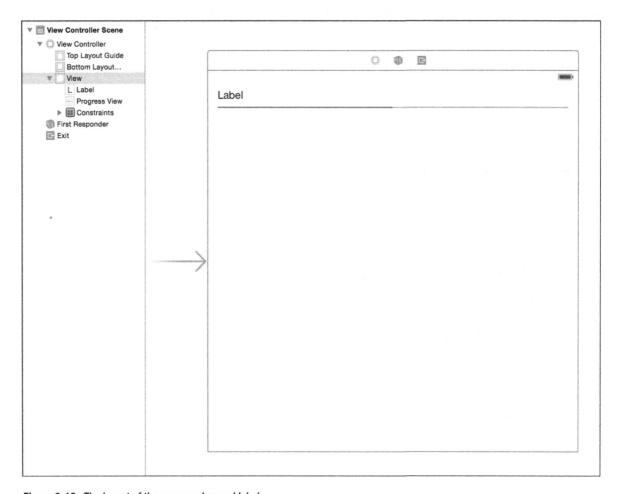

Figure 9-13. The layout of the progress bar and label

Now create two IBOutlets, either in ViewController.m (Objective-C) or in ViewController.swift (Swift), called label and progressView. Connect them in Interface Builder to the label and progress bar you just added. Listing 9-66 shows what to add to ViewController.h, and Listing 9-67 shows what to add to ViewController.swift.

Listing 9-66. Adding Outlets to ViewController.m

```
@interface ViewController ()
@property (nonatomic, strong) Persistence *persistence;
@property (nonatomic, strong) NSManagedObjectContext *managedObjectContext;
@property (nonatomic, weak) IBOutlet UILabel *label;
@property (nonatomic, weak) IBOutlet UIProgressView *progressView;
@end
```

Listing 9-67. Adding Outlets to ViewController.swift

```
@IBOutlet weak var label: UILabel!
@IBOutlet weak var progressView: UIProgressView!
```

Now update viewDidAppear: to reflect the report status to the UI. We set the label to the textual version of the status, and we move the progress bar along appropriately. Since we're calling the reportStatus method from a thread that's not the main thread—the thread used by the UI—we need to make sure we dispatch updates to the main queue in order for them to be executed by the main thread. All interface updates should be done from the main thread. It's not just in the Core Data arena that proper thread handling is important!

Listing 9-68 shows the Objective-C version of the code, and Listing 9-69 shows the Swift version.

Listing 9-68. Updating the UI to Show Progress (Objective-C)

```
-(void)viewDidAppear:(BOOL)animated {
  [super viewDidAppear: animated];

  dispatch_async(dispatch_get_global_queue(DISPATCH_QUEUE_PRIORITY_DEFAULT, 0), ^{
    [self writeData];
  });

  dispatch_async(dispatch_get_global_queue(DISPATCH_QUEUE_PRIORITY_DEFAULT, 0), ^{
    CGFloat status = 0;
    while(status < 1.0) {
      status = [self reportStatus];
      dispatch_async(dispatch_get_main_queue(), ^{
        self.progressView.progress = status;
        self.label.text = [NSString stringWithFormat:@"%lu%%",
            (unsigned long)(status * 100)];
      });
    }

    NSLog(@"All done");
  });
}
```

Listing 9-69. Updating the UI to Show Progress (Swift)

```swift
override func viewDidAppear(animated: Bool) {
    super.viewDidAppear(animated)

    dispatch_async(dispatch_get_global_queue(DISPATCH_QUEUE_PRIORITY_DEFAULT, 0), { () -> Void in
        self.writeData()
    })

    dispatch_async(dispatch_get_global_queue(DISPATCH_QUEUE_PRIORITY_DEFAULT, 0), { () -> Void in
        var status : Float = 0
        while (status < 1) {
            status = self.reportStatus()
            dispatch_async(dispatch_get_main_queue(), { () -> Void in
                self.progressView.progress = status
                self.label.text = NSString(format: "Status: %lu%%", Int(status * 100))
            })
        }
        println("All done")
    })
}
```

Now launch the app again and watch the UI update with the textual percentage and the moving progress bar as the write operation progresses to completion.

Initializing the Stack on a Different Thread

It's a good practice to consider initializing your Core Data stack on a thread other than the main thread. While initializing Core Data is typically fast, you will find that it may take a long time in some cases, especially if there is a large store migration involved. If you initialize in `application:didFini shLaunchingWithOptions:` and it takes a while, the app will crash. If you initialized in a controller like we did, the UI will become unresponsive. Either way, it's bad. For this reason, we encourage you to consider initializing on a different thread.

Let's put all of this into practice with our MultiThread app. First, we'll simulate a long start by adding a 10-second pause. Open `Persistence.m` or `Persistence.swift` and add the code shown in Listing 9-70 to the end of the `if` block in the `init` method (Objective-C), or create the `init` method shown in Listing 9-71 (Swift).

Listing 9-70. Faking a 10-Second Migration (Objective-C)

```objc
NSLog(@"Pretending to do a migration");
[NSThread sleepForTimeInterval:10];
NSLog(@"Done with pretending...");
```

Listing 9-71. Faking a 10-Second Migration (Swift)

```swift
init() {
    println("Pretending to do a migration");
    NSThread.sleepForTimeInterval(10)
    println("Done with pretending...");
}
```

Now launch the app and notice how long the splash screen shows before the interface appears, leaving your user to wonder what might be happening.

Let's address this by launching the Core Data stack initialization on a different thread in the initWithCoder: method of ViewController as shown in Listing 9-72 (Objective-C) or Listing 9-73 (Swift).

Listing 9-72. Initializing Core Data on a Separate Thread (Objective-C)

```
- (instancetype)initWithCoder:(NSCoder *)aDecoder {
  self = [super initWithCoder:aDecoder];
  if(self) {
    [self addObserver:self forKeyPath:@"managedObjectContext" options:NSKeyValueObservingOptionNew
context:NULL];

    dispatch_async(dispatch_get_global_queue(DISPATCH_QUEUE_PRIORITY_DEFAULT, 0), ^{
      self.persistence = [[Persistence alloc] init];
      dispatch_async(dispatch_get_main_queue(), ^{
        self.managedObjectContext = [self.persistence createManagedObjectContext];
      });
    });
  }

  return self;
}
```

Listing 9-73. Initializing Core Data on a Separate Thread (Swift)

```
required init(coder aDecoder: NSCoder) {
    super.init(coder: aDecoder)

    dispatch_async(dispatch_get_global_queue(DISPATCH_QUEUE_PRIORITY_DEFAULT, 0), { () -> Void in
        self.persistence = Persistence()
        dispatch_async(dispatch_get_main_queue(), { () -> Void in
            self.managedObjectContext = self.persistence?.managedObjectContext
        })
    })
}
```

A couple of things are happening here. First, we add an observer (using the Key-Value Observer (KVO) API) of the managedObjectContext property in the Objective-C version of the code. Because everything will happen on a different thread, we can no longer count on this value being set in viewDidAppear:, so we'll launch our "write" code when we get notified instead. We then dispatch the initialization code to another thread. When Core Data finishes initializing, we set the managedObjectContext property on the main thread. Why do we need to set it on the main thread? Because as we stated before, the managed context must be created on the thread that will use it. Since we will be using the managed object on the main thread, we set it on the main thread.

When we set the managed object context property value, the KVO notification will fire so we also need to observe it and launch the "write" code when the property changes. We do this differently for Objective-C than for Swift, since the semantics of these languages differ. For Objective-C, move all your code from viewDidAppear: to a new method called observeValueForKeyPath:ofObject:chang e:context:, which will be automatically called when the managedObjectContext property that we're observing changes. Listing 9-74 shows the code.

Listing 9-74. Observing the Change in managedObjectContext (Objective-C)

```objc
- (void)observeValueForKeyPath:(NSString *)keyPath ofObject:(id)object change:(NSDictionary *)change
context:(void *)context {
    dispatch_async(dispatch_get_global_queue(DISPATCH_QUEUE_PRIORITY_DEFAULT, 0), ^{
        [self writeData];
    });

    dispatch_async(dispatch_get_global_queue(DISPATCH_QUEUE_PRIORITY_DEFAULT, 0), ^{
        CGFloat status = 0;
        while(status < 1.0) {
            status = [self reportStatus];
            dispatch_async(dispatch_get_main_queue(), ^{
                self.progressView.progress = status;
                self.label.text = [NSString stringWithFormat:@"%lu%%",
                                     (unsigned long)(status * 100)];
            });
        }

        NSLog(@"All done");
    });
}
```

For Swift, we create a didSet observer for the managedObjectContext property that calls a new method we create called initiate. Listing 9-75 shows the code.

Listing 9-75. Observing the Change in managedObjectContext (Swift)

```swift
var managedObjectContext: NSManagedObjectContext? {
    didSet {
        self.initiate()
    }
}

func initiate() {
    dispatch_async(dispatch_get_global_queue(DISPATCH_QUEUE_PRIORITY_DEFAULT, 0), { () -> Void in
        self.writeData()
    })

    dispatch_async(dispatch_get_global_queue(DISPATCH_QUEUE_PRIORITY_DEFAULT, 0), { () -> Void in
        var status : Float = 0
        while(status < 1) {
            status = self.reportStatus()
            dispatch_async(dispatch_get_main_queue(), { () -> Void in
                self.progressView.progress = status
                self.label.text = NSString(format: "Status: %lu%%", Int(status * 100))
            })
```

```
            //println(NSString(format: "Status: %lu%%", Int(status * 100)))
        }

        println("All done")
    })
}
```

In both languages, the `viewDidAppear` method should now be gone from your code. The last step, to keep everything clean, is to make sure we have default values for the UI elements. We set initial values in `viewWillAppear:`, as shown in Listing 9-76 (Objective-C) and Listing 9-77 (Swift).

Listing 9-76. Setting the UI Elements to Default Values (Objective-C)

```
- (void)viewWillAppear:(BOOL)animated {
  [super viewWillAppear:animated];

  self.progressView.progress = 0;
  self.label.text = @"Initializing Core Data";
}
```

Listing 9-77. Setting the UI Elements to Default Values (Swift)

```
override func viewWillAppear(animated: Bool) {
    super.viewWillAppear(animated)

    self.progressView.progress = 0
    self.label.text = "Initializing Core Data"
}
```

Now launch the application and notice how the splash screen displays only briefly before the application UI appears and displays "Initializing Core Data" for about 10 seconds, while our fake migration occurs, and then the progress marches from 0% to 100%.

Summary

From uniquing to faulting to caching managed objects, Core Data performs a significant amount of data access performance optimization for you. These optimizations come free, without any extra effort on your part. You should be aware of the optimizations that Core Data provides, however, so that you make sure to work with, not against, them.

Not all Core Data performance gains come automatically, however. In this chapter, you learned how to use techniques such as prefetching and predicate optimization to squeeze all the performance from Core Data that you can for your applications. You also learned how to analyze your Core Data application using the Instruments application, so you can understand how your application is using Core Data and where the trouble spots are. Finally, you learned how to use multiple threads to improve the responsiveness and perceived performance of your applications.

Other iOS programming books might do an excellent job showing you how to display a spinner and a "Please Wait" message when running long queries against your persistent store. This book shows you how to avoid the need for the spinner and "Please Wait" message entirely.

Index

Get the eBook for only $10!

Now you can take the weightless companion with you anywhere, anytime. Your purchase of this book entitles you to 3 electronic versions for only $10.

This Apress title will prove so indispensible that you'll want to carry it with you everywhere, which is why we are offering the eBook in **3 formats** for only $10 if you have already purchased the print book.

Convenient and fully searchable, the PDF version enables you to easily find and copy code—or perform examples by quickly toggling between instructions and applications. The MOBI format is ideal for your Kindle, while the ePUB can be utilized on a variety of mobile devices.

Go to www.apress.com/promo/tendollars to purchase your companion eBook.

Apress®
THE EXPERT'S VOICE™